State, Power and Politics in the Making of the Modern Middle East
Second Edition

Roger Owen has fully revised and updated his authoritative text to take into account the considerable developments in the Middle East in the 1990s. As with the first edition, this book explores the emergence of individual Middle Eastern states since the fall of the Ottoman Empire at the end of the First World War and some of the key themes that have characterised the region.

State, Power and Politics in the Making of the Modern Middle East, Second Edition:

- has been updated to take into account the end of the Cold War, the Gulf War, and the Israeli–Palestinian peace process;
- covers almost all Middle Eastern countries, including the twenty member states of the Arab League, Iran, Israel and Turkey;
- explores such key themes as the state and its formation, the role of the military within the political system, the politics of economic restructuring, democracy and electoral practice, and the changing relationship between religion and politics; and
- includes a new chapter looking at the role of non-state actors such as workers, women, and Palestinians in the West Bank and Gaza.

It continues to serve as an excellent introduction for newcomers to the modern history and politics of a region that is usually portrayed as mysterious, unpredictable and violent.

Roger Owen is A. J. Meyer Professor of Middle Eastern History at Harvard University and a former Director of the Center for Middle Eastern Studies, Harvard University.

State, Power and Politics in the Making of the Modern Middle East

Second Edition

Roger Owen

London and New York

First published 1992
by Routledge
11 New Fetter Lane, London EC4P 4EE

Simultaneously published in the USA and Canada
by Routledge
29 West 35th Street, New York, NY 10001

Reprinted 1993, 1994
Second edition 2000

Reprinted 2001, 2002, 2003

Routledge is an imprint of the Taylor & Francis Group

Typeset in Baskerville by Taylor & Francis
Printed and bound in Great Britain by Biddles Ltd, Guildford and King's
Lynn

British Library Cataloguing in Publication Data
A catalogue record for this book is available from the British Library

Library of Congress Cataloguing in Publication Data
State power & politics in the making of the modern Middle East/Roger
Owen – 2nd ed. Includes bibliographical references and index.
1. Middle East – Politics and government. 2. Africa, North – Politics and
government. I. Title.
DS63.O94 2000   99–047864
320´956–dc21

ISBN 0–415-19673–6 (hbk)
ISBN 0–415-19674–4 (pbk)

For Ben

About thirty years ago there was much talk that
geology ought only to observe and theorise: and
I well remember someone saying that at this
rate a man might well go into a gravel pit and
count the pebbles and describe the colours.
How odd it is that anyone should not see that all
observation must be for or against some view if
it is to be of any service.

(Charles Darwin to Henry Fawcett, 1861)

Contents

Illustrations

Preface

The first edition of this book was almost entirely written in the late 1980s. It has now been revised to take account of the major events which have taken place in the Middle East since then, notably the impact of the end of the Cold War, the Gulf War and the Israeli–Palestinian peace process and the intensification of moves towards greater economic and, in some cases, greater political liberalisation. Revision has also allowed me to benefit from the helpful criticism of many of those who have read it or used it for teaching.

For my purposes, the region is defined in large terms to include the twenty member states of the Arab League (less Mauritania and Somalia), Iran, Israel and Turkey. This is more or less the area known in Britain as the Near and Middle East until the Second World War when reference to the Near East was dropped in most official documents, following a lead from Winston Churchill. As for its history, I have decided to confine myself almost exclusively to the twentieth century, limiting reference to earlier periods only when this seems necessary for a proper understanding of the present. Lastly, I have included Turkey as a Middle Eastern state, partly on the grounds of its long historical connection with the region, partly because, during the 1990s, it forged a number of important new connections with its non-European neighbours: first with those areas with a significant Kurdish population such as northern Iraq, then with Israel.

It is also important to say something about my intended audience. The book is aimed at the non-specialist, or 'first time', western reader who wants to understand more about a part of the world which, although constantly in the news, continues to be presented as mysterious, unpredictable and subject to its own, usually violent, laws of motion. I am well aware that those who try to present a deeper, more realistic, more rounded picture run all the usual risks of persons who set themselves up as cultural middlemen, attempting to explain one set of political practices to people who live and work in terms of quite another. This is a project with many pitfalls, as Edward Said and others have forcefully pointed out. But there are also ways of trying to minimise such dangers. One that I have tried to practice above all others is constantly to ask myself whether the picture I present is one that would be recognisable to Middle Easterners themselves. This is, after all, how we in the west tend to judge the work of outsiders writing about ourselves.

My aim is to provide a good general introduction to the recent political history of the Middle East. I have done this by being both selective and interpretive. Those who want a more simple, chronological account will have to look elsewhere. In my own teaching I have found it useful to direct students either to M. E. Yapp's *The Near East Since the First World War* (London: Longman, 1991) or to William L. Cleveland's *A History of the Modern Middle East* (Boulder, CO: Westview Press, 1994). Other helpful sources are *The Middle East*, published annually in Washington, DC by the Congressional Quarterly Inc., and *The Times Guide to the Middle East*, edited by Peter Sluglett and Marion Farouk-Sluglett (3rd edn, London: Times Books, 1996).

My first major theme in the book is the emergence of the individual Middle Eastern states, the creation of their particular national institutions and the interaction between them. This is treated in historical fashion in Part I, with special emphasis on the construction of the state system following the break-up of the Ottoman Empire at the end of the First World War, the influence of British and French colonialism, the enormous increase in centralised political and administrative power in the early independence period and, finally, the particular pattern of inter-state relations that came to dominate the region from the 1930s onwards. There is also a chapter dealing briefly with the historical developments in Iran, Turkey and Israel which took a somewhat different course from those in the majority of the Arab states. Lastly, I have added a new chapter entitled, 'The remaking of the Middle Eastern political environment after the Gulf War', to cover significant region-wide developments during the 1990s.

Some of the major themes arising from this analysis are then treated in greater detail in Part II. These include the changing role of the military within the political system; the politics of economic restructuring; questions relating to democracy and electoral practice; and the changing relationship between religion and politics in a number of Middle Eastern countries. Here, too, I have added one last chapter: a look at a variety of non-state actors including workers, women, and the Palestinians in the West Bank and Gaza.

There are a number of reasons for adopting such an approach. The first is that the region contains too many states to permit the conventional country by country treatment. Second, it is my belief that there are a number of significant issues – for example, how are elections conducted? where are the boundaries between the religious and the secular? what are the main political obstacles to economic restructuring? – which are much better analysed on a comparative basis, with examples from a variety of different countries.

A third, and more important reason, derives from the attempt to tackle one of the most vexatious questions involved in analysing the politics of any particular region of the world: what, if anything, do the various states and societies have in common? As far as the Middle East itself is concerned, this problem is usually treated in an essentialist and reductionist fashion which sees the key to the whole region as being a shared element of religion, race and geography. From such a perspective – and to parody it only slightly – what unites the Middle East, as well as providing an explanation for almost everything that happens there, is the fact that the majority of its people are Arabs and Muslims who, until becoming rich from oil, lived as tribes in deserts. This view has then often been combined with the second, equally unhelpful, notion of an unchanging East in which, underneath the hectic pace of superficial movement, things remain much the same, whether in terms of tribalism, dictatorial rule or the local people's compulsion to kill each other in the name of religion.

For me, such views are simplistic, say nothing about historical change and explain very little. Nevertheless, they are still so often deeply embedded in much of the contemporary work on the Middle East – by Middle Easterners as well as by outsiders – that they require a major effort to counter them. It is my belief that this is best done from a perspective that sees the region first and foremost as part of the Third, or non-European, World, and subject to most of the same universally historical processes, from colonial rule, through the era of planning and control, to the much more eclectic contemporary combination of opening economies and continuing monopolistic political practice. Such an approach has many advantages. It opens up the Middle East to international comparison, and in so doing can draw on a much larger body of works of comparative political and socio-economic analysis. It suggests a number of universal themes for closer examination, such as development of authoritarian government and the challenge to single-party systems of rule. It moves away from the idea of the region possessing a distinctive form of political, religious and social behaviour. And it provides an index against which to measure those types of explanations which stem from the notion of Middle Eastern exceptionalism: for example, the idea that it is Islam which encourages tendencies towards military rule when, in fact, the politically ambitious soldiers, like so much else in the region, is essentially a Third World phenomenon.

A final note: as this book is intended primarily for readers of English, I have tried to cite the majority of references in that language, using those in French and Arabic only when it seemed absolutely necessary.

Roger Owen,
Harvard University, July 1999.

Acknowledgements

This book relies not only on the usual printed and documentary sources, but also, and more importantly, on the people I have met in the region since my first visits to Israel, Jordan, Lebanon and Egypt in 1955/6. I also owe a special debt of gratitude to the many friends and colleagues with whom I have discussed Middle Eastern politics over the years, whether at St Antony's College, Oxford, Harvard, the MERIP offices in Washington, or during the regular meetings of the Middle East Discussion Group in Britain and the Joint Near and Middle East Committee of the Social Science Research Committee in New York and elsewhere.

I would also like to give special thanks to Joel Beinin, Caglar Keyder, Charles Tripp and Jenny White for their helpful comments on particular chapters; to Israel Gershoni, Ann Lesch, Elizabeth Picard, Yezid Sayigh, Michael Shalev and the late Nazih Ayubi for lending me some of their ideas; and to Talal Asad, Huri Islamoglu, Ghassan Salamé, Tim Mitchell and Sami Zubaida for their influence on my thinking throughout the book. They are, of course, in no way responsible for the final brew.

Abbreviations

ACC	Arab Cooperation Council
ANAP	Motherland Party (Turkey)
ASU	Arab Socialist Union (Egypt)
CIA	Central Intelligence Agency (United States)
CGT	Confédération Générale du Travail (France)
CU	Constitutional Unionists (Morocco)
DMC	Democratic Movement for Change (Israel)
DISK	Confederation of Revolutionary Workers Unions (Turkey)
DP	Democrat Party (Turkey)
DSP	Democratic Left Party (Turkey)
EU	European Union (formerly European Economic Community)
FDIC	Front pour la Défense des Institutions Constitutionnelles (Morocco)
FIS	Islamic Salvation Front (Algeria)
FLN	National Liberation Front (Algeria)
GCC	Gulf Cooperation Council
GIA	Groupe Islamique Armée (Algeria)
GPC	General People's Congress (Libya)
IAF	Islamic Action Front (Jordan)
IDF	Israel Defence Force
IBRD	International Bank for Reconstruction and Development (World Bank)
IMF	International Monetary Fund
IRP	Islamic Republic Party (Iran)
JP	Justice Party (Turkey)
MAN	Movement of Arab Nationalists
MDS	Mouvement des Démocrates Socialistes (Tunisia)
MHP	Nationalist Action Party (Turkey; successor to NAP)
MIA	Mouvement Islamique Armée (Algeria)
MTI	Mouvement de Tendence Islamique (Tunisia)
MU	Magrheb Union
NAFTA	North American Free Trade Area
NAP	National Action Party (Turkey)

NDP	National Democratic Party (Egypt)
NGO	Non-governmental Organisation
NIF	National Islamic Front, later National Congress (Sudan)
NRP	National Religious Party (Israel)
NSP	National Salvation Party (Turkey)
NUC	National Unity Committee (Turkey)
OYAK	Armed Forces Assistance Fund (Turkey)
PDRY	People's Democratic Republic of Yemen (former South Yemen)
PKK	Kurdistan Workers' Party (Turkey)
PLO	Palestine Liberation Organisation
PNA	Palestine National Authority
PSD	Parti Socialiste Destourien (Tunisia)
PSP	Progressive Socialist Party (Lebanon)
RCD	Rassemblement Constitutionnel Démocratique (Tunisia)/ Rally for Culture and Democracy (Algeria)
RNI	National Independents' Rally (Morocco)
RPP	Republican People's Party (Turkey)
SHP	Socialist Democratic Populist Party (Turkey)
SODEP	Social Democratic Party (Turkey)
SPLA	Southern People's Liberation Army (Sudan)
SPLM	Southern People's Liberation Movement (Sudan)
SSNP	Syrian Socialist Nationalist Party
SSU	Sudan Socialist Union
TUSAID	Turkish Industrialists' and Businessmen's Association
UAE	United Arab Emirates
UC	Union Constitutionnel (Morocco)
UGTT	Union Général des Travailleurs Tunisiens
UMT	Union Morocaine du Travail
UNFP	Union Nationale des Force Populaires (Morocco)
UNL	United National Leadership (Palestine)
UNTT	Union Nationale des Travailleurs Tunisiens
USAID	United States Agency for International Development
USFP	Union Socialiste des Force Populaires (Morocco)
WTO	World Trade Organisation

Part I

States and state building

Introduction

The first five chapters of Part I are concerned with the establishment and consolidation of the various modern Middle Eastern states which emerged out of the Ottoman Empire and Persian Empires at the end of the nineteenth and beginning of the twentieth centuries. This is then followed by a chapter describing what I call the 'remaking' of these same states in the 1990s. My approach to the concept of 'state' employed here requires some initial explanation.

The word 'state' itself has two distinct meanings in everyday usage even though the two are often conflated. One use refers to sovereign political entities, i.e. those states with international recognition, their own boundaries, their own seat at the United Nations and their own flag. The other refers to that set of institutions and practices which combines administrative, judicial, rule-making and coercive powers. While the use of the word in the first sense is absolutely clear, and can be used in a Middle Eastern context to refer directly to the Arab states, Israel, Turkey and Iran, that of the second is more problematic and requires further elaboration.

Recognition of the existence of an entity called the 'state' goes back in European political thought at least as far as Machiavelli. However, the most important period of thinking began in the late eighteenth century when the concept was defined and re-defined by a series of thinkers from Hegel onwards culminating in what probably remains the most influential definition of all, Max Weber's notion of the state as 'a human community that (successfully) claims the monopoly of the legitimate use of physical force within a given territory'.

Nevertheless, it also has to be admitted that there is no general consensus concerning this, or any other, single definition and the word 'state' exists today as an essential component of a number of different political vocabularies used to talk about, analyse and to justify a great variety of different political situations, positions and arguments throughout the modern world. One of the most common is its place within a set of binary opposites – state/society, public/private, formal/informal – which are an indispensable part of contemporary political discourse. But there are many other forms of usage. For some, for example the World Bank in its 1997 *World Development Report*, 'state' is to be taken to be more or less the equivalent of government.[1] For others, it is used as though coterminous with dynasty or regime. And none is problem free.

To give just one example of some of the conceptual problems involved, let us return to the notion of the state as part of the set of binary opposites just proposed. Does this mean that the state is a one single thing and society another? If so, what constitutes the boundary between them? And is this the same boundary that exists, say, between the public and the private? For some purposes and in some discussions all this does not matter very much. This would be true, for example, of many contemporary political arguments about the role of the state and whether it should hive off a number of its present functions to private business. But in others, say in any serious analysis of what is usually called 'corruption' or of the black or informal economy, such simplistic assumptions get in the way of an understanding of a much more complex reality where boundaries are porous or non-existent, rules are unclear and many actors shift easily from one role to another with little or no official or legal hindrance.

We should also note the strong tradition which goes back at least as far as Karl Marx of viewing the apparent coherence of the state as either an illusion or, in some versions, a kind of confidence trick played on the public by those in charge who wish either to increase their own power or to disguise the fact that this apparently mighty entity is much less cohesive, much more the tool of competing factions and sectional interests, and, in general, much more chaotic than they want outsiders to believe.[2]

Matters become still more complex when we turn to the non-European world in general, and to the Middle East in particular. By and large most of the political writing concerned with defining the state, together with an associated vocabulary involving such key terms as 'legitimacy', 'hegemony' and 'authority', took place not only in Europe but also on the basis of an evaluation of a purely European experience. Some of this thinking was then transposed to a discussion of the state outside Europe without any great concern as to whether it made sense in what was obviously a different historical and cultural environment. Hence Middle Eastern states were, and are, supposed to possess much the same structure, role and trajectory as western ones, increasing their power over society in wars, as western states seem to do, and decreasing it in line with the contemporary western consensus that markets are better allocators of resources than central planners. It follows that they must also be amenable to much the same analyses of their strengths and weaknesses – according to their taxing or war-making powers or their abilities to penetrate and reshape their societies – as their European neighbours.[3] And as always this helps to create a counter-position: the view that western-type states are inappropriate for the Middle East, that they lack roots and cultural meaning and therefore are bound to perform badly and, indeed, to make the difficulties of government a great deal worse.[4]

Now, having discussed some of the problems involved in thinking about the word 'state' in its second usage, let me set out how I propose to approach the subject in the rest of this book. First, it seems important to begin with some general definition even if it has to be admitted that it is bound to be too narrow as well as, on occasions, an actual barrier to the examination of some important features of Middle Eastern political life. I will borrow such a definition from Joel Migdal, on the grounds that his seems better tailored to analysis of non-European political entities than any of its competitors. A state, according to Migdal, is:

> an organisation, composed of numerous agencies led and coordinated by the state's leadership (executive authority) that has the ability to make and implement the binding rules for all the people as well as the parameters of ruling making for other social organisations in a given territory, using force if necessary to have its way.[5]

I should also note that I prefer this definition to Nazih Ayubi's notion of the state as an 'abstract concept' which, though calling attention to the theoretical nature of much of our social science vocabulary, seems to deny the existence of something which most people in the Middle East experience as real, 'fierce' (in Ayubi's own conception) and possessing considerable power for good or ill.[6]

Second, when it comes to the question of whether or not Middle Eastern states are the same as western states I follow Sami Zubaida in maintaining that they are 'like' western states in the sense that, from the nineteenth century onwards, organisations of this type constituted what he calls the 'compulsory model' for establishing new political units outside Europe, if only for lack of any viable alternative.[7] It is also true to say that Middle Eastern states are also 'modern' states in the sense that the majority of them rest on socio-economic foundations – for example, urbanisation – which are the necessary outcome of modern capitalist development and that, as Talal Asad notes, they now employ distinctive practices and ways of organising the societies they control characteristic only of the twentieth century world.[8] That said, however, it is important to underline the fact that they came into existence in quite different historical circumstances from their western counterparts and, in most cases, in a quite different relationship to the majority of their citizens. It follows, of course, that their further development cannot be predicted simply in terms of European models alone.

Third, it is particularly necessary in a Middle Eastern context to stress the conceptual difference between state, regime and government, even though the lines are usually quite blurred in practice. As far as the Arab countries are concerned, it is useful to consider them as lying on some kind of spectrum, with Egypt at one end where the distinction is most apparent, and those of the Gulf at the other, where state, regime and government are so closely identified as to suggest that if one shaikly regime disappeared, the political entity it had created and ruled would most likely disappear as well. This, in turn, makes analysis of their legitimacy difficult. In the Arab countries, as well as in Iran and, at times, in Turkey, it is the regimes themselves and their varied attempts to create ideological justifications for themselves that have attracted the bulk of both political and academic attention, not the states they control, as in the classical

Weberian paradigm. And it is those regimes which continue to remain suspicious of the loyalties of their citizens that most readily use prison and torture to supplement whatever small amounts of acceptance they have managed to create.

Fourth, the Middle Eastern state has a special and problematic relationship with another constructed entity, the nation. In the Middle East, as elsewhere, state formation took place during a period when local peoples were being encouraged to imagine themselves, and very often to act, as members of a variety of different possible communities, some tribal, religious or territorial, others of the pan-Arab, pan-Turkish or pan-Islamic variety. Different regimes then attempted to accommodate and to control this process in terms of the practices they developed towards frontiers, passports, systems of law and taxation, while all the time being pushed towards the establishment of one fixed and singular identity for their putative citizens. This process was usually aided by the construction of what Zubaida has called a 'national political field' within which, after independence, all significant political activities are then focused.[9] Surrounded by the new international boundary, this field acted to inhibit cross-border relationships and to redirect all assertions of local power or interest towards the capital city where most major political battles were now won and lost.

The process of state creation, in the twin sense of creating both new sovereign entities and of new centres of power and control, has been mostly the work of the twentieth century. It is to this history that I will now turn. This section is divided it into three successive stages – the colonial state, the immediate post-independent state and the authoritarian state – each with its own particular politics, practices and policies. Chapter 1 looks at the first two of these phases as far as the major Arab countries are concerned, and Chapters 2 and 3 the third. This is followed by a fourth chapter that examines the pattern of interaction between the many Arab states in terms of the various solidarities that their peoples shared, and of the contradiction between their desire for greater political unity and their fear of its many consequences.

The twentieth century histories of the three non-Arab states, Iran, Israel and Turkey, are dealt with in Chapters 1 and 5. These states followed a somewhat different historical trajectory from the Arab states. All three were deeply affected by their experience of foreign intervention and control. But in each case the actual creation of the states themselves was the work of powerful groups within their own national societies, often drawing on a considerable pre-history of organisation and political development. This at once provided them with a greater continuity than most Arab states enjoyed, as well as a greater latitude when it came to their efforts to institutionalise state/society relations. Lastly, Chapter 6 introduces the notion of the 're-making' of the Middle Eastern political systems and the pattern of interstate relations during the last decade of the twentieth century.

Notes

1   The World Bank, *World Development Report 1997 (Summary): The State in a Changing World* (Washington, DC: The World Bank, 1997), p. 1.
2   For example, Philip Abrams, 'Notes on the difficulty of studying the state', *The Journal of Historical Sociology* I/1 (March 1988), pp. 63–4, Timothy Mitchell, 'The limits of the state: Beyond statist approaches and their critics', *American Political Science Review*, 85/1 (March 1991), pp. 77–96.
3   For example, Joel Migdal, *Strong States and Weak Societies: State-Society Relations and State Capabilities in the Third World* (Princeton, NJ: Princeton University Press, 1988); Michael Barnett, *Confronting the Costs of War: Military Power, State and Society in Egypt and Israel* (Princeton, NJ: Princeton University Press, 1992). For an interesting variant see, Thierry Gongora, 'War making and state power in the Middle East', *International Journal of Middle Eastern Studies*, 29/3 (1997), pp. 323–40.
4   A good example is Bertrand Badie, *Les deux états: pouvoir et société en Occident et en terre d'Islam* (Paris: Fayard, 1986). See also the critique of Badie's position by Sami Zubaida, *Islam, the People and the State* (London and New York: Routledge, 1989), pp. 131–7.
5   Migdal, *Strong Societies and Weak States*, p. 19.
6   Nazih N. Ayubi, *Overstating the State: Politics and Society in the Middle East* (London and New York: I.B. Tauris, 1995), pp. 30–3, and Chapter 12.
7   Zubaida, *Islam, the People and the State*, p. 145.
8   Talal Asad, 'Conscripts of Western civilization?', in Christine Ward Gailey (ed.), *Dialectical Anthropology: Essays in Honor of Stanley Diamond* (Tallahassee, FL: University Press of Florida, 1992), vol. 2.
9   Zubaida, *Islam, the People and the State*, pp. 126, 162.

1 The end of empires

The emergence of the modern Middle Eastern states

The break-up of the Ottoman Empire

At the beginning of the twentieth century the Middle East was still dominated by the Ottoman Empire, a world empire that had existed for some 400 years. Although its main strength derived from its provinces in Europe, it also controlled extensive territories in the Arab land of the eastern end of the Mediterranean including what are now known as Syria, Iraq, Lebanon, Jordan, Northern Yemen and Israel/Palestine. Furthermore, it maintained a foothold in North Africa round Tripoli and Benghazi in Libya, although it had lost control of the rest of its possessions along the African coast, either to the British (Egypt) or to the French (Algeria and Tunisia). Only the lands on the very frontiers of the region, Persia and the central Arabian peninsula in the east and Morocco in the west, had managed to resist the exercise of direct Ottoman power. Everywhere else in the Middle East, centuries of rule by governors who owed their ultimate allegiance to Istanbul had produced a legacy of Ottoman administrative practice and Ottoman culture which continued to affect political life in countless important ways.

Nevertheless, for all its size and importance, the rulers of the empire had spent the last hundred years trying to confront the growing power of a Europe driven on by the influence of the two great revolutions that it had experienced at the end of the eighteenth century: the political revolution in France from 1789 onwards; and the Industrial Revolution in Britain. One result was the nibbling away of the frontiers of the empire in Africa and West Asia, marked by the establishment of European colonies and spheres of influence. Another was the repeated attempts to reform and to revive the Ottoman imperial structure the better to defend itself against foreign domination. By the beginning of the twentieth century these reforms had done much to transform the legal, military and administrative practices throughout the empire but only at the expense of allowing Europe an increasing economic and cultural presence, and of stirring up incipient nationalist movements among many of its subject peoples, for example the Armenians of Anatolia and the Maronite Christians of Mount Lebanon.

The effect of these processes intensified greatly in the years just before 1914. A series of Balkan wars led to the loss of most of the empire's remaining possessions in Europe, while the Italians took advantage of Ottoman weakness to make a sustained attack on the region around Tripoli in North Africa. Meanwhile, the Young Turk Revolution of 1908 had brought to power a group of officers and officials dedicated not only to the accelerated reform of Ottoman institutions but also to an incipient Turkish nationalism which threatened to drive a wedge between the Turks who controlled the empire and the Arabs who had previously been regarded as their main partners. This placed something of a strain on the loyalties of many Arab army officers and civil servants, although very few of them went so far as to argue the need for a state, or states, of their own. It was difficult for them to imagine a world without the Ottoman sultan as their political and (if they were Muslims) their religious leader. It was equally obvious that the Ottoman state – with its army, its flag and its embassies in Europe – was their only protector against further European encroachment. Nowhere was this better understood than in Palestine, where Arab concern that the Ottomans were not doing enough to contain Jewish immigration and Zionist colonisation was tempered by the realisation that turning away from the Ottomans to a great power like the British or the French for support would be like jumping from a familiar frying-pan into a still more dangerous fire.

The Ottoman military defeat by the British and French during the First World War produced a radical change throughout the whole Middle East. As a result of treaties negotiated during the war itself, the Arab provinces of the empire were carved up into a number of successor states, each of them under the control of one or other of the victorious powers: the new Syria and Lebanon under the French; the new Iraq, Palestine and Trans-Jordan under the British. However, there was also a half-hearted attempt by Britain and France to bring the Arabs themselves into the picture. This was partly because some Arabs, notably the Hashemite rulers of the Hijaz, had become their military allies against the Ottomans during the war; and partly as a concession to what the British sometimes referred to as 'the spirit of the age', a phrase that suggested the need to come to terms with the emphasis that the Americans and some of the founders of the new League of Nations were now giving to such powerful notions as freedom and self-determination. The result was the invention of a new instrument of political control, the mandate, which was used to legitimise British and French government of their Middle Eastern possessions. This had many of the features of an old-fashioned colony but it also required the mandate holders to submit to certain internationally sanctioned guidelines, notably the need to establish constitutional governments in the new states as a way of preparing their peoples for eventual independence. Another of these important guidelines applied specifically to Mandatory Palestine, where Britain was required by treaty to implement the provisions of the Balfour Declaration of November 1917 calling for the establishment of a Jewish national home.

The new order in the Middle East was not accepted tamely by many of its inhabitants. There was a serious revolt against Britain in Iraq in 1920, and anti-British, as well as anti-Jewish, disturbances in Palestine in the same year. Meanwhile, France's attempt to take up its mandate in Syria was challenged, first by the Arab government that had established itself in Damascus after the Turkish retreat, then by a series of rural revolts culminating in the country-wide uprising of 1925–7. All such challenges were contained in the mandated territories themselves. But in Egypt, where Britain had declared a protectorate in 1914, the rebuff given to nationalist attempts to send a delegation – or *wafd* – to the Paris Peace Conference stimulated a widespread revolt in 1919 that was serious enough to cause a major change in British policy and a unilateral grant of qualified independence in 1922. There was even stronger resistance in Anatolia, where efforts by a number of European powers to create military spheres of influence led to a rallying of Turkish forces behind General Mustafa Kemal (later Ataturk) and the creation of the Turkish Republic in 1922. Much the same happened in Persia where Reza Khan (later Reza Shah) used his army to regain control of the whole country from the British, the Russians and the tribal forces that established themselves in many of its provinces during and after the war.

Nevertheless, in spite of all local resistance, there is no doubt that by the mid-1920s the British and the French were the masters of the Middle East. It was they who determined almost all of the new boundaries; they who decided who should rule, and what form of governments should be established; and it was also they, in association with the Americans, who had a major say in how access to the region's natural resources should be allocated, particularly the oil fields that were just beginning to be discovered along the Persian Gulf and in the Mosul district of northern Iraq. Such was Britain's and France's strength that even the rulers of nominally independent countries like Turkey, Egypt and Persia (renamed Iran in 1925) were forced to recognise the new boundaries and the new order, while those like Abd al-Aziz Ibn Saud, who aspired to create a new state in Arabia after his defeat of the Hashemites, knew that he could only achieve this goal with British assistance and support. Writing in the early 1960s, Elizabeth Monroe could refer to the period 1914 to 1956 as Britain's 'moment' in the Middle East.[1] And short as this period now seems, it was then that the basic framework for Middle Eastern political life was firmly laid – together with many of its still unsolved problems involving disputed boundaries, ethnic and religious tensions and the existence of national minorities which either failed to obtain a state of their own, like the Kurds, or were prevented from doing so by *force majeure*, like the Palestinians.

The political practices of a colonial state

Strictly speaking there were only a handful of real colonies in the Middle East in the twentieth century: Aden (British), Libya (Italian) and Algeria (French). For the rest, imperial power was exercised under a variety of different names, most notably mandates and protectorates but also by treaty (as in Trucial Oman) and in one case by condominium (the Anglo-Egyptian Sudan) (see Figure 1). There were important differences, too, in types of government: for example, monarchical or republican; in the degree of direct and indirect rule; and in the political importance of local European settler communities, whether of the same nationality as the ruling power, like the French in Algeria, or another, like most of the Jews in Palestine.

Nevertheless, for the purpose of analysing the Middle Eastern political systems of the post-First World War period, a useful starting point is provided by the observation that there existed a particular pattern of control known as the 'colonial state'.[2] This can then be used to highlight a number of general features that shaped the exercise of power and defined the political arena in most of the countries created or dominated by the Europeans. I will group these features under three headings: central administration; the policies of the colonial power; and colonialism as a conduit for external influences.

Central administration

As far as the Middle East was concerned, it was generally the dominant colonial power that first created the essential features of a modern state, by giving it a centralised administration, a legal system, a flag and internationally-recognised boundaries. In some cases this was done on the basis of some pre-existing administrative entity, as in Algeria; in others it involved either detaching a part of a former Ottoman province (for example, Trans-Jordan) or, more usually, adding several provinces together (for example, Syria and Iraq). This gave many of the new states a somewhat artificial appearance, with their new names, their new capitals, their lack of ethnic homogeneity and their dead-straight boundaries that were so obviously the work of a British or French colonial official using a ruler. However, this point can be pushed too far. Very often there was an administrative logic which defined, if not the boundaries, then at least the area to be controlled from one central location like Baghdad or Jerusalem. Very often, too, some of the vital processes thought essential to state building were already under way in the late Ottoman period, for example, the creation of bureaucracies, large regional markets and the beginnings of the breakdown of what are usually called 'traditional' social units like the tribe or the extended family. However, this is a hotly debated point, particularly among Arab nationalists, for whom the notion of 'artificiality' is a key argument in favour of Arab unity, and also among orientalist historians, many of whom continue to see religious and ethnic communities as more basic forms of political organisation and reference than citizenship or local nationality. I will return to this important argument many times in this and later chapters.

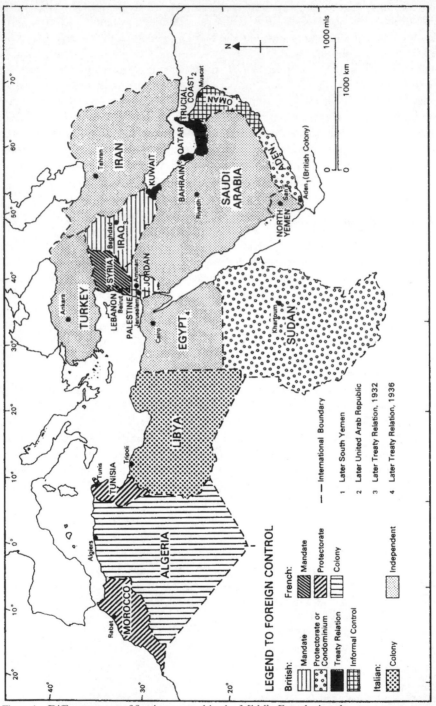

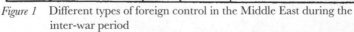

Figure 1   Different types of foreign control in the Middle East during the
inter-war period

Once a specific territorial state was established, other developments quickly followed. One was the attempt to enumerate, control and define the people who lived there. This involved, among other things, the organisation of a census and the passage of a law laying down the principles by which the nationality of its subjects was to be defined. In the case of the new Arab states, the latter was usually based on a combination of the notion of territory (that is, all people living within the new boundaries at a certain point in time) and family (that is, people descended from someone born in the country before a certain date), as in the Trans-Jordanian nationality law of the late 1920s. A second consequence was the need to control and police the new borders in order to prevent incursions, smuggling and illegal migration. And a third was the conclusion of treaties with neighbouring states involving rights of passage and the extradition of persons wanted for certain kinds of illegal activity. Naturally, few of the early efforts in any of these directions were immediately very effective, and tribes and nomads continued to wander across borders and in and out of the new states as if none of the new controls existed. Nevertheless, over time, they had an important part to play in consolidating the role of the political centre, and paved the way for the emergence of the much stronger and more powerful regimes of the post-Second World War period.

The new states were also given new bureaucracies and a new emphasis on homogeneity and equality. There was now to be one centre of authority, issuing standard rules and regulations which were supposed to be applied equally to all those who lived within its boundaries as citizens. However, as in many other aspects of state building, this ideal took many years to establish, the more so as the colonial regimes and their successors had their own security to think of, as well as facing a number of obvious constraints such as the existence of white settlers with entrenched privileges, the commitment given to the League of Nations to protect religious minorities, and so on. One important instance of this concerned religious identity. In theory, at least, a modern state is implicitly secular, in the sense that laws are made by the civil, not the religious authorities, and are supposed to apply equally to all, whether members of a dominant religious community or not. In the Middle Eastern context, however, the effect of such principles was considerably diluted as groups defined in religious terms were not only given special rights of self-management but were also allocated a place within the political system on a communal rather than an individual basis. Hence seats were reserved for minorities in most colonial legislatures, a process that was taken to its extreme in Lebanon, where representation in parliament and appointment to the bureaucracy were based almost entirely on membership in one of the specified religious communities to which all Lebanese, by definition, had to belong.

Table 1.1   Expenditure of colonial governments in the 1920s by purpose (per cent)

	India 1921–30	Cyprus 1923–38[a]	Iraq 1921–30	Trans-Jordan 1924–31	Syria 1923–40	Avg[b]
General administration	19.7	32.0	34.6	20.8	35.4	28.5
Defence and public safety	33.8	17.5	34.4	45.8	28.1	31.9
Economic and environmental services	20.1	10.5	14.5	7.7	7.2	13.2
Public works (development)		13.9	7.0	8.6	15.1	11.2
Social welfare services	7.2	20.1	9.5	10.3	8.9	11.2
Domestic debt service and unspecified expenditure	19.2	n/a	n/a	6.8	5.4	10.5
Total domestic expenditure	*100.0*	*100.0*	*100.0*	*100.0*	*100.0*	
Administration and safety	53.5	49.5	69.0	66.0	64.5	60.4
Economic, environmental and development	20.1	30.4	21.5	16.3	22.3	24.4

Source: Nachum T. Gross and Jacob Metzer, 'Public finance in the Jewish economy in interwar Palestine', Table 18, *Research in Economic History*, 3 (1978), p. 83.

Notes:
[a]Average of the years 1923, 1924, 1934, 1935, 1973, 1938.
[b]Arithmetic mean of each line: last two lines are summations.

A last important feature of the administrative systems established in the colonial period was their particular emphasis on police and security. No doubt this is a feature of all new states. However, in the case of the colonial powers it was, for obvious reasons, considered to be the key to continued political control. This can easily be seen by an examination of the budgets of the period in which, typically, some two-thirds of total expenditure was security related (see Table 1.1). Most of this was spent on creating and developing a police force, and sometimes a rural gendarmerie as well. Less importance was attached to a local army, partly for financial reasons, partly because the colonial power itself accepted the major responsibility for external defence. Nevertheless, small military formations of a few thousand men or so were organised in all colonial states, and even though they were given few heavy weapons and were used mainly for internal security, patterns of recruitment and politicisation were established which were to play a significant role in the immediate post-independence period (see Chapter 10).

Such emphasis on security left little money for education, public health and welfare. Even so, enough was still spent on secondary schools and technical institutes to produce a growing number of activist youths who were willing recruits into the first anti-colonial movements of the 1920s and 1930s (see Table 1.2).

Table 1.2   The growth in the numbers of schoolchildren and students in certain selected Arab countries, 1920–50

Country	Educational establishment	Numbers (1921/2)	Numbers (1948/9)
Egypt[a]	Elementary	342,820	1,069,383
	Preparatory/Primary	126,066	321,315
	Secondary	15,442	90,353
	University	2,282	26,740
		Numbers (1920/1)	*Numbers (1939/40)*
Iraq[b]	Elementary	8,001	89,482
	Secondary	110	13,959
	College	99	1,218 (1940/1)
		Numbers (1945/6)	
Syria[c]	Primary (state)	99,703	
	private	50,431	
	Intermediary (state)	8,276	
	Secondary (private)	4,385	
	University	1,058	

Sources:[a]   Donald C. Mead, *Growth and Structural Change in the Egyptian Economy* (Homewood, Illinois: Richard D. Irwin, 1967), p. 299.
  [b]   Hanna Batatu, *The Old Social Classes and the Revolutionary Movements of Iraq* (Princeton, NJ: Princeton UP, 1978), p.25n.
  [c]   International Bank for Reconstruction and Development, *The Economic Development of Syria* (Baltimore: The John Hopkins Press, 1975), p. 457.

Colonial policy

If there were certain principles underlying the creation of the colonial state, there were also a number of typical colonial practices. One was the attempt to create an alliance, implicit or explicit, with the large landowners and, in some cases, the tribal shaikhs who controlled much of the rural areas. Such men were soon identified as a conservative social force which could be won over to support the colonial position, even when, as in Syria and Iraq, many of their number had participated in the rebellions against the British and the French just after the First World War. Their importance was seen as twofold. First, they could be used to maintain rural security at a time when the government had neither the money nor the administrative resources to maintain a comprehensive police coverage. Second, in those states where constitutional government and general elections – based on some type of manhood suffrage – had been introduced in the 1920s, the large landowners could be relied upon both to manage the rural vote and, in many cases, to put themselves forward as candidates for the new parliaments. This could be made even safer when, in countries like Syria and Iraq, the Ottoman system of two-tier elections was re-introduced, in which the male electors voted for members of a small and easily manipulable local electoral college who, in turn, chose one of their number as the district's representative. To seal this alliance, large landowners were given a host of special privileges like tax exemptions and legal powers over their peasant tenants, as well as being able

3 ideas

to take good advantage of some of the more general benefits of colonial policy such as property registration and improved irrigation.

A second, equally important, feature of colonial politics was the attention paid to sectarian, ethnic and tribal divisions, generally for the purpose of some strategy of 'divide and rule'. This was as true of the French in Morocco, with their special emphasis on the distinction between Arabs and Berbers, as it was in the mandated territories in the east. Such policies could take many forms. They could find expression in different legal systems, as in Morocco or the tribal courts in Trans-Jordan; or in actual administrative separation, for example, the French division of Syria into, among other things, a mini-state for the Alawis along the Mediterranean coast and another for the Druze. Inevitably this did much to counter the centralising, homogenising processes emanating from other parts of the colonial system.

Last, but by no means least, was the particular pattern of colonial economic management. Even if colonies did not pay, they were supposed to balance their books and to be able to get along without loans from the centre in all but very special circumstances. This constraint, together with the emphasis placed on security, left little money for development other than the small amounts spent on public works projects like roads, railways, ports and improved irrigation. Colonies were also subject to a particular type of fiscal and monetary regime, with their currency tied to that of the colonial power and managed by a currency board in the metropolis. This obviated the need for a central bank which, had it existed, would have been able to regulate the money supply or to alter the rate of interest in such a way as to expand or dampen local demand. Meanwhile, throughout most of the ex-Ottoman Empire, the new states remained subject to nineteenth-century commercial treaties, which, until they ran out in 1930, prevented them from setting their own tariffs. The result was the creation of more or less open economies, subject to influences stemming from the metropolis and the world at large, over which the individual state had little or no control. Criticism of what was seen as this unsatisfactory state of affairs formed an essential component of the anti-colonial, nationalist argument, the more so as it could also be used to counter the colonial powers' attempt to justify their rule by an appeal to the many economic benefits that it was supposed to have intro-duced.

External influences

Another essential component of the colonial state was the way in which it acted as a conduit for powerful forces from outside. This was most obvious in the political field, where British and French policies were made in London and Paris and subject to all the pressures of the various parties and interest groups to be found there. As far as the colony, or dominated country, itself was concerned, it meant that its own political life was greatly affected by events like changes of government in Britain and France, or even defeats in wars, over which it had no control. It also meant that it was subject to a variety of often quite contradictory influences and examples, for instance, the ambiguous lessons to be learned from the practice of pluralism and democracy at the centre combined with the day-to-day experience of dictatorial and arbitrary government in the colony itself. In these circumstances, local politicians cannot be blamed for learning as much about how to fix elections as they did about the virtues of pluralism or judicial independence. And, of course, both types of lessons proved useful to those who became leaders of movements of national opposition or ministers in any of the cabinets they were allowed to form.

The role of the colonial state in mediating between the colony and the international economy was just as important. By and large, the British and French attempted to manage affairs in such a way that they monopolised these relations, awarding contracts and concessions to their own nationals, looking after the interests of their own merchants and, in general, attempting to keep the colony as their own economic preserve. Once again, there were often international constraints that made this more difficult, for example, the fact that what were known as 'A' mandates, that is, Syria, Iraq and Palestine, were technically independent countries and could not be included, legally, in any scheme designed to promote imperial preference at the expense of third parties. Nevertheless, this was far outweighed by the benefits to be obtained in terms of control over the Middle East's oil resources or access to each mandate's reserves of hard currency placed securely in the Bank of England and the National Bank of France.

The colonial state as a framework for a new type of politics

The boundaries of a colonial state and its administrative structures defined the arena in which most of the political life now took place, as well as doing much to give it its own particular dynamic.[3] Both points require elaboration. As far as the new arena was concerned, it was largely dominated by the drive to obtain influence or, better still, paramountcy over the institutions created at the new political centre – the capital city. It was also a site for the new rules and new possibilities stemming from the day-to-day realities of colonial practice. To this end, many pre-existing associations and social solidarities were reorganised the better to be able to exert direct pressure on government, or new ones created. Furthermore, just as there was a change in organisation and in focus, there was also a change in the political vocabulary, with words that had their origin in more traditional discourse now having their meaning stretched or altered to meet the challenge of the new situation. One good example of this is the slide in the definition of the Arabic word, *umma*, from meaning the whole religious community to meaning the Arab nation in general, and then just a part of it, for instance, Egypt or Syria. Meanwhile, good use could be made of the opportunities presented by a process of accelerated economic and social change which detached people from their old communities and old loyalties and allowed them to participate as individuals in new types of, mainly urban-based, political activity.

Once again, the point is a controversial one. In many analyses of Middle East politics, the so-called 'traditional' categories of tribe, sect or clan remain fixed and unchanging, giving them a timeless quality in which the same conflicts over differences in communal allegiance and belief are endlessly repeated in patterns that have little to do with national boundaries or national politics. Or, if the creation of new and larger loyalties is allowed, these are supposed to transcend the new boundaries by encouraging the creation of pan-Islamic or pan-Arab forms of organisation with region-wide aims. From this follows the still influential observation that politics in the Arab world continue to be a struggle between groups that are concerned with issues that are either smaller than those to be found at the state level or larger. In this view too, tribes are always competing with tribes, even if the word itself now has to embrace units as widely different as a sect like the Alawis or men from a particular provincial town like Takrit, the birthplace of many of the leaders of Ba'thi Iraq, while slogans and identities continue to be expressed in terms of what are supposed to be a fundamentally unchanging religious or 'traditional' vocabulary.

Against this I would like to argue the counter proposition, that methods of political organisation and styles of political rhetoric are largely defined by their context and that, from the colonial period on, this context was created by the territorial state. Certainly it took time for its effect to be felt throughout the whole of a particular society; certainly there were groups that continued to act as though they were still fighting their neighbours or some distant government to which they owed nothing. However, for the most part, those who wanted power, access to resources or simply self-aggrandisement had to organise themselves in a way that made sense in terms of the new realities, while those who did not, for example, the military raiders from Arabia known as the Ikhwan, or the Arab nationalist politicians who tried to use Trans-Jordan as a basis for anti-French agitation inside Syria in the early 1920s, were soon marginalised or destroyed.

Three other points about the nature of this new arena are important. First, once the initial rural, anti-colonial, revolts had been put down, the main focus for the new politics became largely urban and, in many cases, was confined almost exclusively to the capital city. As a result it came to be dominated by members of a small elite who provided leadership for the growing number of educated town dwellers who were drawn into national political life. In Egypt, for example, the activists were drawn largely from the 53,000 or so people who had been identified as professionals in 1937, the vast majority of them schoolteachers.[4] But there was also a tendency to try to increase the strength of any political movement by seeking recruits among organisable groups elsewhere in the city, such as workers or students, who could be used in the orchestrated series of strikes, demonstrations and boycotts that came to be seen as an essential feature of contemporary political life.[5]

A second important feature was the difference between a monarchical and a republican system of government. As far as Britain was concerned it was the former that was much preferred. This was because a king, constrained by a constitution, was seen as a vital support for the British position, since he provided an important element of continuity and could always be used to dismiss any popularly elected government of nationalists that threatened to tear up or amend the arrangements – usually summed up in a treaty – defining Britain's rights. Such a case clearly existed in Egypt, where King Fuad (1922–36) repeatedly dismissed governments based on huge majorities obtained by the Wafd Party in the preceding elections. Paradoxically, his son, King Farouk (1936–52), had to be coerced into appointing the same party to power in 1942, when new conditions demanded a different British strategy of using the nationalists to keep a neutral Egypt quiet for the duration of the Second World War.

Whatever the British interest, however, such a system inevitably turned the monarch into an important political actor with some powers of veto and, at the very least, great influence over the local politicians and their competition for domestic resources. Later, as independence approached, a great deal depended on whether a king managed the difficult transformation of putting himself at the head of the local nationalist movement – something achieved by the kings of Morocco, Mohammed V (1957–61) and Hassan II (1961–99) and by King Hussein of Jordan (1953–99) – or whether they became so closely associated with the structures of colonialism that they did not long outlast them, for example in Tunisia, Libya, Egypt and Iraq. The French for their part, were more willing to countenance republican forms of government, as in Lebanon and Syria, and to forgo the sometimes uncertain advantages of monarchy for a more easily managed system led by a docile president.

A last significant feature affecting the politics of the colonial period was the presence of a white settler community in Palestine and all of North Africa. Its role can be seen in its classic form in the French colonies and protectorates, where, having strong connections with the mother country, the settlers were able to obtain a privileged position, with their own political advisory bodies, an extra-market system for obtaining control of the best land and, for a long time, their own exclusive trade unions to which, for example, native-born Algerians and others were not admitted. In these circumstances, a major part of the settlers' efforts were directed towards preserving and expanding these privileges against both metropolitan and local nationalist pressures, something that inevitably brought them into conflict with the colonised population at both the political and the economic level. Much the same was true of Libya, although there the period of Italian control was much shorter; not more than two decades in Tripolitania, and only one in Cyrenaica, where a colonial campaign against the Senussi religious order and the tribes continued well into the 1930s.

In Egypt, however, the major component in the European population was provided by Greeks and Italians who, although protected by the capitulatory treaties until the 1930s, and by the special mixed courts for trying foreigners, never received sufficient support from the country's British occupiers to obtain privileged access to land or the power to institutionalise a split-labour market with higher wages for themselves. Perhaps because of this, their relations with the Egyptian nationalists were relatively harmonious and they played only a marginal role in the political life of the colonial period. Palestine was different again. Although the Zionist settlers received initial support from the British, it was later realised that their project of establishing a national home ran counter to the interests of the native Palestinians. Thereafter the mandatory authorities tried to play a balancing role between the two communities, thus incurring the increasing hostility of both sides. In these circumstances there was little chance of introducing common political institutions, leaving the Jews and Arabs to develop their own organisations, forged largely in direct conflict with one another.

Apart from the creation of a political arena, a second way in which the colonial state engendered a new type of political practice was by providing a fresh focus for political struggle. What it did, essentially, was to give birth to the familiar dialectic by which imperial rule cannot help but generate the nationalist forces that will eventually drive it out. In the Middle Eastern context this meant that, throughout most of the region, the colonial powers provided both a sufficient challenge and a sufficient opportunity for a local political movement to develop, until such time when it proved easier to give way to it than to try to resist it for ever. However, to make matters more complicated, by offering posts to local politicians and officials, and by providing new resources to compete for, via control over an expanding bureaucracy, the colonial state also encouraged another type of struggle, this time among the different local groups or factions themselves.

Independence and after

Just as the First World War had created the conditions that led to the grant of formal independence to Egypt in 1922, so too did the Second World War pave the way for the end of colonial domination in many other parts of the Middle East. Expectations of freedom were raised. The defeats suffered by France and Italy, and the emergence of the United States and Soviet Russia as world superpowers, severely damaged the prestige of the old imperial countries. And in Palestine the growth of Jewish economic activity during the war, and then the revelations about the Nazi extermination camps, made the drive for Jewish statehood virtually unstoppable. The result was that Syria and Lebanon obtained their formal independence in 1943 and Trans-Jordan (re-named Jordan) in 1946. Next, Israel emerged out of the military partition of Mandatory Palestine after the British withdrawal in 1948, leaving most of the areas assigned by the United Nations to an Arab entity soon to be taken over by the Jordanians. And, in 1951, Libya was established as an amalgamation of the former Italian colonies of Tripoli, Cyrenaica and the Fezzan.

There was then a brief interval while Britain and France tried to renegotiate their position in Egypt and Iraq (both of which had been virtually reoccupied by British troops during the war) and in North Africa. But the Free Officers' coup of 1952 soon opened up the way for the 1954 agreement on the final withdrawal of the British forces from Egypt, and the independence of Sudan in 1956. At the same time, efforts to contain the Algerian revolt that broke out in 1954 led the French to cut their losses and to grant freedom to Tunisia and Morocco, also in 1956. Hence, just over a decade after the end of the Second World War all the states in the region had obtained their independence, with the exception of Algeria, which had to wait until 1962, and the British colonies and protectorates round the southern and eastern coasts of Arabia.

Patterns of transfer of power differed enormously. In some cases there was a year or so of preparation, capped by an election to decide which political group was to form the first post-independence government. In others, like Syria and Lebanon, French troops lingered on, and it was only in 1946 that they were finally persuaded to leave. Another even messier route was followed in Palestine, where the British made no serious effort to hand over power to anyone, leaving the Palestinian Arabs in confusion and allowing the Jews to proclaim a state based on the significant parastatal institutions they had developed in the inter-war period.

Nevertheless, whatever the conditions in which they had obtained power, the rulers of the newly independent Middle Eastern states faced many of the same problems as their colonial predecessors. It was one thing to create a nationalist coalition against the retreating imperial power, quite another to obtain the allegiance of all of its new citizens. There were also huge problems posed by poverty, illiteracy, religious and social division and the need to find money for development. As a rule, nationalist parties had elaborated quite a powerful critique of the economic policies of their colonial masters before independence in terms of their failures to support industry, to spend money on education or to allow the creation of certain key institutions like national banks. Now, having achieved power themselves, this critique was generally recycled as a programme for immediate action. However, it then had to be carried out at a time when local state structures, deprived of the cohesion provided by the colonial presence, were relatively amorphous and fluid, with fragmented and highly politicised bureaucratic structures. Meanwhile. it was also necessary to find funds for expanding and re-equipping the colonial armies that were now needed not just for internal policing but also for external operations, for example, during the Palestine War of 1948.

In these difficult circumstances, it was perhaps inevitable that there was a great deal of initial instability leading, in a number of cases, to military coups. In Syria, Iraq and Egypt, the first governments, consisting essentially of an alliance of city notables and professionals supported, in the rural areas, by the large landowners, were dominated by well-to-do men who, for all their nationalist credentials, had often been closely associated with the British and the French. In Sudan the major politicians were the leaders of the country's three main religious sects. All found it difficult to meet the political challenge of running relatively poor states. They were also open to accusations that their class position made them particularly unreceptive to questions of income redistribution and social justice. In return, they defended themselves against attack by manipulating the electoral system to their advantage in such a way that forced their radical

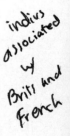

(handwritten margin note: indius associated by Briti and french)

critics to the conclusion that they would never be allowed to obtain enough seats in parliament to form a government. Given such barriers, it made obvious sense for the opposition to turn to the military for help. Frustrated army officers were only too willing to oblige, although usually on their own terms. This happened first in Iraq in 1936, and was repeated in Syria in 1949, in Egypt in 1952, in Iraq again in 1958 and in Sudan in the same year.

The regimes that managed to survive the early independence period problems do not seem to have had a great deal in common. In some cases a royal family was able to mobilise just sufficient resources to beat off, or outwit, the almost inevitable military plots, for example, in Jordan in the 1950s and Morocco in the 1960s and early 1970s. In another, Tunisia, the Neo-Destour and its leader, Bourguiba, were skilful enough to use the years immediately before and after independence to build up a one-party monopoly over the state and all the co-opted groups and associations within the society, sufficient to pre-empt early opposition. Lebanon presents the example of a third route forwards, its pluralist, confessional system lurching uneasily from crisis to crisis but only finally coming unstuck as a result of the accumulation of external as well as internal challenges in the early 1970s.

Many political analysts of the Middle East seem to have had little difficulty in accounting for the early instability of the independent Arab states in terms of explanations derived from a combination of religious and historical factors supposedly specific to the region. One example would be the role of Islam, which, in some arguments, makes all regimes illegitimate, either because they are secular or because they stand in the way of the creation of a community that embraces all believers. Another is Arabism, which is often supposed to play much the same role. But although religious or trans-national allegiances always have to be taken into account, the difficulties experienced in the first post-independent decades do not seem markedly different from those to be observed elsewhere in the non-European world, where ambivalent commitments to pluralism and parliamentarianism also tended to give way to military or one-party rule. It also has to be pointed out that in the Middle East, as in many other regions, political instability was overcome largely as a result of the general process of the expansion of the power of the central bureaucracy and of the security forces. This development will form the main subject of Chapter 2.

The creation of centralised state systems in Turkey and Iran

The creation of centralised state systems in Turkey and Iran had a number of important features in common. Both were based on the ruins of dynastic empires which had been challenged by constitutional and reformist groups in the early twentieth century, occupied by foreign troops and finally overthrown by regimes led by military officers who had seized power in alliance with nationalist forces in the early 1920s. Both were then refashioned through the creation of national armies, centralised bureaucracies and secular legal systems, according to models based very largely on western European experience. Both became the site for statist development projects in which reforms were imposed on society with very little discussion or debate.

Nevertheless, as far as their political histories and types of political practice were concerned, there were also many significant differences between the two. I will deal with these in the light of four of the most important variables: foreign influence and foreign domination; the role of the bureaucracy; the interventions of the local bourgeoisie; and the presence or absence of a ruling party.

The main institutions of the Turkish Republic were created in two stages.[6] The first of these was in the period when Mustafa Kemal was organising his resistance to foreign invasion in Ankara, when it was necessary to persuade leading politicians, officials and others to transfer their loyalties away from the British-dominated rump of the old Ottoman government still ruling in Istanbul. To this end Mustafa Kemal created what he called the Grand National Assembly, with a council of state drawn from among its own members to exercise government on a day-to-day basis. The fact that it represented a wide spectrum of political and social beliefs meant that its authority was accepted throughout most of Turkey, and it became an ideal vehicle for the creation of a new order based on the transfer of government from Istanbul to Ankara and the abolition of the Ottoman sultan's temporal power in 1922. Nevertheless, from Mustafa Kemal's own point of view it possessed certain drawbacks, not the least being that it contained a majority of members who still saw the sultan/caliph as the ideal religious leader of an Islamic constitutional state. This led him to take measures to dominate the assembly, first through the creation of a new party (the People's Party), then through his intervention to ensure that it had great success in the 1923 elections. As a result he was able to force through the abolition of the caliphate in 1924 and, more generally, to use the new party – soon renamed the Republican People's Party (RPP) – to isolate his major opponents and then to push through a series of radical reforms aimed at laying the foundations for a modern, secular nation state. One important step taken at this time was to insist that military officers could only take part in political life if they resigned their commissions, thus isolating those who chose to remain in the army from participation in the decision-making process.

The second stage involved the establishment of the RPP at the centre of what was, essentially, a one-party system. This was greatly assisted by the law for the maintenance of order passed at the beginning of the Kurdish and religious revolt of 1925, which was used to prevent all political activity outside the party itself. It was followed, in the early 1930s, by more positive steps to turn the RPP into a national organisation with an elite membership and an ideology. The former allowed the party to dominate the two-stage election system so as to ensure that it always had huge majorities in the assembly. As for the ideology, this was provided by the six principles of Kemalism introduced in May 1931 – republicanism, nationalism, populism, statism, secularism and something that can be translated either as permanent revolutionism or reformism.[7] These moves were not only supposed to define the basic character of the state but were also part of an attempt to create a political consensus around 'unchanging' guidelines which were beyond criticism and to which all political actors had to owe allegiance. From then on there was little practical difference between party and administration, even when, as after 1939, there were rules preventing party officials from holding state office. The hold of the party was further demonstrated by the way in which its nominee, Ismet Inonu, was so quickly elected as president, and then as chairman of the RPP, following Ataturk's death in November 1938.

A last ingredient of the new system was the statist tradition inherited from the Ottoman period and eagerly continued by Turkey's civilian bureaucratic elite. In these circumstances there was no great problem in presenting the state as a single, coherent, autonomous enterprise, the more so as rival social forces, like the large landowners, remained relatively weak. In these circumstances the beginnings of the growing challenge to the RPP's monopoly of power represented by the creation of the Democrat Party in 1946 is best explained in terms of intra-elite rivalry.[8]

Nevertheless, there were also powerful factors at work that ensured that the opposition received widening popular support all the way up to its overwhelming victory in the 1950 general election. One of these was a growing dissatisfaction with RPP rule, particularly its heavy-handed management of the economy during the Second World War and, in the rural areas, its challenge to Islamic religious practice. A second was the mounting American pressure for political change once Turkey had become reliant on its economic and military assistance after the Second World War. Finally, there was the impact of the RPP's policy of encouraging the enlargement of a native Turkish bourgeoisie, something begun on purely nationalist grounds but which received an important fillip from the statist development plans of the 1930s with their emphasis on joint public/private ventures as a way of building an industrial base. Certain members of this class within the RPP developed into vocal critics of those definitions of the Kemalist principle of 'statism' that emphasised the need for government control over all major aspects of economic life and, in the years after 1945, they became spokesmen for the many entrepreneurs who were anxious for more freedom to run their own affairs, large numbers of whom defected to the Democrats.

The RPP's willingness to surrender the government to the victorious Democrats in 1950 marked the start of a new era of multi-party activity in Turkish politics. However, as elsewhere in the non-European world, the long period of single-party rule had created structures that made life difficult for its successors, notably the close association between the RPP and its supporters in both the army and the bureaucracy, a point I will return to in Chapter 5.

Resistance to foreign occupation and the establishment of a new order in Persia also owed much to the efforts of one man, this time Colonel Reza Khan, who took advantage of the political crisis of the early 1920s to manoeuvre himself into such a position of personal dominance that he was able to have a constituent assembly depose the previous Kajar ruler and offer him the imperial throne in December 1925. Thereafter, however, his method of rule showed significant differences from that of Ataturk. For one thing, Iran possessed only a weak bureaucratic tradition, while the central government remained heavily dependent on the support of the large landowners and tribal shaikhs who dominated the rural areas. For another, Reza Shah chose to browbeat and control a captive parliament (the Majles) by means of personal domination rather than the creation of a single party. To this end he employed all the powers and the patronage that accrued to him as ruler. The result was a species of dictatorship which he used to push through some of the same reforms as Ataturk, although never with the same degree of administrative and organisational single-mindedness. Hence, although he too attacked the powers of the religious establishment by expanding the sphere of the secular educational and legal system, he still left the mullahs and the ayatollahs in possession of both large endowments and an influential system of religious education which ensured that most of their important resources remained intact.

Another very important way in which the history of Iranian politics differed from that of Turkey stemmed from the re-occupation of the country by British and Soviet forces in 1941 and the deposition of Reza Shah in favour of his son, Mohamed Reza. This at once paved the way for an incoherent period of political pluralism in which Persian politicians vied with each other for power in an arena heavily dominated by the representatives of the occupying powers and by the young shah, stripped of much of his father's power but still able to count on the loyalty of much of the army. To make the situation more complicated, the practice of politics had also to come to terms with the effects of an upsurge in tribal and provincial separatism, industrialisation and a huge expansion of education, the result of which was to produce a variety of social forces, none strong enough to dominate the centre like the Turkish bourgeoisie, but all demanding some kind of parliamentary representation.

In these circumstances, politicians were grouped together in loosely co-ordinated factions rather than parties, and the resulting instability produced an enormously rapid turnover of cabinets, with an average of a new prime minister every eight months between 1941 and 1953.[9] Meanwhile, the best that the few skilled political leaders could manage was to create short-lived coalitions based on a temporary coincidence of interest. But a sustained effort to dominate the system long enough to build up a permanent political force which could change the balance of power was impossible. The most obvious example was that of the prime minister, Mohamed Mossadeq, who was unable to take advantage of the explosion of popular nationalism following the Iranian takeover of the Anglo-Persian Oil Company in 1951 to establish a constitutional regime dominated by his own political alliance, the National Front. Instead, he was himself under-mined by a combination of royalist, religious and foreign opposition, paving the way for the dramatic return of the shah from his temporary exile, and the creation of a new imperial dictatorship based on what Abrahamian has styled a 'military monarchy'.[10]

Notes

1 Elizabeth Monroe, *Britain's Moment in the Middle East 1914–1956* (London: Chatto and Windus, 1963).
2 For useful discussions of the political and economic practices of the colonial state see, Hamza Alavi, 'The state in post-colonial societies: Pakistan and Bangladesh', *New Left Review*, 74 (July/August 1972), pp. 59–81; and A.G. Hopkins, *An Economic History of West Africa* (London: Longman, 1973), Chapter 5.
3 The arguments in this section draw heavily on those of Zubaida, *Islam, the People and the State*, pp. 145–52.
4 Figures from Jean-Jacques Waardenburg, *Les universités dans le monde Arabe*, quoted in Ahmed Abdalla, *The Student Movement and National Politics in Egypt 1923–1973* (London: Al-Saqi Books, 1985), p. 19.
5 For example, Philip Khoury, *Syria and the French Mandate: The Politics of Arab Nationalism 1920–1945* (London: I.B. Tauris, 1987), especially Part V. Also his 'Syrian urban politics in transition: The quarters of Damascus during the French Mandate', *International Journal of Middle Eastern Studies*, 16/X (November 1984), pp. 507–40.
6 Feroz Ahmed, *The Making of Modern Turkey* (London: Routledge, 1992), Chapter 4.
7 Ibid, p. 63.
8 Metin Heper, 'Transitions to democracy reconsidered: A historical perspective', in Dankwart A. Rustow and Kenneth Paul Erikson (eds), *Comparative Political Dynamics: Global Research Perspectives* (New York: Harper and Row, 1990).
9 Fahkreddin Azimi, *Iran: The Crisis of Democracy* (London: I.B. Tauris, 1989), Chapter 1.
10 Ervand Abrahamian, *Iran Between Two Revolutions* (Princeton, NJ: Princeton University Press, 1982), p. 441.

2   The growth of state power in the Arab world

The single-party regimes

Introduction

A huge expansion in the power and pervasiveness of the state apparatus is a common feature of the post-independence Middle East. This was largely a result of growth in the size of the bureaucracy, the police and the army, as well as, in many cases, the number of public enterprises. Similar types of expansion took place in many other parts of the Third World at the same time, and for many of the same reasons. These included the need to maintain security after the departure of the colonial power; the drive to establish control over the whole of the new national territory; and the desire to use the state to promote large programmes of economic development and social welfare. Once started, such processes were given further stimulus by foreign aid, by bureaucratic empire building and by the natural predilection of nationalist politicians for technological rather than political solutions to the problems of rapid modernisation.

There were specific Middle Eastern reasons for administrative expansion as well. These included: the implementation of programmes of land reform in a number of Arab countries in the 1950s; the apparent failure of the private sector to meet the challenge of development in the early independence period; and the sudden exodus of many hundreds of thousands of foreign officials, businessmen and agriculturalists that took place in Egypt during the Suez crisis of 1956 and in French North Africa immediately after the end of colonialism. The drive for Arab unity was another locally specific feature, with the Egyptian regime speeding up the process of state expansion in Syria during the three years of union between the two countries, 1958–61, and then encouraging the same process in Iraq in 1963/4, which it demanded as a necessary precondition for any possible union between Cairo and Baghdad. Oil wealth, too, played its part, financing the development plans of populous countries like Algeria and Iraq and forcing the rulers of the smaller desert states like Libya, Saudi Arabia and the Gulf shaikhdoms to begin to create modern systems of administration and to spend part of their new wealth on programmes of welfare for their own citizens.

In this chapter I will deal with the process of administrative expansion and control as it affected those five, well-populated, Arab countries that came under the direction of one-party regimes dedicated to state-led development under the banner of some form of Arab socialism: Algeria, Egypt, Iraq, Syria and Tunisia. All shared many features, notably the increase in state power and the particular type of politics that this produced. Some of the same processes were also at work in Sudan, with its Arab Socialist Union created in the early 1970s, and in the two Yemens both before and after their union in 1990. Chapter 3 will then examine the same topic in the context of a number of the less populated countries ruled by monarchs and royal families, like Jordan and the desert oil producers, as well as of the somewhat anomalous case of Libya.

As for the period under examination in this chapter, most of what is said about Egypt, Syria and Tunisia will concentrate on the years of 'socialist' management up to 1969/70, after which all three experienced what was variously described as a 'correction' or 'rectification' which introduced important new features into their economic and political systems. However, in Algeria and Iraq where the process started later, and could be sustained for longer as a result of increasing oil revenues, examples will be drawn from the 1970s as well.

Expansion in the size of the state apparatus and of its ability to regulate and control

From a chronological point of view, the first country to experience a process of large-scale bureaucratic expansion was Egypt. This followed closely upon the military coup of 1952 that brought Colonel Gamal Abdel Nasser and his fellow officers to power. Immediate attention was paid to increasing the strength of the police and public security while, as soon as British agreement had been obtained to evacuate its troops from the Suez Canal in 1954, the new rulers began to enlarge the armed forces and to re-equip them with more modern weapons, a process that was further intensified as a result of the Anglo-French and Israeli invasion of 1956, the Egyptian intervention in Yemen in the early 1960s and the disastrous Middle East war of 1967. The new regime also took immediate steps to institute measures of economic development based on ideas that had been elaborated by some of the more radical civilian politicians in the last years of King Farouk's monarchy. These included the land reform of 1952, the decision to build the Aswan High Dam and the inauguration of the Helwan Iron and Steel Complex in 1954. The nationalisations of foreign property during the Suez invasion then produced a further stimulus to state-led development, culminating in the first five-year plan, 1960–5, and the nationalisations of Egyptian private banks, factories and other enterprises in 1960/1.

The effect of this on the size and the role of the state apparatus can best be demonstrated by looking at a variety of key indices. As far as the numbers

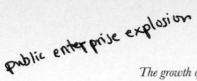

employed in the bureaucracy and the public enterprises were concerned, these rose from some 350,000 persons in 1951/2 to over 1,000,000 in 1965/6, an expansion far in excess of the growth of general employment, production or the population as a whole. Meanwhile, the number of government ministries had nearly doubled, from 15 to 29, during the same period.[1] Hence, by the time of the 1960 census, the government employed about a third of Egypt's non-agricultural labour force.[2] As for the armed forces, the total number of soldiers, sailors and airmen increased from 80,000 in 1955/6 to some 180,000 in 1966 plus about 90,000 paramilitary police.[3] A final index is that of government expenditure as a proportion of Egypt's gross national product which grew from 18.3 per cent in 1954/5 to 55.7 per cent in 1970 (including defence).[4]

In Syria the main period of expansion took place in the 1960s as the result, first, of the export of Egyptian systems of economic and political management during the brief period of the United Arab Republic, then of the statist policies of the Ba'th Party onwards. As a result, the number of state employees rose from 34,000 in 1960 to some 170,000 civil servants in 1975, with another 81,000 in the public sector.[5] If we add that there were also 180,000 men in the armed forces in this latter year, it means that about a quarter of those in urban employment, were then on the state payroll.[6]

Much the same process took place in Iraq after the revolution of 1958; in Tunisia, where the number of local Muslim employees jumped from 12,000 to 80,000 between 1956 and 1960; and in Algeria after independence in 1962.[7] Figures in Table 2.1 provide an illustration of this expansion in terms of huge increases in the proportion of government expenditure to gross domestic product during the 1960s. The only significant difference between the countries concerned spending on defence, where the Tunisian regime of Habib Bourguiba made a determined effort to limit the size of the army as a way of preventing possible coups. No such option existed for the Algerians, with their serious border dispute with Morocco, nor for the Iraqi military regimes of the 1960s, which were forced to confront the revival of Kurdish militancy in the north after the return of the exiled leader, Mustafa Barzani, in 1958. The result was a growth in the size of Algeria's armed forces from 40,000 in 1962 to 65,000 in 1965, and of Iraq's from 40,000 in 1955 to some 80,000 at the end of the 1960s.[8]

An important component in state expansion was the increased spending on education and welfare. Both are very labour intensive in terms of the numbers of

Table 2.1 The increase in the expenditure of central government and public enterprise as a proportion of GDP in certain Arab countries during the 1960s

	1960 (%)	*1970 (%)*
Algeria	25.0 (1963)	42.8 (1969)
Egypt	29.7	55.7
Iraq	28.4	44.2
Syria	23.5	37.9
Tunisia	20.7	40.7

Source: C.H. Moore, 'The consolidation and dissipation of power in unincorporated societies: Egypt and Tunisia', mimeo.

doctors, teachers and health workers who have to be employed to provide comprehensive national programmes. And, in the case of education, it was the huge increase in the size of the school population that first provided staff for the growing civil service and then encouraged the creation of more and more posts to accommodate unemployed school leavers. As far as Egypt was concerned, the number of young people in all types of education rose from 1,900,000 in 1953/4 to 4,500,000 in 1965/6 and 5,900,000 in 1972/3. Of these, 54,000 were in universities at the beginning of the period and 195,000 at the end.[9] Figures in the World Bank's annual World Development Report show the same process at work in Syria, where the proportion of school-age children enrolled in secondary education rose from 16 to 48 per cent between 1960 and 1975, and in Iraq from 19 to 35 per cent. Progress was initially slower in North Africa but then accelerated dramatically. To look only at Algeria, the numbers of children in secondary schools there jumped from 164,000 in 1966/7 to 742,000 a decade later.[10]

The process of expanding administrative control can also be seen at work in policies towards agriculture and industry. As far as agriculture was concerned, the regimes in all five Arab countries took quite considerable amounts of rural land into public ownership, usually as part of a programme of expropriating the larger estates for redistribution to small proprietors and landless peasants. In the Egyptian reforms of 1952 and 1961 a seventh of the total cultivated land was expropriated in this way; in Syria in 1958, and then from 1963 onwards, about a fifth; and in Iraq after 1958 almost half.[11] As it turned out, only in Egypt did the bulk of this land pass directly into peasant hands. However, even where only a part of it was redistributed, as in Syria and Iraq, the rest remained under state control and provided the occasion for the central government to extend its power throughout the rural areas, reducing the role of the old landed class and replacing it with a system of direct administration by the police, the ministries and the party.

Events followed a slightly different course in Tunisia and Algeria, where the first extension of state ownership was mainly as a result of the seizure of lands left by the departing French colonisers. However, in Algeria this was then followed in the early 1970s by the expropriation of 1,300,000 hectares owned by absentee landlords, some 16 per cent of the total cultivated area.[12] As elsewhere, this allowed the state to play a much closer role in rural affairs, usually through the establishment of various types of supervised co-operatives.

Programmes of nationalisation and of large-scale industrialisation provided the state with further opportunities for expansion and control. As everywhere else, the creation of an industrial base was seen as the essential component of economic modernity. And as elsewhere, a process of import substitution, beginning with relatively simple consumer durables and ending up, it was hoped, with the production of iron and steel and then machines, seemed to offer an easy way forward. The result was what Albert Hirschman has referred to in the Latin American context as the 'exuberant phase' of industrialisation, when Arab politicians and planners were too easily satisfied by the way in which local demand for many products was so quickly met by an increase in local production.[13] Only later, in Egypt and Tunisia in the late 1960s, and in Iraq and

Algeria in the late 1970s, did the problems inherent in such a strategy – the drain on scarce currency reserves to buy foreign machinery and raw materials, the lack of attention to agriculture and exports, the problems of managing huge industrial plant – begin to demand serious attention (see Chapter 7). Meanwhile, there was a large increase in the numbers of new factories and in the size of the industrial labour force, providing new jobs and new opportunities for profit and placing the state right at the centre of the drive for economic advance.

A last point of note is that the whole process of expanding state involvement in the economy was justified by the need for rapid development and for a more equitable distribution of a rising national income. This provided an important source of legitimation for the regimes, as well as allowing them to bolster their authority and to reduce the possibility of challenge by asserting the expertise of their official scientists and planners. Such notions could be expressed in fine-sounding technological language or in the more idealistic discourse of Arab socialism. Speeches by the leaders of all five countries leaned heavily on both vocabularies, although they were always careful to make it quite clear that, in a Middle Eastern context, socialism had nothing to do with the dangerous notion of social division and class struggle. Only very rarely was it suggested that any local class or group was no longer to be considered as part of the national community. And even then, as in the occasional references to feudalists or parasitic capitalists, the impression was usually given that such persons were either foreigners or else so closely allied with the forces of reactionary imperialism as to have lost the right to be called citizens. In this way, the emphasis on socialist planning provided an essential ingredient for the public ideology of regimes heavily embarked on statist, integrative pro-grammes of national development and control.

Management of so large an apparatus with such extensive commitments gave the small numbers of individuals at the apex of each regime enormous power. The result was a type of system best classified as authoritarian.[14] This is one in which power is highly centralised, pluralism is suspect and where the regime seeks to exercise a monopoly over all legitimate political activity. Something of its logic in an Egyptian context can be seen from the vehemence with which President Nasser and his supporters denounced the emergence of what they termed 'an alternative centre of power' around Field Marshall Abd al-Hakim Amr, the Chief of the General Staff, in the years just before the 1967 war. As their speeches at that time suggest, it was enough simply to draw attention to the enormity of such a development without ever needing to explain why a multiplication of such centres was actually so wrong.

Authoritarian systems are different from totalitarian ones, however, as they lack the powerful institutions that would be needed to control or to transform society by means of bureaucratic methods alone. As a result, people have to be mobilised, different groups integrated, opposition contained, by a variety of methods which range from terror and brute force (the stick) to economic inducement (the carrot), and from the use of personal, ethnic or group affiliations to the compulsory membership of carefully constructed unions and professional associations designed to keep all those at work in the modern sector strictly in their place. In these circumstances it is only possible to describe some of the major strategies employed in these five Arab states.

When it comes to organised groups within the society, the ideal strategy for an authoritarian regime is to destroy those that it cannot control, and to remake and reorder those that it can. This in fact was the policy first employed in Egypt and Tunisia, whose societies were relatively homogeneous and where bureaucratic structures were already well-developed by the time the Nasser and Bourguiba regimes came to power. Independent political parties were soon suppressed or forced to disband while existing unions and associations were either banned or driven to reorganise themselves according to new sets of rules and regulations. The result was a monopoly of political activity for the regime's single party or national rally: the Neo-Destour in Tunisia; the Liberation Rally, followed by the National Union and then the Arab Socialist Union in Egypt. At the same time, a tightly controlled trade union structure was created under the Union Général des Travailleurs Tunisiens (UGTT) and the Confederation of Egyptian Workers. This was paralleled by the establishment of a number of associations for students, women, peasants and others, while the existing professional associations for doctors, lawyers, journalists and the like were brought under state control, with new leaders installed and, in Egypt, membership in one or other of them made compulsory for all university graduates.

Once in place, such a structure was used not only to ensure the controlled collaboration of the groups in question but also to define the way in which they were able to present their demands and to be represented politically at the national level. In the case of trade unions, for instance, industrial disputes or negotiations about pay and conditions could not be pursued by strike action and were subject to rigid processes of arbitration. More generally, the division of so much of the population into unions and associations allowed the regime to define the role their members were expected to play in the general process of modernisation and national integration. Where women were concerned, for example, it would usually stress the need for them to go out to work, an appeal tempered, as the occasion demanded, by reference to their other role as wives and mothers.

Outside the large cities, state control was initially represented by such centrally appointed persons as the village policeman and the village schoolteacher. Later, however, all the regimes used the mechanism of the land reform and the co-operative to create new institutions at a local level. These could include a village council, a branch of the party and, in Iraq and Syria, a branch of the Peasants' Union as well. In addition, the government was usually represented directly by officials of the ministry of agriculture or agrarian reform who were responsible for providing instructions about the type of crops to be grown, the methods to be employed and the way they should be marketed. In such circumstances, the balance between local initiative and central guidance varied greatly according to the degree of village-level input that was either tolerated or actively encouraged. To speak very generally, whereas the Syrian Ba'thi regime seems to have made the most strenuous efforts to encourage the recruitment of active party cadres, perhaps because of its own strong rural base, this strategy was only employed briefly in Egypt in the 1960s and hardly at all in Iraq, where the party approached the agricultural sector in a much more heavy-handed way based on fixed ideas about how it ought properly to be managed.[15] The Algerian case was different again. There the production and service co-operatives created to assist the beneficiaries of the 1971 land reform were granted a great deal of autonomy in theory but then found themselves heavily circumscribed by the fact that their peasant members were required to cultivate their land according to the country's national plan, as well as by their need to rely on certain state monopolies to supply agricultural inputs and to market certain of their crops.[16]

A second type of strategy was used to extend state control supervision over both the educational and legal systems and the religious establishment. In all three cases, the main incentive was to combine control over the political space that the school and university, the court and the mosque might offer to the regime's opponents, combined with an attempt to appropriate their ideas and practices to serve regime purposes. In the case of the educational system, this was effected quite simply by establishing a national curriculum and then either by forbidding student political activity entirely or steering it into the safer channels provided by the party and by government-controlled youth organisations. As for the law, the courts were brought under control by a dual process of coercing or replacing the existing judges and by drastically restricting the scope of the system by delegating responsibility for much of the adjudication and enforcement to a host of extra-legal authorities, for example, the military, the internal security forces, the managers of state enterprises or the village councils. The shrinkage of the legal system was pushed still further in certain countries by the development of the notion that there existed a higher socialist, or revolutionary, legality, which, whenever applied, superseded the ordinary laws of the land.

Religion seemed to prove no more of an obstacle to state control, at least during the process of bureaucratic consolidation. No regime felt able to abandon Islam entirely for this would have been to cut the most important single ideological and cultural link between it and the bulk of its population. Neverthe-less, all of them explicitly or implicitly asserted the primacy of the political over the religious. And all relied heavily on two important legacies from the Middle East's nineteenth-century past. One was the Ottoman practice of bringing the religious establishment under state control by paying the *ulama* (the clergy) official salaries, by creating a government ministry to manage its property, and by building up a secular educational and legal system to challenge its previous monopoly over these two important areas. The other was the use of the dominant modernist strand in Sunni Islam to obtain official legitimation for state policy. Algeria's establishment of a ministry of traditional education and religious affairs would be an example of the first type of policy; President Nasser's ability

[handwritten: obtain religious opinion justifying decisions]

to obtain a *fatwa* (religious opinion) justifying many of his major policy decisions is a good example of the second. This structure of control was further reinforced by rules making membership of independent religious parties and associations, like Egypt's Muslim Brothers, illegal. Such policies seemed to work smoothly for a while but came under increasing attack in the new political atmosphere of the 1970s (see Chapter 9).

Control over the educational system and the religious establishment, as well as over the press, radio and television, gave the regimes one further advantage, and that was the capacity to establish an ideological hegemony in terms of a statist, universalistic, discourse based on notions of nationalism, socialism and populism, which was then used either to drive out or to subdue alternative political vocabularies. This gave them the power to set the terms of any debate, to direct discussion and, in general, to make it absolutely clear what could and could not be said. It is only necessary to read the accounts of the meeting of any national assembly or any party congress to see what a powerful weapon this could be.

The bottom line as far as state control was concerned was the presence of the army and the police, backed up by the many intelligence services, the secret courts, the torture chambers and the prisons.[17] This is not to say, however, that some of the regimes were not popular to begin with, even if they themselves then proceeded to destroy all the methods that would have made it possible to test such an opinion. President Nasser, President Bourguiba and the National Liberation Front (FLN) in Algeria won real battles in their struggles against the old colonial powers. Furthermore, the enforced retreat of the foreign business communities offered great advantages to local entrepreneurs, while the land reforms and the expansion of the educational systems provided obvious opportunities for a better life for millions of people. Nevertheless, no regime was prepared to share power with more than a limited number of chosen collaborators; organised opposition was ferociously crushed; and all rulers were careful to cultivate an atmosphere of arbitrariness and fear. As in the political system described by the Hungarian novelist, Georg Konrad, the system itself required political prisoners.[18] And whereas some, like the Egyptians, the Tunisians and the Algerians, were able, in Konrad's words, to 'create great order with little terror', others, like the Ba'thi regime that came to power in Iraq in 1968, used violence and fear of violence as a basic instrument for maintaining its control.[19]

[handwritten: create perception of violence and fear]

Given the existence of these types of large, powerful, durable, authoritarian structures, it was inevitable that the ordinary citizen encountered the state at every turn, whether in the Mugamma, the huge building in central Cairo where it was necessary to go for passports, identity cards, export visas and the like, or out in the villages, where the local co-operative had replaced the old landlords as a provider of seeds, fertiliser and credit. Meanwhile, regime policies were shaping people's lives by opening up new possibilities, providing new resources, forcing them into new organisations and creating new relationships between employers and employees, owners and tenants, parents and children, and even men and women. A few chose to confront the state; others tried to ignore it or to imagine that it could be made to go away. Nevertheless, for the vast majority, there was no alternative but to try to use, manipulate or exploit it where possible. For the population at large, access to the channels of influence that led to a job or a loan or a licence was all.

Politics in an authoritarian state

Authoritarian states pose particular problems for political analysis. One of the ways in which the regimes that control them try to give an impression of coherence and of concentrated power and might is to cloak themselves in secrecy. Decisions are generally taken behind closed doors. Divisions are hidden away in the interests of presenting a united front. Everything seems to be locked up inside a vast, opaque, bureaucratic apparatus. Meanwhile, on the outside, there are few spaces for independent political activity, and it is only on rare occasions that a university, factory or mosque escapes from state control long enough to create its own leadership and its own rival political platform. Any other type of organised opposition is forced into an underground existence. There are no polls, and the various controlled elections or referendums provide only fragmentary evidence about what a public might be thinking.

The search for a way of locating the politics within this particular type of system has generally taken one of two forms. Perhaps the most influential has been to focus on the activities of rival factions among the political elite.[20] A second is to concentrate on the way in which the struggle for access to state resources is structured in terms of groups based on ties of region or sect rather than of class.[21] Both approaches are said to be justified on the basis that the authoritarian systems to be found in the Middle East possess four major, and related, characteristics. One, they cannot tolerate organised groups within their own structures. Two, they tend to deal with the people not as individuals but as members of some larger regional, ethnic or religious collectivity. Three, they systematically inhibit the development of an active class consciousness, for example, by preventing the development of free trade unions. Four, they subordinate economic policies to measures of political control.

Nevertheless, it is easy to quarrel both with the restricted nature of such approaches and with the premises on which they are based. The criticism that has been levelled against studies that focus simply on a narrow political elite is well known: they allow the political leaders too much freedom to make decisions without constraint; they reduce politics to a battle for power; they neglect the economic interests of those involved. Moreover, factions are not a single type of unit, they do not remain the same over time and, most important of all, they cannot be said to constitute a self-contained system of political activity, being embedded in a structure of institutions, classes and interests that is very much larger than themselves.[22] Focus on the role of groups is open to many of the same challenges. They certainly existed but in such a bewildering variety of forms – tribes, regional affiliations, sects and so on – that they resist simple classification, while their role in the political life of the Middle East is equally various and very much more obvious in some countries than others. Moreover, there were many more ways of access to state power and resources than simply by being a member of some collectivity, for example, through institutions like the party or the army, or through formal economic or professional associations like chambers of commerce.[23]

Lastly, the characterisation of Middle Eastern political systems upon which such theories are based is equally oversimplified, and leaves out much too much. Classes did exist as political actors, whether in an active manner, where a sense of common consciousness is present, or in a more passive way, as when a whole elite chose policies based clearly and obviously on the notion of private, rather than public, property. It follows that the point about the primacy of political over economic considerations also requires further elaboration. Viewed simply from the angle of the immediate decision, it obviously existed, just as it does everywhere else in the world. But there is another sense in which policies involving rapid industrialisation or the attempt to earn scarce foreign currency through the development of tourism had their own logic and a dynamic that often affected huge areas of economic life, regardless of political attempts at control.

In these circumstances it is better to start afresh by focusing on two general questions: What is politics? And where does the process of political activity take place? This has the major virtue of encouraging us to take a large view of the subject and then forcing us to have to specify the different types of actors and different types of arenas involved, as well as their different orders of importance. In the case of the former, this will involve consideration of individuals, of unofficial as well as of organised groups, of classes, and so on. In the latter it necessitates a discussion of the various locations – bureaucratic, institutional, provincial, local – in which political activity used to, and still does, take place. Viewed from this perspective, there cannot be any one answer to the initial set of questions, and analysis will have to take account of many different levels, arenas and types of situation. I will begin by looking at the state apparatus itself.

Given the concentration of power in an authoritarian, one-party state, the most important political actor was clearly the president. As a rule he was, and sometimes still is, not only head of state but also commander-in-chief of the armed forces and party chairman as well. Typically he made most key decisions on his own in the light of his own version of the public interest. He did not have to seek advice, and took good care to ensure that no one else within the system could accumulate sufficient power to challenge his authority. Further power came from his ability to stand above the various institutions of state, and the various factions they contained, and to adjudicate between them. Once the five Arab regimes had managed to consolidate themselves, only two presidents, Ben Bella and Chadli Benjedid of Algeria, were ousted by their colleagues, and only two others, Ahmed Hassan al-Bakr of Iraq and Habib Bourguiba of Tunisia, were eased out towards the end of their lives by ambitious younger men. On the

evidence so far, death is the only certain way in which, in an authoritarian   *death*
system, a president's rule can be brought to an end.

Nevertheless, presidents could not do exactly what they wanted, and
their power was subject to significant constraints. On the whole, they had the
least freedom in certain areas of domestic policy given the fact that none of
them had a strong enough political or social base simply to impose his ideas on
the rest of the country, and all had to make concessions to important groups
of supporters like the Alawi notables in Syria or the landowners from the
Sahel region in Tunisia who were so close to President Bourguiba. It was
also necessary to delegate enough power to certain individuals and groups simply
to get things done. Presidents might prefer cabinets full of technocrats with no
power base of their own, or a system of institutional balances in
which one ministry or one agency was set up to check another, but, when faced
with a major crisis, all of them seemed to realise that this was a recipe
for impotence and immobilism.

The president presided over a state apparatus that consisted, in the first
instance, of its major component institutions: the military, the party, the security
services, the bureaucracy and the economic enterprises. All had their own
organisational reasons for obtaining resources, influencing policy and
preserving as much as possible of their autonomy. Examples abound of major
institutional rivalries in which, for example, a party might try to seek to extend
its influence into an army and be strongly resisted. More examples will be
given in later chapters. In addition, certain ministries tended to represent
particular economic and social interests that they sought to protect and expand,
for instance, the link between the ministry of labour and the unions or the
ministry of agriculture and the various groups of landowning peasants.

The state itself then provided the major arena for political activity. It contained all the major institutional actors involved in national issues and the
distribution of national resources. Here, too, were the major individual actors;
the men (and a few women) who controlled these large institutions or who
represented significant interests inside and outside the state apparatus. As a
rule the most important came from the group of colleagues who established
the regime in the first place, the Free Officers in Egypt or the so-called Oujda
group of close military associates of President Boumedienne of Algeria. It is
they who were given control over the key posts like the ministry of defence and
the ministry of the interior. However, over time, their numbers tended to
dwindle and they were replaced by others who had worked their way into senior
positions in the party, the army and intelligence. On the whole, the politicians
who were invited to run the domestic side of the economy were much
less powerful, controlled less important ministries and were subject to a
much higher rate of turnover. A last source of power was identification with,
and possible support from some major outside actor, perhaps the embassy
of a superpower, like the USSR before 1990 or the United States, or perhaps
a powerful Saudi prince with enough influence to direct large sums of
money towards the regime.

The more durable of the major regime politicians inevitably became patrons of quite large networks of clients. As a rule these consisted simply of people who had attached themselves to them for reasons of ambition or in order to use them to protect or extend some particular interest. But it might be that the network was also held together by some kind of shared political or ideological position. Important patrons would then try to ensure that their clients obtained high level posts, perhaps as ministers or chairmen of economic enterprises, in exchange for their co-operation in helping them with policies or schemes of their own. This is a reminder that patronage can be a two-way process, that patron and client both need each other, and that it is also something that has to be worked at, attended to, over time. There are scarcely any analyses of network building in the Arab world written from this particular perspective. One of the few scholars who have examined the process in detail in its Algerian context, Bruno Etienne, suggests that a possible dynamic is one that leads a patron whose position in national politics depends initially on the support of a particularly important interest group to try to reduce this dependence over time.[24] Another of Etienne's important insights concerns the way in which different networks may coalesce for a while to form factions when their major interests coincide.[25]

The political role of classes and other social groups in homogeneous and divided societies

An analysis of the role of classes and other social groups within authoritarian systems presents particular problems. Some of these arise from the usual difficulty in locating and defining each particular class, especially in a situation in which the rapid increase in educational opportunity and state employment was bound to make for considerable mobility and general fluidity. In addition, the authoritarian state itself often played an active role in shaping or denying expressions of class interest. In some cases, particular classes were either destroyed or very much reduced in economic and social power (for example, the large landowners in Egypt, Iraq and Syria). In others, parties, associations and unions that might otherwise act as vehicles for class politics were either banned or reorganised as part of the apparatus of state control. As Ahmed Ben Saleh, the Tunisian labour leader, noted after his dismissal from government office in 1969, 'My behaviour is to be explained by my dual membership in party and trade union', a divided loyalty which inhibited him from being able to represent working-class interests when they clashed with those of the regime.[26] For all these reasons, class conflict, the main motor force for developing class conscious-ness, was permitted only muted expression.

Nevertheless, the expression of class interests cannot be made to disappear entirely. As far as the private sector is concerned, whether in industry, trade or agriculture, an essential component of the ownership of property, and of the employment of workers, is an implicit conflict between capital and labour. It also follows that both sides are likely to organise themselves, if they can, either for the purposes of direct confrontation or, more usually, in order to obtain the intervention of the state on their own side.

Working-class activity in the state sector has sometimes been more difficult to discern. However, in Egypt, as elsewhere, groups of workers were often able to obtain sufficient independence from official control to organise strikes and sit-ins or to develop a local leadership which was independent of the official union structure. Workers' representatives were also able to use their presence at the numerous official economic conferences called by government or party to defend their interests in job security, a minimum wage and participation on the board of state enterprises against management efforts to curtail their privileges. On other occasions they found champions among senior regime politicians, aware of their strategic position within the economy and the vital role they had been given in government development programmes. Lastly, there were a few instances of overt opposition at the national level some of which will be described in Chapter 11.

An identification of the political role of the middle class is equally complicated, and depends largely on being able to establish a link between the continued existence of private property and the political practices of senior officers, high level bureaucrats and others aspiring to a bourgeois lifestyle within the regime.[27] Such a link is seen most clearly in the case of rural land, where ownership of quite substantial holdings, often held in defiance of the government's reforms, constituted a common bond between important figures within many regimes, affecting both their policy towards the agricultural sector and, more generally, making them keen defenders of their country's rural elite.

More generally, writers like Hugh Roberts and Jean Leca have argued for the existence of a fundamental link between state officials and private property based on the desire of significant numbers of the former to augment their own, and their family's, resources, as an insurance against the possible loss of a job that gives them regular access to state resources.[28] This encouraged them to establish links with the private sector, a task made easier, according to Roberts, by the fact that the boundary between public and private was so fluid as to allow all kinds of profitable arrangements between bureaucrats, managers of public enterprises and private companies and individuals.[29] Rules governing such transactions were usually not well-enforced, and the major risk that their practitioners ran was the malevolence of their political enemies or the occasional official campaign against an ill-defined notion of 'corruption'. It was the existence of such links, based on shared interest and aspirations to a common lifestyle, that played an important role in skewing public policy in directions favourable to private accumulation, whether in the area of income tax (kept low), support for local companies against foreign competition, or access to scarce foreign exchange.

Another aspect of state policy that has received considerable attention is the way in which regimes inhibited the development of class solidarities by structuring their system of access to political power, and of distributing resources in such a way that people benefited, 'not on the bases of class affiliation but as

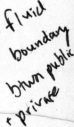

fluid boundary btwn public & private

individuals, families, particular communities, villages or regions'.[30] In the case of the five states in question, this would seem to have been truer of Syria, Iraq and, to some extent, Algeria than of Egypt and Tunisia. One obvious difference is that the former are much less homogeneous societies with regimes that were based very obviously on support from particular regions and, in the case of Syria after 1966, from one particular sect, the Alawis. This can easily be demonstrated by looking at the social composition of the states. In Iraq just after the Ba'th seizure of power in 1968, for example, all the members of both the Revolutionary Command Council and the Regional Command of the party were from the small, predominantly Sunni, region between Baghdad and Takrit.[31]   And,   although   efforts   were   later   made   to widen the circle of leadership to include Shi'is and Kurds, as well as persons from the rural areas, the fact that so many of the top personnel continued to come from the same small region gave some of its inhabitants great privileges, as can be seen from the fact that, in the 1980s, so many of the country's leading public works contractors also came from Takrit.[32] By the same token, major acts   of   resistance   have   been   launched   by   groups   from regions or sects that have felt themselves systematically disadvantaged by the new regimes, for example, the Sunni inhabitants of Hama in Syria who provided major support for the Muslim Brothers' revolt in 1982, or the Berber leaders of the strikes and demonstrations that broke out in the Kabyle region of Algeria in 1980.[33]

It is probably also significant that the development of different classes had proceeded much further in Egypt and Tunisia before the creation of the authoritarian state than it had in Algeria, Syria and Iraq. As Joel Beinin notes of the Egyptian case, there was an underlying continuity in the workers' movement before and after 1952, even though it has often been concealed in the literature by books which treat labour history as simply the institutional history of the official trade unions.[34] The same is true of the Tunisian working class, whose power and organisation continued to assert itself well after independence and in spite of all Bourguiba's efforts to bring it under control. Industry and commerce were less well developed in Syria and Iraq, with few large concerns to take into public ownership and a much smaller number of well-organised workers. In the case of Iraq the political consequences of this situation were masked for a while by the ability of the local Communist Party to mobilise large numbers of followers in street demonstrations in the 1950s. However, its lack of a solid class base in Iraqi society was soon revealed when it quickly succumbed to the assaults of its enemies from 1959 onwards. And if it was invited to join the Ba'th-dominated National Progressive Front for a few years in the mid-1970s, this was mainly because it was still better able to command the allegiance of certain rural communities than its Ba'thi rival. As for Algeria, here local industrialisation was deliberately held up by the French so that regionalism, rather than class identity, remained the major basis of solidarity.

Against the reification of the state

For many writers, the huge size of the bureaucracy in most Middle East and Third World countries has been taken as a sign of a very strong state. And this, in turn, has led them to pose the question as to how anything so formidable could have achieved so little success when it came to pushing through much-heralded programmes of economic development and social transformation.[35] However, this is to ask the wrong question, and then to look for answers in the wrong place.

Arguments that seek to explain the apparent paradox of a strong state with weak powers rest on two misleading assumptions. One is that the state is a coherent entity with a single intent. The other is that this same entity inevitably tries to penetrate and transform a second entity called 'society'. However, as already argued in the introduction to Part I, the state's apparent coherence is more a matter of presentation than reality. This is how most regimes wished things to be. They based much of their legitimacy on their role as the masters of a well-defined path towards modernisation, a claim that not only reinforced their appearance of single-mindedness but also justified whatever interferences and interventions in existing social structures and relations they might choose to make.

perception, not reality

However, when it comes to an analysis of how policies were actually made and executed, what is revealed is a whole range of often contradictory aims and conflicting interests which intersected with those of the wider society in such a way as to blur boundaries and to call into question the whole notion of one distinct entity acting upon another. One good example among many is that of the Egyptian land reform programme. This is usually presented as a major instrument of rural social transformation but in reality it proved to be something much more various and complex.[36] To begin with, the first reform law was passed only six weeks after the Free Officers came to power in 1952, and cannot be regarded as a well-thought out piece of social legislation. Further negative evidence comes from the fact that very little effort was made to see whether the reform had improved agrarian productivity. It is also notewor-thy that, for most of the 1950s, the main focus of administrative attention was directed towards solving the problems of Egyptian over-population and landlessness, not by redistribution but by bringing large quantities of new land into cultivation, for example, in the so-called 'Liberation' Province between Cairo and Alexandria, to be provided with water by the construction of the High Dam at Aswan.

Looked at from this perspective, even the more thorough-going Egyptian agrarian reform law of 1961 is best seen not as a major piece of socio-economic engineering but as just another rather limited attack on landlord power, passed hurriedly as a response to the alleged role of Syrian feudalists and capitalists in the break-up of the union of the two countries in the United Arab Republic. Hence, when the Nasser regime took up the matter of the persistence of 'feudalism' in Egypt itself, as revealed by the investigations following the killing of a peasant activist at the village of Kamshish in 1966, it experienced the greatest difficulty in reaching a consensus about what, if anything, had gone wrong and so what ought to be done.[37] It did not help matters that in such a case the boundaries between what were defined as state and private interests were clearly very indistinct, and that allegations of corruption and other wrong-doing could be backed up not only by appeals to a bewildering variety of different notions of legality and of interpretations of public policy but also by sheer political expediency.

In all this, the idea of the supposed coherence of the state as a single actor with a systematic programme of social transformation is impossible to sustain. What we have instead is the various bits and pieces of the Egyptian version of Hobbes' great Leviathan, acting and reacting in ways that can only be understood through a process of disaggregation which challenges the conventional dichotomies of state versus society, legal versus illegal, or scientific planning versus private self-interest. It is not a question of testing the strength of a supposed single entity – the state – or of its ability to mould another – society. Rather, it is a question of how to interpret the meaning of what was revealed at such moments, when the veil of omnipotence created around itself by an authoritarian regime fell away to expose the bundle of competing, and often contradictory, interests that had always lain just behind.

Notes

1 Nazih N.M. Ayubi, *Bureaucracy and Politics in Contemporary Egypt* (London: Ithaca Press, 1980), p. 189.
2 Clement H. Moore, 'Authoritarian politics in unincorporated society: The case of Nasser's Egypt', *Comparative Politics*, VI/2 (January 1974), p. 199.
3 Elizabeth Picard, 'Arab military in politics: From revolutionary plot to authoritarian state', in Adeed Dawisha and I. William Zartman (eds), *Beyond Coercion: The Durability of the Arab State*, (London: Croom Helm, 1988), p. 119.
4 Moore, 'Authoritarian politics', Table 2, p. 199.
5 Nazih Ayubi, 'Arab bureaucracies: Expanding size, changing roles', in Dawisha and Zartman (eds), *Beyond Coercion*, p. 19.
6 Picard, 'Arab military', p. 119.
7 For Tunisia, see Lisa Anderson, *The State and Social Transformation in Tunisia and Libya 1830–1980* (Princeton, NJ: Princeton University Press, 1985), pp. 235–6.
8 Picard, 'Arab military', p. 119.
9 Abdalla, *Student Movement*, Tables 6.1 and 6.2, p. 102.
10 Mahfoud Bennoune, *The Making of Contemporary Algeria 1830–1987* (Cambridge: Cambridge University Press, 1988), Table 9.3, p. 225.
11 E.R.J. Owen, 'Economic aspects of revolution in the Middle East', in P.J. Vatikiotis (ed.), *Revolution in the Middle East and Other Case Studies* (London: George Allen & Unwin, 1972), Table 1, p. 53. Elisabeth Longuenesse gives a smaller proportion for Syrian expropriation (25 per cent) in her 'Structures sociales et rapports de classe dans les sociétés du Proche Orient', *Peuples Méditerranéens* (July/September 1982), pp. 167–85.
12 Bennnoune, *Making of Contemporary Algeria*, p. 176.
13 A.O. Hirschman, 'The political economy of import-substituting industrialization in Latin America', *The Quarterly Journal of Economics*, 82/1 (February 1968), pp. 11–12.
14 A key work on the subject is Samuel P. Huntington and Clement H. Moore (eds), *Authoritarian Politics in Modern Societies: The Dynamics of Established One Party Systems* (New

York: Basic Books, 1970). See also Guillermo O'Donnell, *Modernization and Bureaucratic Authoritarianism* (Berkeley, CA: Institute of International Studies, 1973); and, in a Middle Eastern context, Moore, 'Authoritarian politics in unincorporated society', pp. 193–218.

15 Compare Raymond H. Hinnebusch, 'Local politics in Syria: Organization and mobilization in four village cases', *Middle East Journal*, XXX/1 (Winter, 1976), p. 124; Ilya Harik, *The Political Mobilization of Peasants: A Study of an Egyptian Peasant Community* (Bloomington, Indiana and London: University of Indiana Press, 1974); and Robert Springborg, 'Baathism in practice: Agriculture, politics and political culture in Syria and Iraq', *Middle Eastern Studies*, 17/2 (April 1981), pp. 191–206.

16 Gauthier de Villers, *Problèmes d'emploi rural en Algérie* (Geneva: ILO Progamme Mondiale d'Emploi, December 1978), pp. 17–19.

17 The best sources are the many Amnesty International reports on the Middle East. See, for example, *Iraq: Report of an Amnesty International Mission* (London, 1983); *Syria: Report to the Government* (London. 1983); and *Syria: Torture by Security Forces* (London, 1987).

18 Georg Konrad, *The Loser* (London: Penguin Books, 1984), p. 205.

19 Ibid.; Samir Al-Khalil, *The Republic of Fear: The Politics of Modern Iraq* (London: Radius, 1989), Chapters 1 and 2.

20 For example, Robert Springborg, *Family, Power and Politics in Egypt* (Philadelphia, PA: Pennsylvania University Press, 1982), p. 83; and William Zartman, 'L'élite algérienne sous le President Chadli Benjadid', *Maghreb/Machrek*, 106 (October/November/ December 1984), p. 39.

21 For example, Bruno Etienne, *L'Algérie, cultures et révolution* (Paris: Editions du Seuil, 1977); and Jean Leca, 'Social structure and political stability', in Dawisha and Zartman (eds), *Beyond Coercion*, p. 165.

22 This point is acknowledged in Zartman, 'L'élite algérienne', p. 39; and Leca, 'Social structure and political stability', pp. 164–83.

23 I take this to be Hanna Batatu's argument when, after careful analysis, he says that he can find 'little evidence' that, when it came to economic policies, President Asad 'gave a marked preference to the interests of the Alawi community' in Syria, *Syria's Peasantry, the Descendents of its Lesser Rural Notables and their Politics* (Princeton, NJ: Princeton University Press, 1999), pp. 227–9.

24 Etienne, *L'Algérie*, pp. 92–106.

25 Ibid., pp. 40–5.

26 Quoted in Bassam Tibi, 'Trade unions as an organizational form of political opposition in Afro-Arab states: The case of Tunisia, *Orient*, 24/4 (December 1979), p. 88.

27 This topic is analysed by John Waterbury, *The Egypt of Nasser and Sadat: The Political Economy of Two Regimes* (Princeton, NJ: Princeton University Press, 1983), pp. 247–60; and by Hugh Roberts, 'Political development in Algeria: The regime of Greater Kabylia', unpublished D.Phil. thesis (Oxford University, 1980), pp. 69–74.

28 This analysis draws heavily on ideas put forward by Roberts in ibid., pp. 73–5.

29 Ibid., p. 84. Also Leca, 'Social structure and political stability', pp. 166–9.

30 Zubaida, *Islam, the People and the States*, p. 165.

31 Amatzia Baram, 'The ruling political elite in Ba'thi Iraq, 1968–1986: Changing features of a collective profile', *International Journal of Middle Eastern Studies*, 21/4 (November 1989), pp. 450–2.

32 Marion Farouk-Sluglett, 'Iraq's capitalism in transition', *MERIP*, 14/6, 125–6 (July/September 1984), p. 52.

33 Raymond A. Hinnebusch, *Authoritarian Power and State Formation in Ba'thist Syria: Army, Party and Peasant* (Boulder, CO: Westview Press, 1990), pp. 286–90; and Hugh

Roberts, 'The unforeseen development of the Kabyle question in Algeria', *Government and Opposition*, 17/3 (Summer, 1982), pp. 312–4.

34 'Labor, capital and the state in Nasserist Egypt: 1952–1961', *International Journal of Middle Eastern Studies*, 21/1 (February 1989), p. 72.

35 For example, Ayubi, *Bureaucracy and Politics*, Chapter 2. See also, Midgal, *Strong Societies*, pp. 4–15.

36 For example, Hamied Ansari, *Egypt: The Stalled Society* (Albany, NY: The State University of New York Press, 1986), particularly Chapters 1 and 3; and Leonard Binder, *In a Moment of Enthusiasm: Political Power and the Second Stratum in Egypt* (Chicago, IL and London: University of Chicago Press, 1978), Chapter 14.

37 Ansari, *Stalled Society*, pp. 34–8, 42, 102, 137–8. See also Waterbury's description of the 'revisionist' account of the events at Khamshish, *Egypt of Nasser and Sadat*, p. 340n.

3 The growth of state power in the Arab world under family rule, and the Libyan alternative

Introduction

The growth in the size and pervasiveness of the central government apparatus was not confined to those states with single-party regimes but took place under a variety of other systems as well, most notably those subject to monarchical or family rule in Morocco, Jordan and throughout most of the Arabian peninsula. The most dramatic example of this is to be found in the tiny Gulf shaikhdoms, where oil was found either just before or just after the Second World War, and which used their new-found wealth to create large bureaucracies and comprehensive welfare facilities for their growing populations. In Kuwait, for instance, the number of government employees increased from 22,073 in 1966 to 113,274 in 1976 and 145,000 in 1980 – nearly a quarter of the total labour force.[1] Growth was just as rapid in Saudi Arabia, where the civil service grew from a few hundred in the 1950s to about 37,000 in 1962/3, 85,000 in 1970/1 and 245,000 in 1979/80.[2] As elsewhere, the expansion of educational opportunities was an important component of this growth; by 1980 there were 1,280,000 pupils in Saudi primary and secondary schools and 42,000 in the new universities.[3]

Oil revenues were not the only encouragement to bureaucratic expansion, however. In the Hashemite Kingdom of Jordan, the ruling family had access to large external subsidies, first from the British, then from the richer Arab states, which it used to develop both their army and their central administration. By 1982 there were 59,000 persons in regular government employment, or just under 15 per cent of the labour force, with another 70,000–100,000 in the armed forces.[4]

Bureaucratic expansion of this size placed great power in the hands of each ruling family but also subjected them to great pressure. Both King Hussein of Jordan and King Hassan II of Morocco narrowly avoided military coups on a number of occasions, while many of the regimes of the Arabian peninsula experienced considerable difficulty in coping with intra-family rivalries exacerbated by their new found wealth and competition for high office. Nevertheless, even where individual rulers were deposed, as in Saudi Arabia in

1964, Abu Dhabi in 1966, or Oman in 1970, the families themselves survived to establish an unusual form of palace politics characterised by a great concentration of highly personalised power, a marked reluctance to permit the existence of political parties, trade unions or similar organisations (except in Morocco), limited social mobilisation and a basic commitment to private economic enterprise. Only in Kuwait was a whole ruling family temporarily removed by *force majeure* as a result of the Iraqi invasion of August 1990.

A discussion of the various types of family rule will form the major theme of this chapter. In addition, I will look at a particular state which passed from the monarchical type to one in which there was a deliberate attempt to create a new species of political and administrative structure – Libya. The period covered will end with the Gulf War of 1990/1 which produced significant changes in the policies pursued by most of the Arab ruling families. These will be discussed in Chapter 6.

The politics of family rule: some general observations

At the end of the colonial period nineteen Arab states or statelets had as their head of state a king, amir, shaikh, sultan, bey or imam drawn from a family that had either established or been given hereditary right to rule. Five of these were then deposed in the 1950s and 1960s – in Egypt, Tunisia, Iraq, Libya and North Yemen – leaving fourteen to survive until the present day – in Morocco, Jordan, Saudi Arabia, Kuwait, Bahrain, Qatar, Oman and the seven members of the United Arab Emirates.[5] At first sight this may seem something of an anachronism. Nevertheless, on closer inspection there are many reasons why these particular families managed to survive, most notably their ability to concentrate power in their own hands, to contain their own internal rivalries and to resist demands to share the process of decision-making with more than a tiny elite of loyal politicians. In doing this they have shown that family rule in the Middle East possesses certain functional advantages which were not so apparent to earlier writers, who relied overmuch on Samuel Huntington's notion of what he termed the 'king's dilemma', that is, his observation that 'the centralization of power necessary for promoting social, cultural and economic reform [would make] it difficult or impossible for the traditional monarchy to broaden its base and assimilate new groups produced by modernization'.[6] However, in actual practice this proved much less of a problem than was once thought. On the one hand, power sharing was rarely attempted, on the grounds that it might pose too many possible challenges to family authority. On the other, as Huntington himself pointed out, monarchs had a possible way out of the dilemma, by taking on the role of chief modernisers themselves and then by slowing down the process in such a way as to keep dislocation, as well as demands for participation, to a minimum.[7]

What were these advantages? And how could they be realised? Certainly the first point to make is that in a Middle Eastern context monarchy conferred none of the legitimacy that had once stemmed from the European notion of the divine right of kings. Indeed, only three of the rulers called themselves kings at all in Jordan, Morocco and Saudi Arabia and for reasons that had more to do with their determination to obtain the respect of the former great powers like Britain and France than it had to do with impressing their own people. Indeed, all three of them habitually used other titles as well, for example, 'shaikh', 'amir' or 'imam', which possessed much more resonance in terms of local custom. Meanwhile, in Saudi Arabia at least, the employment of the vocabulary of monarchy continued to provide a residual sense of embarrassment because, for some Sunni Muslims, and many Shi'is, it suggested a language that ought rigorously to have been confined to Allah himself. As King Faisal is reported to have told other members of his family in 1964, 'I beg of you, brothers, to look upon me as both brother and servant. "Majesty" is reserved to God alone and "the throne" is the throne of the Heavens and Earth.'[8] The Ayatollah Khomeini made the same point more forcefully in his polemics against the Saudi monarchy in the 1980s.

In Middle Eastern circumstances the right to rule resided not in the institution of kingship itself but in a combination of individual and family virtues, including noble lineage, honoured deeds, qualities of leadership and, in the case of the kings of Jordan and Morocco, descent from the Prophet Muhammad himself. Indeed, one of the strengths of the system was the fact that legitimacy was based on a bundle of factors, any one of which could be brought into play on the proper occasion and all of which could be used in various permutations to create powerful myths of origin that connected the family, its past achievements and its present strengths to the territory over which it now ruled.[9] It had the further advantage of not tying a ruler to one particular source of legitimation, which might, in certain circumstances, prove embarrassing or act as a major constraint. A good example of this would be the anxiety of certain Saudi rulers, notably King Abd al-Aziz Ibn Saud himself, not to identify themselves too closely with the religious establishment, even though it was this that provided a fundamental pillar of their family's right to rule.

Another type of flexibility stemmed from the interplay between the family as a whole and the individual ruler, a relationship that allowed an aggregation of the traditional virtues represented by the one and the more modern qualities required to be successful as the other. It is probably no accident that the states where family rule survived were those in which the leading families of nomadic tribes had played a prominent role in the recent past. Nevertheless, this did not absolve contemporary monarchs from developing the skills required to master large bureaucracies or to conduct complex international diplomacy. If the right balance could be found, the position of the family was correspondingly strengthened.

It would be wrong to suggest, however, that the maintenance of family rule was not without its problems. One of the most obvious and the most difficult has been the need to keep the family itself united. This involved finding ways of dealing with the question of succession, as well as with other potential sources of rivalry such as access to power, position and wealth. In large families where the founder, or founders, had many sons by many different wives, there was the additional problem of defining who was, and who was not, to be considered royal, and then who among them was to be considered as a candidate for high office. In Saudi Arabia, where there may be anything up to 4,000 males with a claim to be called 'prince', the question was first tackled by King Abd al-Aziz himself in 1932 when he decreed that only his own offspring and those of his brothers and of families related to his by common history and marriage were to be considered 'royal' and given a stipend. Later the list was twice pruned by King Faisal after 1958 and a number of names were removed.[10] As for the Gulf states, by the 1980s a number of them had written constitutions which defined who was a member and so who was a possible candidate for the succession.

Succession itself can be by primogeniture or by some version of the formula of the ruler's eldest, 'capable', male relative. Both methods possess advantages and disadvantages. Primogeniture is easy to apply and centralises power and decision-making in one single family line. However, it can also produce a monarch who is still a minor or unfit to rule. In addition, it automatically cuts out all the other lines, something that may well increase tensions, particularly in large families. The alternative, that of the eldest capable relative, is more or less bound to produce rulers who are old enough to have had considerable administrative experience. It also encourages family solidarity by allowing more lines to participate in rulership – or, at least, in the realistic anticipation of rulership. The downside is that it generally leads to short reigns and, as in the case of Saudi Arabia, where there were still thirty-one sons of King Abd al-Aziz alive in the mid-1970s, a long list of brothers and half-brothers to go through before it is possible to move on to the next generation.[11] A final point concerns the question of assessing the competence of any potential ruler. Not only is this a highly subjective matter but it is also something that is bound to change over time, depending on the degree of economic development and on the problems that the country faces.

In actual practice, different ruling families have applied different rules, as well as, on occasions, switching from one method to another. Among those that had institutionalised primogeniture by the 1980s were Morocco, Bahrain, Qatar, Abu Dhabi and Dubai.[12] Elsewhere different versions of the formula of the eldest competent male relative were in place, almost always supplemented by the nomination of a crown prince so as to reduce the possibility of a family quarrel breaking out immediately after the existing ruler's death. And in Saudi Arabia a mechanism had also been developed for indicating who was to be considered next in line after the crown prince, the person in question being appointed as second deputy chairman of the Council of Ministers. Nevertheless, all such systems can be subject to change and to family bargaining. Jordan had no less than three crown princes during the reign of King Hussein – two of his (younger) brothers and one of his sons – while in Sharjah in the United Arab Emirates the 1987 dispute between the ruler and his brother was settled by changing the order of succession to make the latter the heir apparent.

If intra-family disputes could be kept to a minimum, a ruler possessed a pool of loyal personnel for use as advisers and in manning the higher offices of state. Where families were large, as in Saudi Arabia and the Gulf, it remained usual for the ruler or his designated successor to be the prime minister and for the major positions in his cabinet to be held by other close relatives. Even where families were smaller, as in Jordan and Morocco, the king's uncles and cousins held important posts like commander-in-chief of the army or were delegated important areas of policy-making like planning and development. Indeed, one of the advantages of family rule is that such appointments do not carry the stigma of nepotism as they must do in a republic. Against this, it is often difficult to remove or transfer a close relative from a position of power, so that senior family members tend to remain in the same post for long periods of time.

A second problem that faced the Arab monarch or family ruler in the past was how to obtain sufficient resources to avoid overmuch dependence on important social groups and to build up support for himself by the distribution of largesse. This was especially the case in the poorer Arabian states before the oil era, and in those like Jordan and Morocco where the monarch was kept on a tight financial leash by the colonial power, with only a small civil list and limited opportunities for accumulating land or other valuable assets. Independence, or oil revenues, or both, provided almost all rulers with a way out. Those with oil now had an expanding income, part of which they could distribute to their own family in various ways, part of which they used to develop the infrastructure and the social services for the benefit of their own citizens. Meanwhile, growing economic activity gave them the option either of permitting their own relatives to go into business or, as in Kuwait, of striking a deal with the powerful merchant community, by which the latter was persuaded to limit its demands for political participation in exchange for a free hand to make money. As for those without oil, independence freed them from dependence on colonial subsidies, while allowing them to find alternative sources of financial support from outside (for example, aid from other Arab states) or, like Hassan II of Morocco, to go into business on his own account.[13] In either case, the tacit association of family rule with private enterprise allowed the rulers to build up a significant business clientele.

A third problem faced by family rulers was their relationship with the army. With the exception of the Bey of Tunis, who was eased out by President Bourguiba just after independence, the other four Arab monarchs who lost their thrones in the 1950s and 1960s were all deposed by military coups. And the same fate could well have overtaken the kings of Jordan, Morocco and Saudi Arabia if they had not been lucky or skilful enough to survive plots organised among their own armed forces. When confronting this problem, family rulers had two possible options. The first, open for several decades to those in the Arabian peninsula, was to have only a very small army, often with a high proportion of foreign mercenaries, and placed under the direct supervision of loyal relatives. The other, forced upon those like the Moroccans and Jordanians who needed a large army for their own defence was for the king to play an active role as commander-in-chief, often wearing military uniform and constantly attending parades and manoeuvres. This strategy is particularly apparent in Jordan, where King Hussein showed great skill in obtaining the loyalty of his army after he had dismissed its British commander, General Glubb, early in 1956 and where, a decade later, he was said to address individual soldiers by their first name 'as if he knows them all'.[14] More generally, it can well be argued that the institution of monarchy provides a better mechanism for maintaining the allegiance of an army than a republic, on the grounds that it makes more sense for a soldier to pledge himself to a person than to something abstract like a flag or a state.

A last problem, specific to ruling families that obtain part of their legitimacy from their close identification with religion, was how to benefit from this connection without being too constrained by it. By and large this involved many of the same techniques as those used in the Arab republics: government control over religious appointments and funds, the close monitoring of the Friday sermon, and so on. Another option was what might be called the 'management of tradition', for example, the introduction of certain practices that carried with them the aura of the past, such as the enforcement of what was considered proper Islamic conduct by the specially created Saudi religious police, the *mutawa*.

The existence of the ruling families and their courts produced a type of politics that differed in a number of significant aspects from that in other types of system. For one thing, it involved the relationship between the family members themselves, a process of interaction in which questions of personality, ambition, state policy and the control of state institutions were inevitably mixed together. What made matters still more complicated was the fact that, in many cases, the senior princes or amirs were also in charge of the most important government ministries, which they could exploit as their own particular fiefs or power bases in support of their own particular interests. In these circumstances, the maintenance of family harmony was bound to be more important than a willingness to take difficult decisions. Nevertheless, the situation may not have been quite as unsatisfactory as many commentators have argued. Ruling families were able to cover serious disputes with a discreet veil of secrecy and were rarely required to explain what their policies were or how decisions had been reached. Furthermore, the existence of rival points of view is not necessarily evidence of a struggle for power. Indeed, rather than being a weakness, it is probably better seen as a source of strength as long as it is kept within reasonable bounds. Certainly a situation in which all the members of a ruling family habitually shared the same approach towards major issues of policy would have ensured that issues were not properly aired and, in general, would have been a recipe for disaster.

Another special feature of family rule is the existence of the royal court, with its own particular atmosphere and its own particular dynamic. Some of its features seem timeless and are just as easily illustrated in the works of Machiavelli or Shakespeare as they are in the books of contemporary political scientists.

There is the advice offered to the medieval courtier, to find out what a ruler wanted and then to go to him with suggestions as to how it might be carried out. There is King Lear's understanding of the importance of gossip, when he says that he desires to 'talk of court news … who loses and who wins; who's in, who's out'. All this in its modern Moroccan context is well described by Waterbury, with his observation that access to the king became the be-all and end-all of political manoeuvring, that palace-watching and second guessing becomes an elite obsession, that evidence of royal favour is sought in the length of a meeting or the sight of a smile.[15] Nevertheless, court life is not just the stuff of a rarefied political drama; its pattern is structured by the dictates of a system in which rulers need political servants to advise them and to carry out their orders, and find it easier to draw them from a small, loyal, continuously circulating elite.

For the public at large, courts or open councils also provide a stage for a continuous performance of what might be called the theatre of legitimacy, in which every event provides an occasion for some highly charged ritual designed to remind the people of their ruler's power and justice as well as of his noble lineage, his generosity and his devotion to his religion. 'To be invisible is to be forgotten' as Bagehot wrote of the nineteenth-century British royal family.[16] Once again Waterbury provides a good example of this aspect of royal behaviour, with an extract from a speech given by King Hassan II of Morocco on the occasion of the release of some prisoners.

> This clemency is proof of the innate nature of our family characterized by its profound wisdom, its great nobility and the solid communion which unites us ultimately with our people. Moreover, if we have adopted this attitude impregnated with wisdom and clemency, it is because we have answered to the humanitarian mission handed to us by the saviour of our nation and the liberator of our citizens, our late Father, Muhammad V, may God bless his memory.[17]

A final feature of note is the natural alliance between ruling families and the more conservative elements within a society, both of whom see themselves as beneficiaries of a system under threat from certain movements and ideologies associated with modernity and rapid economic development. Both tend to admire tribal and rural values. Both tend to be suspicious of political parties and trade unions. One result is that royal courts still contain a disproportionate number of members of the older, notable families. Another is that royal policies have a tendency to favour private property and private enterprise, as against nationalisation, land reform or other collectivist solutions to economic problems. I will give illustrations of all these features of family rule in the next two sections of this chapter.

favoring of elitists

The politics of royal family rule in Jordan and Morocco

The political histories of Jordan and Morocco since independence have much in common. Both countries experienced a short period when their kings attempted to rule as constitutional monarchs before engineering a showdown with the nationalist parties and concentrating power in their own hands. Both had moments of serious military unrest. Both possessed monarchs who deliberately set themselves up as leaders of their respective national movements and as managers of their country's modernisation. Nevertheless, the contexts in which these developments took place were very different. The modern history of Jordan has been dominated by its involvement with Palestine, its relations with its own large Palestinian population, and by its close proximity to Israel; while King Hassan II of Morocco has focused nationalist attention on the incorporation of the former Spanish Sahara into his domain and made loyalty to this policy a touchstone for participation in the political process. Again, Morocco has always been a much more economically diversified country than resource-poor Jordan. Perhaps because of this, it has always contained a greater diversity of political and trade union organisations, which the king has been able to use but has never been quite able to bring under control.

The turning point in King Hussein of Jordan's centralisation of power came in April 1957, with his dismissal of Sulaiman Nabulsi's cabinet dominated by members of parties opposed to many basic features of Hashemite rule. This was immediately followed by the establishment of his authority over the army after averting the threat of a military coup a few days later, and then by the arrival of the first American aid and the financial subsidies sent by a number of Arab states as a replacement for the money previously provided by the British. From that point on political parties were outlawed, and the lower house of the Jordanian parliament was rarely in session (it met only once between 1974 and 1984) giving space for the king to perfect a system that allowed him to make all the major decisions affecting foreign affairs and external security while leaving the execution of policy in other areas to a small group of loyal politicians who circulated between his own royal Hashemite *diwan* (or royal cabinet) and the regular cabinet in charge of day-to-day administration.[18]

As laid down in the constitution, the King of Jordan is head of state and supreme commander of the armed forces. He also appoints the prime minister and, in consultation with him, the cabinet. Historically, both prime ministers and their cabinets were rotated rapidly, lasting an average of only seven months between 1947 and 1974 and for two years from then to the mid-1980s.[19] On appointment, each cabinet received a public letter from the king setting out the main guidelines it would be expected to follow. Its role was essentially executive. Key decisions were taken in consultation with a small group of advisers; notably the chief and the minister of the royal *diwan*, the commander-in-chief of the army, and the prime minister, whose main allegiance was to the king rather than his own cabinet. And particular prime ministers were often chosen just to carry out specific short-term political tasks, one, for example, being known for his ability to establish good relations with the Syrians, another for his willingness to take a tough stand against the Palestinians.

Members of the political elite who staffed the two cabinets came from a small group of several hundred families.[20] Before independence this elite was composed largely of persons who had been brought into Trans-Jordan (as it then was) by the British or who had moved there from Palestine. It then expanded after the annexation of the West Bank to include representatives of the major Palestinian families that were not tainted by their connection with King Abdullah's arch rival, the Mufti of Jerusalem. Later it was enlarged still further to include the heads of important Jordanian families: tribal leaders, merchants and members of the two most significant minorities, the Circassians and the Christians. In this way appointment to one of the two cabinets came to serve a representative function, bringing the king in touch with various regional and social groups in a manner that might otherwise have required the existence of small political parties. It was also a way of organising and maintaining support. Such was the importance attached to having good relations with the palace that members of this elite were almost always content to be dismissed from office without protest, knowing that if they avoided public display they would be recalled to favour on some future occasion.

Jordanians outside this small elite had little or no opportunity to influence policy at the national level. General elections were only rarely held before 1989, and all political organisations were banned. In these circumstances, those wanting to make their opinions known had either to do so by means of personal contact with a member of the elite or to engage in some form of illegal activity. Even so, strikes and demonstrations were very infrequent and the only occasion on which the king had to face anything like a concerted opposition from local Jordanian groups was during the months leading up to the armed confrontation with the Palestinian resistance movement, which began in September 1970.

During the 1970s efforts were made to introduce a system of limited decentralisation. Municipal elections were held regularly from 1976, while some power was devolved to local governors, mayors and the heads of village councils. However, as such elections were closely monitored and most of the persons concerned were either civil servants or retired soldiers with close ties to the government, this only opened up a tiny space for the type of competitive politics that could reflect either national or local issues. What it did allow in some municipalities, however, was a challenge to the existing alliance of government officials and local notables by the election of a few educated technocrats and some men either identified with one of the banned political parties or close to the Muslim Brothers, the single mass organisation tolerated by the royal regime. But, once again, they were forced to operate within very strict limits, as can be seen by the strenuous attempts to prevent the re-election of certain members of the Irbid Council alleged to have been involved in the student demonstrations at Yarmuk University in May 1986.

Opposition to the rule of the kings of Morocco was very much more consistent and difficult to contain. Nevertheless, King Mohammad V and his son,

King Hassan II, were able to develop a system of government that allowed them to concentrate great power in their own person and to act as arbiter between the country's other political forces. In Zartman's schema, the history of this process can be divided into three periods.[21] In the first, from independence in 1956 to 1965, the two kings attempted to create a strongly centralised constitutional monarchy, only for Hassan to abandon the project when he was unable to secure the co-operation of the major parties like the Istiqlal and its more radical offshoot, the Union National des Forces Populaires (UNFP), and was then faced with a major outbreak of popular opposition leading to widespread rioting and demonstrations in Casablanca and elsewhere. Parliament was dissolved during this second period and the king ruled through cabinets of technocrats until the attempted military coups of 1971 and 1972 persuaded him of the danger of establishing his rule on too narrow a base of patron–client relations and senior army officers alone.

Finally, in the third period, which began effectively in 1974, Hassan II was successful in creating a new system of highly controlled democracy in which a number of parties were persuaded to take part in regular elections and to participate in government on his terms. As it developed, his new formula involved a combination of a number of elements. Loyal politicians were encouraged to form pro-monarchical political groupings like the RNI (National Independents' Rally) and the Constitutionalists' Union (CU). Meanwhile, other parties were allowed to contest the elections in 1977 and in 1984, provided they actively supported his highly nationalistic campaign to incorporate the former Spanish colony of the Western Sahara into Morocco. Finally, the elections themselves were subject to considerable manipulation by the state including tight control over what could and could not be discussed during the campaign.

Surrounding the king was a small elite of politicians and notables, and the leaders of various labour unions and other economic interest groups who, according to Entelis, numbered no more than a thousand.[22] As in Jordan, Hassan II was personally acquainted with most of them and very much aware of their personal idiosyncrasies and rivalries.[23] Like Hussein he was adept at keeping them all in play. It was they who provided his advisers, the executors of his policy and his eyes and ears for observing the rest of Moroccan society. A key part of this system was his ability to grant favoured courtiers and politicians access to the business opportunities that he could offer in his double role of manager of a large public sector and the country's leading private-sector entrepreneur.[24]

Given the presence of such a relatively small elite surrounding the royal court, it has been easy for analysts to limit their study of Moroccan politics to an examination of the leading personalities involved and their varied types of patronage networks. But, as in the case of the single-party authoritarian regimes, this is to ignore the interventions of major institutions like the army, as well as the existence of the mechanisms necessary to solve substantive disputes over major policy issues concerning both domestic and foreign policy. In the Moroccan context it also tends to overlook the role of the parties and trade unions in developing distinctive followings among different sections of Moroccan society which look to them to represent some of their particular interests.[25]

The practice of family rule: Saudi Arabia and the Gulf states

The practice of family rule that developed in Saudi Arabia had many of the same features as in Jordan and Morocco, with the important proviso that the Saudi royal family was much larger and thus able to dominate all the senior civil and military posts itself. Otherwise there was a similar division between the cabinet (or in this case the council of ministers) and the royal court, and a similar tendency for the king and his close advisers (the senior princes) to pay special attention to matters of foreign affairs, defence and internal security (as well as the religiously sensitive issues of justice and education), leaving other matters like economic development either to American-educated princes of the third generation or to non-royal technocrats with no power base of their own.

Such a system permitted only a small group of major, political actors drawn from some of the sons of Abd al-Aziz, members of related families like the Jilwis and the al-Shaikhs, and a few tribal leaders and senior clergy. Membership of this group depended largely on the family of origin, seniority, prestige and an active desire to take part in public life. In addition, the significance attached to such membership could rise or fall according to political necessity, while the importance of tribal leaders suffered a decline over time as their followers settled on the land and became more directly subject to the central administration. However, unlike Jordan and Morocco, the family was large enough to keep members of the new educated elites resolutely out of policy-making, with the exception of certain rare individuals like Zaki Yamani, the minister of oil for most of the 1970s and 1980s. There was also no serious attempt to create representative institutions of any kind, while incorporation as a subsidiary member of the ruling elite was based almost exclusively on loyalty to the family and a shared perception of the values of Saudi culture and pride in its own special achievements.

The development of the main features of monarchical rule can be best understood by a rapid survey of recent Saudi political and administrative history.[26] At the time of the death of Abd al-Aziz Ibn Saud in 1953 the country was still ruled much as it had been in the 1930s, with only a minimal bureaucracy of a few hundred officials and advisers, supported on occasion by the considerable resources of the oil company, ARAMCO, from in its enclave in the eastern province. However, before he died, the king made two important preparations for the future. One was his attempt to regulate the succession and to provide leadership for the future by ensuring that his eldest son, Saud, became king but worked in close co-operation with his second son, Faisal, who had important diplomatic and administrative skills that Saud lacked. The second was the creation of a council of ministers to direct the work of the inevitable expansion of the bureaucracy as oil royalties began to mount. Given their different talents, the new king, Saud, worked to consolidate his hold over the royal court while Faisal built up the council as a major institution of state, using it to provide senior princes with administrative experience and to supervise the activities of the various ministries.

Competition between Saud and Faisal came to a head in the period between 1958 and 1964, when Saud's mishandling of a series of diplomatic and financial crises threatened the whole basis of family rule. These included near bankruptcy through the wasteful use of oil revenues, and a failure to find ways to meet the challenge posed by the increasing power of President Nasser of Egypt, made more threatening in 1962 by the dispatch of an Egyptian military force to assist the officers who had overthrown the neighbouring imam of North Yemen. Nevertheless, in spite of these great dangers, the transfer of power from Saud to Faisal was a lengthy process as it took time for the majority of the senior members of the family to accept the need for taking such a serious step. In all this a key role was played by three princes whom Faisal himself had introduced into the council of ministers: Khalid, who was appointed deputy prime minister in 1962; Fahd, who became minister of education in 1953; and Abdullah, who was made commander of the national guard in 1963. In the process of consolidation that took place after Saud had been deposed and Faisal made king (and prime minister) in 1964, Khalid became crown prince (while continuing as deputy prime minister) with Fahd next in line, a position signalled by his appointment to the newly created post of second deputy prime minister in 1967. All this required complex intra-family negotiations, particularly with respect to Abd al-Aziz's next son, Prince Muhammad, who was older than the other three and who took some time to agree to surrender his place in the succession to his full brother Khalid.

Once firmly in power and sure of full family support, Faisal proceeded to provide himself with new instruments of rule, notably the creation of a higher committee of senior princes, which advised him on all major decisions, leaving the council of ministers to deal with more routine matters of administration including the planned development of the economy that began in earnest in the late 1960s. He also took advantage of the death of the grand mufti of Saudi Arabia in 1970 to create a new ministry of justice which brought the important sphere of Islamic jurisprudence within the framework of cabinet control. Finally, he pursued a deliberate policy of introducing western-educated, third generation, princes into government posts, having taken the lead in sending his own son, Saud al-Faisal, to school and then university in the United States in the 1950s. This was important in preventing the family from having to rely too heavily on the advice and skills of Saudi technocrats in the future. But it also had the effect of accelerating a process that Samore has called the development of 'power fiefdoms' among the senior princes, some of whom remained in control of the same ministry, or the same institution, for many years, if not decades.[27] This placed limits on the king's own power, made joint decisions more difficult to reach, and increased the possibility that institutional interests and intra-family rivalries would become dangerously intermixed. A good example of this occurred after the discovery of an ill-planned coup attempt among air force officers in 1969, when family decision-making processes seemed paralysed for months and the king was subject to fiercely conflicting advice about whether to push forward with more reforms or to permit the religious establishment greater control over morals and values. In the end he decided to do both at once.

Faisal's assassination by one of his nephews in 1975 led to a period of more collective family rule, first under King Khalid (1975–82) and then under King Fahd (1982–). Once again this sometimes made consensus difficult, particularly when facing an acute crisis like the seizure of the Grand Mosque in Mecca in 1979 by a group of Muslim religious extremists in the misguided hope that this would act as a spur to popular revolt against the monarchy. Nevertheless, such was the grip that the family and its allies had established on all the major centres of power, that its rule was never seriously threatened, even when it was challenged by the powerful forces of the Islamic revolution in neighbouring Iran.

As Samore notes, the continuous accumulation of wealth and expansion of the state structure greatly facilitated the resolution of structural tensions within the family, as well as between the family and the rest of Saudi society.[28] Meanwhile, the non-royal Saudis who were required as technical experts could easily be absorbed as individuals into the various family patronage networks without the need to admit them into the inner circles of power or to provide them with the support of even the most rudimentary representative institutions. When they felt threatened, as after the Mosque attack in 1979, the king and the senior princes might attempt to build up popular support for themselves by a promise to explore the possibility of creating a popular consultative council. But once it became clear that the majority of family members were against any such arrangement for sharing power the matter was quietly dropped. With all the institutions of government so firmly in the hands of one family, with political parties and trade unions banned, with opposition confined to a few tiny underground groups, the practice of politics at the national level remained an almost exclusively royal monopoly.

Nevertheless, even when so well entrenched at the centre and in the provinces, the Saudi ruling family, like any other, was not able to make policy in a vacuum and was forced to base important parts of its policy on detailed negotiations with powerful interest groups like the religious establishment and the wealthier merchants and businessmen. This could be seen with particular clarity in government efforts to clear up the difficult problems involving bankruptcy and the failure to meet obligations on loans, which came to prominence during the economic contraction that accompanied falling oil prices from 1985 onwards. So complex were the various negotiations regarding such highly contentious issues as the charging of interest that laws and decrees had constantly to be revised in the light of new pressures from the clergy and the business community.

The ruling families in Kuwait, Bahrain, Qatar, Oman and the seven constituent states of the United Arab Emirates (UAE) formed in December 1971 were also able to keep power largely in their own hands during the oil era. This involved a similar process of consolidation and of sorting out problems of succession and of access to high government office. Once this was done it was possible to use family members to dominate the most important posts in the various councils of ministers. In the mid-1980s, the office of prime minister in Kuwait, Bahrain, Qatar and the UAE was held either by the ruler or the crown prince, while the ministries of foreign affairs, the interior and defence (where they existed) were also controlled by senior relatives, the one exception being the ministry of foreign affairs in the UAE, which was in the charge of a commoner. Family dominance was equally apparent in Oman, even though its small size entailed a somewhat different system of administration.[29]

The families in question were able to achieve this type of dominance as a result of two main factors. One was the protection they enjoyed, first from the British presence in the Gulf before its withdrawal at the end of 1971, then from Saudi Arabia and the United States backed up by the system of mutual support they developed for themselves through the creation of the Gulf Cooperation Council (GCC) in 1981. The second was access to profits from oil which largely freed them from financial dependence on the local population for tax revenues or on the local merchants for loans. It also allowed them to distribute great largesse, beginning with their own extended family and then extending throughout the rest of their small populations. This took various forms: cash handouts; state purchase of privately-owned lands for public development at inflated prices; and, in an institutionalised form, by the development of a wide variety of welfare services such as free education and health care and the provision of highly subsidised electricity, water and housing.

The expansion of the bureaucracy and the economy allowed further opportunities for obtaining popular support by providing jobs, loans and the possibility of participating in a whole range of profitable enterprises. A key feature in all this was the creation of particular monopolies that were available only to people defined by the very restrictive nationality laws as local citizens. In most of the Gulf states these monopolies included the sole right to own property and to open a business. The result was a situation in which a privileged group of local nationals was well placed to take advantage of all the openings for making money that stemmed from oil, as well as from the presence of the many millions of non-nationals drawn to the Gulf in search of work.[30]

Given their large, independent, financial resources and their protection from external attack, the Gulf ruling families were free to establish links with all sections of their own societies – the merchants, the clergy, the Shi'i minorities, the settled tribal elements – but on their own terms. In some cases, as in Kuwait, this might include a tacit bargain by which, for example, the merchants agreed to keep out of politics while the royal family kept out of business.[31] In others, it needed to be no more than an extension of a particular set of privileges to a particular group, such as the regular employment of tribesmen in the army and the police. As a rule such arrangements worked with relatively little friction. However, there were always strains during periods of economic slowdown, when oil royalties declined. At such times the families had to undertake the difficult task of managing not the distribution of money and jobs but of decisions concerning the allocation of financial contractions and relative hardships. This was particularly apparent in Kuwait after the collapse of the unofficial stock-market known as the Suq al-Manakh in 1982, when investors, some of whom included prominent members of the royal family, were faced with huge debts running into many billions of dollars. The government took several years to produce an agreed policy, and even then there were inevitable accusations of favouritism as some individuals and companies received very much more in official compensation than others. The situation was only finally resolved after the Gulf War in the early 1990s.[32]

As a rule, relations between Gulf rulers, governments and people were conducted along informal, personal, lines, with only minimal reference to institutions. The only two states to attempt to create formal representative assemblies were Kuwait and Bahrain, just after independence in 1962 and 1973 respectively. However, even there parties were banned, the electorates were confined to only a small proportion of the male population with full citizenship, and the elections themselves were usually subject to considerable government interference. Furthermore, both national assemblies ran into predictable problems stemming from the fact that they contained important members of the ruling family, either ex officio as cabinet ministers or as elected representatives. Tensions between the family and the opposition led to the Bahrain assembly being dissolved in 1975 after two short sessions. The one in Kuwait lasted somewhat longer, with periods of co-operation being interspersed with ones of great friction between some parliamentarians and a government dominated by members of the ruling house of al-Sabah. It was first dissolved in 1976, reopened again in 1981, and then dismissed for a second time in 1986 following the forced resignation of the minister of justice, on the grounds that he had misused his office for personal gain, and fierce criticisms of two other ministers including the minister for oil who happened to be the half-brother of the ruler.

Libya: from monarchy to a new type of state, the *jamahiriyyah*

Libya gained its independence in 1951 as a federal state consisting of the three very different provinces (Tripolitania, Cyrenaica and the Fezzan) and as a constitutional monarchy under King Idris al-Sanusi. In some respects its political history echoed that of Jordan and Morocco, with an early showdown with the main nationalist political party, the Tripolitanian National Congress, in 1952, after which the king took all power into his own hands and ruled through a series of loyal politicians, while keeping parliament firmly under control. There was also a similar system of rule, with a royal cabinet containing a mixture of men from the tribal nobility and from the major families in the towns, and a ministerial cabinet in which the portfolios of finance, defence and the interior were kept firmly under the king's control.[33] Furthermore, the federal system, with its four administrations, provided large numbers of posts for loyal supporters before it was replaced by a centralised system of government in 1963, while the discovery of oil in the late 1950s provided the monarchy with a source of considerable financial largesse.

There were obvious differences as well, some of them significant enough to account for the overthrow of the monarchy by the military coup of 1969 led by Captain Muammar al-Qadhafi. The first involved the size and cohesion of the ruling family. As a result of a confrontation with dissident relatives in 1954, one of whom had killed his senior adviser, King Idris confined the succession to his brothers and members of his own line, depriving all the remainder of their royal titles and of the right to hold public office. This at once removed a large pool of loyal family talent. To make matters worse, he had no son of his own to succeed him, so that succession had to pass through his brothers to the very lacklustre nephew he named as crown prince. Second, the king showed none of the energy of a Hussein or a Hassan in constantly reinforcing his legitimacy and in reminding his subjects of his authority by endless public performance, preferring instead to hide himself away in a distant palace and to manipulate the political system from afar.

A third difference was the king's failure to maintain personal control over the regular army or to impose an acceptable standard of behaviour on either his close relatives or his main advisers when it came to nepotism and corruption. Lastly, King Idris showed little skill in distancing himself from the British and the Americans, both of whom had military bases in the country. Hence by the time he had begun to try to improve his Arab nationalist credentials in the aftermath of the 1967 Middle East war – by his use of oil royalties to support the defeated Egyptians and Jordanians – his support had crumbled away beyond repair. In an important sense he could be said to have delegitimised both himself and the whole system of monarchical rule, and it was only a matter of timing and good fortune as to which of a number of groups of military conspirators would be able to launch their coup first.

The leaders of the Libyan Free Unionist Officers' Movement that came to power in September 1969 promptly constituted themselves as an Egyptian-style Revolutionary Command Council under the chairmanship of Qadhafi, who was immediately promoted to colonel and commander-in-chief of the army. For the first four years they attempted to reorganise the government along the lines laid out in Egypt by Colonel Nasser and his colleagues, centralising power in their own hands, creating new administrative structures to limit the influence of the country's rural elites and then a mass rally, the Arab Socialist Union, to mobilise popular support. By April 1973, however, they were beginning to look for a new organisational formula, which they discovered in the notion of the people's committees to be elected in all villages, schools, popular organisations and foreign companies. To begin with, these committees were only allowed to play a significant role in local and provincial government, where they assumed some administrative and legislative functions. But in yet another initiative announced in September 1975 their activities found expression at a national level with the creation of a General People's Congress (GPC), with Qadhafi as its secretary general and representatives from the district people's committees, supported by the Arab Socialist Union and the new work-based unions to which all Libyans were now supposed to belong.[34]

It was this structure that formed the basis for the final mutation of the Libyan system triggered by the publication of the first volume of Qadhafi's Green Book, *The Solution of the Problem of Democracy* (1976), and his March 1977 announcement that henceforward the country was to become a *jamahiriyyah*, a 'state of the masses'. What this actually meant in practice presents considerable problems of analysis. For one thing, it was subject to considerable experimentation itself, including the creation of a new set of revolutionary committees in 1979 which were established first in schools and universities, and then in parts of the bureaucracy, turning many of the existing ministries into so-called people's bureaux. These existed side by side with the older people's committees, and reported directly to Qadhafi himself, who in 1979 had resigned from his post as secretary general of the GPC to assume the new post of 'leader of the revolution'. For another, the late 1970s also saw the start of a concerted attack on economic privilege, leading to the nationalisation of large numbers of private firms. However, it seems clear that, throughout all these changes, power remained firmly in the hands of Qadhafi and a few close aides who controlled the essential levers of the state.

As a result, by the early 1980s the structure of the Libyan state showed considerable differences from that to be found anywhere else in the Middle East. It is true that it had at its centre a large bureaucratic apparatus backed by an army which had increased to some 55,000–65,000 in 1981 and a sizeable force of policemen, militia and other persons concerned with domestic security.[35] However, this organisation, although ultimately answerable to Colonel Qadhafi and his colleagues, was supervised in a novel way by a combination of the permanent secretariat of the GPC, various revolutionary committees and, in some places, the remains of previous administrative hierarchies to be found in the military and some of the ministries, now renamed people's bureaux. This, in turn, had important consequences for Libyan politics. Whereas all the major Arab regimes had tried to create mechanisms for bringing their populations under their administrative control, not one of them had gone anything like so far as to combine this with the encouragement to popular participation provided by the committees. The result was a multitude of new types of political practice, few of which have been open to inspection by outsiders.[36]

How all this had come about also poses problems in terms of historical explanation. Clearly the presence of large sums of money from oil exports had something to do with it, at least in terms of providing the funds to support such a comprehensive and continuous process of economic, social and administrative engineering. The fact that Libya had only a small population of some two to three millions and had experienced such a short history of centralised bureaucratic structures is also significant. Nevertheless, the personalities and expectations of the small group of middle-ranking army officers who made the coup cannot be ignored. As John Davis, one of the shrewdest observers of the Libyan

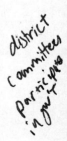

scene, has noted, *The Green Book* seems to have been written by a man who felt deceived and frustrated by the day-to-day experience of government.[37] Born in a tent pitched in the open desert, and with only minimal contact with any type of bureaucracy before he joined the army in 1964, Colonel Qadhafi shared none of the commitment to regular administrative procedures shown by a Nasser or an Asad. He also lacked their patience and their attention to detail. The result was a freedom – perhaps even a compulsion – to experiment, something which remained an essential feature of Libyan political and organisational practice.

Notes

1 Nazih Ayubi, 'Arab bureaucracies: Expanding size, changing roles' in Adeed Dawisha and I. William Zartman (eds), *Beyond Coercion: The Durability of the Arab State*, (London: Croom Helm, 1988), p. 17. Ayubi's figures for 1980 probably exclude military and diplomatic personnel which accounted for another 14,227 in June 1982. The total labour force amounted to 491,641 in 1980. But of this only just over 100,000 were Kuwaiti citizens. See State of Kuwait, Ministry of Planning, Central Statistical Office, *Annual Statistical Abstract 1983* (Kuwait: November 1983), pp. 105–6, 132–3.

2 Ibid., p. 17. But note that the Ministry of Planning using a different definition of employment gives a figure of just under 400,000 in civilian government employment for 1400 AH /1980, or 13.2 per cent of the total labour force. Kingdom of Saudi Arabia, Ministry of Planning, *Fourth Development Plan* (Riyadh, 1405 AH/1985), Table 2–6, p. 32.

3 John A. Shaw and David E. Long, *Saudi Arabian Modernization: The Impact of Change on Stability* (Washington, DC: Praeger, with Center for Strategic Studies, Georgetown University, 1982), p. 26.

4 Ayubi, 'Arab bureaucracies', p. 19: Mary C. Wilson, 'Jordan's current malaise', *Current History* (February 1987), p. 85.

5 I have excluded the rulers of the tiny statelets in the hinterland of South Yemen, formerly known as the Aden Protectorate, all of whom were swept away soon after the British withdrawal in 1967.

6 Samuel P. Huntington, *Political Order in Changing Societies* (New Haven, CN: Yale University Press, 1968), pp. 171–91.

7 Ibid.

8 Quoted in Mordechai Abir, 'The consolidation of the ruling class and new elites in Saudi Arabia', *Middle Eastern Studies*, 23/2 (April 1987), p. 156.

9 For example, King Fahd's speech on 2 March 1992 as quoted in Madawi al-Rashid, 'God, the King and the nation: Political rhetoric in Saudi Arabia in the 1990s', *Middle East Journal*, 50/3 (Summer, 1996), pp. 359–71.

10 Abir, 'Consolidation of the ruling class', p. 157.

11 G.S. Samore, 'Royal Family politics in Saudi Arabia (1953–1982)', unpublished Ph.D. (Harvard University, 1984), pp. 308ff.

12 Rosemary Said Zahlan, *The Making of the Modern Gulf States* (London: Unwin Hyman, 1989), pp. 83, 88, 98ff.

13 For example, Rémy Leveau, 'Aperçu d'évolution du système politique morocain depuis vingt ans', *Maghreb/Machrek*, 106 (October/November/December 1984), pp. 15–18.

14 Quoted in Samir A. Mutawi, *Jordan in the 1967 War* (Cambridge: Cambridge University Press, 1987), p. 16.

15 John Waterbury, *The Commander of the Faithful: The Moroccan Political Elite – a Study in Segmented Politics* (London: Weidenfeld and Nicolson, 1970), p. 162.

16 Walter Bagehot, *The English Constitution* (London: Chapman and Hall, 1867), pp. 63, 70–1.

17 Waterbury, *Commander of the Faithful*, p. 150.

18 The paragraphs on the Jordanian political system draw heavily on Mutawi, *Jordan*, especially Chapter 1. Also the slightly fuller account to be found in the same author's Ph.D. thesis, also called 'Jordan in the 1967 War', Reading University, September 1985. Additional information from Marius Haas, *Hussein's Königreich: Jordaniens Stelling im Nach Orient* (Munich: Tuduv Verlagsgessellschaft, 1975).

19 Sune Persson, 'Exile and success: Palestinian exiles in Jordan', *mimeo* (Department of Political Science, University of Göteberg, Sweden, October 1985), p. 21.

20 Ibid., p. 22.

21 I. William Zartman, 'Political dynamics in the Maghrib: The cultural dialectic', in Halim Barakat (ed.), *Contemporary North Africa* (Washington, DC: Center for Contemporary Arab Studies, Georgetown University, 1985), p. 289.

22 John P. Entelis, *Comparative Politics of North Africa: Algeria, Morocco and Tunisia* (Syracuse, NY: Syracuse University Press, 1980), p. 65.

23 Leveau, 'L'évolution du système politique morocain', p. 236.

24 Ibid., p. 18.

25 For example, David Seddon, *Moroccan Peasants: A Century of Change in the Eastern Rif 1870–1970* (Folkstone: Dutton, 1981).

26 In this section I draw heavily on Samore, 'Royal Family politics'; and Summer Scott Huyette, *Political Adaptation in Saudi Arabia: A Study of the Council of Ministers* (Boulder, CO and London: Westview Press, 1985).

27 Samore, 'Royal Family politics', pp. 235, 286–7.

28 Ibid., p. 490.

29 Zahlan, *Making of the Modern Gulf States*, Chapter 8 and Appendix.

30 Roger Owen, *Migrant Workers in the Gulf* (London: The Minority Rights Group, Report no. 68, September 1985), and sources cited there.

31 Jill Crystal, *Oil and Politics in the Gulf: Rulers and Merchants in Kuwait and Qatar* (Cambridge: Cambridge University Press, 1989), p. 75.

32 Alexei P. Kiriyev, 'An analysis of Kuwait's debt collection program', in Nigel Andrew Chalk *et al.*, *Kuwait: From Reconstruction to Accumulation for Future Generations* (Washington, DC: IMF Occasional Papers, 150, April 1997).

33 Ruth First, *Libya: The Elusive Revolution* (Harmondsworth: Penguin Books, 1974), p. 78.

34 Nathan Alexander, 'Libya: The continuous revolution', *Middle Eastern Studies*, 17/2 (April 1981), pp. 212–19.

35 Figures from Lisa Anderson, *The State and Social Transformation in Tunisia and Libya 1830–1980* (Princeton, NJ: Princeton University Press, 1985), p. 266.

36 One of the rare examples of direct observation is John Davis' description of an election for one of the new popular committees. See his 'Théorie et practique du gouvernement non representatif: les élections aux comités populaires d'Ajdabaiyah', *Maghreb/Machrek*, 93 (July/August/September 1981).

37 Ibid., p. 39.

4 Arab nationalism, Arab unity and the practice of intra-Arab state relations

Introduction

The fact that the vast majority of newly independent states contained largely Arabic-speaking populations and that they consciously identified themselves as Arab has played a major role in twentieth-century Middle Eastern politics. Nevertheless, for many years, attempts to try to define this role and to work out whether the practice of intra-Arab state relations differ markedly from that between other groups of states in, say, Latin America or East Asia, did not prove markedly successful. For one thing, much of the writing on the subject has always been highly political and concerned to make polemical rather than academic points. Perhaps because of this, few writers took much care to distinguish between the various types of Arabism, which have run all the way from a sense of shared history, culture and, sometimes, religion to the creation of parties and movements that have placed Arab nationalism and Arab unity at the centre of their programmes of political action. There was a similar disinclination to distinguish between the different types of national solidarities to be found among the Arabs; for example, the strong sense of local identification to be found among Egyptians or Moroccans, or the several kinds of Palestinianism that developed among Palestinians with quite separate experiences of occupation, exile or foreign rule.

Matters started to change in the 1980s with writers on the Middle East increasingly influenced by the lively debate between the exponents of different theories or explanations of nationalism, as well as by the work of those like Sami Zubaida who argue that nationalism itself does not constitute a 'unitary general phenomenon' and therefore that no such theory is possible or appropriate.[1] It began to be observed that the greater part of the writing on Arab nationalism had been by those who saw it, first and foremost, as an ideology, a set of ideas to be interpreted and analysed for what they say about the relationship between history, culture, society, politics and the right ordering of a future, united, Arab nation. And that this was usually done by isolating the work of a handful of Arab intellectuals, politicians and polemicists who were then somewhat arbitrarily defined as being the most significant nationalist thinkers, even if, at its best, such an approach might also seek to locate them within the wider currents of the social and political thought of their time.[2] It was further observed that, as a rule, those who concentrated their attention on nationalist writings tended to an 'idealist' view of history, in which ideas are the motor force of historical change, while those who were more concerned with nationalism as a political movement exemplified a more 'materialist' approach, in which change is largely the product of economic and social developments within each society and in the world at large.[3]

In what follows I will identify myself with those who have adopted this more critical approach, paying particular attention to the differences between the various types of Arab nationalist movements, as well as on their impact, not only on the politics of the separate Arab states and of the Palestinians, but on Middle Eastern inter-state relations as well.[4]

From Arabism to Arab nationalism

At the end of the nineteenth century large numbers of people living in the Middle East had claims to be called Arabs, for linguistic, cultural and historical reasons. They spoke Arabic and, what was more important, those who could read and write had access to a language that had resisted major dialectisation and could be understood from Morocco to the Persian Gulf. They were also heirs to a common culture and a common historical experience based on memories of the Arab and Ottoman Empires. And the vast majority of them who were Muslims possessed not only a common religion but also a set of religious practices, like the pilgrimage, that brought significant numbers of them together at the same revered holy sites.

Nevertheless, Arabness was just one of a number of possible identities at this time, and usually much less important than that of belonging to a particular family or tribe or region or town. And even when the first nationalist writers in the Syrian provinces of the Ottoman Empire began to write in praise of Arabism and to try to get people to think of themselves, first and foremost, as Arabs, they had to compete with a number of other national, religious or regional identities which had already begun to assume political importance. As has often been remarked, it was the Arabs and the Turks, of all the peoples in the empire, who came last to a national movement of their own, many decades after the Greeks and Armenians and others. But like all such latecomers, they had immediate access to a well developed vocabulary based not only on notions of patriotism and national rights but also on associated concepts like citizenship and political representation which could be seen as the properties of any people strong and united enough to have established a nation state of its own.[5]

Writers like Benedict Anderson, Ernest Gellner and Tom Nairn have tried to set out some of the specific historical conditions that allow national movements to appear and to gather strength.[6] These include certain processes that tie significant groups of people together into what Anderson calls an 'imagined community', for example, the development of local or regional economies and the spread of printing and newspapers. This in turn encourages a transition from a situation in which people possess a cluster of identities based on religion, or some other primary loyalty, to one based on culture – which may then be conceived of, either partially or wholly, in secular terms. Typically this involves a concern with language, folklore and popular history, either real or invented. And it often starts with the works of poets, artists and lexicographers who have a particular interest in stressing cultural homogeneity. From there it can quickly develop into a strongly-held political belief that the people who are identified as sharing a particular culture should also live together in a particular state on a particular piece of land.

For writers who argue in this way, all nationalisms generate a very similar type of political theory, using very much the same language. They are concerned with a common problem of national definition: What is the national essence? How was it maintained through history? Where are its boundaries? Their writings are also to be seen much more as a call to action than a coherent, philosophically satisfying, statement. Their purpose is to start a movement, not to fill libraries. If they are to succeed they have to persuade all the people they have defined as being Turk, or Persian, or Arab, or whatever, to act as though that was their primary identity and to place it at the centre of their political lives. This is often best done by a combination of rhetoric and poetry, and by an appeal to the memory of a glorious national past and to the dream of an equally glorious national future.

Just what class or group first takes up the call and tries to mobilise the rest of a national population differs from case to case. Some writers assign this role to the educated elite, others to the middle class. But neither of these groups is usually defined with any precision. There is more general agreement that, in a Third World context, national movements arise most obviously as a result of a desire to throw off imperial control and of a recognition that, in a world of nation states, the only way a people can protect itself is to obtain a state of its own. Whether they succeed will then depend not only on an ability to mobilise large sections of this same population and to keep it unified but also on a whole variety of historical, geographical and political accidents such as wars, great power rivalries and the strength of other groups competing for the same territory.

As far as the Arabs at the eastern end of the Mediterranean were concerned, they followed a roughly similar historical path, from an emphasis on language and culture to the emergence of the first overtly political groups that appeared just before the First World War, calling for the separation of the Arab provinces from an Ottoman Empire which was seen as being run, increasingly, by Turkish-speaking officials and which seemed woefully deficient at standing up to both European and Zionist encroachment. Members of some of these same groups, including many former Ottoman army officers, came together to take part in the Hashemite-led revolt against the Turks in the First World War and then in the short-lived Arab kingdom established by the Amir Faisal in Damascus in 1919/20.

Nevertheless, in spite of the fact that its apologists try to present Arab nationalism as a single movement with a single objective, there was, from the outset, no general agreement about how Arabism should be combined with the more local loyalties to be found in Damascus, Baghdad and the other cities of the Fertile Crescent.[7] This problem was made yet more difficult by the fact that not only was the eastern Arab world split up into separate states by the colonial powers but that these same states also developed their own local laws, symbols and practices which provided an alternative focus for Arabist loyalties. This can be seen very clearly in Iraq, the first of the eastern Arab states to achieve its official independence in 1932 (and a seat at the League of Nations), where efforts to create a sense of Iraqi patriotism were deliberately introduced by the very same king and set of politicians who were also busy with schemes for wider Arab co-operation and even unity. Examples of the former range all the way from the establishment of a competition among poets and musicians to provide words and music for the first Iraqi national anthem to the arguments in favour of universal military service and the politically orchestrated appeals to Iraqi national feeling designed to put an end to the divisions engendered by the tribal revolts of 1935/6.

However, if the colonial period saw the creation of new frontiers dividing the new Arab states from each other, it also saw the development of powerful countervailing tendencies as well. One that followed from the normal processes of economic modernisation was the growing importance of newspapers, broadcasting stations, films and foreign travel in reinforcing the sense of an Arabism that transcended the new political boundaries. This was accompanied by the introduction of intra-Arab conferences of various kinds, and by the development of institutions like banks, with branches in a number of separate states. The policy of employing Palestinian-Arab teachers, doctors and legal experts in Iraq, Kuwait and Bahrain was part of the same trend. A second countervailing tendency was the assistance given to those fighting against the colonial presence, for example, King Faisal's offer of employment to two Syrian, anti-French, activists who sought refuge in Baghdad in the early 1930s. But certainly the most important factor was the growing Arab support for the Palestinians in their struggle against both the British and the Jewish settlers, culminating in the active involvement of politicians and publicists during the anti-British revolt of 1936–9. As Yehoshua Porath correctly observes, from then on events in Palestine constituted the 'single most important factor contributing to the growth of pan-Arab ideology'.[8]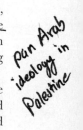

In these circumstances it was relatively easy to keep a sense of Arabism alive and to stress the links that united the Arabic-speaking peoples across what could be made to seem like wholly artificial, foreign-imposed, borders. As Said Bensaid notes of one of the deputies attending the first Syrian constituent assembly in 1928, he felt unable to swear an oath of allegiance to something as vague as the notion of a country (*watan*) called Syria.[9] For him, as for many others, the Arabs belonged to a state with much larger and more generous frontiers than the British and the French had allowed.

The new Arab states: between co-operation and competition

The contradictory necessities of state building versus Arabism were reflected in the policies of the various Arab regimes as they gained their independence, first in the east, then in North Africa, then in the Gulf. All were aware of the many cross-border ties that linked them to their neighbours, and sought to profit from them. However, all were equally aware of the dangers these same ties imposed and the possibilities they offered for external interference in their political life. Not only was it virtually impossible to control the free flow of people and ideas but there were also a multitude of tribal and family, of cultural and commercial, connections that linked Arabs on both sides of any border. In these circumstances, the new regimes began to use a heightened, political, Arabism to win local support, to enhance their own legitimacy and to protect themselves from attacks by the growing number of groups advocating greater Arab co-operation against the colonial powers or against the Jews in Palestine. Meanwhile, for the Hashemite rulers of Iraq and Trans-Jordan in particular, the spread of Arab nationalist sentiments allowed them to dream of expanding their own power to include union with neighbouring states like Syria and Palestine.

A good example of the type of politics this involved took place in Iraq in 1932, when King Faisal tried to get the British to give their approval to his holding an Arab congress in Baghdad, using the argument that Arab support would help to reduce Iraqi weakness and to overcome the dangers threatening the integrity of Iraqi society. This in turn was countered by Humphreys, the British High Commissioner, who argued that such a move might actually provoke the hostility of its neighbours and so encourage the very dangers that the king feared. In his own opinion, the best way to serve the Arab cause would be through Iraq's attention to its own economic and cultural progress.[10]

More than sixty years after the event it is possible to see the merits of both sets of arguments. A parade of Arabism might have both positive and negative consequences, depending on circumstances. In this particular, Iraqi, case it could have been used to increase support for the regime. It could just as easily have stimulated opposition, either from the local Shi'is, who tended to see Arabism as a way of bolstering Sunni supremacy, or by the leaders of other Arab states like Saudi Arabia who resisted anything they saw as an Iraqi bid for leadership over the rest of the Arab world.

In this situation, the way chosen by most Arab regimes in the 1930s and 1940s was one of encouraging greater co-operation on a state-to-state basis. It can be seen in the treaties of friendship, arbitration and extradition that were signed between them from 1931 onwards. It can also be seen in the creation of what was officially entitled the 'League of Arab States' in 1945, with Syria, Iraq, Saudi Arabia, Egypt and Lebanon as its first members. Although there were quite serious difficulties between the advocates of closer union (notably Egypt) and those who wanted a looser type of arrangement (mainly Lebanon and Saudi Arabia), all agreed that what was needed was a framework permitting greater co-operation between what were, basically, independent sovereign states.[11] Indeed,

greater state-to-state cooperation

as Bahgat Korany points out, the word 'state', in its territorial sense, appears forty-eight times in the twenty articles of the Arab League charter.[12]

Nevertheless, there were simultaneous pressures to move towards greater integration as well. The defeat of the Arab armies in Palestine in 1948/9, the struggle against what was left of the British and the French presence and the growing competition between the Americans and the Russians for Middle Eastern influence all seemed to underline the advantages of such a move. Further emphasis came from President Nasser's assertion of Egyptian independence, leading to his nationalisation of the Suez Canal and his survival against the Anglo-French and Israeli invasion of October/November 1956, which he immediately set out to exploit as a great 'Arab' victory. In this atmosphere it was easy to mobilise large crowds behind nationalist and anti-colonial slogans throughout most of the Arab world. Popular enthusiasm reached its peak with the formation of the United Arab Republic between Egypt and Syria in 1958, and then again with the unity talks of 1963, during which enthusiastic crowds carried flags through the streets of Cairo with four stars representing the countries that were supposed to form the new super-state: Egypt, Syria, Iraq and, in some formulations, North Yemen.

The search for greater political unity failed, however, largely due to the disparity in power between the different Arab states and regimes. One example is provided by the central role assumed by President Nasser and by Egypt. Given Egypt's economic and military predominance in the Arab world at this time, closer integration could not help to be to its own great advantage. But this was exactly what worried the other Arab leaders, particularly when the Egyptian regime showed no compunction in appealing to their people over their own heads. 'If as a state Egypt recognizes boundaries in its dealing with governments,' wrote a columnist in *Al-Ahram*, the official mouthpiece of the Nasser regime on 29 December 1961, 'Egypt as a revolution should never hesitate or halt before these boundaries but should carry its message beyond its borders to the people in order to initiate its revolutionary message'.[13] Such fears were further intensified by the actual experience of Syrian union with Egypt, which left many important persons, the future President, Hafiz al-Asad, among them, determined never to allow their country to be manoeuvred into such a subservient position again.

The Palestine issue also possessed the capacity both to unite Arabs and to divide them. For the first ten years after the creation of the state of Israel and the expulsion and flight of some 750,000 refugees, the two Arab states most closely involved, Egypt and Jordan, were more preoccupied with trying to recruit Palestinian support against the other than in preparing a plan for joint Arab action against the Israelis.[14] There was also little willingness to encourage the Palestinians themselves to play a role in the future liberation of their own land.[15] Things changed in the early 1960s, however, when the idea of creating what was known as a Palestinian 'entity' among refugee Palestinians began to gather support and was finally agreed by the Arab leaders themselves, meeting at the first Arab summit in January 1964. This in turn paved the way for Ahmad al-Shuqairi to establish the Palestine Liberation Organisation (PLO) at the initial meeting of the Palestinian national council held in Jerusalem the following May. For most observers, rivalry between Egypt and the new revolutionary regime of Brigadier Qasim in Iraq, 1958–63, was the main reason for the decision. But some also saw it as aimed against Jordan, which was bound to feel threatened by an organisation that offered an alternative leadership to the many Palestinians living under its own control.

Meanwhile, in these very same years, Yasser Arafat and a few friends were preparing to start guerrilla operations against Israel with their new Fatah organisation which they had formed in a deliberate attempt to allow Palestinians to gain control over their own destinies after years of neglect by the Arab states. In the end it was Fatah's greater militancy that not only played a role in precipitating the disastrous confrontation with Israel leading to the 1967 Middle East war but that also allowed it to obtain a major influence in the PLO, leading on to Arafat's election as chairman of its executive committee in February 1969.

Tension between the Palestinians and the Arab states also points to another reason behind the inability to unite, and that is the fact that, by the 1950s, the main exponents of Arab nationalism were the Arab regimes themselves. By and large such regimes were only willing to contemplate union when they were weak and under threat – a situation which, in Malik Mufti's argument, promoted tendencies towards what he terms 'defensive unionism' – putting it quickly aside when they began to feel more strong.[16] Unable to contemplate any of the reductions in their own power and sovereignty that a real union would involve, they were also worried that unbridled support for Arab nationalist goals could involve them in a dangerous war with Israel as well. For both reasons, they were particularly wary of the smaller, pan-Arab, groups like the Movement of Arab Nationalists (MAN) founded in Beirut in the early 1950s, whose demands for union and for immediate confrontation with the Israelis were worryingly insistent. After some initial hesitation, MAN supported President Nasser's drive for Arab leadership until 1965/6. However, it then began to adopt a more critical stance towards Nasserist policies and to argue that it was the regimes themselves that were the main obstacles to Arab unity and which should either be forced to change their ways or be removed by revolution from below.[17] The road to the liberation of Jerusalem, they now argued, was through Damascus, Cairo and Amman.

In the highly charged atmosphere that followed the 1967 war, it was the PLO, the guerrillas and their various Arab radical supporters that seemed, for a moment, to show the Arab world an alternative way forward. Soon, however, the existing states began to assert themselves, to strengthen their defences and to regain some of the initiative. In all this they were greatly assisted by access to the oil wealth that Saudi Arabia, Libya and the Gulf states agreed to distribute at the Khartoum Arab summit in 1967. This was followed by Jordan's successful confrontation with the Palestinian resistance movement in 1970/1 and then by the much better performance of the reorganised Arab armies in the 1973 war against Israel. Thereafter, the drive for union was much diminished and the separate states were left free to develop their own particular identities within the larger Arab political environment.

Arabism in the 1970s and the 1980s

In a well-known article published in 1979, Fouad Ajami proclaimed the 'end of pan-Arabism'.[18] By this he seems to have meant that the power of the individual states to resist pan-Arab appeals had become much greater and therefore that such appeals were now much more difficult to make. This is undoubtedly correct as far as it goes. However, as I have tried to show in the previous section, the drive for unity was always more ambivalent than is usually presented. Just as important, any scheme for greater interstate co-operation was underpinned by a basic Arabism, a sense of kinship between the Arabic-speaking peoples, which remained a central fact of Middle Eastern life whatever else might be going on. Seen from this perspective, what Ajami is trying to describe is not the end of Arabism itself but an important change in the way it was interpreted and put to political use.

Apart from the immediate fallout from the 1967 war, the Arab environment changed in a number of important ways during the 1960s and early 1970s. One factor was the decline of Egyptian power and prestige as a result of military defeat, economic exhaustion and the death of President Nasser. A second was the growing financial influence of Saudi Arabia, and a third the new political importance of Syria following the consolidation of President Asad's regime in the early 1970s. If we also add the large increase in the numbers of independent Arab states, we see an Arab world where power was very much more diffused and, consequently, in which it was very much more difficult for one leader, or one regime, to exercise influence or control.

Another important factor accounting for the changed Arab environment was what has been termed the increasing 'durability' of the Arab regimes and the existing Arab states.[19] After the numerous coups of the 1950s and 1960s, no regime or ruling family was overthrown by force in the 1970s and 1980s, with the exception of that of President Nimeiri of Sudan, who was ousted as a result of widespread popular (and army) opposition in 1985. Other enforced changes, like President Sadat's assassination in 1981 or President Bourguiba's deposition in 1987, did not lead to any basic change in the way each country was run. As has already been argued, the major reason for this durability lies in the growth of state power. Only Lebanon provides solitary testimony to the inability of a government to contain the conflicting forces at loose on its national terrain, a situation made even more difficult by the way it also became the victim of intra-Arab and Arab/Israeli rivalries which could be played out, with much less danger, on the land of a weaker neighbour.[20]

The new situation permitted regimes to exploit some of the possibilities inherent in Arabism without having to surrender control over policy or, worse still, their own state sovereignty. An obvious strategy was to proclaim a strong attachment to unity while avoiding any scheme that might involve closer political union with another Arab country or actual military confrontation with Israel. Two of the regimes that practised this approach most assiduously were the Ba'thi ones established in Syria in 1966 and Iraq in 1968.[21] Both were helped by the fact that one of the three major principles of Ba'thism, 'unity', implied such a strong commitment to Arabism, almost by definition, that it was unnecessary to demonstrate this commitment by actually undertaking potentially self-defeating actions in its support. As an additional precaution, both regimes resorted to periods of rhetorical overkill, adopting such extreme positions in support of the Palestinians and against Israel as to make it extremely dangerous for any of the other Arab leaders to consider either uniting with them or following their lead.

A second change in direction involved each regime placing more and more stress on its own local territorial nationalism. This was relatively easy for the countries of North Africa, Libya apart, where the existence of separate states had never been seen to be in any sort of major conflict with the demands of Arabism or greater Arab co-operation.[22] As for Egypt, President Sadat was able to derive advantage from the genuine mood of war weariness that followed the October war with Israel and the local feeling that the country had spilled more than enough of its blood in the Arab cause. Hence his decision to return to the use of the name Egypt, in place of the United Arab Republic, aroused little popular opposition.

Matters were somewhat more difficult in the eastern part of the Arab world, where the existing states still seemed somewhat artificial entities to many of their own people and where most of the separate regimes had traditionally relied on political appeals to Arabism to augment their own legitimacy. However, in Iraq and Jordan there began a process of subtle linguistic change designed to reinforce the vocabulary of a local territorial nationalism while, elsewhere, it was loyalty to the ruling family that generally stood proxy for a primary attachment to the state within its narrow boundaries.[23] Only in South Yemen, where appeals to either Arabism or Yemeni nationalism were deemed politically and ideologically inappropriate, was a third authority, that of Marxist-Leninism, employed as an alternative focus for popular loyalty until its sudden rejection in favour of Yemeni unity at the end of the 1980s.[24]

One index of the shift towards a more localised set of symbols and practices that linked particular Arabs to particular pieces of land was the construction in capital cities like Amman of tombs of local unknown soldiers. Another was increased attention to the celebration of specific national days, few of which had any symbolic pan-Arab component.[25] This process was carried furthest in Iraq during the war with Iran in the 1980s, when the regime encouraged the use of a specifically local history and geography calculated to stress its differences with its Arab neighbours. A good example is the frequent pictorial representation of the Iraqi landscape as an oasis of richly watered date palms surrounded by an obviously Arab desert.[26]

Such moves clearly reinforced the existing tendencies towards greater separateness among the Arab peoples that were already expressed in the different passports, the different educational and legal systems and the different rules governing migration and citizenship. Nevertheless, in spite of the obvious diminution in the calls for unity, Arabism continued to express itself in a variety of ways, for example, by the joint action to expel Egypt from the Arab League after its peace treaty with Israel in 1979, or the support given to Iraq by Egypt and Jordan during its long war with Iran from 1980 to 1988. In each case, the unity of the Arab ranks was broken, the first time by Egypt, the second by Syria, who sided with Iraq's adversary, Iran. But in each case, too, the ties of Arabism were strong enough to encourage a high degree of co-operation between the great majority of the other Arab states.

The same tendencies were reinforced in the 1970s by the oil boom, which encouraged a whole new breed of schemes of intra-Arab co-operation based on the planned redistribution of wealth from the richer countries to the poorer in the interests of the more rapid economic development of the Arab region as a whole. Even more important were the decisions to use oil revenues in support of the so-called 'front line' states in the wars against Israel and to bolster the resolve of those opposed to the Camp David agreement of 1978. As a result, Syria was promised $1.8 billion a year for ten years, Jordan $1.2 billion and the PLO and the Palestinians of the occupied West Bank and Gaza $150 million each.[27] However, it should also be noted that, as a result of falling oil revenues, the financial demands of the Iraq/Iran war and the changes in political relationships between donors and recipients, it is very unlikely that all this money was actually delivered.

The specificities of intra-Arab relations

In international law, as well as in their own perceptions of themselves, the individual Arab states are sovereign entities. This is officially recognised in the title as well as the charter of the League of Arab States. As Article VIII forcefully asserts: 'Each state participant in the League shall respect the existing regime obtaining in the other League states, regarding it as a (fundamental) right of those states, and pledges itself not to undertake any action tending to alter that regime'.[28] Nevertheless, in terms of actual practice, the League acted as though the Arab states should conduct their relations more in terms of notions of brotherhood than of protocol. This can be seen very easily in the League's lack of any mechanism for settling disputes about interference in each other's internal affairs. The matter was raised forcibly on two occasions in 1958. In the first, Lebanon lodged an official protest against propaganda attacks against it by the media of the United Arab Republic (then consisting of Egypt and Syria), and against intervention across its borders by armed bands. Instead of examining the protest in detail and trying to assign blame, the other members passed a resolution which simply called upon both states to end the disturbances between them. As the Sudanese delegate explained, this approach was based not on the notion that the League was a court of justice adjudicating between two parties but on the need to encourage a reconciliation between brothers. A few months later, a Tunisian speech of complaint against Egypt for harbouring a group of political exiles which, it alleged, had plotted against the government was rejected, again without examination, as largely 'offensive' to the League of Arab States and derogatory to one of its members.[29]

The reason for the absence of an official mechanism for settling interstate disputes stems obviously from the assumption that the Arab states were so similar in kind that such a mechanism was both unnecessary and inappropriate. As leader of the revolution, Muammar Qadhafi stated forcefully to President Mubarak in December 1989: 'I am against diplomatic representation (between Egypt and Libya) because the ultimate aim must be a united Arab nation where there is no need for the exchange of such missions.'[30] Occasions of this kind also provide an important clue to the way in which intra-Arab relations were (and are) actually conducted. As a rule, they were attended to, personally, by the president or head of state, often on the telephone to his opposite number or by personal visit, with only minimal reference to his own foreign ministry or his diplomatic representatives in the other capital. Another feature was the important role assigned to senior members of a regime with significant personal contacts in other Arab states, for example, Anwar Sadat in the Nasser period, who was regarded as having good relations inside most Arab states, or Rifaat al-Asad, the Syrian president's younger brother, who had close ties with Prince Abdullah of Saudi Arabia.

Just as important, there was a general disregard for borders and for national sovereignty when it came to trying to influence an Arab neighbour, to put pressure on it or to try to stop it from pressuring you. Over the years this has taken the form of direct military intervention, assassinations, kidnappings, bombings, sabotage, newspaper and radio campaigns, and support for the political opponents of rival regimes. A few examples of the most flagrant acts of interference, taken more or less at random, would include: King Saud's plot to kill President Nasser in 1958; Egyptian attempts to destabilise King Hussein between 1958 and 1960, including the assassination of his prime minister; the brief Syrian invasion of northern Jordan in 1970; Jordanian and Iraqi support for the Muslim Brothers in their struggle with the Syrian regime from 1979 onwards; Algeria's provision of base facilities for the Polisario Front during its fight against the Moroccan army in the Western Sahara; and Libyan encouragement of armed incursion into Tunisia in 1980. As all such activities were organised by senior military officers or members of an intelligence agency, their origins are inevitably shrouded in great secrecy and their exact purpose difficult to discern. Nevertheless, they are certainly testimony to a habitual willingness to act across international borders that seems unparalleled elsewhere in the non-European world.

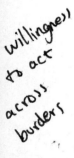

Attempts to reduce such behaviour to a set of underlying principles or patterns have not proved particularly successful.[31] Nevertheless, it is possible to hazard a few generalisations about the practice of intra-Arab state relations, its aims and its consequences. The first is the general assumption that boundaries are porous and that neighbours will attempt to interfere. This forces regimes to be much warier than they might otherwise be and, often, to try to pre-empt such interference by making a first move themselves. More generally, this assumption has often led to attempts to weaken a difficult neighbour as a way of reducing its capacity to make trouble. Second, it follows that there is also an assumption of potential conflict even when no objective reason for one exists. Third, the close involvement with events and processes across Arab borders means that there is less of a difference between domestic and foreign policy than in other parts of the world. Regimes habitually attempt to find support, and even legitimacy, across such borders while having to pay close attention to rival attempts to do just the same.

The role of Israel and the Palestinians in intra-Arab relations

Apart from the influence of Arabism on intra-Arab relations, another specific and unusual influence has been that of the Israeli/Palestinian conflict. As far as the particular role of Israel was concerned, this stemmed largely from the fact that, for the first thirty years of its existence, its relations with its Arab neighbours were conducted almost exclusively by force and by threat of force, a policy developed by its long-time prime minister, David Ben-Gurion, and his defence establishment in the early 1950s. At different times this was aimed at pre-empting an Arab attack, at preventing Arab support for Palestinian and other guerrillas and at trying to get rid of a hostile Arab leader like President Nasser.[32] Israel's Arab neighbours, for their part, were unwilling either to sign a peace treaty or to normalise relations and were thus left with the choice of preparing for war or seeking some kind of unofficial *modus vivendi*. As a rule, Egypt and Syria took the former path, and Jordan and Lebanon the latter.

This unresolved conflict was largely responsible for a Middle Eastern arms race, a series of wars, and the Israeli occupation of the West Bank, Gaza and Egypt's Sinai peninsula in 1967, as well as numerous lesser clashes. The Palestinian factor added an extra dimension, particularly after the increase in the size and bellicosity of the guerrilla organisations in the late 1960s. The consequence was to bring Lebanon and Jordan more directly into the conflict as a result of Israeli raids against the bases established on their territory. However, Israel's policy towards the two states soon diverged. No sooner had King Hussein decided to expel the guerrillas from Jordan than Israel reverted to its traditional policy of support for the Hashemite monarchy as a conservative force on its eastern flank. At the same time, intervention against the Palestinians in Lebanon became ever more intense, leading up to the Israeli invasion of the country in 1982, the military defeat of the Palestinians and the brief attempt to engineer the establishment of a friendly regime dominated by the Lebanese Forces and controlled by the newly-elected President, Bashir Gemayel. Even though politically unsuccessful, Israel's invasion triggered off a series of changes in the internal balance of power between Christian, Shi'i and Druze militias that were to make their own major contribution to the further disintegration of Lebanon's fragile social system.

One reason why the Israelis were able to exercise their power in Lebanon was the fact that the Egyptians had already signed a peace treaty with them in 1979. From President Sadat's point of view this involved a considered decision to normalise relations with his powerful neighbour. It also involved the implicit decoupling of the political equation that implied that support for the Palestinians and hostility to Israel were two sides of the same coin. For most of the other Arab regimes, however, this was seen as a gross betrayal of the Arab cause, even if the majority of them soon began, cautiously, to follow the Egyptians along the same path. The alternative strategy employed by Syria was to build up its military capacity so as to be able to confront Israel, while, at the same time, seeking to control the Palestinian resistance movement in such a way that its policies became subservient to the requirements of Syrian security. This too aroused considerable Arab hostility, particularly when it involved Syria's military confrontation with the PLO's forces in Lebanon in 1976 and then its later attempts to divide the Palestinians and to promote an alternative leadership to Yasser Arafat after 1983.

Analysis of the influence of the Palestinians on Arab politics and interstate relations is even more complex than that of Israel. For most of the first two decades after 1948 they were without a state of their own, and largely under the control of several different regimes. However, once they began to assert their own independence of action in the late 1960s they inevitably posed major problems for those Arab states they asked for support. One, of course, was the danger of inviting a harsh Israeli response. Another was the twin appeal that the Palestinian leadership was willing and able to make, both to the regimes and to their people. Although one of the main principles of Fatah's political creed was to maintain the movement's freedom of action by avoiding interference in the internal affairs of Arab states, this was often ignored in practice. In some cases, as in Jordan in 1970 and in Lebanon a few years later, it meant direct attempts to destabilise the regime in association with opposition forces; in others, there was pressure to follow a revolutionary logic that placed Arab unity and the necessity of constant confrontation with Israel above everything else. As a result, the leaders of most Middle Eastern regimes could have been forgiven for supposing that, while Palestinians saw their own nationalism as perfectly compatible with a wider Arabism, they were quite ready to ride roughshod over Jordanian or Egyptian or Lebanese national self-interest if this was believed to stand in the way of their own objectives.

In addition to their own nationalism, the Palestinians also developed an evolving strategy for achieving their political aims. This began with great stress on the primacy of armed struggle. But, as in the case of most movements of national liberation, it turned progressively towards an emphasis on diplomacy and a negotiated settlement. The first major stage in this transformation was completed in 1974 when the Twelfth Palestinian National Congress agreed on what was called an 'interim' or 'phased' programme by which it was decided that an 'independent national authority' was to be established over any part of Palestinian national territory that could be liberated from Israeli control –

generally understood to refer to the West Bank and Gaza. Twelve years later this process reached its culmination with the political statement issued by the Nineteenth National Council held in Algiers in November 1988 that affirmed the determination of the PLO to arrive at a 'political settlement' of the Arab–Israeli conflict by means of an international peace conference at which all parties would be represented on an equal basis.[33]

The process just described owed much more to developments within the various Palestinian communities inside and outside the West Bank and Gaza than it did either to Arab diplomatic activity or to obvious Arab self-interest. Indeed, a number of Arab regimes did their very best to split the movement, to marginalise its leadership or to make their own political arrangements with the Israelis without reference to the PLO. This was true, for example, of the Egyptians, whose separate peace with Israel in 1979 lacked any sure guarantee that Palestinian rights would be respected. Nevertheless, the leadership of the PLO managed to overcome these threats in a number of ways. It was able to rebuild the unity of the movement, whenever this was required to launch a new political initiative. It also made skilful use of the disagreements between the various Arab states to find new allies for itself and to avoid falling under the influence of any one potentially hostile regime. By so doing it was in a position to take maximum advantage of the revolt against Israeli rule on the West Bank and Gaza, the *Intifada* when it broke out in December 1987 and to use it as a launching pad for a renewed drive towards an independent Palestinian state.

The politics of Arab economic integration

During the early independence period it was a natural assumption that the drive towards greater political co-operation among the Arab states should be accompanied by one towards greater economic integration as well. Such feelings were influenced by developments during the Second World War when a large part of the region had been run as a single unit by the Anglo-American Middle East Supply Centre based in Cairo, and then by the early signs of progress towards the establishment of a European Common Market. Supporters of the move also saw it as a way of promoting intra-Arab economic exchange, which had been greatly diminished as a result of the creation of the separate national economies by the colonial powers.

There were, however, significant difficulties. Opportunities for increasing trade were seriously limited by the fact that most of the newly independent Arab states produced roughly the same range of agricultural and industrial products, the only major exception being oil which had already become far and away the most important contributor to intra-Arab exchange. In addition, most of the Arab regimes were unwilling to lower tariffs, being heavily reliant on them to protect their own infant industries, to raise revenue, or both. There were important political difficulties as well, notably the fear that the economically weaker states felt towards integration with the strong, and the very considerable problems involved in setting up an Arab international secretariat to monitor and to manage any new arrangement.

Efforts to promote Arab economic integration took four main forms.[34] The first of these, which was attempted in the early 1950s, can best be characterised as the free trade phase, when an initiative was taken to use the Arab League and some of its associated institutions to reduce barriers to the exchange of goods, services, capital and labour. Its main achievement was the Convention for Facilitating Trade and Regulating Transit between the states of the Arab League, which was agreed at the first conference of Arab economic ministers in 1953. One of its strongest exponents was Lebanon, which had a special interest in securing access to Arab markets as a way of reducing its dependence on Syria following the break-up of the customs union between the two countries in 1950. The convention led to some progress in the mutual abolition of tariffs on agricultural goods and oil but little on the industrial goods that almost all the signatories were concerned to protect.

This phase was followed in 1957 by a sustained attempt to create an Arab common market with a single external tariff. Leadership came from Egypt, anxious to build on the momentum created by the defeat of the Anglo-French invasion of Egypt, which, thanks to Saudi financial assistance it was able to present as an economic as well as political victory for Arab solidarity. Agreement in principle to establish such a market was reached at the Arab League's economic council in January 1958. But it was not until August 1964 that Egypt, Iraq, Jordan, Kuwait and Syria signed a treaty binding them to establish the Arab common market on 1 January 1965 and to work towards the progressive abolition of all duties and quantitative restrictions on trade between them by January 1974. In the event, the treaty was only ratified by four of the states concerned – not Kuwait – and it proved extremely difficult to reach agreement on the goods on which tariffs and quotas were to be reduced. There was a similar lack of progress towards the establishment of a common external tariff. Arguing with the benefit of hindsight, it would seem that the various states concerned agreed to enter the union for largely political reasons and that, far from promising them tangible economic benefits, it was soon seen as a threat to their existing programmes of industrialisation based on the protection of their own national markets. However, in mitigation it should also be noted that many other non-European regional groupings ran into exactly the same kind of problems, for example, the Latin American Free Trade Association started in 1960.[35]

The third move towards greater economic integration began during the oil boom of the early 1970s and involved the creation of a multiplicity of funds and banks to invest some of the new wealth in the oil-poor Arab states. Here at last was a significant complementarity to exploit, with the oil-rich states in need of labour and expertise to create modern institutions for themselves, and the remainder desperately anxious for the capital necessary to develop their economies. It also opened up the prospect of combining Arab resources in a whole host of joint ventures, from banks to shipping agencies, from metallurgical plants to huge schemes designed to improve the agricultural output of Sudan. The basic institutional model was provided by the Kuwaitis, whose Kuwait Fund for Arab Economic Development had been established at the time of independence from Britain in 1961. Its aim was as much political as economic: a desire to underpin the city state's rather fragile legitimacy by showing that it was prepared to share its wealth in co-operative ventures with its poorer Arab neighbours. This pattern has been followed, since 1970, by the creation of several hundred other Arab enterprises, staffed by a growing group of officials who owe their allegiance to Arab as much as to local state interests.

The fourth and final form of Arab economic integration is the various subregional groupings, of which the Gulf Cooperation Council (GCC) was certainly the most successful. The idea was first introduced in the form of the abortive North African (Maghreb) Union, established with a consultative council at Tunis in 1966. However, as with the Arab common market, efforts to remove barriers to local trade were thwarted by the existence of the separate national plans and national planning agencies, as well as by the pull of the European Economic Community with which individual trade agreements seemed preferable. The GCC, established in 1981, offered quite a different model, with many more obvious advantages. This was a union between economically underdeveloped states all of which had ambitious plans to build a variety of modern industries based on the existence of cheap energy, a programme that was much more likely to succeed if the states could manage to agree on how to share their growing local market between them.[36] Later, in 1989, the creation of two more subregional groupings was announced: the Arab Maghreb Union (MU), embracing Algeria, Libya, Mauritania, Morocco and Tunisia; and the Arab Cooperation Council (ACC), consisting of Egypt, Iraq, Jordan and North Yemen. However, in each case the political reasons for their establishment were very much more obvious than the economic, causing the ACC to collapse as a result of the Iraqi invasion of Kuwait in August 1990 and leaving the MU moribund given that both Libya and Algeria were largely cut off from normal international relations for most of the 1990s.

Was there an Arab 'order'?

Enough has probably been said to sustain the argument that the Arab states interact in a way that is unusual, to say the least, in the modern world, on account of their close ties of language, region and culture. A last question to ask therefore is whether their pattern of interaction was, and perhaps still is, sufficiently regular, predictable and mutually well-understood to constitute something that it would be useful to call an 'order'. Here the terminology itself is less significant than the process of uncovering those permanent structures that inform the thinking of all the major actors and so influence their policies and the way they practice day-to-day inter-state, and inter-regime, relations.

To answer this question it is necessary to consider several important features of the Middle East's regional context. The first is the growth in the number and

variety of independent Arab states, from the five that signed the original Arab
League charter to the present-day twenty-one (plus the Palestinians). This at
once suggests that strategies designed to exercise leadership and influence have
had to become very much more complex. There has also been the obvious
tendency towards the development of sub-regional groupings in both North
Africa and the Gulf, leaving a much more fluid situation in the old heartlands of
Arabism at the eastern end of the Mediterranean.

The second feature is the growing importance of relations with local non-
Arab states, beginning with Israel and then extending to Iran, Turkey and some
of the North African countries like Ethiopia. In all cases such states have passed
from being simply enemies, or, at the least, difficult and unruly neighbours, to
allies of one or more of the Arab regimes in their disputes with other local Arab
rivals. At one stage, in the 1950s, President Nasser was able to marginalise a state
like Iraq simply because it had entered the Baghdad Pact of 1955 with Britain
and some non-Arab neighbours. But this solidarity in the face of the non-Arab
world was certainly broken in the late 1970s and early 1980s by the peace
agreement between Egypt and Israel and then by the strategic alliance between
Syria and revolutionary Iran.

The third and fourth features involve the role played in the region by the
superpowers, on the one hand, and the European Community, on the other. As
far as the superpowers were concerned, a key moment was the American
decision taken in the mid-1950s to abandon its brief search for alliances with
secular nationalist Arab leaders like President Nasser and to base its Middle
Eastern position on its support of conservative, or 'moderate', monarchical
regimes like the Saudis, Jordanians and Moroccans, none of which posed any
threat to its major partner, Israel. This at once gave the Soviet Union an
opportunity to gain major influence by offering military and financial aid to the
more radical regimes like the Egyptians, the Syrians and the Iraqis. However,
once the latter had been so comprehensively defeated by the Israelis in 1967, this
left the field clear for the United States to exercise an almost unrivalled
hegemony for two decades, before the Soviet Union began to make a small
comeback in the early Gorbachev era. European political influence was very
much less important but it did play an important role in the economic field by
forcing an increasing number of Arab states to band together in order to
improve the terms on which they might hope to obtain access to the Common
Market.

Looked at in these terms it would seem that if there was an Arab order it must
certainly have been an evolving one that was strongly influenced by the changing
balance of Middle Eastern, as well as international, power. Three phases suggest
themselves. The first is obviously marked by the growing power of Nasser's
Egypt, which, although often challenged, was strongly enough based to allow it
to dictate the terms on which major Arab policy decisions were to be made. This
was initially effected through the Egyptian control over the Arab League in the
1950s, then by President Nasser's domination of the Arab summits of the early
1960s. The second phase, ushered in with such dramatic intensity by the Israeli

although USSR supported radical regimes (defeat '67) gives US unbridled hegemony

1) Egypt under Nasser (50s and 60s)

2) Israeli military hegemony (~ 1967 to 70s)

3) Arab unity

victory in 1967, was one of Israel's military hegemony, bolstered in the early 1970s by its strategic alliance with the United States. This was used constantly to keep the individual Arab states divided and off balance. The third, and final, phase began in the mid-1980s with the increasingly successful attempts to unite the Arabs, first in support of Iraq in the Gulf War, then behind the Palestinian *Intifada*. One sign of this was the Amman summit of November 1987, the first to be held since 1982. Another was the restoration of diplomatic relations between Egypt and most of the Arab states which had been severed in 1979. This phase then came to an abrupt halt with the Iraqi occupation of Kuwait with its stimulus to new forms of Arab disunity and division.

Notes

1 Sami Zubaida, 'Theories of nationalism', in G. Littlejohn *et al.* (eds), *Power and the State* (London: Croom Helm, 1978).

2 For example, Sylvia G. Haim (ed.), *Arab Nationalism: An Anthology* (Los Angeles, CA: University of California Press, 1962), Introduction; and Albert Hourani, *Arabic Thought in the Liberal Age 1978–1939* (Oxford: Oxford University Press, 1962), particularly Chapter 11.

3 Ernest Gellner provided an excellent example of the difference between an idealist and a materialist approach to nationalism in a seminar on 'Nationalism' given at St Antony's College, Oxford, 18 October 1980, when he observed that just as Marx had turned Hegel's idealism on its head, he proposed to do the same with Elie Kedourie's assertion that it is ideas about nationalism which create cultural homogeneity when, in his opinion, exactly the reverse was true. The same point is repeated in Gellner's *Nations and Nationalism* (Oxford: Basil Blackwell, 1983), p. 358.

4 In what follows I have been particularly influenced by C. Ernest Dawn, 'The formation of pan-Arab ideology in the interwar years', *International Journal of Middle Eastern Studies*, 20/1 (February 1988), pp. 67–91; Eberhard Kienle, *Ba'th Versus Ba'th: The Conflict Between Syria and Iraq* (London: I.B. Tauris, 1990); and Malik Mufti, *Sovereign Creations: Pan-Arabism and Political Order in Syria and Iraq* (New York and London: Syracuse University Press, 1996).

5 Said Bensaid, 'Al-Watan and al-Umma in contemporary Arab use', in Ghassan Salamé (ed.), *The Foundations of the Arab State* (London: Croom Helm, 1987), pp. 152–9.

6 Benedict Anderson, *Imagined Communities: Reflections on the Origins and Spread of Nationalism* (London: Verso, 1983); Tom Nairn, 'Marxism and the modern Janus', *New Left Review*, 94 (November/December, 1975), pp. 3–29.

7 For a subtle analysis of the competing nationalism present in Damascus just after the First World War, see James L. Gelvin, *Divided Loyalties: Nationalism and Mass Politics in Syria at the Close of the Empire* (Berkeley, CA: University of California Press, 1998).

8 Yehoshua Porath, *In Search of Arab Unity, 1930–1945* (London: Frank Cass, 1986), p. 162.

9 Bensaid, 'Al-Watan and al-Umma', p. 152.

10 Khaldun S. Husri, 'King Faysal I and Arab unity 1930–33', *Journal of Contemporary History*, 10/2 (April 1975), pp. 324–5.

11 Ahmed Gomaa, *The Foundation of the League of Arab States: Wartime Diplomacy and Inter-Arab Politics* (London and New York: Longman, 1977), pp. 247–8.

12 Bahgat Korany, 'Regional system in transition: The Camp David order and the Arab world 1978–1990', in Barbara Allen Roberson (ed.), *The Middle East Regional Order* (London and Basingstoke: Macmillan, 1992).

13 Quoted in Adeed Dawisha, *The Arab Radicals* (New York: Council on Foreign Relations, 1986), p. 24.

14 Moshe Shemesh, *The Palestinian Entity 1959–1974: Arab Politics and the PLO* (London: Frank Cass, 1988), pp. 11, 19, 21.

15 For example, Helena Cobban, *The Palestine Liberation Organisation: People, Power and Politics* (Cambridge: Cambridge University Press, 1984), p. 23; and Andrew Gowers and Tony Walker, *The Man Behind the Myth: Yasser Arafat and the Palestinian Revolution* (London: W.H. Allen, 1990), p. 25.

16 Mufti, *Sovereign Creations*, pp. 10–16.

17 Walid Kazziha, *Revolutionary Transformation in the Arab World: Habash and His Comrades from Nationalism to Marxism* (London: Charles Knight, 1975), Chapter 4; and Fred Halliday, *Arabia Without Sultans* (Harmondsworth: Penguin Books, 1975), pp. 21–5.

18 Fouad Ajami, 'The end of pan-Arabism', *Foreign Affairs*, 57/2 (Winter, 1978/9), pp. 355–73.

19 This is part of the subtitle of Adeed Dawisha and I. William Zartman (eds), *Beyond Coercion: The Durability of the Arab State* (London: Croom Helm, 1988).

20 Georges Corm, *Fragmentation of the Middle East: The Last Thirty Years* (London: Hutchinson Education, 1988), Chapter 6.

21 Kienle, *Ba'th Versus Ba'th*, Chapter 4.

22 Elbaki Hermassi, 'State-building and regime performance in the Greater Maghreb', in Salamé (ed.), *Foundations of the Arab State*, pp. 76–7.

23 For example, Amatzia Baram, 'Qawmiyya and Wataniyya in Ba'thi Iraq: The search for a new balance', *Middle Eastern Studies*, 19/2 (April 1983), pp. 188–200.

24 I owe this idea to Professor Michael Cook.

25 Emmanuel Sivan, 'The Arab nation-state: In search of a usable past', *Middle East Review* (Spring, 1987), pp. 25–8.

26 Amatzia Baram, 'Mesopotamian identity in Ba'thi Iraq', *Middle Eastern Studies*, 19/4 (October 1983), pp. 426–55. Also his, *History and Ideology in the Formation of Ba'thist Iraq, 1968–89* (London and Basingstoke: Macmillan/St Antony's, 1991), especially Chapters 6 and 7.

27 Patrick Seale, *Asad: The Struggle for the Middle East* (London: I.B. Tauris, 1988), p. 313.

28 Muhammad Khalil, *The Arab States and the Arab League: A Documentary Record, II, International Affairs* (Beirut: Khayats, 1962), p. 59.

29 Ibid., p. 203.

30 Quoted by Middle East News Agency, 12 December 1989.

31 Still one of the best examples is Patrick Seale, *The Struggle for Syria: A Study of Post-War Arab Politics* (Oxford: Oxford University Press, 1965). For another view, see Bahgat Korany and Ali E. Hilal Dessouki (eds), *The Foreign Policies of the Arab States* (Boulder, CO: Westview Press and Cairo, Egypt: The American University of Cairo Press, 1984).

32 Dan Horowitz, 'The Israeli concept of national security and prospects for peace in the Middle East', in Gabriel Sheffer (ed.), *Dynamics of a Conflict: A Re-examination of the Arab–Israeli Conflict* (Atlantic Highlands, NJ: Humanities Press, 1975).

33 Extracts from the English translation of the text can be found in *Middle East International*, 339 (2 December 1988), pp. 22–3.

34 For an expanded version of the same arguments see Roger Owen, 'Arab integration in historical perspective: Are there any lessons?', *Arab Affairs*, 1/6 (April 1988), pp. 41–51.

35 For example, M.J.H. Finch, 'The Latin American Free Trade Association', in Ali M. El-Agraa (ed.), *International Economic Integration* (London and Basingstoke: Macmillan, 1982).

36 Abdullah Ibrahim El-Kuwaiz, 'Economic integration of the Cooperation Council of the Arab States of the Gulf: Challenges, achievements and future outlook', in John A.

Sandwick (ed.), *Gulf Cooperation Council: Moderation and Stability in an Independent World* (Boulder, CO: Westview Press, 1988); and Michael Cain and Kais Al-Badri, 'An assessment of the trade and restructuring effects of the Gulf Cooperation Council', *International Journal of Middle Eastern Studies*, 21/1 (February 1989), pp. 51–69.

5 State and politics in Israel, Iran and Turkey from the Second World War

Introduction

This chapter examines the political process after 1945 in the three major non-Arab Middle Eastern states – Israel, Iran and Turkey. The history of these countries has little in common except in the most general terms, for example, the central importance of the American alliance and American aid (except to Iran after the 1979 Islamic Revolution) and, in the Israeli and Turkish cases, the problems of sustaining a multi-party democracy through decades of rapid socio-economic change. Beyond this, there is little value in a search for similarities, and I will simply provide a brief account of what I take to be the salient features of each system in terms of state construction and the distribution of power in the period up to 1990. I will also place considerable emphasis on the point that, in each country, this process was a fluid one and continually contested.

Israel

The state of Israel officially came into existence in May 1948, towards the end of a bitter civil war between the Arab and Jewish populations of Mandatory Palestine, which in turn was triggered off by the precipitate British military withdrawal. By this time the Jews were in control of most of the areas allocated to them under the United Nations partition agreement of November 1947, with the exception of the Negev Desert in the south. However, they still had to face invasions by small Arab armies, as well as a complex struggle with the Hashemite Kingdom of Jordan, a struggle that eventually was to leave what was later to be called the West Bank in Jordanian hands and a divided Jerusalem. By the time the fighting came to an end with the armistice agreements of 1949, the new state of Israel had been purged of all but 160,000 of its original Palestinian population of some 850,000.[1]

According to the declaration of independence issued by its provisional council, Israel was stated to be a 'Jewish state established by and for the Jewish people'. As Nira Yuval-Davis notes, while this declaration had no legal authority, it was of great symbolic value as it represented the widest possible consensus among the different trends and groups within the Zionist movement that had worked to establish just such an entity.[2] Nevertheless, the differences between these same groups were too great to permit agreement on the balance between those religious and secular principles which would have formed the core of a permanent constitution. What happened instead was the creation of a system of government based on an amalgamation of different institutions, laws and practices, some of them based on the Jewish organisations established in Mandatory Palestine, others owing more to the political exigencies of the first few months of independence and the fact that politics continued to be dominated by the Mapai party under its powerful leader – and Israel's first prime minister – David Ben-Gurion. The political history of this period provides a fascinating, if complex, insight into the way in which a modern state comes to be constructed, something that Mitchell has aptly described as involving a process of 'coordination and renaming'.[3]

An essential feature of the process was the degree of choice that came to be exercised by the leading politicians over what was, and what was not, officially defined as being part of the central state apparatus. In some cases the decision was more or less straightforward, as when they simply took over most of the organs of the colonial state, together with those of its laws that did not conflict with central Zionist goals; striking out, for example, the mandatory government's regulations limiting Jewish immigration and Jewish land purchase. Much the same applies to specifying those major offices and institutions named in the transitional law of February 1949 that established the presidency, the cabinet and the Knesset (parliament). In other cases, however, certain important organisations were either left as non-state entities or brought under the state umbrella while remaining subject as much to party as to central bureaucratic control. As everywhere, the reasons why such and such a choice was made depended on the struggle between different political interests, as well as on certain Zionist imperatives such as the desire to attract more Jewish immigrants, relations with world Jewry and an increasingly hostile attitude to Israel's remaining non-Jewish inhabitants.

We should also note that, although some of this process was carried out in terms of Ben-Gurion's newly coined concept of 'mamlachtuit' – the need to subordinate pre-state organisations and party-based institutions to control by a Jewish state which he regarded as the highest expression of Zionism – this can equally well be interpreted as being aimed at improving his own position and that of his party as well. As Yoram Peri notes, the Mapai leadership gained great advantage in its competition for public support from being able to speak in the name, not only of itself, but also of the government, the state and the nation.[4]

Moving now to specifics, it will only be possible to give a few of the more important examples of this process. I will choose those that relate most directly to the central questions of citizenship, stateness and the creation of new sets of practices that allowed the exercise of a high degree of centralised control by Israel's major political groups.

For most political historians, the creation of a new Israeli army represents the clearest example of Ben-Gurion's drive to establish statist, or national, institutions divorced from their previous particularist, party, affiliations. Hence, out of the pre-state Haganah, the Palmach and the smaller militias like the Irgun came the IDF (the Israeli Defence Force), a unitary military organisation whose members were supposed to possess no social or political allegiance except to the government through the minister of defence.[5] The significant features of this process were further emphasised by the introduction of such notions as professionalisation and depoliticisation, which, in turn, were taken up by the military itself as part of its own organisational image.[6] However, as Peri demonstrates, Ben-Gurion was also able to use this process as a cover for his personal control of the military as prime minister and minister of defence, promoting officers loyal to himself and to his party, weeding out others associated with his political rivals, and preventing effective supervision by the Knesset and the cabinet in the name of the higher necessity of national security.[7]

The new status of another major pre-state institution, the Histadrut (or General Organisation of Jewish Workers in Palestine, founded in 1920) was subject to a more openly political logic. In this case it was decided that it should remain outside the official apparatus of the state but only after surrendering some of its functions – for example, control over its schools – to the new ministries like the one dealing with education. Here the rationale is said to have involved the transfer of those Histadrut services that had previously served as a base for Mapai's major political rival, Mapam, while leaving it with other functions that either assisted Mapai to steer the economy or to reach out to large sections of the population, including new migrants, through its provision of social welfare via its sickness and pensions funds.[8] Given the fact that the Histadrut not only represented workers' interests but was also a major employer and the owner of important enterprises like the construction company, Sol Boneh, the manufacturing company, Koor, and Israel's second largest bank, its usefulness to a government trying to manage a poor economy was further augmented by its role in recruiting Mapai voters from among the new entrants to the labour market it employed or the new immigrants it supported. A last significant asset was provided by its ability to divide and control the Arab workers once they were forced to seek jobs in the Israeli economy in the 1950s.[9]

A third type of formula was applied to the two other major pre-state Zionist organisations, the Jewish Agency (responsible for relations with world Jewry) and its land purchase arm, the Jewish National Fund. In this case it was decided that their role in promoting further migration and settlement should be exercised in the name of the whole Jewish people rather than the Israeli state. One reason was that it allowed the agency to receive funds from the United States which could only benefit from tax exempt status under American law if they were channelled for use by a philanthropic organisation and not by a foreign state.[10] Even more important, it permitted the adoption of certain exclusionary practices towards the Arab population – for example, land owned by the fund could not be sold or rented to non-Jews – which, as Michael Shalev argues, made it

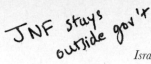

possible to discriminate in favour of the Jewish population without having to call attention to the fact by incorporating it into the public laws of the state.[11] Having said all this, however, both the Agency and the Fund remained firmly under the control of the major Israeli political parties that were represented on their management in proportion to the votes they had received in the 1946 elections to the pre-state national assembly – a practice known in Israeli parlance as the 'key'. The notion of the key also played an important role as a guide to the distribution of the funds received from overseas, which were divided among the parties in just the same proportion.[12] Seen from this perspective, the fact that both the Agency and the Fund are often referred to by Israeli political scientists as 'quasi-state' enterprises captures some of the reality of their position, without suggesting the further point that, in any country, the boundary between what is, and is not, defined as belonging to the state is always fluid and subject to political manipulation.

The system constructed in the first few years after 1948 possessed a number of important features which remained central to the practice of Israeli politics at least until the 1967 Middle East war. First, power continued to reside with the leaders of Mapai (later the Labour Alignment), which, although never able to obtain a clear Knesset majority in elections held under the system of proportional representation inherited from the pre-state period, consistently obtained twice as many seats as its nearest rivals.[13] It also benefited from its pivotal position in the left/right spectrum, which meant that it was impossible to consider forming a coalition without it. In these circumstances Mapai was always able to provide a government with the prime minister, the foreign minister, the ministers of the treasury and (for all but a few months) of defence. Furthermore, its capacity to govern was enhanced by its control over such important organisations as the military and the bureaucracy as well as over the Histadrut and the Jewish Agency, both of which gave it access to a huge variety of extra resources ranging from the former's newspaper, publishing house and bank to the latter's funds raised in North America and elsewhere.[14] Lastly, as Shalev notes, Mapai was able to play a hegemonic role in one other important sense, in that the party's interpretation of Israel's national mission, of its military strategy and of its principal economic objectives was soon accepted by the vast majority of the country's Jewish citizens.[15]

Second, Mapai was willing to share office and to distribute resources through the construction of coalitions which were wider than those that would have been strictly necessary to ensure a Knesset majority. One way of describing this process is to use Itzhak Galnoor's phrase, 'the politics of accommodation'.[16] However, in reality it was much more than this. For one thing, it encouraged the other parties to try to recreate themselves in Labour's image, seeking access to resources from government as well as from their own banks and credit institutions, their own economic and social organisations and their own links with Jewish communities overseas.[17] For another, the parties themselves became essential links between the various official and quasi-official bodies that made up the Israeli state.

A third feature of Israel's first two decades was the existence of a strong executive controlled by a party that provided most of the senior members of the cabinet, including a strong prime minister with wide, and purposefully ill-defined, powers. It was the party and the cabinet that initiated most of the new legislation, with only rare challenges either from the Knesset or from the judiciary. Borrowing from British precedent, the former was provided with formidable sovereign powers, at least on paper. Hence, according to the Knesset basic law of 1958 (introduced as a substitute for part of a permanent constitution), no other body can veto Knesset laws, while only the Knesset can dissolve itself. However, as in the British case as well, strong party control over the members of parliament was easily able to render these privileges virtually meaningless.

Fourth, the government, and the institutions it controlled, pursued highly interventionist economic policies. In part these were necessary to build up the defence establishment and to cope with the mass immigration of the first four years after independence, when the Jewish population nearly doubled. However, such policies were also encouraged by the lack of private investment in the Israeli economy at this period and by the government's access to large funds from outside. According to figures quoted by Joel Beinin, Israel received over $6 billion in capital imports between 1948 and 1965, two-thirds of which consisted of unilateral transfers from world Jewry, from the United States and from the post-war reparations paid by the West Germans.[18] As a result, the government was able to contribute two-thirds of all capital invested in Israel in the 1950s and two-fifths in the 1960s. This, in turn, gave it extra control over a public sector that, together with the Histadrut, employed some 40 per cent of the labour force, as well as over the private sector through its ability to award loans, concessions and contracts.[19] More power came from Mapai's ability to use the Histadrut to control relations between workers and employers, making it easier to steer the economy and also to enjoy the many political rewards that went with it.[20]

A last feature of Israel's early political life was that it took place within the context of an aggressive security policy towards Israel's Arab neighbours. This in turn was used to justify the treatment of the country's own Arabs as what Erik Cohen has called 'members of a vanquished enemy population'.[21] They were placed under martial law until 1965, they lost much of their remaining land and, although they were given the vote, they were not allowed to form their own political parties. Hence, while they were formally members of the Israeli democracy, they were in actual fact subject to a wide range of controls which rendered them subordinate to the will of Jewish politicians and bureaucrats.[22] The resulting contradiction between the notion of a state with equality for all and the practice of denying equality to some remained largely hidden until 1967, when the Arabs still formed less than 10 per cent of the total population. But it was to assume greater salience once Israel obtained control over the much larger numbers of Palestinian Arabs in the West Bank and Gaza during the 1967 war.

For many Israeli analysts, their army's unexpected, and overwhelming, victory in 1967, and its rapid conquest of places steeped in ancient Jewish

prohibited formation of parties

history, like East Jerusalem and the West Bank, marks a watershed in their country's politics. There is certainly some truth in this. As Galnoor notes, it led to an immediate revival of the highly charged debate about Zionist objectives concerning boundaries and the treatment of the large non-Jewish population they now controlled, which soon paralysed the Labour Party, devalued Labour Zionism and gave an immediate advantage to those religious nationalists who seemed to be able to provide clearer ideological answers to current problems.[23] Nevertheless, as Galnoor also argues, the war itself is better seen as a 'catalyst' for trends that had already begun to manifest themselves before 1967.[24] Three of these are of particular importance.

The first trend involved the influence on politics of certain processes of economic and social change which had begun to gather momentum in the early 1960s. One concerned the fact that a substantial portion of Mapai's historic base of support – the Ashkenazi working class (of European origins) – was promoted into managerial or clerical roles after 1948 and their place taken by oriental Jews from Asia and North Africa, and later by Palestinian Arabs. This and other factors then encouraged the growing political involvement of these same Orientals, whose share in the total population rose from a third in 1951 to over half by the 1970s. As their numbers increased, and as the second generation immigrants began to feel less dependent on Mapai and the Histadrut for jobs, houses and social security, they became much more resentful of the wide educational and cultural gap that separated them from the Jews of European origin. To take only one example, only three cabinet ministers of oriental origin were appointed between 1948 and 1973.[25] An oriental drift away from Labour is visible before 1967, even if it did not begin to become a flood until Menachim Begin's Likud bloc began to look like a viable alternative in the 1970s. Arabs, too, started to use the power that they had obtained from their entry into the Israeli labour market, and could no longer be relied upon to vote for Mapai in the way they once had.

A second trend already apparent before 1967 was the growing disenchantment of some of the younger members of the National Religious Party with their inability to exercise more than a marginal influence over Israeli life while serving as one of Mapai's regular coalition partners. This was to have important effects after the war when they forced their party to interest itself in broader national questions, for example, the establishment of Jewish settlements on the West Bank, just as it was already beginning to abandon its earlier role as mediator between the government and the majority of the observant community.[26]

Third, Mapai, like any party that had been in power for several decades, was beginning to show signs of stress and strain, manifest most obviously in intra-party splits, over-centralisation and a general loss of enthusiasm and intellectual vigour. To make matters worse, it also experienced growing difficulty in managing its various constituencies and in finding them the necessary resources. Symptoms of this malaise can be seen in the resignation of its long-time leader, Ben Gurion, in 1963 and his founding of a rival party, Rafi, as well as in the large number of anti-government strikes during the 1966/7 recession. All this

BG resigns in '63

was made much more difficult after 1967 when there was a huge surge in private capital investment from outside, expanding sectors of the economy like the growing military-industrial complex over which the party was able to exercise much less control.[27]

Nevertheless, as far as major shifts in voting patterns were concerned, these only began to reveal themselves in the general elections held after 1967.[28] In 1969 the Labour-Mapam alignment (Ma'arach) was still able to obtain 46.22 per cent of the vote (and 56 seats out of 120). By 1973 this had been reduced to 39.7 per cent and 51 seats. And there are some who even argue that its totals would have been even less than this if the election had been held, not in the immediate aftermath of the 1973 October Middle East war, but a few months later when evidence of the government's unpreparedness for the Egyptian and Syrian attack was more widely known. Then came a new challenge to the alignment in the shape of the creation of the Democratic Movement for Change (DMC), which took 11.6 per cent of the vote in the 1977 election, enough to reduce the Ma'arach to 26 per cent and to let in the Likud (33.4 per cent) in coalition with the National Religious Party and the DMC.

Coming as it did after so many decades of Mapai dominance, the shock produced by the Likud victory of 1977 was aptly described by Dan Horowitz as more than just a 'change of government'.[29] However, while it is easy to see that the stable voting patterns of the old era had come to an end, it has proved much more difficult to work out just what replaced them. Looking at the electoral data on their own, it would seem that what emerged is best described as a 'two-coalition' system, with the regular increase in the Likud vote being halted in 1984, to be replaced by something like a stalemate, with Likud and Labour obtaining 41 and 44 seats respectively in that year's general election and 40 and 39 in 1988. Given the fact that this gave neither group a clear majority to govern at what was widely perceived to be a time of great national crisis, and that the increasingly strident demands of the smaller parties made the traditional practice of coalition building very difficult, both of the larger groups resorted to the new formula of cabinets of 'national unity' in which the major offices were shared between them according to predetermined rules. This introduced many of the practices associated with the formation of coalitions in two-party systems elsewhere in the world: difficulty in formulating clear policies; mutual suspicion; and the sense that at least one of the partners was always looking for the right occasion to bring down the government and to fight another general election on terms favourable to itself. In the Israeli case, however, what kept the cabinet of national unity together until the spring of 1990 was its popularity, at least in its first two years; the succession of economic, religious and political crises ending with the Palestinian *Intifada*; and, at least as far as the party leaders were concerned, their perception that they were better off inside the government, with access to posts and resources, than outside.

Meanwhile, the coherence once associated with the exercise of state power in the period of Labour hegemony was very much reduced. This can be seen by an examination of any number of new factors.[30] One was the diminished authority

emergence of national unity gov'ts)

of the parties themselves, whose role in representing a wide range of political interests was increasingly challenged by powerful new organisations, as well as by pressure groups like Gush Emunim, which acted as a champion of the Jewish settlers on the West Bank. This was accompanied by a similar reduction in the power of quasi-state institutions like the Histadrut, many of whose business enterprises began to experience severe difficulties during the long period of economic stagnation during the late 1970s and the 1980s. The result was a process of fragmentation which, by 1990, had greatly reduced the power of any one group to steer Israeli policy on its own.

Iran

Iran was occupied by British, American and Soviet forces during the Second World War, who deposed Reza Shah in 1941 and replaced him with his son, Mohamed Reza. In these circumstances the throne lost much of its power and authority, and was exposed to considerable pressure from political groups within the Majles anxious to curtail its powers still further and to turn it into something of a constitutional monarchy. The struggle was at its most intense over control of what were seen as the two essential props of the regime, the army and the ministry of the interior, the latter being responsible both for the police and for the appointment of provincial governors-general and the local councils that supervised elections. Beyond this, power in the countryside was shared with the large landowners and tribal chiefs, only some of whom were loyal to the shah. Meanwhile, in the towns, the weakening of monarchical authority, combined with the growth of economic and social tensions produced by the war, permitted radical organisations like the Marxist Tudeh party (established in 1941) a space within which to recruit, to publicise their policies and, in the case of the Tudeh itself, to create a nation-wide party with strong links with the trade unions and an increasing capacity to mobilise large numbers of people for demonstrations in the major cities.[31]

Once the war was over, however, and foreign troops withdrawn, the shah was able to move quite rapidly to re-establish monarchical control. He increased the size of the army, repressed the Tudeh, built up support from the members of landowning families in the Majles and then, in 1949, took advantage of an attempt on his life to proclaim martial law and to convene a tame constituent assembly which voted at once to increase his powers.

Moves towards a further build-up of palace power were then interrupted by three years of prolonged crisis, 1950–3, triggered off by popular opposition to the proposals put forward for the renewal of the 1933 agreement with the Anglo Iranian Oil Company. In these circumstances the shah had little option but to appoint a government led by an old opponent of the monarchy, Dr Mohamed Mossadeq, who not only nationalised the oil industry but also went on to use his coalition of anti-monarchical forces, the National Front, to strip the ruler of most of the powers he had been able to win back since 1941. However, Mossadeq's

[margin handwritten note: Mohammed Reza, post-war builds up army quick]

own support soon began to wane, making it easier for him to be overthrown in a coup organised by Iranian army officers with assistance from the American CIA.

With power back in his own hands, Mohamed Reza Shah moved quickly to crush all centres of opposition and then to establish a strongly centralised military dictatorship. Its base lay in the further expansion of the bureaucracy and the army, together with a more efficient security apparatus based on the intelligence-gathering and supervisory agency, SAVAK (National Information and Security Organisation), set up in 1957. In all this he obtained great advantage from a high level of American aid as well as from increasing money from oil sales, which grew from 11 to 41 per cent of total government revenues between 1948 and 1960.[32] However, even if, as exponents of the notion of Iran as a rentier state assert, such large amounts of income from outside allowed the shah to expand his bureaucracy, to spend money on public works and to lessen his dependence on key social groups like the large landowners, it also produced negative consequences such as inflation and a tendency for the economy to make sudden lurches from periods of boom to ones of deep depression.[33]

A good example of the disadvantages of dependence on external income can be found in the period of political instability that took place between 1960 and 1963. A combination of falling revenue, widespread shortages and inflation in the late 1950s led, first, to an outbreak of strikes and other symptoms of popular discontent, then to a period of enforced austerity when much-needed loans from the United States and the International Monetary Fund could only be obtained in exchange for the promise of a programme of extensive economic retrenchment. Pressure from Washington for more comprehensive reform followed, as part of the new Kennedy administration's general campaign to persuade America's authoritarian allies to pre-empt popular opposition by social reform. The shah's response was to proclaim what he called a 'White Revolution' in 1962, the most important feature of which was an extensive programme of land redistribution. This in turn encouraged an increasingly vocal opposition from a wide range of urban groups united by their dislike of American interference and the shah's dictatorial ways. They included a revived Tudeh Party and National Front, as well as a group of radical clergy led by the Ayatollah Khomeini. The movement culminated in three days of huge popular demonstrations in Teheran and other major cities in June 1963, which were dispersed by the army with considerable loss of life. Once again the shah moved quickly to crush the rest of the opposition, while Khomeini himself was deported to Turkey, from where he moved on to a more permanent refuge in the Shi'i holy city of Najaf in Iraq.

Renewed American support, ever-increasing oil revenues and the programme of land reform that destroyed the power of the rural magnates provided the basis for a further attempt to consolidate the shah's regime. It was based, as before, on a continuous expansion of the army, the bureaucracy and the security services, with the number of civil servants doubling between 1963 and 1977.[34] Increased state power allowed the regime to maintain a tight grip on all possible sources of opposition, as well as to extend its control over new areas of society in both town and country. One instance of this is the role played by SAVAK in setting up, and

then supervising, government-sponsored trade unions; another is the incorporation of a wide range of village headmen and others into a system of rural control.
Meanwhile, the central position occupied by the state in the management of the
economy provided the regime with enormous scope for supervising and
controlling private-sector entrepreneurs by means of subsidies, credits and access
to government contracts.

Nevertheless, given the emphasis on manipulation and control exercised
without any form of political participation, the shah's programmes failed to
create the type of support that similar initiatives had produced elsewhere. An
obvious example is the programme of land reform itself, which, although
distributing small plots to two million peasants, negated much of its positive
effect by trying to force many of them to surrender these same plots to form part
of large and, it was thought, more efficient co-operative farms. As Fatemeh
Moghadam observes, while few such farms were actually created, the legacy of
bitterness that the whole episode left behind meant that the regime lost all
possibility of obtaining political support from the direct beneficiaries of the
reform.[35]

The shah's system of government also remained highly sensitive to external
shocks. This was amply demonstrated in 1975/6, when the economic boom
promoted by the quadrupling of oil prices in the early 1970s began to peter out
amid evidence of widespread corruption and the misuse of resources. The shah's
response to this was the creation of a new instrument of control, the Rastakhiz
(Resurgence) Party, a mass organisation to which all of Iran's bureaucrats and
persons of influence and importance were first encouraged, and then forced, to
belong.[36] Whatever the real aim of this initiative in terms of bridging the gap
between the shah's regime and the wider society, the most significant effect of the
use of the party as an agent of supervision and mobilisation was to intensify fear
and resentment within a wide range of groups, some of which had remained
more or less untouched by government regimentation until this time. These
included the clergy, whose control over their own religious endowments and
system of education now came under attack, and the merchants of the bazaar,
who found themselves subject to fines and arrest as part of the government's
anti-inflation campaign aimed against excessive price rises and profiteering. It
was at this time too that the shah himself began to come under great pressure
from the new American administration of President Jimmy Carter, aimed at
stamping out some of the worst excesses of SAVAK and the other security
services in the name of improved human rights.

Most writers date the beginning of the last great wave of opposition to the
shah to 1977, when signs of economic discontent started to appear in tandem
with a growing willingness to criticise a regime that was perceived to be losing
American support.[37] They are also agreed that the massive popular protests
represented the start of a revolutionary process that not only sapped the
foundations of the shah's regime but also went on to express itself in a sustained
experiment aimed at creating a new political order. As for the importance of the
roles played by the different components of the anti-shah coalition, here there is

more disagreement. Some stress the importance of the near general strike that paralysed the oil industry, the banks and government offices in 1978.[38] For others, it was a mainly religious phenomenon, with everything from day-to-day tactics to overall leadership and ideology provided by the clergy.[39]

The reality was more complex. For one thing, the process of undermining the shah's government was the work of a variety of social forces usually with quite different interests. For another, the clergy itself was by no means united. A third important point concerns the role of Khomeini himself. Although his leadership of the anti-shah movement was vital throughout 1978, its impact was of much more than purely religious significance. It was his single-minded insistence that there could be no negotiations with the shah before he left the throne that prevented any of the other leaders of the opposition from breaking ranks and trying to make a deal with the regime. He was also a master of a type of populist rhetoric, with its emphasis on such central themes as anti-imperialism, democracy and social justice, that seemed to provide a consensus around which all opponents of the shah could come together. As Zubaida notes, a central feature of his thinking involved a call to the 'people' (certainly not a traditional Islamic concept) to rise up against an unjust and Godless tyranny. And he goes on to make the essential point that this same appeal constituted the core of a species of popular nationalism that saw Islam 'as the identifying emblem of the common people against the "alien" (and pro-western) social spheres in their own country which had excluded and subordinated them'.[40]

A final aspect of Khomeini's leadership was that it was aimed at seizing, and then utilising, the institutions of the Iranian state as they existed in the 1970s and not in trying to return Iran to the type of political order that had existed in seventh-century Medina under the leadership of the Prophet Muhammad. This can be clearly seen in the speed at which he and his allies took over the army, the broadcasting service and the government ministries, purging officers and officials whose support for the revolution was deemed to be unsound. Khomeini's next task was to stabilise the new situation as quickly as possible by introducing a constitution which established the main agencies of the new Islamic government and its senior personnel. If all had gone according to the original plan, the constitution in question would have been an amalgam of the 1906 Iranian one and that of France under the Fifth Republic. It was only when this first draft was challenged by some of the few liberals in the assembly of experts (which was acting as a constituent assembly) that it was revised in such a way as to include a very much greater degree of direct clerical supervision as well as specific reference to the key notion justifying religious involvement in politics: Khomeini's doctrine of the *velayat-e faqih* (the rule of the just jurist).[41]

It is the way in which the constitution of the Islamic republic was conceived and drafted that explains much of its ambiguity. At one level it contained features typical of a nineteenth-century European liberal constitution, with its emphasis on the separation of powers between the executive, the judiciary and the Majles, or legislature. As political leaders like Ali Khamenei, the second president of the republic, were later to explain, they were convinced at the time

of the need for a system of checks and balances in order to avoid any more dictatorships like that of the shah.[42] However, at another level, the constitution contained references to religious institutions and personnel, and ideas that set limits on those of a more secular or universal nature. An example of this can be found in Principle 26, which asserts that 'the formation of parties, groups and political and professional associations … is free, provided they do not harm the principles of freedom, sovereignty, national unity, Islamic standards and the foundation of the Islamic republic'. Just as important, the constitution created new supervisory bodies, like the twelve-man Council of Guardians that was charged with ensuring that all legislation was in conformity with 'Islamic decrees' (Principle 96).

Given the separation of powers and the existence of so many parallel institutions like the revolutionary courts, cohesion was only possible when implemented by Khomeini himself as the Faqih and leader of the revolution. However, in practice, the ayatollah was slow to come down on one side or another in the various factional disputes that ensued, and he tended to be used as a decision-maker of last resort who might, in certain circumstances, be persuaded to come up with an unambiguous judgement when prompted. For the rest, the only other instrument of governmental cohesion was the IRP (the Islamic Republic Party), which was established in 1979 in time to win a majority of seats in the 1980 Majles election. Once it had grown strong enough for its members to take over the presidency (after President Bani-Sadr's ouster in 1981) and most of the cabinet ministries, as well as being powerfully represented in the parliament, its leaders were in a position to make whatever policies that could obtain a consensus among the politically active clerics. But this was not always easy. There were immediate divisions over the question of relations with foreign powers and over the extent to which private property could be sacrificed to the needs of the community or of social justice. Such was the strength of conservative feeling that a bill proposing only a moderate act of rural redistribution involving uncultivated land was held up as un-Islamic by the Council of Guardians from 1980 onwards.[43]

The war with Iraq encouraged sufficient unity to allow the machinery of government to operate with some cohesion until the middle of the 1980s. However, once oil revenues began to fall dramatically in 1986, followed by a number of serious military reversals, major divisions among the leadership began to emerge. These intensified after the decision to agree to a cease-fire in the summer of 1988 and tended to focus, in the first instance, on what became known as the question of leadership. As debated in the years just before the Ayatollah Khomeini's death in 1989, this had two parts. One was the question of the role of the Faqih after Khomeini's expected demise. The subject became even more complex after Khomeini's own attempt to redefine, and also to expand, the powers of the Faqih in January 1988, as a way, it would seem, of freeing himself from the religious authority of the senior theologians on the Council of Guardians then being used to justify vetoes over legislation of which he himself approved (see Chapter 9). The other was the problem posed for

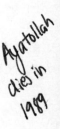

policy-makers by the constitutional separation of powers between executive, Majles and judiciary. According to President Ali Khamenei, in a sermon preached in April 1988, such a separation might have been justified at the beginning of the Islamic revolution but it had gone on to produce a harmful 'dispersion and diffusion' of control that now had to be urgently addressed.[44]

In the event, Khomeini's own death, and the fact that he was succeeded as Faqih by a relatively junior theologian with little religious authority – the same Ali Khamenei – meant that the Ayatollah's attempted redefinition was made redundant. Nevertheless, the question of the separation of powers was tackled directly in the constitutional referendum that was held at the same time as the presidential elections in August 1988. This permitted the new president, Ali Hashemi Rafsanjani, to combine the posts of prime minister and president in one, a measure that facilitated his efforts to build up a single, centralised source of authority and policy-making. Many problems still remained, however. President Rafsanjani was repeatedly defeated in his efforts to amalgamate the revolutionary guards into the regular army. And the fact that Iran remained a theocracy, governed and administered by mullahs, meant that criticisms of his policies by political rivals could still be couched in terms of a symbolic and religious rhetoric that continued to command an important constituency within the government itself.

Turkey

As in any country, the transition from single-party rule to the practice of multi-party competition was not an easy one in Turkey. In spite of their overwhelming victory in the 1950 general election, the leaders of the new Democrat Party retained a justified suspicion that many of the senior bureaucrats and army officers would retain their historic loyalty to the RPP in opposition. This does much to explain the increasingly strong measures that they took to try to curb their rival's power and influence, most notably their proposal to establish a committee to investigate allegations that the RPP was engaging in subversive activities, a plan that was one of the major causes behind the anti-Democrat military coup of 1960.[45]

A second example of the difficulties of transition concerned the impact of multi-party competition on the relations between the parties, the central administration and interests to be found in the wider society. As Caglar Keyder points out, politics before 1950 were the preserve of a small elite within the bureaucracy and an even smaller number of entrepreneurs and businessmen, almost all known to one another.[46] Now, after the first open elections, Turkey's politicians were forced to respond to a large national constituency and to find ways of maximising the distribution of resources and the rewards of office on a much wider scale. Attempts to analyse this phenomenon frequently attach an exaggerated importance to the Democrats' often rhetorical support for the notion of free enterprise. But in fact the period in which they attempted to pursue liberal economic policies was relatively short and, as early as 1954, they were already returning to more openly statist measures involving a reinforcement of bureaucratic control over a significant proportion of economic activity. In addition, the Democrats extended two new avenues of patronage to their supporters and potential clients. One was a system of protective tariffs and quotas which could be used, selectively, to favour particular interests or individuals. The other was their successful programme of opening up Turkey's rural areas by means of roads, electricity and new forms of transport.

The officers' coup of 1960 was clearly aimed at ousting an increasingly authoritarian Democrat Party from power. However, beyond that, there was little coherent purpose among the military plotters, while influential groups of intellectuals and officials took advantage of the situation to introduce programmes of reform of their own. One was the replacement of the 1923 constitution by a new one more in keeping with current democratic practice, as well as the introduction of new laws permitting the formation of labour unions and the institution of collective bargaining between employers and workers. Another was the effort to centralise previously haphazard economic interventions within a new state planning organisation with power to allocate cheap government credit and scarce foreign exchange. Such measures resulted both in a growth in administrative power and in the multiplication of interest groups with more pressing demands. They also helped to intensify a process of rapid economic and social change marked by an increase in industrialisation, urbanisation and labour migration abroad. The result was the creation of new social strata (including an increasingly militant working class), new relationships between interest groups and government and, at a national level, a new political and electoral geography.

↑admin power + ↑interest grps

The immediate beneficiary of these processes was the Justice Party (JP), a successor to the dissolved Democrat Party which, in spite of military efforts to hold it back, won more votes than its RPP rival in every general election between 1961 and 1971. Initially it was forced to join a series of short-lived coalitions with the RPP. But after its convincing victory in the 1965 election it was able to form a government of its own under its new leader, Suleyman Demirel. Demirel it was who consolidated the party's organisational strength by using his control over what remained essentially a highly politicised programme of planned economic development.[47] But it was also Demirel who saw this same strength weaken as elements on the right defected from his leadership to form new organisations like the National Action Party (NAP) and the Islamist National Order Party. One reason generally put forward to explain this phenomenon points to the further multiplication of often contradictory economic interests that could no longer be represented by a single political organisation, for example, the growing opposition between the representatives of the larger enterprises that benefited from rapid industrialisation and those of the small artisans and craftsmen who did not.[48] Another concerns the growing militancy of a number of workers' and leftist student organisations, which aroused a variety of hostile responses from their opponents on the right.[49]

contradictory economic interests

It is clear that many army officers shared this same fear of growing worker activism and were only too happy to launch a second intervention in 1971 designed to put an end to a situation of growing administrative chaos caused by strikes and political violence. However, once again, the senior generals who took charge of events had no agreed programme of reforms, and contented themselves with minor constitutional amendments aimed at curbing some of the freedoms granted in 1961. Of more significance for the future was the split within the RPP over its leader's support for the military coup, and its take-over by Bulent Ecevit, who immediately used his position to push it in a more leftward direction, seeking new constituencies among working-class and minority groups. This in turn paved the way for a much greater polarisation of Turkish politics once parliamentary life was again restored in 1973. With the Justice Party vying with the NAP and the National Salvation Party (NSP, the successor to the Islamic National Order Party), for support on the Turkish right, and the RPP trying to pick up votes among radical groups on the left, the stage was set for an increasingly heated ideological confrontation which soon spilled over into the streets of towns throughout Turkey. To make matters worse, neither the RPP nor the Justice Party was able to obtain a clear majority in any of the elections held from 1973 onwards. This left them the unsatisfactory choice of either forming a minority government or having to patch together a coalition with one or more of the smaller parties.

Given the highly politicised atmosphere in Turkey in the 1970s, and the fact that it resulted in yet another military intervention in 1980, it is probably inevitable that analysts tend to offer a whole range of different explanations for the lack of firm government, the politicisation of most parts of the state administration and the growing political violence. For some the chief blame attaches to the squabbling of the politicians, made worse by the defects in the Turkish party system and the country's constitutional structure. Others concentrate more on the underlying stresses and strains posed, first by a period of rapid social transformation, and then by a long period of economic crisis from 1973 onwards, when high oil prices combined with a loss of American aid after the invasion of northern Cyprus and a decline in the remittances sent back by Turkish workers in Europe to produce a crippling shortage of foreign exchange. Others again point to the existence of various groups on both the right and the left that seemed determined to seize power by violent, extra-parliamentary means.

In the event, of course, all these factors played their part. Nevertheless, it should also be noted that by 1980, the year of the third military intervention, the economic situation had much improved as a result of the introduction of the economic stabilisation plan agreed with the IMF in January 1980 and the revival of United States military aid once the American administration had decided that it needed a strong Turkey as an ally against the forces unleashed by the Iranian revolution.[50] In addition, as Feroz Ahmad notes, the martial law declared in thirteen provinces in December 1978 should have done much more to reduce political violence than it actually did.[51] Why this did not happen remains a puzzle, the more so as the military was able to bring the situation under control immediately it took power in September 1980. It may have had something to do with the fact that the generals were not unhappy to allow matters to deteriorate so as to provide a better justification for their own coup, as Ahmad suggests.[52] But it may also be that the police force had become so highly politicised and so heavily infiltrated by NAP supporters before 1980 that it was no longer capable of effective action. The same could also have been true of those municipalities and other local administrations that had passed into the control of the NAP or some other extremist group.

There is no doubt that the army's intervention in 1980 had widespread popular support. However, this does not mean that the majority of the Turkish people were prepared to put up with a long period of military rule. Indeed, it is reasonable to suggest, as Ahmad does, that one of the main explanations for the unexpected success of Turgut Ozal's new Motherland Party (ANAP) in the 1983 elections was that it was viewed by many as the organisation least closely attached to the generals and so the most likely to engineer a return to full civilian rule.[53] The fact that ANAP went on to dominate Turkish politics for the rest of the 1980s can be ascribed to three particular sets of reasons. The first was the partial success of its domestic policies aimed at transforming Turkey from a protected, inward-looking economy to one based on the export of manufactured goods to the highly competitive world market. Fortunately for the Ozal government, the policy of export promotion was launched just at a time when the Iran/Iraq war was producing a surge in demand for Turkish goods. Moreover, the country's ability also to make substantial inroads into the west European market was assisted in large measure by the way in which the previous military government had destroyed all the institutions protecting workers' interests, making it easier for manufacturers to keep wages low. Just why the great militancy shown by the unions in the 1970s collapsed as quickly as it did in the face of such military pressure is unclear but it may be that it had something to do with the fact that the Turkish industrial working class was of a relatively recent formation and had only a short tradition of political activism.[54]

The second reason for ANAP's success was Ozal's ability to disengage himself, his party and then the whole political system from military tutelage (see also Chapter 10). This was a gradual process which involved the re-establishment of successor parties to the old ones dissolved by the generals, and the return of almost all the old politicians after the 1987 referendum that put an end to the ten-year banishment imposed on them under the 1982 constitution. It also involved the establishment of a de facto division of responsibilities between the Ozal government and the army, in which the former was allowed to manage the economy while the latter retained most of its control over domestic security. The result was a situation in which the checks on Turgut Ozal's freedom of action were gradually removed until he was in a position to use an ANAP parliamentary majority to have himself elected as president in 1989. This in turn gave him sufficient authority to continue to dominate his party and parliament, as well as to seize the opportunity offered by the Gulf crisis that opened the next summer to increase his powers still further.

The third and last reason was the weakness and division of the opposition. As happened in many other countries, the party that was best positioned to offer solutions to the economic crisis of the 1970s was able to set the political agenda and to manoeuvre its opponents into a situation in which all they had to offer was a pale imitation of its own policies. In addition, the coalition of politicians that had come together to form ANAP in the first place brought with it constituencies among a variety of religious, nationalist and regional groups which gave it a wider appeal than its competitors. Finally, the old politicians who restarted their old parties in a new guise seem to have incurred much of the blame for the violence of the 1970s and the military intervention that followed.

All this was enough to ensure ANAP's victory in the 1987 election, albeit with a greatly reduced popular majority. However, due to the vagaries of the 1983 electoral law and some clever amendments to it just before the election itself, the party's third of the vote translated into two-thirds of the seats in the Grand National Assembly. This, in turn, allowed Ozal's own election as president, as well as permitting him to withstand pressure from the opposition to dissolve the assembly after ANAP's share of the vote in the 1989 municipal elections had fallen to only 21.7 per cent, significantly less than that of its two major rivals.

ANAP's domination of the political process during the 1980s also led to a profound change in the role and character of the Turkish bureaucracy. In spite of attempts by the major parties to politicise it during the previous decade, for example, by bringing in their partisans to top posts in the ministries of finance and trade, senior civil servants had managed to preserve the autonomy of a number of key state agencies.[55] In the case of the Motherland Party, however, economic decisions with important ramifications for particular business enterprises, such as the provision of export subsidies or subsidised credit, began to be made much more by the ministers themselves (and often the prime minister) than as a result of normal bureaucratic process. Although this was generally justified by the need to cut red tape and to speed up official procedures in a time of economic liberalisation, there is no doubt that it was used to favour party supporters while punishing those who had voted for its rivals. The same trend can also be observed in the award of central government resources to municipalities and other organs of local government, which varied according to the political coloration of the institution concerned.

Notes

1 For a detailed examination of the 1948/9 fighting, see Benny Morris, *The Birth of the Palestinian Refugee Problem: 1947–1949* (Cambridge: Cambridge University Press, 1987); Avi Shlaim, *Collusion Across the Jordan: King Abdullah, the Zionist Movement and the Partition of Palestine* (Oxford: Clarendon Press, 1988), Chapters 71–2.

2 Nira Yuval-Davis, 'The Jewish collectivity', Khamsin, 13, *Women in the Middle East* (London: Zed Books, 1987), pp. 62–3.

3 E. Roger Owen, 'State and society in the Middle East', *Items*, 44/1 (March 1990), pp. 10–14.

4 Yoram Peri, *Between Battles and Ballots: Israeli Military in Politics* (Cambridge: Cambridge University Press, 1983), pp. 45–6.

5 For example, Dan Horowitz and Moshe Lissak, *Origins of the Israeli Polity: Palestine Under the Mandate* (Chicago, IL and London: Chicago University Press, 1978), pp. 190–1; Don Peretz, *The Government and Politics of Israel*, (2nd edn, Boulder, CO: Westview Press, 1983), p. 144.

6 Peri, *Between Battles and Ballots*, pp. 39–40.

7 Ibid., p. 48.

8 Horowitz and Lissak, *Origins*, pp. 193–4.

9 Michael Shalev, 'Jewish organized labor and the Palestinians: A study in state/society relations in Israel', in Baruch Kimmerling (ed.), *The Israeli State and Society: Boundaries and Frontiers* (Albany, NY: State University of New York Press, 1989), pp. 103–13.

10 Horowitz and Lissak, *Origins*, pp. 194–5.

11 Shalev, 'Jewish organized labor', p. 93; Uri Davis and Walter Lehn, 'And the Fund still lives', *Journal of Palestine Studies*, VII/4 (Summer, 1978), pp. 4–16.

12 Dan Horowitz and Moshe Lissak, *Trouble in Utopia: The Overburdened Polity in Israel* (Albany, NY: State University of New York Press, 1989), p. 35.

13 For a history of Israel's electoral system and the difficulties in changing it see Misha Louvain, 'The making of electoral reform', *Jerusalem Post*, 13 April 1977.

14 Dan Horowitz, 'More than a change of government', *Jerusalem Quarterly*, V (Fall, 1977), pp. 14–15; Michael Shalev, 'The political economy of Labor Party dominance', in T.J. Hempel (ed.), *Uncommon Democracies: The One Party Dominant Regimes* (Ithaca, NY and London: Cornell University Press, 1990), pp. 104–7.

15 Shalev, 'Political economy', pp. 85, 118.

16 Itzhak Galnoor, 'Israeli democracy in transition', *Mimeo* (1987), pp. 28–35.

17 Horowitz and Lissak, *Origins*, pp. 206–10.

18 Joel Beinin, 'Israel at forty: the political economy/political culture of constant conflict', *Arab Studies Quarterly*, 10/4 (Fall, 1988), pp. 437 and Table 1.

19 Ibid., pp. 440–1.

20 Shalev, 'Political economy', pp. 122–5.

21 Erik Cohen, 'Citizenship, nationality and religion in Israel and Thailand', in Kimmerling (ed.), *Israeli State and Society*, p. 72.

22 Shalev, 'Jewish organized labor', pp. 110–15.

23 Itzhak Galnoor, 'Transformations in the Israeli political system since the Yom Kippur War', in A. Arian (ed.), *Elections in Israel 1977* (Jerusalem: Jerusalem Academic Press, 1980), p. 123.

24 Ibid., pp. 123–4.

25 Peretz, *Government and Politics*, p. 62.

26 Galnoor, 'Israeli democracy in transition', pp. 12–13.

27 For example, Michael Shalev, 'Israel's domestic policy regime: Zionism, dualism and the rise of capital', in Frances G. Castles (ed.), *The Comparative History of Public Policy* (Cambridge, MA: Polity Press, 1989), pp. 131–2.

28 For the figures, see Peretz, *Government and Politics*, pp. 80–1.

29 This is the title of Horowitz's article in the *Jerusalem Quarterly* (Fall, 1977).

30 Here I follow the argument in Galnoor's, 'Israeli democracy in transition', pp. 35–43.

31 Abrahamian, *Iran Between Two Revolutions*, 1982), pp. 281–305.

32 Hossein Mahdavy, 'Patterns and problems of economic development in rentier states: The case of Iran', in M.A. Cook (ed.), *Studies in the Economic History of the Middle East* (Oxford: Oxford University Press, 1970), Table 2, p. 430.

33 For Mahdavy's over-optimistic evaluation of the economic advantages of oil rentierism, see ibid., p. 432.

34 Abrahamian, *Iran Between Two Revolutions*, p. 438.

35 Fatemeh E. Moghadam, 'An historical interpretation of the Iranian Revolution', *Cambridge Journal of Economics*, 12 (1988), p. 413.

36 Fred Halliday, *Iran; Dictatorship and Development* (Harmondsworth: Penguin Books, 1979), p. 47.

37 For example, Henry Munson Jr, *Islam and Revolution in the Middle East* (New Haven CT and London: Yale University Press, 1988), pp. 126–7.

38 Halliday draws attention to the 'modernity' of the Iranian revolution as compared to the Russian and the French, citing the Iranian revolutionaries' use of the general strike as one example of this. Fred Halliday, 'The Iranian Revolution', *Political Studies*, XXX/3 (September 1982), p. 438.

39 For example, Hamid Algar, *The Roots of the Islamic Revolution* (London: The Open Press, 1983), pp. 123–4.

40 Zubaida, *Islam, the People and the State*, pp. 18–20, 33.

41 A more detailed analysis of Khomeini's thought can be found in Chapter 9 of this book. The translation of the word *faqih* as 'just jurist' can be found in 'The Constitution of the Islamic Republic of Iran', *Middle East Journal*, 34/2 (Spring, 1980), pp. 181–204.

42 See Ali Khamenei's Friday Prayers sermon of 28 April 1989 in British Broadcasting Corporation (BBC), *Summary of World Broadcasts*, ME/0447 A/1 (1 May 1989).

43 Asghar Schirazi, *The Problems of Land Reform in the Islamic Republic of Iran: Complications and Consequences of an Islamic Reform Policy* (Berlin: Free University of Berlin, Forschungsgebietsschwerpunkt, Occasional Papers, 10, published by Das Arabische Buch, Berlin, 1987), pp. 13–22.

44 Ali Khamenei's Friday Sermon of 28 April 1989.

45 Feroz Ahmad, *The Making of Modern Turkey* (London: Routledge, 1993), pp. 110–14.

46 Caglar Keyder, *State and Class in Turkey: A Study of Capitalist Development* (London and New York: Verso, 1987), p. 117.

47 Ahmad, *Making of Modern Turkey*, pp. 138–9.

48 Ibid., pp. 142–4.

49 Ahmet Samim, 'The ordeal of the Turkish Left', *New Left Review*, 126 (March/April 1981), pp. 72–6.

50 Tosun Aricanli, 'The political economy of Turkey's external debt: The bearing of exogenous factors', in Tosun Aricanli and Dani Rodrick (eds), *The Political Economy of Turkey: Adjustment and Sustainability* (London: Macmillan, 1990), pp. 230–49.

51 Ahmad, *Making of Modern Turkey*, pp. 175–6.

52 Ibid., p. 176.

53 Ibid., pp. 189–90.

54 This is the argument developed by Ayse Oncu, 'Street politics: Comparative perspectives on working class activism in Egypt and Turkey', *mimeo* (Paper prepared for workshop on 'Socio-economic transformation: State and political regimes in Turkey and Egypt', Istanbul, July 1990).

55 Here I follow the argument of Korkut Boratav, 'Contradictions of "structural adjustment": Capital and state in post-1980 Turkey', *mimeo* (Paper prepared for workshop on 'Socio-economic transformation: State and political regimes in Turkey and Egypt', Istanbul, July 1990).

6 The remaking of the Middle Eastern political environment after the Gulf War

Introduction

The fortuitous coincidence of the Gulf War of 1990/1, the collapse of the Soviet Union and the end of the Cold War provided a catalyst for a process which I think is best described as a 're-making' of the Middle East's structures of government and of the pattern of relationships between individual states and with the outside world. As far as the region as a whole was concerned, this process had three main features. The first was the inauguration of a serious diplomatic effort to solve the Arab/Israeli dispute, leading, in turn, to a considerable reduction in the proportion of national expenditures devoted to military spending after 1990 (see Table 10.2). The second was the Gulf states' decision to rely on the United States for their own security rather than on some local or pan-Arab arrangement. And the third was the great increase in the number of agreements between Middle Eastern states and international organisations such as the European Union, the World Trade Organisation and the World Bank, committing them to a staged opening up of their economies and so, over time, to the surrender of many of their existing powers of management and control.

Meanwhile, at the domestic level, the post-Gulf War decade was one of an increasing Arab reliance on the principle either of regular elections or, among the Gulf states, increased consultation between rulers and the members of a variety of newly established advisory councils. Iran, too, became the site of a significant attempt to introduce notions of pluralism and accountability into the authoritarian form of government created after the Islamic revolution. In Israel and Turkey, by contrast, the attempt to liberalise economically while also dealing with such major national issues as relations with the Palestinians or the Kurds was made much more difficult by social divisions exacerbated by a series of relatively weak coalition governments. Only at the end of the decade did their electoral systems create the conditions for the stronger coalitions necessary to tackle such problems with any hope of permanent success.

While it is tempting to see all these changes as part of a general process of domestic liberalisation, the reduction of regional tensions and of increased integration into the global economy, they actually represented a much more complex reality, suggestive not so much of a single, unidirectional movement but of a more indeterminate transformation of local structures as a result of pressures both from within and without. Hence, even while the dangers of war between states declined dramatically, there remained many serious internal conflicts such as the civil war in Sudan and the anti-government insurrections in Turkey and Algeria. Meanwhile political liberalisation continued to lag far behind economic liberalisation, with the introduction of new laws and new practices which often seemed as restrictive as those they replaced.

I will now review the major developments of the 1990s before returning to the difficult question of their overall shape and meaning.

Regional developments after the Gulf War

At the regional level, Iraq's invasion of a sovereign Arab state in the name of its own version of Arabism, and then the deep divisions which this produced both between the regimes and inside each society, provided a near fatal blow to what was left of the once powerful belief in a unity which could transcend individual local interest. It also left a legacy of considerable mistrust manifest, for example, in the temporary isolation of regimes like the Jordanian, the Yemeni and Sudanese whose leaders had been unwilling to condemn the Iraqi position outright. It encouraged the Gulf states to replace their emphasis on collective security arrangements within the Gulf Cooperation Council (GCC) by bilateral defence agreements with the United States, Britain and France. And it opened the way for direct American involvement in the promotion of an Israeli/Palestinian peace process leading from the Madrid conference of 1991, to the Oslo accords of 1993 and then the establishment of a Palestine National Authority (PNA) in the Gaza Strip and parts of the West Bank in 1994.

As for the non-Arab states, peace with the Palestinians seemed to hold out the possibility of an Israel which was not only universally recognised by its Arab neighbours but also bound to them by multiple commercial and cultural ties as well. In the event, however, the concessions which this required further intensified the divisions within Israeli society itself and did much to produce the poisonous atmosphere which led to the assassination of Yitzhak Rabin, the country's prime minister, in November 1995. The peace process then ran into further difficulties as a result of a series of bomb explosions by Palestinian religious extremists inside Israel in early 1996, followed by the election of a Likud-led government under Benjamin Netanyahu which showed little interest in withdrawing from more parts of the West Bank as laid down in the Oslo Accords. Instead, it placed great emphasis on the intensification of the process of physical separation between Israelis and Palestinians begun during the Gulf War, by means of the increasing isolation of the Gaza Strip from the northern and southern halves of the West Bank.[1]

Turkey also found itself much more closely involved with the Arab Middle East through its growing security interest in the future of the northern regions of

Iraq separated from the rest of the country after the creation of a 'safe-haven' to protect its Kurdish population from Saddam Hussein's reprisals. Such involvement was further increased by its military alliance with Israel which gave it sufficient leverage over Syria to demand the expulsion of the PKK leader, Abdullah Ocalan, from his hide-out there and so to pave the way for his eventual arrest and trial in 1999. Meanwhile, Iran, having failed to reap any significant reward from its neutrality in the Gulf War, began a successful campaign to create new ties with the small Arab states on the opposite side of the Gulf.

The domestic impact of the Gulf War

The Gulf War had a profound impact on domestic political structures as well. In the Arab Gulf the role played by the ruling families during the crisis encouraged considerable local criticism of their policies and their secretive methods of rule. In spite of all the billions of dollars they had spent on military equipment none of them could offer their people military protection against the Iraqi army. This had led, in turn, to the invitation to allow American and other western troops to be quartered on Saudi soil, a decision deeply offensive to much domestic opinion. Some groups tried to use President George Bush's definition of the coalition's war-aims as a fight for democracy and a new world order to put pressure on his local Gulf allies to move in the same direction. Others used the occasion to criticise continued reliance on western military support. The result was a flood of post-war petitions challenging the ruling families' authority and demanding change in a more liberal or a more conservative direction.[2] The rulers' eventual response was either to allow new parliamentary elections, as in Kuwait, or to introduce some form of consultative council with its members nominated so as to represent the major groups and interests within each society.

Elsewhere, those regimes which had taken the western side in the conflict sought to exploit the situation in order to strengthen their economic and military ties to Europe and America. However, in many cases they also had to cope with a fresh surge of religious radicalism, triggered in part by opposition to their participation in the Gulf War alliance. The steps then taken to contain the threat made it much more difficult to accommodate religious parties and religious opinion within the emerging electoral systems which regimes like the Algerian, the Egyptian and the Tunisian had begun to create.

Further domestic developments during the 1990s

The larger Arab republics

The Gulf War came at a time of transition for most of the major Arab states, a moment at which they were beginning to make progress towards greater economic liberalisation, supplemented in some instances by political reform as well. In Egypt, the regime decided to take advantage of its war-time reward – an international offer of partial debt forgiveness in exchange for further substantial

economic liberalization

reforms – to push on seriously with the construction of a more market-oriented economy. However, just as this ambitious programme was getting under way, the country experienced a series of attacks by religious militants against foreign tourists aimed, it seemed, at crippling one of its major sources of revenue. The regime responded with an increasingly harsh crackdown which, over time, extended beyond the arrest, torture and execution of the militants themselves to the harassment of their supposed sympathisers in the professional associations and the Muslim Brothers.

The crackdown on religious militancy had the unfortunate result of strengthening the already well-entrenched authoritarian tendencies within the regime, encouraging its supporters in its National Democratic Party (NDP) to monopolise more and more of the political life of the country. This tendency was much in evidence in the 1995 elections when the NDP obtained 416 of the seats, leaving what was left of the official opposition with a mere 28.[3] To make matters worse, the regime also closed down all those professional syndicates, like that of the lawyers, which might have acted as a source of independent criticism of its actions, while harassing any of the country's human rights activists who drew public attention to its many abuses of police power. As one outspoken foreign journalist noted in April 1999, it seemed as though the Mubarak government had decided that the best way to avoid pressure for more democracy was to have no democracy at all.[4] Hence, by the time the militants had announced their abandonment of armed opposition in spring 1999, the regime's re-vamped authoritarianism was so deeply entrenched as no longer to require justification by an appeal to the dangers posed by religious violence.

Much the same process took place in Tunisia. There the main Islamic grouping, the Nahda, was banned in 1990 and its leader, Rachid Ghannouchi, driven into exile. For a while the campaign against religious militancy was supported by the secular opposition but relations began to break down in 1994 when the opposition was permitted only a minority representation in the National Assembly. From then on, critics of the regime, like Mohamed Moadda, the leader of the Movement of Social Democrats (MDS), were subject to continual harassment. As in Egypt, an authoritarian regime and its elite supporters found it easier to manage the process of economic transition with only token opposition and a highly controlled system of parliamentary representation.

One of the justifications given in both Egypt and Tunisia for their restrictions on popular political activity was the example of Algeria. There the headlong rush towards a multi-party system begun by President Chadli Benjadid in 1989 had led to the first multi-party elections in 1991/2, to military intervention, to a brutal insurrection by Muslim militants in which some 65–75,000 Algerians were killed, and, finally, a long drawn out process of trying to construct a more manageable system of popular representation. Political life was subject to endless manipulation by the generals who held the real power, using elections to secure the return of presidents and politicians willing to serve their purposes while refusing any negotiation with the militant Islamic groups. A military man, General Lamine Zerouel, was elected president in 1995, only to be replaced when he had outlasted his usefulness by another of the generals' candidates, Abdelaziz Bouteflika, in April 1999, in an election boycotted at the last minute by all of Bouteflika's politically-credible opponents.

President Asad of Syria also had his own good reasons for not wanting to accompany his limited economic liberalisation of the late 1980s and early 1990s with anything that could be called political liberalisation as well. He seems to have been keenly aware of the lessons to be drawn from countries like Romania where well-entrenched single-party regimes had been swept quickly away in the heady months following the fall of the Berlin Wall in 1989. Moreover, his whole system of control depended on interlocking sets of, often military-dominated, vested interests many of which would have been seriously threatened by a process of political opening up. Hence, not only were there no more than token moves to allow more independent (i.e. non-Ba'thi) candidates to run for the national elections in 1990 and 1994, but also a resolute determination not to raise popular expectations concerning future reform. Much the same policy was continued through the 1998 parliamentary elections and then Asad's own re-election as president in February 1999, even though there were great efforts to get Syrians to come to the polls for what was, essentially, a meaningless vote. Meanwhile, the only indication that change might be in the offing were the increasing signs that the elderly president was grooming his own son, Bashar, as his successor, giving him increasing executive responsibility while removing some of his more obvious rivals from government service.

Turning finally to Iraq, there were some optimists who put forward the view that the end of the war with Iran would lead to an easing of the tight control exercised by the regime headed by President Saddam Hussein.[5] They based their view on the fact that, as a result of wartime pressure, the government had been forced to allow a great deal more private initiative just to keep the economy going as oil income plummeted and the state's ability to fund, as well as to administer, all its enterprises was under serious strain. In the event, however, Saddam Hussein chose to manage what was obviously going to be a difficult transition to a peace-time economy, not by further liberalisation but by a direct attempt to obtain the money he needed from his oil-rich neighbour, Kuwait.

Thrown out of Kuwait by the allied coalition, with much of his country's infrastructure destroyed by Allied bombing, his economy subject to international sanctions and facing widespread popular uprisings and then the loss of Iraq's northern provinces as a result of the creation of a safe-haven for the Kurds, Saddam Hussein had little option but to concentrate on mere survival from 1991 onwards. Fortunately for him, the circles of defence which he had built around himself since becoming president in 1979, stood him in good stead, allowing him to hang on to power but with little room to manoeuvre. In such grim circumstances, he had no alternative but to supplement his usual harsh measures of torture and repression with limited gestures of conciliation towards his battered population.[6]

The Arab states under family rule

Political developments in the two Arab monarchies, Jordan and Morocco, moved along mutually opposite trajectories after 1990. Like their republican neighbours, both were simultaneously engaged in a process of economic liberalisation and of finding new methods to control the Islamic religious organisations which were assuming greater prominence in local political life. However, the international pressures facing each of the rulers were significantly different. As far as King Hussein of Jordan was concerned, the major issue was, as always, his country's relationships with Israel and the Palestinians. By joining vigorously in the Madrid conference of 1991, and then accepting the Oslo accords and establishing normal treaty relations with Israel in October 1994, he committed himself to a process over which he had little real control. As difficulties with the new Israeli government of Prime Minister Benjamin Netanyahu intensified after 1996, he was led to counter his domestic critics by placing new restrictions on the political freedoms which he had introduced in 1989. In Morocco, it was the other way around. Growing economic and cultural ties with the European Union encouraged King Hassan to create a new system of what he called 'alternance' (rotation) by which members of the opposition parties were eventually allowed to form their own government in March 1998.

The main landmarks in the King Hussein's partial retreat from the establishment of a more open political system in Jordan were as follows. In 1989 he allowed the first free elections for over forty years in which parties were not allowed but candidates could stand as members of identifiable political blocs. The result was a win for those associated with the Jordanian branch of the Muslim Brothers, then one of the King's major supporters. Parties were permitted to put forward their own candidates in the 1993 elections allowing the Brothers to obtain a dominant position in the parliament. However, relations with the Islamists quickly soured as a result of their opposition to the Peace Process and the subsequent treaty with Israel. This led the king to institute a crackdown on the Brothers in 1994/5 and then to amend the electoral law to make it more difficult for their political organisation, the Islamic Action Front (IAF), to do well in the 1997 elections. The result was a boycott of the elections by the Front, mounting tensions, and new government attempts to curb both the local press and the activities of the professional syndicates.

It is also important to note that, in spite of the creation of a more open parliamentary life, the king surrendered none of his important prerogatives, continued to rely on an inner cabinet of close advisers and to remain unaccountable for most of his actions. This situation remained unchanged while Hussein's brother, Crown Prince Hassan, acted as regent when the king himself went to the United States in 1998 for cancer treatment. Then, in a moment of high drama, the dying king flew back to Jordan in January 1999 to announce that he was replacing Hassan by his own eldest son, Prince Abdullah. The open letter he wrote to his brother explaining his actions seemed to suggest two main areas of disquiet: differences over who should rule after Hassan himself and allegations that Hassan had been interfering with the integrity of the army.[7] Abdullah

election in Jordan

acceded to the throne a few days later and, to judge from some of his initial speeches, seemed well-aware of the popular criticisms which had surfaced during his father's last years, offering the possibility of amendments to both the repressive press law of 1996 and the electoral law of 1997. However, given his inexperience, and so his reliance on many of his father's old advisers, few Jordanians believed that they would see any major changes until the peace process between Israel and both the Syrians and the Palestinians had finally been resolved.

Morocco's move in the opposite direction owes something to the changing international context, as noted above, and something to the fact that thirty years of royal management and control had simply worn down the ageing members of a once vigorous opposition to the point where they were willing to take part in what were still partially-managed elections and to form a cabinet in which the king and his allies retained control over defence, foreign policy, internal security and justice. Moreover, such was the imbalance between the well-entrenched position of the king and some of his long-time advisers, on the one hand, and the weak government of Prime Minister Abderrahman Youssoufi, on the other, that over time a number of the powers initially granted to the new government were clawed back. There was also a significant bottom line as politicians were constantly reminded of King Hassan's general unwillingness to go too far along the road towards constitutional democracy. As he had stated forcefully in an interview with *Le Monde* in 1992: 'Islam forbids me from instituting a constitutional monarchy in which I, the King, delegate all my powers and reign without governing.'[8] As in Jordan, the king's sudden death in July 1999 suggested the possibility of movement towards greater royal power-sharing, but only after the new king, Mohammed VI, had had time to build up his own authority sufficiently to challenge the position of his father's long-standing, and highly authoritarian, advisers.

Turning now to the changes in the pattern of government encouraged by the Gulf War, the state most immediately affected was, of course, Kuwait. Almost all the members of the ruling family fled the country to escape the Iraqi occupation and so were able to provide a rallying point for the many thousands of Kuwaitis also in exile. But it was also clear that once the Iraqis had been expelled they would be under considerable pressure to account for their demonstrable failure to protect the country in the months leading up to the invasion, as well as the growing evidence of mismanagement and corruption involving the Kuwait Investment Office which appeared to have run down its holdings by billions of dollars without proper accounts. Hence it was with some reluctance that the al-Sabahs agreed to the holding of the 1992 elections which produced a Parliament in which as many as 33 out of its 50 members were identified as part of the opposition.[9] This led to a period of (by Gulf standards) intense criticism of those senior al-Sabahs who had held key posts before the occupation, particularly the minister of foreign affairs who was finally forced to resign. There was also a constant testing of the limits of the ruling family's own constitutional powers including the National Assembly's successful establishment of its right to review all the government decrees issued during its suspension, 1986–92. Further areas of criticism were opened up by members of the new assembly elected in 1996, including serious allegations of corruption and maladministration.

The al-Sabah family twisted and turned under this assault, always trying to find new ways to protect those of its members under parliamentary attack. One example is the way it engineered the resignation of the whole cabinet in March 1998 to void further questioning of the minister of information, Shaikh Nasser al-Sabah. But this was not enough to prevent a series of mini-crises in which threats to dissolve the assembly were made and then withdrawn, most probably on the grounds that a new parliament was as likely to contain as many of the family's critics as the old. Nevertheless, ruling family patience finally ran out in the summer of 1999 when new elections were called for July, seventeen months before their appointed time. As expected, the election of an assembly with members deeply divided over a number of contentious issues, including an al-Sabah proposal to give women the vote and to let them stand for elected office, provided little assurance that criticism and conflict would diminish. However, given the general context of a continuing threat from Iraq, combined with the loyalty which almost all Kuwaitis feel towards both their rulers and the parliamentary system, there seemed no reason why this state of controlled tension between rulers and ruled should not continue for many years to come.

Elsewhere in the Gulf, the main challenges to the traditional ways of ruling family management came from a variety of different groups using petitions, taped sermons and more direct methods such as the bombing of American military facilities in Saudi Arabia in 1995 and 1996 and the simmering insurrection among parts of Bahrain's local Shi'i population once its call for a revival of parliamentary life had been rejected by the state's al-Khalifa rulers. In Saudi Arabia in particular, the call for reform came from both ends of the religious and cultural spectrum: that is from groups arguing for a more tolerant, open society and those who believed that the al-Sauds had greatly neglected their duties as custodians of the religious law and of the Islamic community in general. Indeed, both sides can be said to have egged the other on, with a liberal petition of December 1990 being immediately countered by a more conservative one in February 1991 signed by a number of the senior religious leaders who clearly felt that their own authority was under direct attack. Nevertheless, it can also be observed that there was a considerable area of overlap between the two positions. Both called for more consultation, more open government and more attention to the rule of law and human rights.

The al-Sauds' response took two main forms. One was the announcement of the establishment of a Consultative Council in March 1992. The other was the use of the pro-Saudi religious leaders to reprimand and, if necessary, discipline those of their number who refused to sign statements condemning the critics and so reinforcing the official view of the proper relationship between the family and the religious establishment. There was then some delay in the selection of the sixty members of the new Council which did not begin work until 1994.[10] Three years later, in July 1997, its membership was increased to ninety. Although its powers were limited to giving advice, there were areas where it was allowed to question ministers and, in the case of its eight standing committees, to make its voice heard when policy was being discussed.

Much the same model was used in establishing the other consultative councils elsewhere. In Oman, for example, a new and enlarged council was introduced in 1991, with members selected from each of the country's fifty-nine *wilayas* (provinces). And although it met in full session only twelve times in its first year, its five committees met regularly every week. Its size was later increased to improve representation while an elective element was introduced by which voters chose two names to go forward for final selection. Nevertheless, as in Saudi Arabia, its role remained purely advisory and may even have served to strengthen the sultan's own power by allowing him to build a wider basis of support while keeping many of his country's more important local leaders in the capital city away from their own regional bases of power while they served on the various standing committees.[11]

As in all systems of family rule, significant political change could only take place in the Gulf states as a result either of a shift in attitude among the ruler and those of his relatives in the top leadership positions or if there was a new ruler. Two examples of the latter were particularly significant during the 1990s. In Saudi Arabia, the increasing incapacity of King Fahd due to illness meant that, from 1997 to 1999, executive power passed largely into the hands of his half-brother, Crown Prince Abdullah, someone with both greater personal authority and powers of decision than Fahd himself. As a result, the Saudi government was galvanised into making a serious response to the serious situation posed by the great fall in oil prices during 1998, placing a moratorium on government hiring, reducing the value of basic subsidies and, in the case of the ruling family itself, putting a stop to many of the ways in which the princes had been able to use state services for free. The second example comes from Qatar where the ruler, Shaikh Khalifah, was deposed by his son, Shaikh Hamad, in 1995 in a bloodless coup. This allowed Shaikh Hamad to embark on a number of innovations including giving votes to women in the February 1999 municipal elections and then making a promise of an elected assembly to come. Given the fact that primogeniture was becoming much more common in family successions in general, the prospects of power passing regularly to eldest sons, as happened in Bahrain in March 1999, suggested that generational change might become a further stimulus to limited political reform.

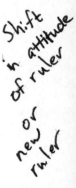

Shift in attitude of ruler or new ruler

Iran, Israel and Turkey

Iran

Iranian politics in the 1990s continued to be dominated by the type of institutionalised factionalism which allowed disputes concerning a whole variety of important issues – from foreign alliances to the proper management of the economy – to be vigorously pursued without posing too great a threat the ultimate stability of the Islamic Republic itself. At the time of the 1992 Majles elections it was possible to identify three major factions known, loosely, as the conservatives, the religious radicals and the reformers, each with its own power bases within different parts of the state structure and each defined by its stance towards economic and cultural issues. To speak very generally, it was the conservatives who were committed to defend what they took to be the status quo under the leadership of the Ayatollah Khomeini, the religious radicals who wanted to use the state to create a more egalitarian society, and the reformers who were committed to many of the same notions of liberalisation, privatisation and the creation of markets which constituted economic orthodoxy for the World Bank and the major western governments. However, all three factions had their own vested interests to defend, all three were committed to maintaining some version of an Islamic society and all three believed that it would be far too risky to try to eliminate one or other of their opponents.

The 1992 elections themselves resulted in what, at first sight, was hailed as an overwhelming victory for candidates associated with President Rafsanjani and the reformers. But, in the event, many of them proved as conservative in social matters as they were liberal in economic ones. This, in turn, paved the way, for a conservative victory over the religious radicals which considerably reduced Rafsanjani's freedom of manoeuvre.[12] Supported as a rule by Khomeini's successor as Supreme Guide, Ali Khamenei, and with strong bases in broadcasting, the mosques, the para-statal institutions like the huge religious foundations, as well as the judiciary, the police and the parliament, the conservative bloc had enough allies in the Majles to obstruct many of the president's proposed reforms as well as to inhibit the development of better relations with the western world on which future economic progress was known to depend. Their position was further strengthened by the fact that, far from reaping any reward for its neutrality in the Gulf War, Iran continued to be treated as an outlaw nation by the United States as well as by some of its European allies, notably Britain.

The result was something of a stand-off between the two main factions in which few new policy initiatives were possible at the national level. However, the situation was then dramatically altered by the surprise results of the 1997 presidential elections which produced a landslide victory of a relative newcomer, the clergyman and former Minister of Information, Mohammad Khatami. Capitalising on a mood of general public discontent, Khatami managed to mobilise support from many of the groups marginalised in the first stages of the Islamic Revolution, such as secularists, Muslim leftists, young people and large numbers of women, behind a campaign which promoted a vision of an Islamic society where dissent and freedom were allowed within the rule of law. He was also helped immeasurably by the divisions within the Rafsanjani camp which prevented the outgoing president from being able to put forward a credible successor.

Khatami's huge popular success combined with the abject defeat of the main conservative candidate gave him a considerable advantage when it came to the selection of his first cabinet and his choice of policy priorities. He also benefited from the discrete support given by former President Rafsanjani from his new position of power as head of what had first been known as the Expediency Council when originally set up in the late 1980s to mediate disputes between the Majles and the judiciary. Later, under its full name, the Assembly for Diagnosing the Interests of the Regime, it had been doubled in size to allow it to play an expanded role in government. As its members now included not only the Supreme Guide and the president but also many of Iran's most important political figures, it was ideally suited to play a mediating role between the factions as well as to ensure that attacks on Khatami's leadership could be blunted and contained. It is also noteworthy that Khamenei himself did not feel able openly to oppose any of the new president's initiatives, perhaps feeling that he lacked the popular authority to do so.[13]

Nevertheless, Khatami's obvious lack of political experience, his failure to make much of an impact on a deteriorating economic situation, together with the fact that the Majles and many of the major organs of government were controlled by his conservative opponents, was enough to ensure that much of his energy had to be taken up with a series of political dog-fights with his clerical foes. One concerned the arrest of one of his most visible supporters, Gholan-hossein Karbaschi, the mayor of Teheran, on allegations of corruption and embezzlement.[14] Another followed the dismissal by the Majles of his minister of interior, Abdollah Nouri, in June 1998. Both incidents provoked counter-demonstrations by pro-Khatami students and others sufficient to alarm the conservative hard-liners who feared that they might have lost control of the streets. And, in each case, Khatami himself was able to fight back, for example by ensuring that Nouri was replaced by another minister of his own choice.

The next great trial of strength came with the municipal elections of February 1999 in which candidates associated with both the Khatami and Rafsanjani groups won control of most of the major cities, including Istanbul where they secured all fifteen of the seats. Just as important was the fact that Khatami's reformist camp was able to prevent the conservative-controlled Election Supervisory Board from vetting candidates in such a way as to reject the applications of many of their leading supporters. Khatami himself then used the result as a platform from which to re-emphasise the main tenets of his reformist agenda: the need to establish what he called an 'Islamic democracy', with accountable government, civil institution and a form of political activity based on parties which could be held formally accountable for their members' actions.[15]

All now seemed set for a second great reformist victory in the general elections due to be held early in the year 2000. But this was then suddenly and dramatically thrown into doubt by the student demonstrations against continuing press censorship which broke out in Teheran and other cities in July 1999. Such an open manifestation of the frustration caused by the slow progress towards Khatami's goal of a more open society, opened up the possibility that the huge reform coalition might not hold together long enough to allow the hoped-for electoral triumph, forcing Khatami himself back into a closer alliance with the very conservative forces which he was planning to overcome.

Israel

Traumatic though the Gulf War was for Israel, with its deliberate isolation from the Allied military coalition and its brief bombardment by Iraqi rockets, it was the renewal of the peace process with the Arab states representing the Palestinians which had the more profound effect on Israeli politics. This was revealed almost immediately by the defeat of the Likud government in the 1992 elections by a Labour party which seemed to represent a less uncompromising stand towards the negotiations.

At the same time, concerns about the weaknesses of the series of the national unity governments from 1984 to 1990 led to the adoption of two significant political innovations, also in 1992. One was the introduction of a modified version of the party primary as a way of electing the leader and determining most of the places on the single national list of candidates to be presented to the electorate. Labour was the first to use it in 1992 just before that year's election. Likud then moved to the same system in March 1993 when Benjamin Netanyahu used his increasing popularity to defeat Yitzhak Shamir as head of the party.

The second innovation was the 1990 amendment to the Basic Law: the Knesset introducing a process of direct election of the prime minister to begin in 1996. This was supposed to ensure that the person thus elected would have sufficient prestige and authority not to have to make too many concessions to his smaller coalition partners. The prime minister's power was further strengthened by a second amendment to the Basic Law to the effect that a vote of no confidence in the Knesset was now sufficient not only to bring down the government but also to force new elections as well. It also provided that the prime minister himself could only be voted out of office by eighty or more of the 120 members of parliament, an overwhelming majority which was clearly going to be very difficult to obtain.

In the event, however, the reforms seemed to have exactly the opposite effect from that intended.[16] Reliance on party primaries increased the independence of the individual candidates now that they were elected by the rank and file members rather than nominated by the leadership. More importantly, it also paved the way for the emergence of a second generation of relatively untried and untested leaders, Netanyahu in 1993 and Ehud Barak who defeated Shimon Peres to head the Labour Party in 1997.

Even more significant drawbacks were to be revealed by the 1996 general election itself. Israelis tended to split their two votes, using one to choose between Peres and Netanyahu, the other to support one of the smaller parties which more nearly represented their own religious, ethnic or sectarian interests. As a result Labour and Likud together obtained only sixty-six of the 120 Knesset seats, their smallest proportion of the total since the creation of the state, with the three religious parties getting twenty-three and the new party formed to represent the huge influx of Russian immigrants, seven. It follows that, at one level, the electorate treated the race as simply between Netanyahu and Peres with Netanyahu scraping a win with just 30,000 more votes than his rival (out of an electorate of some 3,000,000) and so earning the right to form the next government regardless of the fact that Labour had won two more seats. However, on a second, it was able to take advantage of the new arrangements to support Knesset candidates closer to its personal interests. Two striking sets of figures serve to underline the same point: Netanyahu got twice as high a percentage of the vote (50.4) as his own party, the Likud (25.1), including an overwhelming 90 per cent of the religious vote.[17]

Subsequent events also demonstrated the peculiar strengths and weaknesses of a prime minister elected under this new system. As it turned out, Netanyahu was just as dependent on the support of his six coalition partners to maintain his government's slight majority in the Knesset as any of his predecessors, a situation which gave the smaller parties enormous power to demand particular concessions or to block some of his more important initiatives. In these circumstances the Netanyahu government seemed to slide rapidly from crisis to crisis, unable to pursue clear policies towards the two most important questions of the day, the future of the peace process and the further de-regulation of the economy. Finally, its support had sufficiently eroded by December 1998 that, rather than face defeat on a vote of confidence in the Knesset, Netanyahu preferred to call for new elections in May 1999.

The result was a great disaster, not only for Netanyahu himself – who lost the race for prime minister to Ehud Barak by 12 percentage points (or 363,000 votes) – but also for his Likud Party which saw its number of Knesset seats drop from thirty-two to nineteen. Just how much he himself was to blame for this débâcle remained a matter for debate, However, a good case can certainly be made for the fact that his perceived duplicity and untrustworthiness had not only alienated a considerable number of his former political supporters, but also placed the virtues of his uninspiring but well-organised opponent in a much more favourable light.[18] Be that as it may, such a huge electoral victory gave Barak himself sufficient authority to build the coalition he believed necessary to revive the stalled peace talks with the Syrians and the Palestinians. And even though he had to deal with a Knesset in which his own party (now re-named 'New Israel') had only twenty-seven seats, as opposed to thirty-four in the 1996 election, he was able to put together a government in which none of his partners had sufficient power to alter its basic policies by threatening to resign.

Turkey

Turkish politics bear some resemblance to Israel's in the 1990s to the extent that both witnessed a succession of relatively weak coalition governments with slim parliamentary majorities and subject to the strong pull of regional and sectional interests. However, in Turkey's case the situation was also seriously affected by the continued insurrection led by the Workers' Party of Kurdistan (PKK/ Partiye Karkaran Kurdistan) in many of the country's eastern provinces, the growth in popular support for the main Islamic party, Refah (Welfare), and increasing military pressure on the civilian politicians culminating in what many commentators have called the 'silent coup' of 1997.[19]

The decade began with the 1991 electoral defeat of the Motherland Party which had dominated Turkish politics during the 1980s. This was succeeded by a True Path/Social Democratic Party coalition, first under Suleyman Demirel and then, when Demirel was elected president in 1993 following Turgut Ozal's death, under the untried Tansu Ciller. Ciller's administration lasted until 1995 when one of her main coalition partners withdrew its support bringing True Path back to power as a caretaker government to prepare for new elections under another relatively inexperienced leader, Mesut Yilmaz.

The elections themselves, held in December 1995, produced a considerable shock to the whole system as a result of the fact the party which emerged with both the most votes (21.32 per cent) and the most seats (158) was the Islamist party, Refah, led by the political veteran, Necmettin Erbekan. This victory had been on the cards for some time as a result of Refah's growing popular support as manifest, for example, by the elections of one its leading lights, Recep Erdogan, as mayor of Istanbul in 1994. It benefited greatly not only from an excellent organisation dedicated to mobilising grass-roots support but also from the divisions on the Turkish right which split the vote between the Motherland and True Path parties. The weakened state of the left-wing parties was another significant factor for it very much reduced their old ability to deliver welfare to the poor. Nevertheless, in a state run by avowed secularists, this was enough to create such an atmosphere of near panic among many members of the Turkish elite, the military included, that their immediate response was to encourage the formation of an anti-Refah, or blocking coalition, of the Motherland and True Path parties in March 1996 with Yilmaz as prime minister.

However, such was the mutual antipathy between Yilmaz and Tansu Ciller that this new government lasted no longer than June, after which the only half-way viable coalition that could be stitched together was one led by Refah, with Erbekan as prime minister and Ciller's True Path as his junior partner. Yet no sooner had this shaky enterprise managed to defy its critics by staying in power for more than a few months when confrontation between Erbekan and the military members of the National Security Council became inevitable. While he, for his part, seems to have believed that he had received a sufficient mandate from the Turkish people to alter the balance between religion and society, the generals were equally convinced that his mere presence in government posed a basic threat to the values and institutions of the secular state. To make matters worse, Erbekan made a few initial statements which served further to rouse military suspicions. He denounced the new defence agreement which the military had negotiated with Israel. And he seemed ready to explore the possibility of negotiations with representatives of the Kurdish rebels on the basis of an appeal to Muslim solidarity. As a result, the generals not only prevented him from taking any important new initiative but also forced him to agree to an attack first on the religious schools, then on Muslim organisations at large. When he prevaricated about actually implementing the proposed measures, he was forced to resign in June 1997, just a year after first taking power. Worse was to follow as the military persuaded the courts to close down his party and to exclude him from politics for five years beginning in January 1998.

Much the same pressures confronted Erbekan's successor, Mesut Yilmaz, back as prime minister at the head of yet another frail coalition and with only minority support in the Grand National Assembly. He too was forced to agree to place new curbs on organisations suspected of promoting Islamic thought. However, he too resisted the implementation of some of the harsher measures, worried, like all the rest of the politicians, at the thought of alienating the Muslim support he would need in the next election. On occasions he also tried to launch a mild counter-attack, warning the military that it was in danger of carrying out a fourth coup, and insisting that it was the civilian government, not the military, that should decide the best way to curtail Islamic political activism. However, the generals would have none of this and, in so doing, were forced to state their position with increasing force and clarity. Hence, in June 1998 the army's second-in-command issued a statement saying that fundamentalism was the country's number one danger and problem. This was followed a few weeks later by the assertion that the armed forces had a 'legal obligation' to protect the present constitutional order from Islamic agitation.[20]

The Yilmaz government was finally forced to resign after the loss of a vote of censure in December 1998, paving the way for new elections under a caretaker government led by Bulent Ecevit the following April. The results were again a great surprise. Receiving obvious benefit from the nationalist euphoria surrounding the capture of the PKK leader, Abdullah Ocalan, Ecevit's own party, the Democratic Left Party (DSP), won 22 per cent of the vote while the revived National Action Party (now MHP) won 18.2 per cent, allowing its members to take seats in the assembly for the first time since the 1970s. This in turn allowed Ecevit to form a more than usually stable coalition government with the MHP and Yilmaz's Motherland Party.

Middle East political developments in the 1990s: conclusion

Any detailed examination of Middle Eastern political developments during the 1990s reveals something of a mixed picture. On the one hand, there were tendencies which seemed to suggest an unequivocal movement towards pluralism, a freer press and more open discussion in many Arab countries. On the other, there is the undoubted fact that progress in the direction of allowing a real parliamentary opposition to develop in the former one-party states was at best slow and at worst, as in Egypt, non-existent. How then to make sense of this apparent conundrum? Rather than looking at the question of political change in terms of a simple contrast between developments which either helped or hindered the transition to a more liberal polity, it is more useful to begin by viewing the events of the 1990s from a number of different perspectives.

One such perspective relates to the short period of time involved. If European experience is anything to go by, the establishment of even an imperfect democracy is likely to take much longer than ten years. Indeed, it has more usually been the case that progress proceeds in fits and starts over many decades. The reasons for this are also important. Politics is essentially a process of contestation between a wide variety of interests and groups each with their own agendas. Hence, in the Arab countries, there were inevitably going to be powerful forces which preferred monopoly to open competition, and control to criticism and public discussion, with outcomes heavily dependent on the balance of power between them at any particular time.

A second perspective opens up a consideration of the negative side of the equation, that is an examination of what might have happened but, in the event, did not. The drive towards a Middle Eastern peace settlement was not derailed by the serious attack it faced, first from Palestinian radicals and then, much more importantly, from Israel's Netanyahu government. Islamic militants were unsuccessful in their attempt to overthrow a number of individual Middle Eastern regimes. No Gulf ruling family made any moves to dissolve a consultative council once it had been put in place. And the transfer of power in Saudi Arabia, from Fahd to Abdullah, and in Jordan, from Hussein to his eldest son, was accomplished without serious difficulty. In every case, the local balance of forces was such as to protect the developments set in train at the beginning of the 1990s from serious disruption.

A third, and final, perspective involves a comparison between state/society relations at the beginning of the decade and at the end. Within this relatively short period of time most Arab regimes experimented with a somewhat less intrusive form of government permitting a greater degree of press freedom, providing more information about their own performance and seeking ways of keeping their opponents under control short of putting large numbers of them in prison. This, in turn, had something to do with the fact that each regime had, of necessity, to attend more seriously to questions of its own legitimacy. Lacking the resources either to enforce a general consensus or simply to buy support for themselves through the provision of universal welfare services, many regimes switched to an alternative form of justification based on their ability to represent the needs and aspirations of all their people. Then again, every serious effort at economic reform required the introduction of new systems of management and the creation of new sets of relations between groups inside the state apparatus and the local business community. And while much of this involved short-run alliances aimed at monopolising the sale of certain goods and services, the fact that all those concerned were forced to prepare for the progressive opening-up of the economy as required by international treaty meant that such alliances generally possessed a certain fluidity and an ability to change and to grow over time.

Meanwhile, turning to the social side of the equation, the growth of educational opportunity during the previous decades and the increasing access to information from sources other than that of the state provided resources which could be used to create new forms of political pressure and new forums for public debate. In these circumstances it was often human rights groups which emerged as the leading critics of individual regimes, using their foreign connections to publicise local abuses in ways which regimes found embarrassing but often difficult to control. Beyond that, the notions of private initiative and of communal self-help encouraged the formation of a large number of formal and informal associations which could be used to mobilise resources, to lobby for different causes and, in general, to provide a much thicker web of connections between social groups and the state apparatus.

Looked at from a combination of all three perspectives one tentative conclusion would be that most of the processes set in train in the Arab states and Iran during the 1990s were irreversible. Hence, while it would seem likely that, here or there, a single ruler or a single regime might try to take away concessions previously granted, or to close down this or that representative institution, the general trend towards more open governments interacting with more open societies seemed bound to continue. The same conclusion must also apply to Turkey and Israel, although with the obvious proviso that their initial degree of openness was generally much greater than that of their Arab neighbours. Another way of making the same point would be that the problems which Turkey and Israel now face – problems which combine specific local features with more general ones common to most of the world's democracies – will also be the ones which some of the more open Arab states will have to begin to face themselves in the first decades of the twenty-first century.

This is, however, just a provisional conclusion to which I will return after I have looked at many aspects of the subject in greater depth in Part II.

Notes

1 This point is forcefully argued by Amira Hass, *Drinking the Sea at Gaza: Days and Nights in a Land Under Seige* (New York: Metropolitan Books, 1999).

2 Gause characterises this as a 'petition fever'. See F. Gregory Gause III, *Oil Monarchies: Domestic and Security Challenges in the Arab Gulf States* (New York: Council on Foreign Relations, 1993), pp. 98–9.

3 For a useful collection of analyses of different aspects of the 1995 elections see Sandrine Gamblin (ed.), *Contours et détours du politique d'Egypte: Les élections législatives de 1995* (Cairo: Cedej and Paris: L'Harmattan, 1997).

4 Steve Negus, 'Lawyers locked out', *Middle East International*, 9 April 1999, p. 18.

5 See, for example, Kiren Aziz Chaudhuri, 'On the way to the market: Economic liberalization and Iraq's invasion of Kuwait', *Middle East Report*, 170 (May–June 1991), pp. 14–23.

6 For example, Faleh A. Jabar, Ahmad Shikara and Keiko Sakai, 'From storm to thunder: Unfinished showdown between Iraq and US', *IDEO Spot Survey* (Tokyo: Institute of Developing Economies, March 1998), pp. 27–8.

7 An English translation of this letter can be found in 'Word for word: Succession in Jordan', *New York Times*, 31 January 1999.

8 Quoted in Gregory White, 'The advent of electoral democracy in Morocco? The referendum of 1996', *Middle East Journal*, 51/3 (Summer, 1997), p. 396.

9 This is Gause's own calculation, *Oil Monarchies*, pp. 102–3.

10 R. Hrair Dekmejian, 'Saudi Arabia's Consultative Council', *Middle East Journal*, 52/2 (Spring, 1998), pp. 204–10; and Selim Jahel, 'Arabie Saoudite: le Majlis Al-Choura, un parlement selon la Charia', *Arabies* (May 1998), pp. 20–34.

11 For example, Abdullah Juma Al-Haj, 'The politics of participation in the Gulf Cooperation states: The Omani Consultative Council', *Middle East Journal*, 50/4 (Autumn, 1996), pp. 564–5.

12 Farzin Sarabi, 'The post-Khomeini era in Iran: the elections to the fourth Majlis', *Middle East Journal*, 48/1 (Winter, 1994), pp. 104–5.

13 This is the argument of Olivier Roy, 'Tensions in Iran: The future of the Islamic Revolution', *Middle East Report*, 28/2, 207 (Summer, 1998), p. 40.

14 The fact that many Iranians believe that the conservatives were trying to use Karbaschi to get back at Khatami is well illustrated by a newspaper cartoon circulated in Teheran following the mayor's arrest showing him in prison garb with, as his convict number, 2–3-1376, the date of Khatami's sweeping victory according to Iran's Islamic calendar. David Gardner, 'Mayor who made the mullahs see red', *The Financial Times*, 24 July 1998.

15 See, for example, his speech on the second anniversary of his own election as president, 23 May 1999 as reported by Saeed Barzin, 'Cracks in the reform camp', *Middle East International*, 4 June 1999, pp. 16–17.

16 I take this idea from Avishai Ehrlich, 'For land and God: Israel under Netanyahu', *Israel and Palestine*, 203 (n.d.: 1998?), pp. 10–12.

17 Figures from Gregory Mahlet, 'Israel's new electoral system: Effects on policy and politics', *MERIA Journal*, Center for Strategic Studies, Bar-Ilan University, Israel, no. 2 (June 1997); and Sammy Smooha and Don Peretz, 'Israel's 1996 elections: A second political earthquake', *Middle East Journal*, 50/4 (Autumn, 1996), p. 537.

18 This, in general, is the argument put forward by Avishai Margalit, 'Israel: Why Barak won', *New York Review of Books*, 21 August 1999, pp. 47–51.

19 For example, Michael M. Gunter, 'The silent coup: The secularist-Islamist struggle in Turkey', *Journal of South Asian and Middle Eastern Studies*, 21/3 (Spring, 1998), pp. 1–13.

20 Quoted by John Barham in 'Turkish ministers bow to the generals', *Financial Times*, 8 July 1998.

Part II

Themes in contemporary Middle Eastern politics

Introduction

In Part II, I examine some of the themes mentioned in Part I in greater detail. These are: the politics of economic restructuring; the practice of democracy and the evolution of single-party regimes; the impact of the contemporary religious revival (Christian and Jewish as well as Muslim); the changing role of the military; and, finally, the political practices of certain non-state actors such as NGOs (Non-governmental organisations), women's groups and members of populations seeking states of their own like the Palestinians. To do this I draw examples, where appropriate, from most of the Arab states as well as from Israel, Iran and Turkey. Where possible I also try to employ the notion of the state which sees it not as a single entity but as a collection of multiple institutions, practices and sites of contestation, all involved in different ways with the processes I describe.

As far as the time period is concerned, the main focus is on the post-Second World War decades, characterised, first, by the state-building projects undertaken by the newly independent regimes and, then, the challenges posed to them in the 1970s and 1980s. In almost all the countries of the Middle East, a period of enthusiasm for centralisation and planning was followed by a process of enforced readjustment, in which local wars, changes in the international economic climate, shortages of resources and social pressures from below all played an important role. In some cases this led to sharp ruptures in the political process as in the Lebanese civil war and the Iranian revolution or the Turkish military coup of 1980; in others it encouraged an almost equally stressful period in which the introduction of new economic and political strategies threatened to upset many of the previous relationships established between the different institutions of state as well as between the regimes and their people.

An important feature of this whole process was a kind of international demonstration effect in which, in an increasingly globalised world, many of the official changes in policy, as well as the language used to justify them, were heavily influenced by the various types of anti-statist ideologies emanating from Europe and North America, whether the western emphasis on liberalisation and the privatisation of state assets or the eastern ones of economic and political perestroika, glasnost and the end of single-party monopoly. Later, in the 1990s, the notion of globalisation itself began to play an increasingly powerful role, encouraging some groups and interests to embrace it as the only possible way ahead, while alarming others who saw it as a threat to their previous positions or ascendancy or, more generally, as a danger to their culture, religion and way of life. Indeed, the debate came quickly to be polarised between those identified as possible winners and losers. This, in turn, encouraged many regimes, for example the Egyptian, to put themselves into a position to control the pace of change in the interest of social harmony, pulling back those groups which were anxious to proceed too fast, chivvying along those which would have been happy with no change at all. To make matters more complex, the regime's own stance was itself under close scrutiny from international pressure groups concerned with such issues as human rights, the treatment of women and the proper protection of the environment.

All this was to have a profound effect not only on the state itself but throughout society, posing many questions but yielding few obvious answers. What was to be the new balance between the public and the private, the religious and the secular? How much popular participation should be allowed and what were most appropriate arrangements for ensuring it? Where did the military establishment fit in now that the prospect of more Arab–Israeli wars seemed much diminished? In the short run, at least, it was the regimes themselves which attempted to come up with the answers. But these were also regimes which were no longer quite as sure as they had once been of their own power to manage and to control, to shape and to define. Populations could no longer be treated as though they consisted of a single, state-defined, more or less homogeneous, identity. New institutions, with their own new institutional agendas, had to be created to fulfil promises made to international bodies like the new European Union (EU) or the World Trade Organisation (WTO) intent on creating a worldwide regime of good business practice. This left the regimes themselves with little alternative but to control what they could, to prevent debates that seemed to threaten social peace, but to give ground to international and domestic social forces if they must.

7 The politics of economic restructuring

Introduction

During the 1970s many economists began to comment on what they took to be a worldwide trend towards greater liberalisation, privatisation of public sector enterprise and what was often referred to as state 'shrinkage', that is, a deliberate attempt to reduce the proportion of national resources controlled by the state. Not surprisingly, these same phenomena also began to attract the attention of analysts of the Middle East. To begin with, most attention was focused on the Egyptian policy of *infitah* – variously translated as 'liberalisation' or 'opening-up' – announced by President Sadat in 1974. But similar signs soon began to be observed in other countries of the region as well, whether in the Likud bloc's call for deregulation and a reduction in the state's role in economic management in the 1977 Israeli electoral campaign, the structural adjustments inaugurated in Turkey by Turgut Ozal just before the military coup of 1980, or the orchestrated challenge to 'socialist' planning that developed in Algeria as soon as Chadli Benjadid succeeded Houari Boumedienne as president in 1978.

[handwritten margin note: Ozal changes structure beginning in 1980]

Given the fact that similar processes seemed to taking place all over the world outside the Communist bloc, it was natural that many of the explanations that then began to be put forward should either be couched in global terms or else draw heavily on models developed with respect to other regions. Examples of the first type would be those that assert the link between the world recession of the mid-1970s, increased international indebtedness and the policies contained in the economic stabilisation and structural adjustment packages demanded by the International Monetary Fund (IMF) and the World Bank as a quid pro quo for the loans necessary to meet the growing foreign exchange crisis in many parts of the non-European world. Among the many examples of the second type, certainly the most influential have been those which draw their inspiration from the Latin American writer Guillermo O'Donnell and his focus on the notion that such crises were more or less inevitable in countries which based their development strategies on inward-looking policies such as state-led import substituting industrialisation with its typical misallocation of resources and neglect of exports.[1] In a Middle Eastern context, two early works that draw heavily on both types of explanation are Caglar Keyder's *State and Class in Turkey* (1987) and John Waterbury's *The Egypt of Nasser and Sadat* (1983).

Nevertheless, approaches of this type are not without their problems. To begin with, there are usually quite considerable difficulties concerning the establishment of an exact chronology of events, and then in specifying the precise linkage between the world recession and its supposed impact on a particular economy. As far as the Middle East was concerned, the first signs of strain were to be observed in such countries as Egypt and Tunisia in the late 1960s at a time when the international economy was still in its last phase of rapid expansion. Later, the fact that so many Arab states continued to benefit, directly or indirectly, from the high price of oil throughout the 1970s and early 1980s meant that the constraints of indebtedness could be postponed much longer than, for example, in the case of their neighbours, Israel and Turkey. This is not to deny the existence of international links: they are a vital presence, not only in terms of real pressures and influences but also in the minds of all those policy-makers and polemicists whose borrowing from the policies and political vocabularies of other states are all part of a considerable international demonstration effect that helps to spread the influence of powerful ideas like privatisation and deregulation still further. However, it is obviously one thing to observe an Algerian minister in the late 1980s quoting Deng Xiaoping's well-known defence of a revived private sector in China along the lines of 'it doesn't matter what colour the cat is so long as it catches the mice' (i.e. engages in new investment), and quite another to demonstrate in detail how external factors affected the day-to-day politics of the long process of Algerian economic reform.[2]

A second set of problems concerns the whole notion of 'crisis' and of the relationship between its economic and political components. For the most part, what are usually referred to as 'crises' are not simply economic events, with obvious causes and effects, but highly managed political affairs, to be controlled and manipulated in ways that owe more to the balance of social forces within the country and the need either to maintain old coalitions or to build new ones, than to absolute necessities enforced by bankruptcy or the market. Looked at from this perspective, leaders have a fair degree of choice as to whether they justify new policies in terms of the bankruptcy of the old, as Sadat did in Egypt in the 1970s, or Iran's President Rafsanjani in 1991, or simply to adapt quietly to changed circumstances, like President Asad with his tentative introduction of a 'creeping' economic liberalisation in the late 1980s and early 1990s.[3]

What strikes the Middle Eastern observer is just how varied have been the attempts to change statist systems of economic management since the 1970s. Clearly the need for reform itself in no way dictates the type of policies subsequently pursued. Instead, the path actually pursued seems dependent on a whole variety of different variables. The most important would seem to be the seriousness of the initial crisis, and thus the strength of the pressures which could be brought to bear by the IMF, the World Bank and other international organisations in exchange for new loans, the strategic importance of the country concerned to the United States and its Arab allies, and the power of well-established vested interests anxious to preserve their own monopoly over local resources from serious challenge either by private sector or foreign rivals. Another factor of some significance was the size of the local economy, with the smaller ones more easily dominated by a limited number of local monopolies and so in much greater need of international trade and investment to open up their domestic markets to real competition.

In what follows I will begin by examining the situation in North Africa (including Egypt) which contains those Arab states whose trajectory most closely resembled that of other liberalising economies in Africa and Latin America. I will then look at the somewhat different situation that obtained in the other Arab countries much more heavily dependent on oil. Finally, I will turn to the three non-Arab states, Israel, Turkey and Iran, in each of which developments took another path again. However, in each case I will be guided by such central questions as the timing and pace of reform, the relationship between the economic and political interests at work and, increasingly, the impact of external factors, whether pressures from international organisations like the World Bank, the new World Trade Organisation (WTO) and regional groupings like the European Union, or the general influence of the powerful push towards globalisation that emerged in the 1990s.

The result of all such forces was a politics played out in many different institutional settings and at many different levels, the main impact of which can be found in a changing relationship between state and economy and state and society. Unfortunately, this latter development is not well-captured by the still dominant paradigm of 'retreat', except perhaps in instances such as the state's decreasing ability to impose a legal or ideological uniformity on its citizenry at large. Indeed, it will be the major argument of this chapter that what took place in the economic sphere is more accurately characterised as a process of re-regulation in which the state has been re-positioned the better to cope with the new international forces and to safeguard the positions of its major interest groups.

ve-regulation and re-positioning

Economic restructuring in North Africa, including Egypt

The phase of state-led planning based on rapid industrialisation, tight control over foreign capital and a huge extension of public ownership lasted about ten years in Egypt and Tunisia (roughly the decade of the 1960s) and the same amount of time in Algeria (roughly the decade of the 1970s). In each case the incoherence, and often sheer confusion, which marked its early stages were largely hidden by the emphasis on planning as an instrument of scientific management, as well as by the initial success in increasing production for the heavily protected local market. However, even then it was clear to a few that there had been no particular rationale behind the decision to take what was essentially a rag-bag of, mostly foreign-owned, firms into public ownership, nor behind the list of new industrial enterprises which the state was now committed to promote.[4] Later, other more serious problems were revealed, such as the severe economic distortions involved in the abandonment of market relations for a type of planning which paid little attention to cost and price. However, in every case, what provided the initial incentive towards a series of adjustments aimed at a partial opening up of the economies to foreign investment and foreign competition was a growing realisation that the policy of inward-looking development was incapable of generating the revenues required to pay for imports and to finance an ever-expanding welfare state.

The first regime to seek to reverse this process was the Tunisian, beginning in 1969, when the minister responsible for establishing an integrated system of 'socialist' economic management, Ahmed Ben Saleh, was abruptly sacked and a new strategy of more decentralised management introduced. But this was soon overshadowed by the more dramatic change of direction signalled in President Sadat's 'October' working paper of April 1974 with its call for a process of *infitah*, liberalisation, aimed at increasing the efficiency of the Egyptian public sector, revitalising the private sector and encouraging foreign investment particularly from the increasingly wealthy Gulf oil states. Algeria's introduction of a shift in economic direction came a few years later in 1978/9 following the sudden death of President Boumedienne. New policies were immediately unveiled by his successor, Chadli Benjadid, during the discussions leading up to the publication of the next five-year plan, 1980–4, which contained strong criticism of the previous emphasis on heavy industry run by large, inefficient, public sector organisations, calling instead for administrative decentralisation, greater attention to light industry and special encouragement to the private sector.

In spite of their dramatic start, the policies of liberalisation and decentralisation in the public sector developed quite slowly in North Africa. For one thing, the second oil boom of the late 1970s provided enough new finance to blunt some of the pressure from both international and domestic indebtedness. For another, some of the early attempts to reduce food subsidies, and so to raise the price of basic necessities for the bulk of the population, led to such severe riots and disturbances – in Egypt in 1977 and Tunisia in 1984 – as to force regimes to put a temporary halt to the process while providing useful political ammunition to all those who had opposed the reforms in the first place. The fact that the early stages of liberalisation had also led to a growth in unemployment and an increased polarisation of income between rich and poor seemed to provide further evidence of the dangers of proceeding too fast. Much the same situation also occurred in Morocco where an agreement with the World Bank and the IMF led immediately to cuts in subsidies, price rises and the riots of January 1984.

Nevertheless, all three states were pressured into seeking help from the IMF, the World Bank and their international creditors from 1986 onwards following the sharp fall in the price of oil and the subsequent rise in their domestic and international debt. This, in turn, forced them to commit themselves to a return to their earlier policies of economic reform. In Tunisia this took the form of a renewed commitment to the removal of barriers to trade and investment. In

Egypt it involved a standby agreement with the IMF in 1987 in which a series of loans was offered in exchange for an Egyptian promise to meet a set of agreed monetary targets. And in Morocco it led, among other things, to a strong commitment to public sector privatisation in 1989. But certainly the most dramatic change in direction took place in Algeria at the end of the 1980s after several years of forced austerity and falling living standards had led to the widespread riots of October 1988. President Chadli's immediate response was the introduction of policies aimed not only at renewed economic reform but also a complete restructuring of the country's political system as well (see Chapter 8).

Pressure for economic reform intensified after the Gulf War. In Egypt, the regime was quick to seize the opportunity to obtain much-needed debt relief in return for its military and diplomatic support for the Allied attack on Iraq. This involved the strongest commitment to a thoroughgoing structural adjustment yet made, including the announcement of a list of over 300 public companies which were to be put up for sale. It also led, over time, to major cuts in subsidies, the introduction of a new tax system, the revival of the stock exchange, and laws freeing urban property, and then agricultural land, from the systems of rent control enforced during the Nasser period: 'a revolution to end the revolution' as *The Economist* correctly described it.[5] Elsewhere, in Tunisia and Morocco, economic reform was given much greater urgency, partly under pressure from the IMF and the World Bank, partly from the European Union, with both countries signing industrial free trade agreements committing them to reduce tariff barriers over a twelve-year period. Only in Algeria was the process derailed for a while by the military intervention in early 1992 and the subsequent bloody struggle between religious militants and the security forces which wrought great destruction while making it much more difficult to attract international investment outside the highly protected oil and gas sector. Nevertheless, even here the regime submitted itself to a four-year IMF programme, 1994–8, in which it exchanged a promise of better budget discipline for help with access to the international capital market.

At the end of the 1990s the process of economic reform had been going on in North Africa for a sufficiently long period to allow some tentative conclusions about the political dimensions of the whole process. To begin with, it is important to observe that structural adjustment and the liberalisation of the economy is not a single event, as it has sometimes been portrayed, but an on-going process with no obvious end in sight. This can be seen very clearly as far as privatisation is concerned, where, in spite of the considerable efforts involved, the difficulties and resistances were much more challenging than originally imagined. In Egypt, as of 1997, only 80 of the 314 public companies originally slated for public sale had either been sold, wholly or in part, or else put into liquidation.[6] In Morocco, as of 1998, the number was 52 out of the promised 112 enterprises and hotels.[7] As experience in Britain and elsewhere has shown, there are complex technical problems involved in preparing state-owned companies for sale, including the need to reduce work forces, clear unsold inventories and settle their often huge debts. These problems are then greatly magnified in countries like those of North Africa with weak capital markets, limited social security payments for the unemployed and the fact that the public sector had never been particularly well managed in the first place. Governments have been forced to be very creative in finding ways of selling off public enterprises, wholly or in part, to a variety of different combinations of investors, both foreign and domestic. They have also had to develop new methods for insulating the poor from the shock of enforced layoffs by the provision of early retirement packages or workers' share-ownership schemes.

A second important example of the open-ended nature of the structural adjustment process is provided by the fact that all the countries concerned made long-term commitments ether to the Uruguay Round organised by the GATT or its successor, the WTO, as well as, in the case of Tunisia and Morocco, to the EU. Many of these involve a staged process of tariff reductions, the opening up of local markets for services like banking and insurance, and the creation of new regulatory regimes for business. Inevitably the consequences of such promises are difficult to predict in advance, even though it was generally clear that, if implemented to the full, they would create a completely new climate for the conduct of economic business.

All this makes analysis difficult not only for the academic observer but, much more important, for the local actors themselves when it comes to the best ways to position themselves to meet the new opportunities ahead, to defend themselves against future foreign competition or to lobby for new policies designed to protect and enhance their own particular interests. One thing they lack is a generally accepted analytical framework with which to discuss the impact of economic liberalisation in general. For want of anything better this usually means recourse to a very imprecise, and highly politicised, notion of 'globalisation', conventionally interpreted as a threat to national security and to social peace and so a useful argument for those concerned about the possible purchase of state enterprises by foreign investors or the passage of particular laws thought harmful to local business.[8] The resulting polemics give a misleading simplicity to the debate in which the exponents of openness and speed are seen as pitted against those of protection and the defence of existing vested interests. However, it is also a natural expression of a situation in which, on the one hand, the private sector is still not strong enough to challenge the government on major issues while, on the other, the problems ahead are so large and varied that only an alliance with state power itself seems a reliable guarantee by business interests fearful of being overwhelmed by predatory forces coming from the international economy.

It has also not gone unnoticed that governments still retain enormous powers of choice when it comes to the disposition of public assets, the introduction of new regulatory mechanisms, or the types of competition policy they are prepared to enforce. Nevertheless, given the growing complexities of managing a more open economy, as well as of governments' increased reliance on private investment, businessmen with ties to the regime began to find that their advice was not only asked for but being taken seriously into consideration when new policy was being made. Egypt, where at least 45 persons from business were elected as official NDP candidates to the People's Assembly in 1995, is a good case in point.[9] Meanwhile, the growing political influence of business interests also encouraged strategic alliances between public officials and private entrepreneurs, many of which can be accused of fostering corrupt practices, even though the legal definitions of just what constitutes wrong-doing across the public/private divide is usually not clearly stated and even less clearly enforced. A final factor was the weakness of the official trade unions which, even where they were called upon to negotiate new labour laws, often lacked the authority to ensure the support of their own members, forcing many workers to fend for themselves against the growing power of local entrepreneurs.[10]

blurry lines btwn sectors

weak trade unions

Beyond this, among governments as well as public opinion at large, there was also a lively debate about the nature of some of the other basic changes which the restructuring of the economy seemed to require. At one level this concerned the vital question of the relationship between economic and political liberalisation, with the regimes themselves tending to argue that the former might easily be put in danger by too much of the latter, a position which some attempted to reinforce by appeals to the Asian model, at least before the Asian crisis of 1998. Such arguments tended to commend themselves to North African rulers facing the possibility that the inevitable economic discontent among the unemployed and many sections of the poorer classes could be more easily exploited by religious militants if they were given any opportunity to form legal political organisations. They also commended themselves to many of their relatives, supporters and cronies as a way of exploiting the advantages of what, in Egypt and Tunisia, still remained virtually one-party regimes. Such arguments tended also to contain a self-reinforcing element in that, the more the state encouraged corruption and cronyism, the more there was to criticise and therefore the more necessary it was to try to contain such criticism by tougher press laws and tighter control over professional associations. At other levels, there was an obvious concern with the need to upgrade existing plants, to produce more technologically-qualified graduates and to ensure that, in the shift from public to private employment, the number of opportunities open to women should not be drastically reduced.

vicious cycle

The limits of oil wealth: encouraging private profit in Syria, Iraq and Jordan

Syria

In Syria it was the 1960s which witnessed the first major acts of nationalisation and the establishment of state control over much of the economy. This trend was then arrested shortly after President Hafiz al-Asad's seizure of sole power in 1970, when the new ruler attempted to consolidate his position by loosening important restrictions, permitting freer trade and encouraging some of the richer Syrians who had fled the country to return to invest their money at home. The major political gain from this early version of *infitah* was the way that it could be used to forge an alliance between the Alawi-dominated regime and the well-established Sunni merchants of Damascus. This was cemented still further during the economic boom which followed the 1973 Middle East war when certain parts of the Syrian economy, for example much of the service sector, were opened up to both western and Arab capital. The result was ten years of rapid economic growth, sustained until well into the early 1980s by Syria's own oil revenues and the much larger sums which President Asad was able to obtain from Saudi Arabia, Libya and Kuwait.

Raymond Hinnebusch has argued that, had it not been for the increase in authoritarian control needed to contain the severe challenge posed by the Muslim Brothers in the late 1970s and early 1980s, the trend towards economic liberalisation might have been allowed to deepen and to intensify.[11] However, his position is somewhat undermined by his counter-argument that the early Asad years also saw a developing interest between public sector managers, trade unionists, Ba'th party officials and local businessmen which underpinned a statist approach to economic management while preventing any move which might threaten their privileged position.[12] One result of this situation was the emergence of a system of officially tolerated corruption in which public sector managers and private entrepreneurs were able to come together to manipulate the economy for their own profit.[13] And while this gave President Asad the great political advantage of being able to reward loyal supporters and to act as a mediator between competing economic cliques, it also led to serious allegations of financial wrongdoing which helped to fan the flames of the popular discontent which burst out in the late 1970s. Furthermore, it acted to inhibit the creation of the coherent strategy necessary to allow Syria to diversify its economy and so to be able to pay its large military bills out of its own resources. That the economy managed to progress at all during the 1980s was largely due to the fact that the country's stance as the main opponent of Israel and the most direct supporter of the Palestinian guerrillas allowed Asad to continue to obtain large annual subsidies from the oil-rich states.

Over time, however, the persistence of domestic economic difficulties, combined with a reduction in Arab aid and the loss of Syria's captive Russian and East European markets after 1989, began to force the regime into what Hinnebusch has called a 'creeping economic liberalization'.[14] This began when the austerity measures introduced in 1987 were followed by attempts to get private capitalists to carry more of the burden of investment and of the expansion of local exports. Some did it voluntarily, seizing on opportunities to make new alliances with international companies. Others were forced into seeking new business opportunities as their contracts with cash-strapped state enterprises began to decline.[15] The culmination of this process was the passage of Syrian Law 10 of 1991 making it easier for foreign and domestic capital to invest in a wider range of local activities. The result was another period of high growth during the early 1990s, helped, as in Egypt, by a renewal of subsidies from the Gulf states anxious to reward Asad for his pro-Allied Gulf War stance.

What the process of economic opening did not lead to was a simultaneous opening up of the political system. Indeed, President Asad remained resolutely unwilling even to use the word 'liberalisation' at all lest it should excite the kinds of popular expectations which, in his estimation at least, had forced other authoritarian rulers like President Ceaușescu of Romania so precipitately from office.[16] He also seems to have been anxious not to reduce his state of military preparedness *vis-à-vis* Israel nor harm the alliance of forces, both inside the state and outside, which had sustained him in power for so long. Only the economy was allowed to experience a 'selective liberalisation' leading to a slight shift in the balance between the private sector and well-entrenched vested interests designed more to expand the president's own support base than to allow any greater freedom of political manoeuvre to non-state actors.[17]

Iraq

The re-emergence of an Iraqi private sector followed quite a different trajectory. What little private capital that existed was largely obliterated by the nationalisations of the 1960s, so that the new ventures which were allowed to establish themselves in the 1970s were largely the creation of the Ba'thi regime itself, anxious to prevent too much of the oil wealth passing into the hands of the foreign contractors employed on the huge public works schemes which the oil revenues allowed. The main beneficiary proved to be the local construction sector where the hand of the government can be clearly seen in the fact that most of the new firms owed their existence to public loans. Regime favouritism can also be seen in the way in which, according to Issam al-Khafagi, at least half the large enterprises which dominated the sector were owned by families from Takrit and al-Anbar, the original home of Saddam Hussein and many of his close supporters.[18]

A second period of encouraging private economic activity followed in the 1980s, stimulated largely by the shortages of food and other necessities during the long war with Iran. This was started in the agricultural sector where a law of 1983 permitted groups and individuals to rent state land for their own profit, a practice that had been outlawed from some years.[19] It was then extended to other sectors, with a particular boost in 1987 from the introduction of a reform programme involving the sale of certain state-owned enterprises, and the grant of greater autonomy to others, in the hope of increasing their efficiency and so reducing the losses which were imposing such a great drain on the central budget. This was followed, in 1988, by the actual privatisation of various public enterprises including factories and hotels, as well as by the creation of a new state bank, the Rashid, to provide competition for the long-established Rafidain which had previously exercised a complete monopoly over all major financial transactions.

As elsewhere, even such limited reforms met with resistance from inside the public sector itself, a development attested to by President Hussein himself in a number of speeches in which he called for a relaxation of party control over the government and economy in terms which seem to have been deliberately reminiscent of those employed by the supporters of perestroika in the Soviet Union. One example is his ringing assertion in 1987 that 'if there had been no private sector in Iraq it would have been the duty of the leadership to create it' and that 'our brand of socialism cannot live without the private sector whether now or after the war'.[20] No doubt much of this had to do with an attempt to spread some of the costs of the much-needed post-war reconstruction and investment towards those privileged entrepreneurs who had made huge fortunes during the war with Iran itself. But whether this, in itself, would eventually have led to much more than a selective liberalisation of the Syrian variety remains doubtful.[21]

[handwritten margin note: Spread costs of war w/Iran to pvt enterprise)]

In the event, all such conjectures were made redundant by the wholly new situation brought about by Iraq's invasion of Kuwait and the huge destruction wrought to its own economy which followed. What happened instead was a return to such small-scale private activity as was possible under the strict regime of international economic sanctions, a development often promoted by the government itself in its desperate need to maximise whatever local resources could be found. Meanwhile, in the Kurdish 'safe haven' established in northern Iraq in April 1991, the absence of organised state power meant that there could only be private economic activity, much of it heavily taxed by the two main military groups for whom it was their only major source of revenue.

Jordan

Jordan's experience was different again. Although, in theory, the most open of the three Arab economies under discussion, the role of the state remained powerful even after a decade of self-proclaimed liberalisation. And this in spite of the fact that, since 1988, the government worked closely with the IMF to promote a programme, first of the stabilisation needed to bring its run-away debt under control, then of limited structural adjustment aimed at the elimination of subsidies and other market distortions. Such policies were sufficient to provoke serious public disturbances in 1989 and 1996, but no change in the government's basic economic stance. For all this, Jordan had only made modest moves in the direction of privatisation by the late 1990s, a process perhaps best exemplified by the wholly transparent expedient of changing the status of a number of state-owned enterprises into public share-holding companies. Such slow progress is generally explained in terms of the opposition of vested interests and government bureaucrats worried about a loss of power and control.[22] However, it can also be attributed to the particular problems present in a small country with only a narrow local market in which there are legitimate fears that privatisation will lead to a loss of the government's ability to protect local enterprise from fierce foreign competition, particularly from Israel with whom Jordan signed a trade pact in 1995.

Limited movement in the Gulf

The moves towards more open economies in the Gulf states were bound to be different from those implemented elsewhere. From the beginning of the oil era, the ruling families' control had been based on their near monopoly of oil revenues and their ability to distribute these revenues so as to assure maximum public support. In such circumstances, few taxes were necessary and the main flow of funds was from government to population via subsidised food and energy and the provision of free services such as health and education. Many writers now make the point that this was the reverse of the situation which obtained in Europe and North America where there was a historical link between taxation and representation. In the Gulf, they claim, the fact that there was no taxation limited demands for popular representation in government by making them more or less redundant.[23] The rulers' other main service to their citizens was to protect them from foreign competition by a host of rules designed to ensure that local business was able to obtain a large share of the oil-related profits.

Pressure to change the system only became significant in the late 1980s when falling oil prices and the need to maintain high levels of military spending meant that ruling family governments no longer had the resources to maintain a full range of subsidised services or to provide the level of investment which both the oil and the non-oil sectors required. This encouraged tentative attempts to reduce the level of subsidies in the 1990s coupled with renewed efforts to promote greater private sector activity both in terms of business expansion and of the provision of new jobs for the growing numbers of unemployed graduates. In addition, there were even more tentative moves towards privatisation and improving conditions for the foreign investors whose money and technical expertise was needed to upgrade parts of the oil industry and to assist with the extremely capital-intensive business of developing the huge deposits of natural gas to be found in such states as Qatar and Saudi Arabia.

Progress was slow in all areas. By the end of the 1990s some government subsidies had been reduced or entirely removed, public officials were more willing to share information with private businesses, and banking systems were being regularised and encouraged to lend more to local clients. However, for all the talk, no substantial attempt had yet been made to privatise public sector enterprises with only a small start in Kuwait where shares in a number of public companies had been put up for sale. There was slow progress too towards the proposed common external tariff for the countries of the Gulf Cooperation Council (GCC). Although all states remained committed to the target date of 2001, there were difficult structural problems to overcome due to the fact that some relied much more heavily on protective duties than others.

The reasons for this are not difficult to discern. On the one hand, governments were worried about stirring up popular discontent in the highly-charged atmosphere following the Gulf War. On the other, there was a fear of the loss of control expressed at various levels of the royal family and the bureaucratic and business elite. There were public sector and private monopolies to protect. There were concerns about the presence of too many foreign businessmen in sensitive areas of the economy, and an even more general worry that the price to pay for a more vibrant private sector would be greater outside participation and a need for the laws and regulatory mechanisms necessary to ensure international standards of transparency and accountability. Nevertheless, falling revenues and the usual set of commitments made by those Gulf states which had either become members of the WTO or were still seeking admission, ensured that some movement was unavoidable in the short run, with the promise of much faster progress in the decades to come. This, in itself, was enough to promote a lively, if still secretive, form of political activity by a variety of different interest groups attempting either to protect existing positions or to take advantage of the anticipated opportunities to come.

Turkey, Israel and Iran

Turkey

During the 1980s, Turkey was often presented as one of the most successful examples of a highly protected, inward-oriented, economy that, under pressure from a severe balance of payments crisis in the 1970s had launched a sweeping, IMF-supported, programme of structural adjustment and economic liberalisation. Major emphasis was placed on the encouragement of exports which increased three times in value between 1980 and 1987, producing a continuous surplus on the country's balance of trade. This was accompanied by efforts to stimulate private foreign investment and the removal of government control over most agricultural prices. Later, however, Turkey's performance began to be seen in a somewhat less favourable light due to the persistence of high levels of inflation, the continued losses made by many of its major state-owned enterprises and its extremely hesitant progress in the area of privatisation.

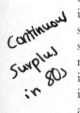

The political context in which these developments took place embraced three quite distinct periods: that of the stalemate between the parties and the high levels of political violence in the late 1970s, the three years of military intervention, 1980–83, and the return to a reformed democracy thereafter. A central figure in all three periods was Turgut Özal who, as president of the State Planning Commission (and a former member of the staff of the World Bank) was largely responsible for the introduction of the programme of economic stabilisation and restructuring in 1979, a programme he continued to manage, first as deputy prime minister under the military government, then as prime minister from 1983 to 1989, and president until his death in 1993. Specific international factors were also important, notably the renewed support of the United States under President Reagan, which saw Turkey as a valuable strategic partner in the struggle to contain the impact of the Iranian revolution.

An essential feature of the 1979 World Bank package was a return to creditworthiness by means of control over government expenditure, and a new emphasis on exports rather than import-substituting industrialisation to be encouraged by deregulation and other measures designed to force Turkish

industry to meet the challenge of international competition. How this programme would have fared without the military intervention is impossible to say.
But given that the generals were determined, for their own political reasons, to
destroy the power of the unions, Turkey's modern industrial sector was well
placed to keep its costs down while it sought to take advantage of the favourable
Middle Eastern market conditions produced by the second oil boom and the
outbreak of the Iran/Iraq war. This advantage continued well into the 1980s,
supported after 1983 by the tight constraints imposed on working-class activism
in the new 1982 constitution and the governments led by Turgut Ozal which
were willing to provide exporters with special loans and guarantees.

The introduction of the programme of economic restructuring, followed so
closely by the military intervention, also had important consequences for the
balance between Turkey's major economic interest groups.[24] Prior to 1979 the
Turkish economy was dominated by a group of state enterprises and large family
companies operating within a highly protected, highly regulated, domestic
market. This provided a context in which the competing political parties could
use access to different areas of the state sector to build up clienteles and to
reward their supporters by giving them jobs or by permitting private entrepreneurs to invest in selected industries for which they received licences and
subsidies. Parties in government found the money for this expensive exercise
either from foreign aid or, when this came to an end in the mid-1970s, from
deficit financing. Another feature of the economy in the 1970s was the division
of both the employers and the workers into often competing organisations. It was
these divisions which prevented any sustained attempt by the two sides to
negotiate their own relationship, independent of government intervention.

The military intervention changed this pattern of interest representation in
two important ways. First, all collective bargaining was suspended and three of
the four trade union confederations closed down. Unionism was dealt a further
blow by the military government's Trade Unions and Collective Agreements
Law, with its introduction of a cumbersome process of collective bargaining
which placed many restrictions on the right to strike. Second, the military's
strenuous efforts to transform the political system involved a conscious –
although only briefly successful – attempt to break the link between the parties
and economic interest groups by outlawing any direct subvention of the former
by the latter.

The new pattern of interest representation that emerged after the military
coup has been analysed by Ilkay Sunar in terms of the renewed fragmentation of
employers' groups and the continued weakness of the highly regulated unions.[25]
As he saw it, the former were briefly united in their liking for the military's
repression of working-class activism before dividing again along familiar lines,
with those in the modern sector benefiting from the Ozal government's policy of
export promotion, and the small- and medium-size manufacturers disturbed by
such obvious political favouritism and worried about their ability to protect their
position in the local market. As for organised labour, this had now come to be
dominated by Turk-Is, the one large union to survive the military period due to

its role as the representative of state sector employees. Nevertheless, in spite of the fact that its members faced a situation of rising unemployment and falling real wages for much of the 1980s, its leadership remained quite passive. As a result labour opposition to the restructuring remained largely ineffectual until it began to obtain support from the revived social democratic and left parties in the early 1990s.

With the decline in the dominating influence of Turgut Ozal ushered in by the defeat of his Motherland Party in the October 1991 elections, the divisions within Turkish society began to reproduce themselves much more strongly at the political level. There were now two right-wing parties, a fragmented left and a growing challenge from the Refah Party with its heavy support from small businesses which felt at a disadvantage in an increasingly open economy dominated by much larger and more favoured enterprises. Such divisions are often used to explain the problems faced by economic reformers in the 1990s and their inability either to contain inflation or to press on purposefully with privatisation in spite of the obvious challenge posed to Turkish business by Turkey's entry into a Customs Union with the EU in 1996. Given the frequent changes of government and the fierce competition for votes, it proved difficult to sustain any coalition capable of producing more than minimal reform. Increased military intervention in the political arena made the problem even worse.

The struggle over privatisation was waged with particular intensity in spite of laws passed by the Ozal government from 1984 designed to provide a legal framework for such a process. Opponents could be found at both ends of the political spectrum with the parties of the right unwilling to surrender an important source of patronage and those on the left, pushed on by the unions, worried about its impact on income distribution and jobs. Proof came, if proof was needed, when the sale of the various state-owned cement works, beginning in 1989, led to a substantial reduction in employees accompanied by an increase in the use of subcontractors.[26] One of the main weapons in the hand of those opposed to privatisation was the constitutional ban on the sale of strategic enterprises to foreigners, a relic of the Ataturk regime's determination to protect Turkish economic independence by refusing more foreign concessions. This was used to brand a 1994 privatisation law as unconstitutional and it was only in 1998 that the matter was finally settled and sales of parts of the state-controlled energy sector were finally allowed to go ahead.

Israel

The Israeli process of structural adjustment was similarly long drawn out and for much the same reasons as in Turkey. In Israel too the power of vested interests to obstruct change was further accentuated by the unwillingness of the major parties to give up such a valuable source of patronage and by a series of weak coalition governments in the late 1980s and early 1990s with insufficient parliamentary power to push programmes through. Beginning with the Likud election victory of 1977, tentative attempts were made to deregulate parts of the economy including the banking system. However, for a number of years these were entirely overshadowed by the pressing need to control a rapid increase in inflation brought on, in part, by the continuous temptation to politicians to win support by increases in spending on the social services. This process reached its peak with the hyper-inflation of 1984/5 which was only brought under control by a drastic deflation engineered by the cabinet of national unity formed after the 1984 elections. The economic stabilisation programme then put in place was very similar to ones previously adopted in Argentina, Bolivia and Brazil and involved a wage and price freeze, a devaluation, and a large cut in government expenditure. But, unlike Latin America, where such plans tended to achieve only a temporary and partial success, rises in Israeli prices were soon reduced to a more manageable 20 per cent a year, with little increase in unemployment and even a limited resumption of growth.[27]

Successful stabilisation was not, however, accompanied by any sustained effort to alter the basic structure of the economy and, in the course of the next few years, wage rates and unemployment began to rise again, while the government continued to prop up unprofitable firms. The result was a second stabilisation programme introduced in 1989 and engineered by Shimon Peres, the minister of finance in the Labour/Likud coalition government, which combined yet another devaluation – aimed at encouraging exports – with an enforced reduction in real wages. Histadrut agreement to the programme on behalf of its union members was the price it had to pay for further government support for several of its ailing enterprises such as Koor and Sol Boneh, as well as its health insurance fund, and many of its associated agricultural *kibbutzim* and *moshavim*.[28]

The late 1980s also saw the beginnings of a process of cutting subsidies to industry, refusing to bail out failing companies and, most spectacularly of all, the national unity government's willingness to summon up the courage to win a showdown with the country's largest defence contractor over the cabinet's decision not to allow it to go ahead with the manufacture of the enormously expensive Lavi fighter. The process was further intensified after the Gulf War and the moves towards a negotiated settlement with the Palestinians. This encouraged progressive cuts in the military budget, a substantial downsizing of the defence industry and then a progressive dismantling of the system of regulations, subsidies and other barriers which were protecting Israeli companies from foreign competition.

As always, privatisation proved the hardest nut to crack, given the difficulties in raising enough capital from domestic sources for the necessary buy-outs coupled with pressures to keep key strategic industries in Israeli hands. However, the break up, and then sale of, the Koor conglomerate in the early 1990s not only helped to reduce the power of union opposition but also paved the way for a number of other big sell-offs by the Netanyahu government which came to power in 1996. These included the government stake in Israeli Chemicals, substantial shares in the four government-owned banks and a minority holding in Bezeq, the giant telecommunications monopoly. What was also new was that most of these sales were conducted privately, rather than as a result of a public auction or issue of shares, and led to a transfer of ownership to members of Israel's own prominent business families. This, in turn, raised the question of how much had really changed. Critics pointed out that not only had the prime minister and his senior advisers been able to retain an enormous discretion as to how and to whom public companies were to be sold, but that there was also much the same degree of monopoly and concentration as before, although under new ownership.[29]

Iran

Finally, we come to the Iranian economy which underwent yet another type of restructuring as a result of the 1979 revolution. Prior to this, the shah's regime, for all its ideological commitment to public enterprise, had used its increasing oil wealth to support a growing public sector. From the 1960s the state had begun to invest heavily in industrial projects which were too large for private business groups to fund by themselves. It also created public monopolies in certain parts of the financial, transport and utilities sectors. This was far more significant than the few half-hearted attempts at the privatisation of state enterprises initiated for largely ideological reasons during the 'White Revolution' of 1963, and then again in the mid-1970s. Nevertheless, the private sector also expanded very rapidly on its own even though it was heavily dependent on the state for licences, subsidies and protection.

A major change took place in this pattern during the first years of the Islamic Republic with the widespread nationalisation of most of the large private factories and mines as well the banks and many other types of business enterprise. The reasons were various and included the expropriation of the property belonging to most of the old industrial and financial elite, the flight of foreign technicians and the threat of economic collapse. As Shaul Bakhash relates, those in control of the Revolutionary Council stepped in to fill the vacuum which their own attack on the shah's entourage had itself created. The result was a series of laws beginning in summer 1979, including one nationalising the banking system and another which promoted a state take-over of most of the country's larger manufactories.[30] Justification was provided by appeal to the revolutionary demand for economic and social justice. As stated in Principle 44 of the Revolution's 1979 constitution, the private sector should 'supplement' the activities of the state and co-operative sectors, while Principle 47 asserts that private property is to be 'honoured' only if obtained by 'legitimate means'. [31]

Nationalisations continued in a more sporadic fashion until 1982 and then stopped. There would seem to have been two main reasons. One was that, with the country now at war with Iraq, a number of senior government officials had come to realise that the state itself was going to have considerable difficulty managing its huge collection of assorted economic enterprises with any degree of efficiency. Thinking of this type culminated in the Ayatollah Khomeini's eight-point decree of December 1982 with its emphasis on the need to respect individual rights and property. Indeed, from 1983 onwards, a few of the nationalised enterprises were even returned to their former owners; although this process was often held in check by the need to find jobs for some of the revolution's own vast army of poorer supporters. By 1986, over 90 per cent of those working in the larger factories were employed in enterprises owned and managed either by the government or official revolutionary organisations (known as the *bonyad*) like the Foundation of the Deprived.[32]

The second reason for the halt to further nationalisation was the emergence of the Council of Guardians as a major defender of private property rights and of the freedom to engage in private economic activity. This was a development of great significance as it blocked almost all the schemes for the redistribution of wealth present in the Majles and elsewhere. Nevertheless, it is also important to note that the political and ideological struggle which it engendered did not affect those nationalisations which had already taken place, and referred more directly to the much more theologically sensitive issues of the ownership of urban and agricultural property and of freedom of trade. It was here, where the rights of private ownership and commercial activity was most clearly stated in the primary rulings to be found in the *sharia*, that the conservative forces represented in the Council of Guardians could most easily make their stand.

In a 1984 speech, Ali Hashemi Rafsanjani, the speaker of the Majles (and later president), identified two basic factions within the Iranian revolutionary regime as far as the economy was concerned: one that supported the 'nationalisation of most industries', the other the 'private sector'.[33] Once both factions had stabilised their positions after 1982, each was able to achieve significant victories while neither was able to obtain the upper hand. If the conservatives could not reverse most of the early nationalisations nor prevent the state from exercising a powerful influence over the economy by means of its control over prices, credit and trade, the radicals were prevented from producing a five-year plan which would have necessitated re-renewed access to foreign loans. Nor were they able to use the narrow majority in the Majles to press on with any further redistribution of income. Meanwhile, the middle ground between the two factions was occupied by a variety of interest groups, like the Teheran Society of the Bazaars and Guilds or the Chamber of Commerce, Industry and Mines, all trying to obtain the Ayatollah Khomeini's ear and to provide their own definition of where the still fluid boundary between public and private economic activity should run.

It took the end of the war with Iraq, the death of the Ayatollah and the election of Rafsanjani as president in 1989 to create the necessary consensus that urgent steps were needed to arrest the continued deterioration of the economy which had led to a halving of per capita income during the revolution's first decade. The capstone of this new policy was the five-year plan for post-war reconstruction, long subject to fierce debate, and finally passed by the Majles in January 1990. This provided the framework for a programme of structural adjustment and economic liberalisation to be promoted by the encouragement of private enterprise, the freeing of restrictions on trade, the phased reduction of subsidies and the sale of many of the non-strategic manufacturing, service and commercial enterprises owned by the state.

Nevertheless, major stumbling blocks remained. For one thing, the plan required a significant injection of foreign capital and, although the Majles finally agreed to permit some limited borrowing from abroad, many senior politicians remained wary of making any concessions to western interests. Their position then received some further justification from the fact that, far from receiving any reward for its neutrality during the Allied attack on Iraq, the country remained subject to economic isolation by the United States and some of its European partners. For another, the regime's attempt to put an end to the significant price distortions that had emerged during the 1980s by unifying the exchange rate in March 1993 had soon to be reversed as a result of a huge drop in the official value of the Iranian riyal.[34] This had the further effect of blunting attempts to limit the privileged position enjoyed by a number of powerful revolutionary organisations which were able to finance much of their activities by obtaining foreign currency at an extremely favourable rate and then either exchanging it for cheap riyals or using it to import foreign goods for resale to local merchants, all at an enormous profit.

What made the whole problem worse was the fact that, for a variety of reasons, including the difficulty of obtaining western financial and technological support, the economy continued to falter, thus providing more ammunition for the regime's still powerful critics in their stubborn defence of the economic status quo. This produced a situation in which successive presidents, Rafsanjani and then the popular Mohammad Khatami who succeeded him in 1997, were unable to produce policies designed either to address the country's growing economic difficulties or to point the way ahead. A very good example is provided by Khatami's own long-awaited economic reform package which he announced at the beginning of his second year in office in August 1998 in which he balanced his call for making it easier for foreign investment by a pledge to retain government subsidies on basic commodities as well as, more generally, to place the need for social justice above that of economic growth. This unwillingness to take a strong line was immediately interpreted as an unsatisfactory compromise between the ideas put forward by his two rival sets of advisers.[35]

Conclusion

The great diversity of the Middle East's experience of economic liberalisation makes generalisation difficult. Nevertheless, given the fact that some form of economic restructuring was attempted throughout the region, and often for the same reasons, there are several common features worth highlighting. First, policies aimed at affecting the basic structure of an economy are highly political events and cannot easily be isolated from their more general context. This is true whether or not they are accompanied by any parallel attempt at greater political liberalisation. What does make a difference, though, is that where political developments lag behind it is much more difficult to identify a single direction of change and so to argue, as many try, that progress in the economic and political spheres will be mutually reinforcing. Such is the situation in all the Arab countries and Iran where the reforms are aimed more at shoring up the position of the current regimes than creating a wholly new relationship between state, society and the economy.

A second point concerns the larger international context. Here developments in the Middle East can be seen to echo some of the political discussions set in train in the United States and western Europe in the 1980s and eastern Europe, and in the former Soviet Union in the 1990s, with their spirited debate about just what the state should or should not do as far as its control and management of the economy is concerned. After a period marked by the highly ideological interventions associated with the Reagan administration in the United States and the Thatcher government in Britain, the 1990s saw a more balanced attempt to identify what the state does most efficiently and what it makes most sense to cede to private initiative. For most of the Middle East the question had just begun to be raised in explicit form. But it was also present, implicitly, in a variety of different contexts where public and private interests were involved in general considerations of the general good. One example is provided by President Mubarak's attempt to cajole the private sector into making specified investments in new public projects or in the construction of new schools.[36] As one of Mubarak's close advisers, Usama al-Baz, put it in March 1998: 'we encourage national capital but we refuse to let them [sic] run the country'.[37]

Indeed, so new was the whole process that the terms of the debate were not only not well understood but also tended to be cloaked by the use of religious or moral language, as in Iran, or by an appeal to national security or to the need to protect national or ethnic identity and culture almost everywhere else. Moreover, many of the central issues involved in a re-ordering of relations between the public and the private sectors remained difficult to define. This was certainly the case with the vexed issue of corruption which retained distinctly different meanings in the religious, legal, administrative and simply political vocabularies in which it was conventionally discussed. To make matters more complex the whole issue remained much too useful a weapon to be easily surrendered, making struggle over its popular, day-to-day, meaning still more intense.

Would-be analysts are thus placed in the position of not knowing exactly where to look, what the key variables may be or even which are the most appropriate concepts needed to define the central relationships involved. This leaves the majority with no option but to employ a perspective which focuses on the contrast between the power of vested interests to prevent further progress, on the one hand, with the forces for change, on the other. As far as the former are concerned, I myself would attach great importance to the always powerful drive for monopoly and control, a force which does much to explain the ways in which quasi-public monopolies have begun to be replaced by quasi-private ones in Israel and Turkey, and which is also likely to be the case in Egypt, Tunisia and Morocco. In countries with relatively small markets and an, often well-founded, fear of foreign domination, domestic competition is quite easily contained provided international competition is kept to a minimum.

Arrayed against the forces of continued monopoly and state control were the growing pressures making for a more open-ended, less manageable change. Much the most important were the commitments to international best practice demanded by the World Bank, the EU and the WTO, forces which would inevitably lead to greater transparency in both business and government, to better protection for private property and private enterprises and to an eventual opening up of protected local markets for services as well as a wider range of foreign products. This, in turn, promised to encourage new types of political activity and argument, including those concerned with the redefinition of national goals concerning education, welfare and social justice, and the promotion of sectional interests involving the position of women, minorities and the long-term unemployed, as well as the protection of the environment.

Where all this might lead as far as the power and position of the state is concerned is another matter. In Israel, where the process of economic liberalisation really took off in the mid-1990s, we can see the emergence of what one analyst has styled a 'leaner, more autonomous' state apparatus.[38] Many versions of the same may also appear elsewhere in the Middle East, as regimes use public resources to reposition themselves in such a way as to best maintain their own power and that of their key constituencies.

Notes

1 Guillermo O'Donnell, 'Reflections on the pattern of change in the bureaucratic authoritarian state', *Latin American Research Review*, 13 (1973), pp. 3–37, and 'Tensions in the bureaucratic authoritarian state and the question of democracy', in David Collier (ed.), *The New Authoritarianism in Latin America* (Princeton, NJ: Princeton University Press, 1979).

2 Quoted in Yves Gazzo, 'Les économies arabes face à la crise: les solutions libérales et ses limites', *Maghreb/Machrek*, 120 (April/May/June 1988), pp. 110–11.

3 For Sadat, see Waterbury, *The Egypt of Nasser and Sadat*, pp. 127–8. For Rafsanjani, see Sohrab Behdad, 'The post-revolutionary economic crisis', in Saeed Rahnema and Sohrab Behdad (eds), *Iran After the Revolution: Crisis of an Islamic State* (London and New York: I.B. Tauris, 1995), p. 112. And for Asad, see Raymond A. Hinnebusch , 'The political economy of economic liberalization in Syria', *International Journal of Middle Eastern Studies*, 27/3 (August 1995), p. 308.

4 Two of the best accounts of this period are by economists who lived in Egypt in the early 1960s and who knew most of the planners personally: P.K. O'Brien, *The Revolution in Egypt's Economic System: From Private Enterprise to Socialism* (Oxford: Oxford University Press, 1966), Chapter 5; and Bent Hansen, with Girgis Marzouk, *Development and Economic Policy in the UAR (Egypt)* (Amsterdam: North Holland Publishing Company, 1965), Chapter 11.

5 *The Economist*, 27 October 1997, p. 45.

6 This figure is taken from Gamal Essam El-Din's article, 'Privatization at the cross roads', *Al-Ahram Weekly*, 23–29 October 1997. Other commentators give somewhat different numbers.

7 Cameron Khosrowshahi, 'Privatization in Morocco: The politics of development', *Middle East Journal*, 51/2 (Spring, 1997), p. 243; Roula Khalaf, 'Stuck in the slow lane', *Financial Times* (Morocco supplement), 26 March 1998.

8 For a useful survey of books in Arabic concerning the threat of globalisation, see Ahmad S. Moussalli, 'Globalization and the nation state in the Arab world', *MESA Bulletin*, 32/1 (Summer, 1988), especially pp. 11–14.

9 See, for example, David Gardner, 'Reformist zeal put to the test', *Financial Times* (Egypt supplement), 11 May 1999.

10 The weakness of Egypt's trade union leadership has been cited as one of the reasons why the negotiations for a new Labour Law, which had been begun in 1993, had still not reached a satisfactory conclusion by the summer of 1999. See Fatemah Farag, 'May Day dilemma', *Al-Ahram Weekly*, 29 April–5 May 1999.

11 Hinnebusch, *Authoritarian Power and State Formation*, pp. 295–6 and 317.

12 Ibid.

13 See, for example, the useful discussion of this point in Batatu, *Syria's Peasantry*, pp. 208–16.

14 Hinnebusch, 'The political economy of liberalization in Syria', p. 308.

15 Ibid., p. 313.

16 Hinnebusch notes reports of a slogan with the word 'Asadsescu' seen on a Damascus wall in 1989, clearly put there by someone who wished Asad to go the same way as Ceauşescu. Quoted in his 'State and civil society in Syria', *Middle East Journal*, 47/2 (Spring, 1993), p. 243.

17 Ibid., p. 315.

18 'The parasitic basis of the Ba'thist regime', in CADRI (Committee Against Repression and for the Democratic Rights of Iraq), *Saddam's Iraq: Revolution or Reaction* (London: Zed Press 1986), pp. 73–88.

19 Robert Springborg, 'Iraqi *infitah*: Agrarian transformation and growth of the private sector', *Middle East Journal*, 40/1 (Winter, 1986), p. 37.

20 Quoted in *Middle East Economic Digest*, 31/13 (28 March 1987), p. 18.

21 For example, the persuasive argument of Marion Farouk-Sluglett in her article, 'Iraq after the war (2) – the role of the private sector', *Middle East International*, 17 March 1989, p. 18. For a slightly different view see, Kiren Aziz Chaudhry, 'On the way to the market: Economic liberalization and Iraq's invasion of Kuwait', *Middle East Report*, 170 (May–June 1991), especially pp. 20–3.

22 For example, Taher H. Kanaan, 'The state and the private sector in Jordan', in Nemat Shafik (ed.), *Economic Challenges Facing Middle Eastern and North African Countries* (Houndmills, Basingstoke: The Macmillan Press; and New York: St Martin's Press, 1998), p.78.

23 For example, Luciani, 'Allocation vs. production states', pp. 75–8, in Hazem Beblawi and Giacomo Luciani (eds), *The Rentier States*, (London: Croom Helm, 1987).

24 The following analysis draws heavily on arguments to be found in Keyder, *State and Class in Turkey*, Chapter IX; and Ilkay Sunar, 'Redemocratization and organized interests in Turkey', *mimeo* (Paper presented to the annual conference of the British Society for Middle Eastern Studies, Exeter, 12–15 July 1987).

25 Ibid.

26 Aysit Tansel, 'Workers displaced due to privatisation in Turkey', Economic Research Forum for the Arab Countries, Iran and Turkey (Cairo), *Working Paper 9719* (1998), Table 2, p. 11.

27 Michael Bruno, 'Sharp disinflation strategy: Israel 1985', *Economic Policy*, 2 (April 1986).

28 Peretz Kidron, 'The pay off', *Middle East International*, 17 February 1989, pp. 10–11.

29 For example, Michael Shalev, 'The contradictions of economic reform in Israel', *Middle East Report*, 28/2, 207 (Summer, 1998), pp. 31–3; and Judy Dempsey, 'Doubts exist over benefits of sales', *Financial Times* (Israel supplement), 26 March 1998.

30 Shaul Bakhash *The Reign of the Ayatollahs* (London: I.B. Tauris, 1985), pp. 178–85.

31 'Constitution of the Iranian Republic of Iran', *Middle East Journal*, 34/2 (Spring, 1980), p. 193.

32 Patrick Clawson, 'Islamic Iran's economic prospects', *Middle East Journal*, 42/3 (Summer, 1988), p. 381.
33 Quoted in Shahrough Akhavi, 'Elite factionalism in the Islamic Republic of Iran', *Middle East Journal*, 41/2 (Spring, 1987), p. 184.
34 For a technical discussion of the pros and cons of the multiple exchange rate, see Massoud Karshenas, 'Structural adjustment and the Iranian economy', in Shafik, (ed.), *Economic Challenges*, pp. 202–24; and Sohrab Behdad, 'The post-revolutionary economic crisis', in Rahnama and Behdad (eds), *Iran After the Revolution*, pp. 115–19.
35 'Khatami promises economic reform', *Financial Times*, 3 August 1998.
36 For example, Mubarak's meeting with thirty-one top businessmen in Steve Negus, 'Mubarak loses his cool', *Middle East International*, 27 March 1998, pp. 12–13.
37 Quoted in ibid.
38 Shalev, 'Contradictions of economic reform', p. 33.

8 Parties, elections and the vexed question of democracy in the Arab world

Introduction

Those European-controlled Arab states which became independent before or just after the Second World War followed much the same political trajectory as in the rest of Africa and Asia. For some this involved a passage from a brief period of competitive elections to several decades of one-party rule followed, in some cases at least, by the revival of a more open political system in the 1980s and 1990s. For others this meant a slightly different path, missing out either the initial multi-party stage, like Tunisia, Algeria and the former South Yemen, or the single-party stage, like Jordan, Lebanon and Morocco. Sudan pursued yet another variation involving three distinct passages from multi-party to military government. Elsewhere, the Gulf states, although subject to large amounts of British influence, were generally unaffected by the same pressures and maintained a pattern of direct family rule with the single exception of Kuwait where there was an elected assembly, but no formal parties, from 1961–76, 1981–6 and 1992 to the present. As for the three non-Arab states, only Israel maintained an uninterrupted period of democratic practice, at least as far as its Jewish citizens were concerned. The Turkish system of competitive elections introduced in 1946 was three times interrupted by the military interventions of 1960, 1971 and 1980, while Iran experienced only brief moments of electoral democracy in the 1940s and a more restricted, Islamic version, from 1980 onwards.

Given this somewhat chequered history there has been a tendency to view the majority of Middle Eastern peoples as being either unwilling or unable to practise the type of open, competitive politics which westerners see as essential for a working democracy. And this, in turn, has led to a considerable literature devoted to an examination of just why this should have been so: couched sometimes in terms of a so-called Arab or Islamic 'exceptionalism' stemming from the existence of specific anti-democratic religious or cultural forces, and sometimes relying on the more conventional explanations which have been applied generally to all other parts of the ex-colonial world.[1] As will be seen in the discussion which follows, I tend towards the latter view. However, I do this in conscious disagreement with the idealised conception of their own democracy put forward by many western commentators as well as in light of the fact that its establishment in Europe was very much more difficult, and more subject to interruption, than the majority of them allow. Even if we employ the most minimal definition of democracy possible – the existence of contested elections in which the defeated party surrenders power – there are many European countries which passed through quite considerable periods of time during the nineteenth and twentieth centuries when no such convention was in place.[2] In other words, the practice of democracy is a difficult business, easily knocked off course by wars, revolutions, social conflict or economic collapse, and requiring to be underpinned by a complex system of legal, organisational and administrative arrangements if it is to function effectively.

In my own discussion I will begin by taking Egypt as the prototypical example of a state which made the transition from multi-party competition through single-party control and then back to a managed system of competition again. I go on to examine some of the variants of this process in other parts of the Arab world, first in those states subject to a one-party system for all or part of the last three decades, then in the family-ruled states such as Jordan, Morocco and Kuwait. Finally, I will look at the particular political history of Lebanon, the one Arab country which maintained a continuous practice of competitive elections for the first thirty years after independence and which it then managed to revive after fifteen years of divisive civil war.

Egypt: the ups and down of the democratic idea

Between its qualified independence in 1923 and the military coup of 1952, Egypt held ten general parliamentary elections. Those in which voters were allowed a free choice generally ended up in a victory for the Wafd Party, the nationalist alliance that had come into being to fight the British protectorate in 1919. However, most attempts at Wafdist rule lasted little more than a few months before being brought to an end by a combination of political enemies including the king, the British High Commissioner (later Ambassador) and the leaders of a number of smaller parties, almost all of them former members of the Wafd itself.

One manifestation of the intensity of Egyptian political competition was the way it encouraged frequent attempts to alter the electoral system so as to make victory more difficult for the Wafd while improving the chances of one or more of its rivals. The result was that almost every election was fought under a different set of rules. Changes included movement between a one and a two stage electoral process, limitations on the original system of complete adult male suffrage and attempts to manipulate the organisation of village-level voting. One example would be Ismail Sidqi's new constitution and electoral law of 1930 which imposed such stringent educational and property qualifications on the electorate that some 80 per cent of the adult population was effectively disenfranchised.[3] This was then reversed by a return to the old constitution in 1935. Another example would be the frequent attempts by the party in power to replace any of those village *umdas* – the people most closely connected with the management of the peasant vote – who were thought to favour their opponents with men loyal to their own cause.

Egypt's electoral history is thus a good illustration of the great importance of the rules and practices by which elections take place and of how easy it was, and still is, to manipulate them for some temporary advantage. It also highlights the special problems of having to run an effective democracy in a predominantly rural, predominantly illiterate, society where the majority of the peasants were easily subject to landlord influence. This, in turn, had a significant effect on the organisation of the parties themselves, discouraging them from being anything more than machines for winning elections, with little need for public meetings and regular membership so long as they could persuade a sufficient number of the scions of wealthy landowning families to stand as their candidates in order to deliver the rural vote.

Given the obvious deficiencies in the practice of Egyptian democracy, as well as the perceived failure of its landlord-dominated parliaments to tackle most of the burning national and social problems of the day, it is not surprising that democracy itself soon came under attack. There is certainly good evidence for this from the 1930s onwards.[4] Nevertheless, it would be wrong to suggest that the majority of the Egyptian elite was ready to abandon a system enshrined in the constitution and supported by so many free institutions like the press and the universities until persuaded to do so by defeat in the Palestine War of 1948/9 and the increasingly desperate struggle against the British military presence along the Suez Canal.[5] Only then did democracy become widely identified as a western initiative designed to promote political and social division at a time when Egypt, like its other Arab neighbours, needed to concentrate all its forces on the major problems of national independence, economic development, social justice and the defence of Palestinian rights.[6]

As one of the first leaders to put such ideas into practice, President Nasser's own personal views are of great significance. Here is a typical sentiment expressed in an interview with an Indian newspaper editor in March 1957:

> Can I ask you a question: what is democracy? We were supposed to have a democratic system during the period 1923 to 1953. But what good was this democracy to our people? I will tell you. Landowners and Pashas ruled our people. They used this kind of democracy as an easy tool for the benefits of a feudal system. You have seen the feudalists gathering the peasants together and driving them to the polling booths. There the peasants would cast their votes according to the instructions of their masters. ... I want to liberate the peasants and the workers both socially and economically, so that they can say 'yes'. I want the peasants and the workers to be able to say 'yes' and 'no' without any of this affecting their livelihood or their daily bread. This in my view is the basis of freedom and democracy.[7]

It then took many years of military-backed, authoritarian rule before some intellectuals, poets and others began to question their own complicity in the sacrifice of the country's political freedoms in pursuit of Nasserite economic and social policies of this kind. In Egypt such views were trenchantly expressed by the writer Tawfik al-Hakim, whose *Audat al-Wai* (*The Return of Consciousness*) consists of an agonised process of self-interrogation as to why he had allowed himself to be so easily beguiled by the Nasser agenda.[8] Others of his colleagues took longer to realise that the wager they had made with themselves that the Nasserite version of nationalism, and then of Arab socialism, would culminate in a revived democracy had turned out to be just plain wrong.

The new Nasser-led regime abolished all Egypt's existing parties in 1953. To fill the gap as far as popular representation was concerned it organised a series of national rallies: the Liberation Rally in 1953, the National Union in 1956, and finally the Arab Socialist Union (ASU) in 1961. All were conceived as mass organisations with a monopoly of legitimate political activity. The choices of names were also significant: in each case the word 'party' was deliberately avoided, given its powerful connotations of division and lack of national purpose.[9]

The basic organisational structure of the most important of these mass organisations, the ASU, was created in 1963/4. At its apex was a higher executive committee which stood in for the type of permanent central committee to be found among the Communist parties of Eastern Europe. Next came the temporary provincial committees which presided over the formation of district-level committees. At the base, the one purely Egyptian addition to this familiar type of structure was the creation of so-called 'basic units' established either in the villages or at a place of work. There were nearly 7,000 of these, each run by a committee of twenty members, and covering most Egyptians except those in the army or the police.[10] When finally in place, this mass, pyramidal structure contained nearly three-quarters of the male electorate.[11]

The ASU never became, and was probably never intended to be, an autonomous political organisation. There was considerable overlap between it and government, for instance, with the same person often holding post in both structures. There was also little attention to creating a regular system of membership nor any attempt to impose party discipline except, on rare occasions, by the threat of expulsion. This latter sanction may have had some influence, however, as ASU membership soon became a necessary requirement for anyone wanting to hold office or to run for a place in the Union's regional or national assemblies.[12]

What the ASU most obviously lacked was a clearly defined role and a coherent ideology. Three areas in particular were the subject of on-going contestation and debate. The first was its relationship to other Egyptian institutions, notably the army, the bureaucracy and the professional syndicates, all of which its leaders aspired, at one time or another, to control. The second was the nature of the 'alliance of working forces' that President Nasser required it to represent. Should this be based on class or on a more corporatist formula defining members in terms of their place and type of work? The last area was that of ideology and focused on the vexed question of what was meant by the socialism the Union was supposed to express. El-Kosheri Mahfouz identifies two main trends inside the ASU, one that wished to place its socialism in an Arab or local Middle Eastern context, the other to take its cue from East European or Soviet practice.[13] Uncertainty on all these counts was one of the reasons why the activities of the ASU so quickly aroused the suspicions of groups within the military and the administration which feared that it had the capacity to develop into something like a Yugoslav or Russian Communist Party with aspirations to total social and administrative control.[14]

President Nasser's own thinking about the ASU was tinged with some of the same misapprehensions. On the one hand, he believed in the need for a mechanism for rallying support for the regime and of isolating its domestic enemies. On the other, he was wary of giving power to groups and organisations not directly under his own control. And like any other leader, he had to maintain a balance between the interests of Egypt's various political constituencies, many of which were deeply disturbed by the ASU's actual, or potential, power. In his own case, although he sometimes put forward proposals to make the Union more effective, particularly after the 1967 defeat, he more usually treated it as simply an extension of the central administration, to be managed by his own loyal political allies.[15]

In the end it was left to President Nasser's successor, Anwar Sadat, to seize the bull by the horns and to find a way of converting the ASU into a tame government party as part of the general process of economic and political liberalisation launched in the early 1970s. In theory, he, like any other new leader of what was essentially a one-party state, was faced by three possible options: he could reform the single party from inside, he could dissolve it outright, or he could refashion it as a vehicle to mobilise regime support in the context of a multi-party electoral system. In the event, he finally opted for the last, but only after several years of discussion and debate which saw him move from the promotion of a number of separate tendencies (or platforms, *minbars*) inside the ASU to allowing three of these same platforms to contest the November 1976 national elections as separate political organisations: his own National Socialist Rally (later the Egypt Party), the Liberal Socialists to the right and the National Progressive Unionists (Tagammu) to the left.

Having created the rudiments of a three-party system it was then necessary to establish the rules to govern electoral practice as well as the formation of any new parties in the future. As far as the 1976 election itself was concerned, the major decisions seem to have been taken by Sadat and his close advisers operating through members of the National Socialist Rally inside the formerly ASU-dominated People's Assembly.[16] In this way it was decided to continue the previous system of 175 two member constituencies, each of which was supposed to contain one candidate identified as a peasant or worker. Meanwhile, opposition efforts to introduce laws designed to prevent government interference in elections were not well supported, leaving the Nationalist Socialist Rally with the overwhelming advantage of having the election itself supervised by the ministry of the interior, and with many of its candidates government officials themselves. This was enough to give it 280 of the 350 seats, with twelve going to the Liberal Socialists, two to the National Progressives, and the rest to independents.

A new Parties Law followed in 1977 specifying that any new party would have to accept the principles of the constitution, the national charter of 1962 and Sadat's '*infitah*' Working Paper of April 1974, and that none could be established on a 'class, sectarian or geographic basis'.[17] This was clearly designed to prevent the establishment of organisations based on localism, religion or on an ability to mobilise the huge constituency of workers, peasants and others who had made important gains during the Nasser period and who now feared that they were all at risk. The result was that Egyptian parties came to represent largely similar ideological trends rather than solid economic, social or cultural interests. It also ensured that important segments of the population, most notably the workers and peasants, were left without a specific organisation of their own and thus effectively disenfranchised.

President Sadat was soon forced to backtrack in his experiment in controlled democracy as a result of growing popular opposition to many of his policies, most importantly his attempt to cut the level of several basic subsidies (which led to the so-called 'bread' riots of January 1977) and his journey to Jerusalem at the end of the same year as a move towards peace with Israel. Critics were harassed while Sadat himself began to substitute the use of parliament as a way of keeping in touch with public opinion by such measures as popular referendums, the placement of his supporters at the head of the professional syndicates and, finally, the introduction of a more tractable representative body, the Majlis al-Shura (Consultative Council) in 1980, with its members only half elected and the rest selected by himself.[18]

Movement towards a more open political system was restarted by President Mubarak but still with a great emphasis on management and control. His first innovation was a 1983 amendment to the 1972 electoral law which established an entirely new system of representation, one still designed to favour the government party but leaving some small scope for a small official opposition. This called for the creation of forty-eight large constituencies instead of the previous 175 smaller ones. Parties wishing to stand in the election could only enter by offering lists in every one of them, a precaution designed to prevent an attempt to concentrate their limited resources on those few constituencies where they might have the most popular support. They were also required to obtain 8 per cent of the vote at the national level before being awarded any seats. Another important provision banned candidates from standing as independents lest this allowed people into the Assembly whose political affiliations were unknown. As the architect of the reformed system, the then prime minister, Fuad Muhieddin, put in private conversation, he did not want 'new men' to be able to stand for election when 'we [the government] don't know them'.[19]

Once the new electoral machinery was in place, it was necessary to persuade opposition politicians, as well as the Egyptian electorate, that there would be enough freedom and openness to make participation worthwhile. The creation of the necessary confidence was managed quite cleverly, first by allowing a government candidate to be beaten in a by-election in Alexandria in November 1983, then permitting the revived Wafd Party to put up lists for the May 1984 national election even though it had not yet been legally constituted as an official party. Manoeuvres of this type were enough to ensure that just under half the registered voters (43 per cent) went to the polls. And even though the government party, now renamed the National Democratic Party (NDP), won 73 per cent of the votes (and 390 out of the 448 seats), the Neo-Wafd did well enough to secure the rest of the seats with its own 15 per cent.[20] The limited Wafdist breakthrough was based, not only on the political skills of its elderly leaders who had participated in contested elections before 1952, but also on an alliance with the Muslim Brothers which brought it important financial and organisational support. Its rivals among the other opposition parties suffered greatly from their own inexperience, as well as from selective government interference, especially in the rural areas.[21] Not surprisingly there were also many administrative problems stemming from the fact that participation in contested elections was still a new experience for many Egyptians, that registers had not been kept up to date and that many people, including at least one government minister, were not even able to find their way to their proper polling station.[22]

Egypt's next general election was held earlier than scheduled, in 1987, as a result of a successful legal challenge to the 1984 ban on independent candidates on the grounds that it violated individual rights enshrined in the 1971 constitution. Realising that this threatened to undermine the legality of the Assembly which had the duty of re-electing him as president later that same year, Mubarak changed the rules to allow one independent to stand in each constituency before calling Egyptians to the polls in April. The NDP obtained 308 seats with 70 per cent of the vote as against the Neo-Wafd which obtained 35 seats with 11 per cent and a new alliance of the Socialist Labour and Socialist Liberal Parties with the Muslim Brothers which obtained 56 seats with 17 per cent. There were also four independents.[23] Once again, the opposition made serious allegations concerning official interference, including the claim that three-quarters of the polling stations had no proper neutral observers.[24] But such claims, though largely true, cannot be taken to mean that, if the election had been really fair and open, the NDP would not still have won. Given its close association with the administration it is likely to have obtained a substantial majority anyway, leaving independent-minded voters only a second-best option of being allowed to select which parties were to form the official opposition.[25]

The 1990 election was the second to be held prematurely, once again as a result of a successful legal challenge to the conduct of the one before. The result was yet another change in the electoral system, highlighted by a return to the two member constituencies in use before 1984 and the removal of all remaining barriers to independent candidates. Opposition efforts to obtain the lifting of the nine-year-old state of emergency, which could be used to impose considerable constraints on their activity during an electoral campaign, proved unsuccessful and led to a boycott by the Wafd and all the members of the Socialist Labour, Socialist Liberal and Muslim Brother alliance. The result was a still more overwhelming victory by the NDP, with opposition limited to just a few members of the Tagammu and a number of independents.[26]

Things hardly improved for the opposition in 1995. This time the government party obtained 94 per cent of the 444 seats with only six for the Tagammu and five for the Wafd; although there were also some Wafd-supporters among the fourteen independents. Such lack of success can be accounted for, in part, by the fact that the legal opposition parties were now so closely tied to the government (via their support for its campaign against the Muslim militants) that their programmes were hardly distinguishable from that of the NDP. They also suffered badly from faults of leadership, limited financial resources and their obvious inability to provide the patronage and access to power which a government party has by right. A particularly telling sign of their general weakness was the Wafd's inability to present candidates for more than 181 of the seats.[27] Once again, government interference was widespread, though not universal.[28] What was more significant was the fact that so many influential government supporters were now struggling to climb on to the electoral band-wagon that it was difficult to find enough seats to accommodate them all.

Nevertheless, there is more to it than that. Why was it that after a brief period, 1984–87, in which the proportion of NDP seats declined, the 1990 and 1995 elections saw it reach such a dominating position that it could afford to ignore the opposition almost entirely? And what does this say about the possibility of further progress towards greater Egyptian electoral democracy? Much of the answer must come from the observation that, by the early 1990s, the country had become more or less a one-party state with the links between government and NDP so strong that there was little political advantage to be gained by opposing it, and every advantage from jumping on the band-wagon, whether officially permitted by the party-managers or not.[29] In such a situation, even though a president might wish for a slightly larger opposition, if only for a kind of international window-dressing, the pressure from grass-roots supporters become too strong to allow it. It follows that there can be little reason to suppose that the opposition had no realistic hopes of doing better throughout the remainder of the Mubarak presidency which, as a result of his re-election for a fourth term in 1999, will run until the year 2005. It also follows that there is nothing to prevent further political marginalisation of those groups and interests unable to find a place under the official umbrella.

Such lack of progress raises the further question of what is the regime's rationale for continuing to employ such a transparently unfair system of representation. One obvious answer is that it helps to secure the very large sums of aid which come from the United States, and, to a lesser extent, from Europe. For the rest, we may observe that similar systems, in which the government party is secure against defeat at the polls, exist in many other parts of the world and have been the subject of frequent examination. According to Guy Hermet, what have been called 'elections without choices' are widely used by regimes to mobilise public opinion and to provide themselves with extra legitimation.[30] They also present an opportunity for the leader of the government party to discipline his supporters by leaving them off his electoral list without the need for frequent, and perhaps embarrassing, purges. The result is a system of controlled, rather than free, elections and, in the Egyptian case, a process of what Kienle has also called 'de-liberalization' with no obvious end to it in sight. [31]

Single-party and multi-party government in North Africa and the Arab east

A number of Arab states followed part of the Egyptian trajectory, either starting after independence with a brief period of contested elections before succumbing to single-party rule (like Sudan, Syria and Iraq) or starting with single parties or rallies and then moving towards a slightly more open system (Tunisia and Algeria).

Of the three countries in the first camp, Sudan's development was the most unusual, passing three times from short periods of parliamentary democracy – 1953–58, 1965–69 and 1986–89 – to longer periods of military government, usually in association with a single political organisation. Another unusual feature was the fact that, on each occasion, the return to contested elections was in terms of the previous electoral system and so of head-to-head competition between the two main political alliances, the Unionists and the Umma Party, rather than an entirely new system of parties and electoral practices. Lastly, Sudan is also unusual in that it has experienced two quite different types of single-party rule. The first was the work of President Nimeiri's Sudan Socialist Union founded in 1972 along the lines of Egypt's ASU as a general method of mobilising popular support. This rather ineffective organisation was then swept away overnight when the Nimeiri regime was overthrown by the military coup of 1985. The second was a much more powerful and effective grouping, the National Islamic Front (NIF), dominated by the Sudanese branch of the Muslim Brothers, which had taken part in elections from 1968 onwards but only managed to come to power on the back of General Omar al Bashir's coup of June 1989. It was the NIF which launched a wholesale programme of Islamisation in 1991, designed to reshape the economy and society of those parts of the Northern Sudan under its control. And all this while the northern government was still in deadly conflict with the Southern People's Liberation Army (SPLA)/ Southern People's Liberation Movement (SPLM) alliance which was continuing its armed struggle in order to obtain greater autonomy for the south.

Both Syria and Iraq also proceeded from a short period of contested, although heavily managed, elections, via military coups to a system of one-party rule. In each case the party was the Ba'th (Arab Renaissance) Party which had been first organised in Syria in the 1940s and then established branches in Iraq in the 1950s. In its early stages it was little more than a small, often clandestine, grouping whose only hope of gaining power was by forming an association with discontented army officers. And it was only after taking over state power in this way, in Syria from 1963 onwards and Iraq from 1968, that both parties were able to turn themselves into nation-wide political organisations with important control and managerial functions over their respective societies.

The founders of both parts of the Ba'th were much influenced by the Soviet model of the party as a revolutionary vanguard, functionally separate from the central bureaucracy, and given the task of supervising the activities of the civil servants, the military and the popular organisations like the workers' and peasants', students' and women's unions. They also adopted various Soviet-style ideological practices aimed at strengthening the party's legitimacy and authority by magnifying its role in the past and stressing its access to a science of politics that gave it a unique insight into present conditions and future developments. To begin with the core of its ideology lay in its advocacy of a secular Arab nationalism. But, over time, this was tempered by an appeal to socialism and then to an eclectic mixture of nationalism, religion and anti-imperialism. Lastly, the leaders of both parties, Hafiz al-Asad in Syria and Saddam Hussein in Iraq, having used the party to cement their own power, took advantage of their monopoly over the levers of power to raise themselves above it, blurring the distinction between party and government and so turning it into just one of a number of interlocking instruments of management and control.

This process of transformation is evident in Syria from 1970 onwards. Once President Asad began to construct his own pyramid of presidential power he was careful to ensure that the more militant and radical features of Ba'thi ideology were watered down and that its organisation played only a subordinate role in government.[32] As he saw it, the party would be most useful to him as an instrument of mobilisation and social control and an aid to the execution of regime policies in certain well-defined areas such as land reform and the management of public sector enterprises. At the same time, he was unwilling to allow it much of a role in internal security or in ensuring the loyalty of the army, where a separate Ba'thi military branch was preserved. The result was a vigorous drive to recruit new party members, particularly in the rural areas, as well as to enlarge the usual popular organisations for workers and others under Ba'thi control. This process was further intensified in an effort to solidify the regime against its various religious opponents from 1979 onwards (see Chapter 9). Party figures for the total involved would suggest that the number of full members increased from some 8,000 in 1971 to 53,433 in 1981 and then nearly 160,000 in 1989, while the much larger cadre of supporters who had some association with the party may have reached almost 640,000 by this last date.[33]

The party's rapid growth, and the fact that it soon contained a large number of opportunists who were recruited along regional or sectarian rather than ideological lines, was a further limitation on its ability to play a vanguard role.[34] Its position was also adversely affected by two other tendencies: the attenuation of its ideology, and the ever increasing personal dominance of President Asad himself, supported by his predominantly Alawite security apparatus. All this makes it difficult to evaluate the Ba'thi's changing position within the Syrian political structure. In Hinnebusch's view, as of the late 1980s, it remained what he called a 'real party' and continued to perform 'crucial political functions'.[35] It still served to legitimise the regime, to facilitate elite recruitment and to provide one possible channel for the choice of successor to the president himself.[36] It also played a limited role in policy formulation and is credited by Hinnebusch with a spirited defence of the state sector and an ability to block incipient moves towards greater economic liberalisation.[37]

In Iraq, members of the tiny Ba'th Party obtained power on the back of yet another military coup in July 1968. To begin with its political base was so narrow that it could only maintain itself by terror, torture and harsh repression. But during the early 1970s, it began to institutionalise its role on the basis of an alliance between President Hassan al-Bakr, who supervised the loyalty of the army, and his vice-president, Saddam Hussein, who supplemented his control over the regime's main security apparatus, the Jihaz al-Khas (Special Branch), by carefully building up a disciplined, civilian party apparatus. Unlike the Syrian Ba'this, he chose to recruit new members at a slow, controlled pace with maximum emphasis on loyalty. According to some sources it could take seven to eight years to pass through the various stages of apprenticeship before being allowed to become a full member.[38] It was also kept a deliberately secretive organisation, holding few congresses – only five between 1968 and 1995 – and with strict rules that forbade any member from revealing information about its organisation, its numbers or its internal discussions.[39]

Once the party organisation had become sufficiently large, Saddam Hussein used it to supervise the military, the educational system, the popular organisations and as large a proportion of Iraqi society as such a secular institution, with strong ties to the dominant Sunni community, could reach. There was then a period of rapid expansion in the late 1970s when the Ba'th began to recruit extensively among the Shi'i as well, in an effort to maintain their loyalty at a time of increasing religious opposition stimulated by the Iranian revolution. Hence, by 1979, the party is estimated to have had some 25,000 full members as well as approximately 1,500,000 associates.[40] A membership of this size then allowed it to place a member or associate in every government department, a party commissar in every military unit, and a party cell in every school, university and neighbourhood, thus greatly extending the scope of its supervision into the home and the classroom where the regular security apparatus was generally unable to reach.[41]

Saddam Hussein's own accession to the presidency in 1979 inaugurated changes in the role of the party which are not always easy to evaluate. From the beginning he made it clear that he was no longer interested in the previous method of collective leadership but only in one based on his individual power. This point was underlined by a bloody purge of opponents within the Ba'th, and then further reinforced by a process of well-orchestrated personal glorification in the early stages of the war with Iran which soon reached the heights of adulation associated with China's Chairman Mao or North Korea's Kim Il Sung. At the party's 1982 congress, for example, it was asserted that it was Hussein who had personally led the fight against Iran in 'all its military, strategic, mobilizational, political, economic and psychological aspects [and] in a creative, courageous and democratic manner'.[42] All this helped to reduce the salience of the party and its ideology, a trend that was intensified during the war against Iran and the invasion of Kuwait in which both the military campaigns themselves, as well as the larger justification in terms of a shifting kaleidoscope of nationalist, religious and historical themes, were managed by the president himself with almost no reference to the party at all. The same trend continued into the 1990s, with Ba'th legitimacy further eroded by its association with the demise of the Soviet and most East European communist parties, leaving it with only various residual supervisory functions over those areas of Iraq still under central government control.[43] Nevertheless, there were occasional signs that Saddam Hussain still had some use for party loyalty, notably as a counter-weight to the problems he was encountering with members of his own disorderly family. Hence the praise he heaped upon it in his speech to its Eleventh Congress in 1995.[44]

So long as it lasted, Soviet and East European communist experience provided a valuable guide to significant trends within the Syrian and Iraqi Ba'th parties as well. As far as ideology was concerned, this underwent a similar process of dilution in which, over time, Ba'thi rhetoric was emptied of almost all its substance. To begin with, when they were still in heated competition with other ideologies such as Nasserism and communism, the spokesmen of both parties were concerned to argue the Ba'thi case in ways that struck a chord with as wide a circle of political activists as possible. This was also a factor in the fierce war of words that broke out between the two parties in the late 1960s and early 1970s, with each side trying to present itself as the sole legitimate heir of the parent organisation founded in Syria some two decades earlier. As was the case with much the same verbal contest between the ideologues of Marxist-Leninism in the USSR and China at just the same time, the authority of Ba'thism was constructed in such a way as to allow only a single source of ideological truth. In other words, if one was the authentic successor, the other could not possibly be so as well. As Eberhard Kienle notes, the intensity of this struggle was not only predicated on a vital concern with regime legitimation but also on the importance both leaderships attached to obtaining the support of a pool of Ba'thi militants within the region who were free to throw in their lot with one regime or the other.[45]

Later, however, as the two regimes obtained more confidence, the struggle became of less practical significance and Ba'thism, as an ideology, lost much of its initial sharpness, just like East European communism. There were a number of locally specific reasons as well. Perhaps the most important was the fact that Ba'thism itself never consisted of more than a number of general principles that proved incapable of meaningful theoretical elaboration. Unlike Marxism, for example, it possessed no major works of philosophy or history that could be used as a basis for such an enterprise. Indeed, the reality was that it was always much closer to a typical Third World nationalism – with its characteristic appeal for a collective struggle to create a modern society – than the complete guide to progressive social development that its leaders sometimes claimed. Furthermore, for all the creation of party institutes for training, indoctrination and research, there was little sign of a desire to produce a coherent body of Ba'thi doctrine, leaving the leaders free to interpret it in almost any way they might choose.[46]

The result was an official ideology which, in its Iraqi context, has been described as 'rhetorical' and 'deliberately repetitious'.[47] However, analysts who concentrate simply on its intellectual content – or lack of it – miss much of the point. As in the case of the Soviet Union before Gorbachev's perestroika, the major function of such an ideology was not to provide intellectual enlightenment but rather to serve as an instrument of political control. This operated in various ways. At one level, the appeal to Ba'thism as a tool of scientific analysis was utilised to provide the leaders with that aura of omniscience which allowed them to claim the ability to see beneath the surface of events, never to be surprised, always so correct in their analysis of the contemporary context that they were incapable of miscalculation.[48] At a second, ideological pronouncements provided a set of guidelines that not only indicated the current party line to its members but also reinforced the leader's power to define just what that line was. In the Iraqi case once again, this can be seen in Saddam Hussein's initial emphasis on ideology as 'the only basis for the life in which the Ba'thi believes', coupled with the party's stress on its leader's 'creativity', a trait at once estimable but impossible to emulate for fear that this would lead the membership into serious trouble.[49]

The monopoly exercised by both presidents over major ideological pronouncements in the name of Ba'thism, the party and the revolution was further reinforced by the development of the cult of the personality. Just why this tends to emerge in some one-party states and not others is difficult to pin down. Looking at the communist world before perestroika there was a huge gamut of practice from the heady adulation of Kim Il Sung to the restrained attitude adopted towards more retiring leaders like Poland's Gomulka. Clearly there is a strong element of choice involved. Even in the most authoritarian state with the most cowed of populations, a leader seems able either to encourage or to discourage such a development. What would seem to be the case with Presidents Asad and Hussein was that both saw a positive political advantage in raising themselves head and shoulders above their supporters, their family and their rivals by stressing the fact that they were personally 'indispensable' (a word often applied to Saddam Hussein) and the sole source of all political wisdom and guidance.

Once such a cult is well established, there is an obvious tendency for the role of both the party and its ideology to diminish further. A man who wants to present himself as the leader of all his people will not wish to discriminate too obviously in favour of party members. He may also come to believe that control is exercised more efficiently if there is a single train of command from the presidency straight to the cabinet and the central administration rather than one which has to pass through the party as well. All these factors were present in both Iraq and Syria even if the adulation for President Asad never went anything so far as that for Saddam Hussein. Once the future of the Ba'th party became so entirely dependent on that of its leader, East European precedent suggests that it would be unlikely to survive any popular movement which swept him away.

Tunisia and Algeria followed the second stage of the Egyptian sequence, moving from single-party systems to ones which were just a little more competitive. In Tunisia the process was begun in a tentative way in 1981 when candidates outside the ruling Parti Socialiste Destour (PSD), established by its first president, Habib Bourguiba, were permitted to stand for election to the national assembly, although none of them were successful. The process was then expanded after Ben Ali had deposed Bourguiba in November 1987, promising to change what he described as a 'corrupt, one-party state' into a more tolerant multi-party one.[50] A year later he called a meeting of representatives of a large number of popular organisations to discuss the necessary guidelines for such a transformation. These were then set out in a National Pact signed by sixteen of the groups concerned which stressed the right to establish parties, to hold free elections and to pursue 'loyal' political competition.[51] Then came a general election in April 1989 based on a modified form of proportional representation designed to favour the government party by awarding all of the seats in any of the twenty-five multi-member constituencies to the organisation which won the majority of votes. The result was an overwhelming victory for the PSD, renamed the Rassemblement Constitutionel Démocratique (RCD), which obtained 80 per cent of the vote and all of the 143 seats. The only significant competition came from members of the unofficial Mouvement de Tendence Islamique (MTI) running as independents who secured 13 per cent of the vote but no seats.

Further progress towards greater political competition was then blocked for two main reasons. First, President Ben Ali refused to allow the MTI – soon renamed the Harakat al-Nahda ('Movement of Renaissance' or 'Re-birth') – to register itself as an official political party on the grounds that Tunisia had no need for a specifically religious organisation. It was then banned completely in 1990. Second, the president proved unwilling to negotiate an electoral system that was agreeable to the officially recognised parties. The result was a series of boycotts lasting until the 1994 elections when the main opposition group, the Mouvement des Démocrates Socialistes (MDS), having decided to take part, was able to obtain nineteen seats as opposed to the RCD's 144. But just a year later, the MDS's leader, Mohamed Moadda, was put on trial and eventually sentenced to eleven years in gaol after the publication of a letter written to criticise the general lack of political freedom. The party then split between the Moadda supporters and those willing to continue co-operation with the regime. Meanwhile, the regime itself, in an effort to meet foreign criticism of RCD domination, engineered a constitutional amendment permitting opposition candidates to stand against President Ali in the 1999 elections, and also guaranteeing them a minimum of 20 per cent of the seats in the Chamber of Deputies elected on the same day.

The process of political restructuring in Algeria was a great deal more violent. It was triggered off by a major series of popular demonstrations against the economic policies of a government still dominated by members of the single official organisation, the Front de Libération Nationale (FLN), in October 1988, leading to the drafting of a new constitution which removed all references to a privileged position for the FLN or for the Algerian socialism which it was supposed to represent. Next came a new parties law in July 1989. As in Egypt, it specifically banned the formation of any party based on region or religion. But, unlike Egypt, this did not prevent a number of such parties from being formed, notably the Front Islamique de Salut (FIS) and the Rally for Culture and Democracy (RCD) representing Berber interests in the north east. Last came a new electoral law based, like the Tunisian one, on a system designed to favour the government party by awarding all the seats in a constituency to the group which obtained the majority of votes. However, when it came to the first multi-party local elections in June 1990 this precaution was not enough to prevent the FIS from obtaining a comprehensive victory, winning thirty-two of the forty-eight provincial councils (as opposed to fourteen for the FLN) and control of all the major cities.[52]

The success of the FIS was more than enough to put pressure on President Chadli to get the FLN leadership to reform its own structure in advance of the national elections scheduled to follow. Only when this was resisted by well-entrenched forces within the organisation did Chadli switch to the more high-risk strategy of actively promoting competition to the FLN, a policy which seriously misfired by helping the FIS to win the first round of the general election of December 1991 and then forcing the army to intervene to prevent its anticipated victory in the second round, removing Chadli himself in the process.[53] All this was sufficient to precipitate the start of a bloody series of massacres by the armed wing of the FIS as well as by members of the even more militant Groupe Islamique Armée (GIA) aimed at undermining the new, military-backed, regime.

The result was an increasingly violent stand-off between the army and the militants, with the hardline generals refusing to negotiate with the jailed leadership of the FIS while attempting, over time, to construct a political system with more manageable political parties and no place for the Islamic Front itself. A first step was taken along this road with the legislative elections of May/June 1997 in which the National Democratic Rally, formed by President Zerouel only two months before, obtained 153 of the 380 seats leaving two tame Islamic parties with 103 seats between them and the FLN, once again under reliable pro-government leadership, 64. The headline given by the *Economist* to its account of this managed event – 'Just what the President wanted' – seemed to say it all.[54] Yet further progress in the same direction was made much more difficult by the presidential elections of April 1999 in which an attempt to increase the legitimacy of the military's candidate, Abdelaziz Bouteflika, by having him run against heavy-weight, and therefore credible, political opponents was thwarted by their last minute withdrawal. This left Bouteflika an easy winner but lacking the popular authority required to address either the question of national reconciliation or the country's huge economic and social problems.

Family rule and elections in Morocco, Jordan and Kuwait

Had the monarchy been overthrown in either Morocco or Jordan, there is little doubt that it would have been replaced by a military government, perhaps with single-party rule support. In the event, however, the two Kings, Hussein and Hassan II, permitted occasional periods of contested elections on the assumption that party competition would allow them to combine some form of popular representation with a method of preventing the politicians from uniting against them. Writing of the Moroccan context, John Waterbury has described such a strategy as one of 'divide and survive'.[55]

Once Morocco had achieved its independence, its monarch, Mohammed V, saw his prime political task as one of preventing the main nationalist party, the Istiqlal, from attaining a position strong enough to challenge his own authority. This he did by denying party members the monopoly of cabinet positions they demanded and then trying his best to cause the party leadership to split, as it did in 1959 when a dissident group was encouraged to break away to form the new Union National des Forces Populaires (UNFP).[56] At the same time, the king took firm steps to ensure his own control over the army, the military and the bureaucracy as well as over the principal sources of political patronage.

Many of the same tactics were continued by his son and successor, Hassan II, who also added the extra precaution of encouraging his own supporters to create yet another new organisation, the Front pour la Défense des Institutions Constitutionelles (FDIC), which went on to win sixty-nine seats in the parliamentary elections of 1963, as opposed to the Istiqlal's forty-one and the UNFP's twenty-eight. Perhaps because of their success in preventing the FDIC from winning an absolute majority, members of both opposition parties were then subject to a campaign of official harassment culminating in the arrest of most of the UNFP leadership after the discovery of an alleged plot against the life of the king. Coincidentally, this was followed by a period of severe economic crisis leading to riots, the proclamation of a state of emergency in 1965 and the abrogation of parliamentary life for the next five years.

King Hassan made a number of attempts to revive the system of controlled multi-party activity, one in 1969/70 which was brought to a swift end by the attempted military coups of 1971 and 1972, and the second in 1977 when a new method of election was introduced combining direct election for two-thirds of the members with selection by an Electoral College for the rest. In the event, 141 seats were obtained by candidates standing as independents as opposed to forty-nine for the Istiqlal. This parliament remained in session until Morocco's fourth general election in 1984, once again held under new rules. On this occasion, 204 seats were subject to direct election and the remaining 102 to an indirect process of selection. There was also a considerable amount of gerrymandering of boundaries to ensure that many mainly urban constituencies contained a large rural vote.[57] This time the largest number of seats, eighty-three, went to yet another party of palace supporters, the Union Constitutionel (UC) formed in 1983, with forty-three to the Istiqlal and the remainder to the six other parties which had been allowed to compete.

It was only in the period following the Gulf War that King Hassan introduced measures to open up the system in such a way as to allow the possibility of an opposition party being invited to form a government under his new slogan of 'alternance' ('rotation'). After an election in 1993 in which the opposition won the majority of directly elected seats only to have this cancelled by a larger number of direct appointments, yet another set of constitutional amendments in 1996 led to a return to a system of direct elections for all seats. And even though the subsequent election, in November 1997, failed to produce an outright winner among opposition parties, the king asked the 73-year-old veteran politician, Abderrahman Youssefi, to form a cabinet supported by a seven-party coalition which took office in March 1998.

Jordan had a brief period of party competition between 1955 and the political crisis of April 1957 when all were banned by King Hussein. Candidates then stood as independents in the few general elections up to 1967 after which the king thought it wise to suspend parliamentary life almost entirely due to the situation of crisis and confusion caused by the Israeli occupation of the West Bank and the period of difficult relations with his Palestinian population which followed. Hence the Lower House did not meet at all for ten years from 1974 onwards, ostensibly on the grounds that this would contravene the resolution of the Rabat Arab Summit of that year that the PLO (and not Jordan) should be the sole representative of the Palestinian people.

Parliament was finally recalled in January 1984 to prepare for new elections. The introduction of a revised electoral law took two more years and the elections themselves were not held until November 1989. By this time the domestic situation had been transformed, first by the outbreak of the Palestinian *Intifada* on the West Bank, then by the riots and demonstrations of April 1989 protesting the price increases imposed as part of the government's austerity package. The temporary cabinet appointed to deal with the situation promised free elections without official interference. This encouraged 1,400 candidates to compete for eighty seats, twelve of them women. And although political parties remained banned, the authorities allowed them considerable latitude in advertising their connection with particular movements or trends. As a result, candidates generally believed to be associated with Jordan's well-organised Muslim Brothers won some thirty-two of the seats, with ten to fifteen going to men representing the various leftist, reformist and Palestinian groups.[58]

The election had two immediate consequences. One was the pressure it placed on King Hussein to define the conditions under which he would permit the existence of legal political parties. His answer was the establishment of a sixty-man Royal Commission to draw up a National Charter. Members were chosen from all the existing political organisations and seem to have agreed in advance to abide by the king's guidelines that the formation of a party was to be made dependent on the announcement of its support for both the monarchy and the constitution.[59] The new Charter was then presented to a national congress in June 1991. The second consequence was a growing conflict between the king and the Islamic opposition in the parliament, made worse by his tentative moves to normalise relations with the west and, later, the Israelis, after the Gulf War. This, in turn, led him to adopt a new electoral law in 1993 designed specifically to make it more difficult for members of the Muslim Brothers to get elected. To do this it replaced the previous system of multiple votes with a single vote one which, together with the continued over-representation of the rural areas, encouraged voting along personal or tribal lines while discriminating against urban-based candidates.[60] The new system had the immediate effect of reducing Muslim Brother representation to eighteen in the November 1993 elections. That the Brotherhood was able to perform even as well as it did must be put down to its developing relationship with Palestinians opposed to the peace process with Israel and with Jordan's underclass of the young unemployed and the poor.[61]

Relations between the king and the Muslim Brothers continued to decline leading to a wave of arrests of Islamist activists in 1994/5 including the increasingly outspoken Layth Shubylat, the head of the Engineers Association, followed by a boycott of the 1997 elections by the Islamic Action Front (the new name for the political wing of the Muslim Brothers) and eight other opposition parties in response to the king's refusal to amend 1993 electoral law. The end result was a parliament which, though containing some representatives from a number of other parties, was dominated by docile supporters of King Hussein.

Kuwait is the other family-ruled state with a substantial history of parliamentary life. Independence in 1961 was followed by the creation of a consultative assembly which drafted the 1962 constitution with its provision for an elected national assembly. The first elections were then held in 1963 with 205 persons standing as independents and competing for fifty seats. Successful candidates included members of the ruling, al-Sabah, family as well as merchants, intellectuals, members of the local Shi'i community and Bedouin.[62] The electorate was kept deliberately small, consisting initially of only 17,000 male citizens, defined by their membership of families which had lived in Kuwait continuously since 1920. One implication was the existence of tiny parliamentary constituencies in which most candidates were known personally to almost all of their electorate. Further elections were held in 1967 and 1975 after which the amir suddenly dissolved the assembly in 1976 for fear that it might encourage tensions inside the country's immigrant Arab population at the start of the Lebanese civil war. Problems had also arisen from the efforts of a small opposition bloc of ten or so deputies to curb some of the powers of the al-Sabahs and to air allegations that the family had interfered in the elections to prevent victory by some of its main critics.[63]

The amir agreed to new elections in 1981. Once again, government interference and the creation of yet smaller constituencies created problems for members of the unofficial opposition. Nevertheless, a few did manage to obtain seats, most notably men who stressed their personal religious credentials as either Sunnis or Shi'is. Another election was held in 1985 and produced an assembly which contained what J.F. Peterson has identified as four 'unofficial groupings' backed by 'readily identifiable organizations' with 'established platforms'.[64] However, this assembly lasted only a year, then finding itself dissolved as result of the heightened crisis which threatened to destabilise Kuwait towards the end of the Iran/Iraq war in 1986. Pressure for a return to democratic life began to build up slowly and, in early 1990, there were elections to a national council, the purpose of which was to discuss a way to revive the National Assembly which would also avoid the regular confrontations between the deputies and the Al-Sabah ministers which had seemed to be one of the inevitable problems of family rule. But this process was immediately interrupted by the Iraqi invasion.

As already noted in Chapter 6, most of the same problem re-emerged with a vengeance in the new National Assemblies elected after Kuwait's liberation in 1992 and 1996 with many deputies trying to hold leading members of the Al-Sabah responsible for their mismanaged diplomacy just before the occupation and for the loss of state funds during and after it. The result was an extended period of confrontation and negotiation in which both sides tried to work towards a new set of understandings regarding parliamentary practice. Certainly the most important of these was the Al-Sabah's attempt to establish a distinction between those family ministers whose actions remained exempt from criticism inside the assembly – specifically the prime minister and the ministers of foreign affairs, the interior and defence – and those who were not.[65] However, given the importance of the issue to both sides, it was unlikely that any such understanding, even if agreed on a temporary basis, could solve the basic problems of political accountability which the use of family as ministers must always raise.

The special case of Lebanon

The reasons for the comparative longevity of the Lebanese system of parliament and parties stems directly from its essential role at the centre of the process of confessional representation and inter-confessional political bargaining which was enshrined in the constitution of 1926 and further validated by the National Pact between the leaders of the Sunni and Maronite communities in 1943. Over time, this came to be underpinned by the widespread belief that some form of democracy was a necessary mechanism for integrating the country's various major sects into the Lebanese political field and then of regulating the often precarious relations between them.[66] Party activity was just one small, but increasingly unruly, component of the whole situation, being contained with some difficulty by the set of not very well-established rules and compromises which governed political life. Great problems arose when these began to break down under the pressure of events set in train by the appearance of growing economic and social inequality exacerbated by the anomalous presence of the

Palestinian militias after 1970 and by the repeated Israeli incursions into the south.

Many writers on Lebanon note the central role of parliament from 1926 onwards but then go on to explain it as the result of the deliberate attempt by men like the political thinker Michel Chiha to provide a mechanism for confessional cohabitation. A more likely explanation would stress the following points. First, there was widespread elite support for a political system based on the principle of sectarian representation.[67] A second point would stress the degree of fit between the system of parliamentary representation devised by those who drafted the 1926 constitution, a weak central administration and the type of *laissez-faire* economic system and inter-confessional arrangements that were already in existence in late Ottoman times. Third, given the French insistence that seats in the new assembly should be allocated to members of the most numerous sects in rough proportion to their numbers within the population at large, it was more or less inevitable that most of those elected would come from the country's leading families whose local influence was based on their control over significant local resources. Fourth, their presence in parliament, and hence their availability for cabinet office, then offered them access to yet more wealth and power; while the fact that this same possibility was open to Muslim notables as well as Christians provided them with great encouragement to downplay their opposition to the division of Lebanon from Syria in the interests of direct participation in the new system.

A final part of this same argument concerns the reasons why the central administration remained weak. This had a great deal to do with the fact that the Lebanese economy was dominated by merchant and banking interests with an antipathy to state control. But it was also the result of a situation in which the ability of the notables to satisfy their political clienteles depended on their capacity to provide them, personally, with the resources and services which a better developed administration would have provided out of central funds.

To begin with, there was little scope in such a system for the organised political party. On the one hand, most economic and social interests could be represented at government level either by the notable politicians or by one of the many sect-based institutions like the Maronite Church or the Maqasid Society, the leading Islamic charity. On the other, an economy based largely on agriculture and services did little to encourage the development of unions or any of the other urban solidarities that provide the basis for most class-based parties. In these circumstances, the majority of the deputies elected to the National Assembly (for example, two-thirds in 1964) ran either as independents or on some notable's electoral list, while the primary form of political grouping remained the parliamentary bloc with little or no general appeal beyond the reputation of its leader.[68]

Political organisations only began to register themselves as parties for the purpose of contesting elections in the first decade after independence. One of the first to do so was the Kataeb (also known as the Phalange), which, according to Frank Stoakes, took the plunge with 'some reluctance' in 1952.[69] By this he means that, although it saw the advantages of having representatives in the National Assembly, the Kataeb was anxious not to have to abandon its military arm consisting of well-trained young supporters. In the event, however, this proved no great worry, as the party's militia was used so effectively in the limited civil war of 1958 that it was immediately catapulted into national prominence as a defender of Christian interests, obtaining nine of the ninety-nine seats at the next elections and a regular place for one of its representatives in the cabinet. Control over the party was exercised by its leader, Pierre Gemayel, working through a political bureau supported by only a handful of specialised function-aries and a tiny staff. Meanwhile, great attention was paid to the recruitment of a disciplined membership which had reached a total of some 60,000 in the early 1960s, some 85 per cent of whom were Christian.[70] Other parties that had sufficient organisational ability to obtain a few seats in the assembly were the Progressive Socialist Party (PSP), the Syrian Socialist National Party (SSNP) and the Armenian Tashnaq Party.

In Lebanon, as elsewhere in the Arab world, groups calling themselves parties or movements existed for many other purposes besides electoral competition. Some represented the interests of local confessional communities, others had close links either with Arab parties or Arab regimes. As violence became a more prominent feature of Lebanese political life after 1967, many also began to organise their own militias, as well as to develop a powerful critique of the parliamentary system. A good example of such a group is Ibrahim Qulailat's Independent Nasserites, in Arabic *al-Murabitun*, which combined the function of social club in many of the poorer quarters of Beirut with a growing emphasis on military recruitment.[71] Their growing strength then allowed many of the more radical groups associated with Kamal Jumblatt's PSP and the Palestine Liberation Organisation to come together to form what was later to be known as the National Movement, with the aim of pushing for major changes in the political system. This was strongly opposed by the leaders of the Kataeb who saw themselves increasingly as major defenders of the existing status quo. It was developments such as these that encouraged the party militias to take up arms during the first rounds of serious fighting in and around Beirut in 1975, pulling in various parts of the army, the Palestinians, and, later, the Syrians, after them.

It was only in 1989, fourteen long years later, that the fighting died down sufficiently to allow representatives of the warring groups to meet in Taif, Saudi Arabia, so as to work out the ground rules for a return to parliamentary life. The main innovation was a recognition of the need to share political office on a fifty-fifty basis between Christians and Muslims as opposed to the 6/5 ratio used before. To do this the number of seats in the National Assembly was enlarged from ninety-nine to 108. The first election held under the new rules in 1992, proved a somewhat unsatisfactory affair given the fact that candidates were given only three months notice, that the electoral rolls were incomplete after the huge movements of population during the civil war and that the Syrian army was still present in much of the country. For these and other reasons there was a boycott by the major Christian groupings, something which helped to account for a particularly low turn out. Nevertheless, this was enough to allow the system to return to some semblance of normalcy, underlined by the presence of eight deputies from the Shi'i Hizbollah movement which had formed a political party in 1990 alongside its military wing. A second national election followed in 1996. Although marred by the usual accusations of widespread interference and manipulation, it obtained extra importance from the fact that it marked the return of most of the Christian parties to the assembly.

Some concluding remarks on the practice of Arab democracy

Even a brief survey such as this is testimony to the variety of electoral experience in the Arab countries and the difficulty of making useful generalisations. Nevertheless, it should be sufficient to highlight the existence of some of the more important variables which have affected Middle Eastern political history during the twentieth century. On the one hand, electoral democracy seems to have survived best in those countries where it played a central role either in mediating communal relations, as in Lebanon, or as part of the ruling family's strategy for standing above a process of orchestrated party competition, as in Jordan and Morocco. On the other, it has had an obviously chequered progress in those countries where post-independence difficulties tended to encourage those regimes which placed primary emphasis on a mixture of rapid economic and social development with political control. There, as elsewhere in the ex-colonial world, the one-party state was taken as the ideal model until its failure to negotiate the problems posed by international indebtedness stimulated a fresh set of leaders to introduce a process of controlled economic liberalisation as far as both politics and the economy were concerned.

It follows that much of the responsibility for democracy's uneven record must lie with those either in power at independence or who seized it from them shortly thereafter. But some responsibility must also attach to those members of each country's political elite who first justified the loss of political freedom in exchange for what was supposed to be the more important goal of national development and then, once an opportunity was offered to form new political parties, proceeded to organise them in a top-down way which more or less replicated the authoritarianism of the regime itself. Meanwhile, decades of statist economic management had created a set of vested interests whose desire to protect their gains made them automatically suspicious of popular government and its accompanying pressures for accountability and an end to corrupt relationships between bureaucrats and businessmen. Lastly, the simultaneous appearance of radical religious movements, each with its own militant wing, made the whole process of creating new forms of political representation that much more difficult. Whether or not Islam *per se* was inimical to democracy is a large question to which there can be no satisfactory answer. But the particular practices of particular Muslim groups were sufficiently ambiguous in this regard as to encourage quite considerable doubts among their more secular-minded countrymen.

All this is enough to raise questions about blanket statements concerning a basic Middle Eastern incapacity with regard to proper democratic practice. If we start by looking at the historical record rather than by reliance on a series of *ex cathedra* observations about what is lacking in Arab society and its political culture, we find a variety of initiatives, some of which showed considerable promise for shorter or longer periods of time, others which, however constrained, were enough to suggest that, given a more favourable local and regional climate, the same country and the same society might well be able to return to a more open political life in the future. At the very least, what history reveals is a living legacy which not only keeps the idea of democracy alive but also ensures that it is subject to continuous lively debate.[72]

Notes

1 There is a huge literature on the subject. I find the most useful contributions to have been made by Ayubi, *Over-stating the Arab State: Politics and Society in the Middle East*, Chapter 11; John L. Esposito and John O. Voll, *Islam and Democracy* (New York and Oxford: Oxford University Press, 1996); Sami Zubaida, *Islam, the People and the State* (London: I.B. Tauris, 1995), Chapter 6; and the contributors to Ghassan Salamé (ed.) *Democracy without Democrats* (London: I.B. Tauris, 1994), particularly the editor himself, Jean Leca, John Waterbury and Gudrun Krämer.

2 The notion of competitive elections is central to Karl Popper's definition of democracy quoted in Charmers Johnson, 'South Korean democratization: The role of economic development', *The Pacific Review*, 2/1 (1989), pp. 3–4.

3 P.J. Vatikiotis, *The Modern History of Egypt* (London: Weidenfeld and Nicolson, 1969), p. 283.

4 For an early example, see Sidqi's own memoirs, *Mudhakkirati* (Cairo: Dar al-Hilal Press, 1950), pp. 119–38.

5 This point is well argued by Israel Gershoni in his 'Confronting Nazism in Egypt – Tawfiq al-Hakim's anti-totalitarianism 1938–1945', *Tel Aviver Jahr-Buch Für Deutsche Geschichte* (Tel Aviv: Institut für Deutsche Geschichte, Tel Aviv University), XXVI (1997), particularly pp. 136–46.

6 For a useful analysis of this trend, see Malcolm Kerr, 'Arab radical notions of democracy', *St Antony's Papers*, 16 (London: Chatto and Windus, 1963), pp. 9–11.

7 Quoted in BBC, *SWB*, 194, 12 March 1957.

8 *The Return of Consciousness*, trans. Bayly Winder (New York: New York University Press; and Basingstoke: Macmillan, 1985).

9 Waterbury, *The Egypt of Nasser and Sadat*, p. 313.

10 Leonard Binder, *In a Moment of Enthusiasm: Political Power and the Second Stratum in Egypt* (Chicago and London: University of Chicago Press, 1978), p. 310; and El Kosheiri Mahfouz, *Socialisme et pouvoir en Egypte* (Paris: Librairie Générale de Droit et de Jurisprudence, 1972), p. 173.

11 Mark H. Cooper, *The Transformation of Egypt* (London: Croom Helm, 1982), p. 31.

12 Clement Henry Moore, *Images of Development: Egyptian Engineers in Search of Industry* (Cambridge, MA and London: The MIT Press, 1980), p. 58; Raymond Baker, *Egypt's Uncertain Revolution Under Nasser and Sadat* (Cambridge, MA and London: Harvard University Press, 1978), pp. 84–5.

13 El Kosheiri Mahfouz, *Socialisme et pouvoir*, pp. 125–7.

14 For an example of the ambition to extend its control, see the interview with the leader of the ASU, Ali Sabri, in ibid., p. 177.

15 Baker, *Egypt's Uncertain Revolution*, p. 108.
16 Cooper, *Transformation of Egypt*, pp. 194–8.
17 Waterbury, *Egypt of Nasser and Sadat*, p. 368.
18 Robert Bianchi, *Unruly Corporatism: Associational Life in Twentieth Century Egypt* (Oxford: Oxford University Press, 1989), pp. 84–6.
19 Information supplied privately by the late Ahmad Bahaeddin.
20 For full results, see *Revue de la Presse égyptienne* (Cairo), 13 (July 1984), pp. 11–27.
21 Bertus Hendricks, 'Egypt's elections: Mubarak's bond', *MERIP*, 14/1, 129 (January 1985), pp. 11–18.
22 The minister was Butros Butros Ghali, then minister of state for foreign affairs, later Secretary General of the United Nations. Private communication from the late Magdi Wahba.
23 For full results, see *Revue de la Presse égyptienne*, 27 (1987), p. 245.
24 Bertus Hendricks, 'Egypt's new political map: Report from the election campaign', *MERIP*, 17/4, 147 (July–August 1987), pp. 23–30; and Adel Darwish, 'Mubarak's electoral triumph', *The Middle East*, 151 (May 1987), pp. 11–14.
25 The argument about the NDP winning any open election can be found in Darwish, ibid., p. 11.
26 Max Rodenbeck, 'Egypt: disdain and apathy', *Middle East International*, 7 December 1990, pp. 15–16.
27 Eberhard Kienle, 'Désélectionner par le haut: Le Wafd dans les élections législatives de 1995', in Sandrine Gamblin (ed.), *Contours et détours du politique en Egypte: Les élections législatives de 1995* (Cairo: Cedej and Paris: L'Harmattan, 1997), p. 136.
28 There is a useful analysis of this point in ibid, pp. 143–7.
29 Kienle, 'Désélectioner par le haut', pp. 48–9.
30 See his 'State controlled elections: A framework', in Guy Hermet, Richard Rose and Alain Rouquié (eds), *Elections without Choices* (London and Basingstoke: Macmillan, 1987), pp. 3–16.
31 Kienle, 'Désélectioner par le haut', p. 147.
32 Hinnebusch, *Authoritarian Power and State Formation*, pp. 145–7, 166–77.
33 Batatu, *Syria's Peasantry, the Descendants of its Lesser Rural Notables and Their Politics* (Princeton, NJ: Princeton University Press, 1999), Table 13–1, p. 178. These totals are generally larger than the totals given by Hinnebusch in *Authoritarian Power*, pp. 178–9.
34 Ibid., pp. 177–85.
35 Ibid., p. 312.
36 Whether or not there is another struggle for the succession as seemed about to break out during Asad's illness in 1984 it is likely that the winner would call a meeting of the Ba'th Party to legitimise his victory. For an account of the 1984 crisis, see Alasdair Drysdale, 'The succession question in Syria', *Middle East Journal*, 39/2 (Spring, 1985), pp. 246–57.
37 Hinnebusch, *Authoritarian Power*, pp. 316–17.
38 For example, Christine Moss Helms, *Iraq: Eastern Flank of the Arab World* (Washington, DC: The Brookings Institution, 1984), p. 87.
39 See, for example, the Ba'th Party newspaper, *Al-Thawra*, 14 February 1980, quoted in Ofra Bengio, 'Iraq', in Colin Legum (ed.), *Middle East Contemporary Survey*, 4, 1979–80 (London and New York: Holmes & Meier, 1981), p. 505.
40 Faleh A. Jabar, Ahmad Shikara and Keiko Sakai, 'From storm to thunder: Unfinished showdown between Iraq and US', *IDEO Spot Survey* (Tokyo: Institute of Developing Economies, March 1998), p. 16.
41 Ibid. See also Youssef M. Ibrahim, 'How the Baath rules Iraq: With a very tight fist', *New York Times*, 11 January 1981.

42 'Statement of the Iraqi Ba'th Party Ninth Regional Congress', 27 June 1982, quoted in, Ofra Bengio, 'Iraq' in Colin Legum *et al.* (eds), *Middle East Contemporary Survey*, 6, 1981–2 (London and New York: Holmes & Meier, 1983), pp. 588–90.

43 Jabbar, Shikara and Sakai, 'From storm to thunder', p. 28.

44 This point is made by Amatzia Baram, *Building Towards Crisis: Saddam Husayn's Strategy for Survival* (Washington, DC: The Washington Institute for Near East Policy, 1998), pp. 40–1.

45 Eberhard Kienle, *Ba'th versus Ba'th: The Conflict Between Syria and Iraq* (London: I.B. Tauris, 1990), pp. 38–46.

46 In Iraq, for instance, Saddam Hussein was regarded as the only major ideologue and by the early 1980s was credited with having over 200 books, articles and essays to his name. Helms, *Iraq*, pp. 105–6.

47 Ibid., p. 104.

48 For examples of such claims, see Saddam Hussein's 'Interviews with Arab and foreign journalists', in *Saddam Hussein on Current Events in Iraq*, trans. (London: Longman, 1977), p. 48; or Tariq Aziz, *The Revolution of the New Way* (n.p., n.d, printed in March 1977), pp. 30, 37.

49 Both phrases can be found in 'Statement of the Iraqi Ba'th Party Ninth Regional Congress', quoted by Bengio, 'Iraq', in Colin Legum (ed.), *Middle East Contemporary Survey*, 4, 1979–80, pp. 616, 618.

50 Fred Halliday, 'Tunisia's uncertain future', *Middle East Report*, 163 (March/April 1990), p.25.

51 Lisa Anderson, 'The Tunisian National Pact of 1988', *Government and Opposition*, 26/2 (Spring, 1991), pp. 244–60.

52 Arun Kapil, 'Algeria's elections show Islamist strength', *Middle East Report*, 163 (March–April 1990), p.13.

53 Many of the main factors underlying these events are still not known. There are, however, many members of the Algerian elite who claim that Chadli was trying to use FIS to get rid of his rivals in the FLN.

54 The *Economist*, 14 June 1997, p. 48.

55 John Waterbury, *Commander of the Faithful*, pp. 145–9.

56 Douglas E. Ashford, *Political Change in Morocco* (Princeton, NJ: Princeton University Press, 1961), p. 97.

57 Mustapha Sehemi, 'Les élections législatives au Maroc', *Maghreb/Machrek*, 107 (January/February/March 1985), p. 25.

58 Lamis Andoni, 'King Hussein leads Jordan into a new era', *Middle East International*, 17 November 1989, p. 3.

59 Lamis Andoni, 'Preparing a national charter' and 'Incorporating all trends', *Middle East International*, 2 February 1990, p. 10 and 13; April 1990, p.10.

60 The difference between the two systems is well explained in Glenn E. Robinson, 'Can Islamists be democrats? The case of Jordan', *Middle East Journal*, 51/3 (Summer, 1997), pp. 373–87.

61 Ibid., pp. 382–3.

62 J.E. Peterson, *The Gulf Arab States: Steps Towards Political Participation* (New York: Praeger, 1988), pp. 39–40; Rosemary Said Zahlan, *The Making of the Modern Gulf States* (London: Unwin Hyman, 1989), pp. 37, 40–1.

63 Ibid., p. 42.

64 Peterson, *Gulf Arab States*, pp. 42–6.

65 See Robin Allen, 'Emir of Kuwait acts on stand-off', *Financial Times*, 12 June 1998.

66 For example, Kamal Salibi, *A House of Many Mansions* (London: I.B. Tauris, 1988).

67 Edmond Rabbath, *La formation du Liban politique et constitutionel: Essai de synthèse* (2nd edn, Beirut: Librairie Orientale, 1986), I, pp. 393–7; Meir Zamir, *The Formation of Modern Lebanon* (Ithaca, NY and London and New York: Cornell University Press, 1985), pp. 207–13.

68 Michael Hudson, *The Precarious Republic: Political Modernization in Lebanon* (New York: Random House, 1968), p. 232.
69 Frank Stoakes, 'The supervigilantes: The Lebanese Kataeb Party as builder, surrogate and defender of the state', *Middle Eastern Studies*, 11/1 (January 1975), p. 215.
70 Ibid., pp. 216–17.
71 Marion Farouk-Sluglett and Peter Sluglett, 'Aspects of the changing nature of Lebanese confessional politics: Al-Murabitun, 1958–1979', *Peuples Mediterranéens*, 20 (July/September 1982), pp. 67–8.
72 For example, Ayubi, *Over-stating the Arab State*, pp. 442–5.

9 The politics of religious revival

Introduction

The establishment of an Islamic state in Iran in 1979 was the major event of the first period of heightened activity by religiously-inspired political movements triggered off by the 1967 Arab–Israeli war. However, long before that, religion had played an important role in the process of state and nation building in the region due to the fact that it was inextricably involved with central questions of identity and of communal values. And it continues to remain of exceptional importance as states and religious organisations of many types vie with one another for influence over basic issues concerning the exercise of power and the creation of a just society. An analysis of its role in the political process is thus essential, but also difficult. I will begin by drawing attention to some of the definitional problems involved.

First and foremost, it is important to note that the study of religion in politics is not the study of religion *per se* but of its influences on the policies and the distribution of power within a modern state. It follows that an examination of particular theologies or systems of religious law is only relevant to the extent that these provide motives and programmes for political action. To use a topical example suggested by Dale Eickelman and James Piscatori, a Muslim woman's putting on a veil is not an inherently political act but 'it becomes one when it is transformed into a public symbol'.[1] This approach has the additional virtue of allowing the subject to be analysed by the usual tools of the social scientist. However, we should also be aware that, although religious phenomena can come to life in connection with a 'complex cluster of other social and cultural vectors' they are not directly caused by them.[2] Hence significant parts of the story are inevitably beyond the scope of such a method: notably the religious experience itself – what William James called the 'individual pinch of destiny' – and the sense of belonging to a community of believers.[3]

A second definitional problem concerns the scope of such an inquiry. In my own opinion it should extend to an examination of the political influence of all three major Middle Eastern religions, that is Christianity and Judaism as well as Islam. For one thing, studies of politico-religious activity that confine themselves exclusively to Muslims tend to exaggerate the specificity of Islamically-inspired political practice, and so suggest that it is more abnormal – and often more violent and obscurantist – than it really is. For another, given the widespread use of religion as an ethnic or political marker, there are many places whose politics cannot be understood without reference to the central role played by the interaction and contestation between peoples of different religious identities, for example in Lebanon, Egypt and Sudan (Muslims and Christians) or Israel and the West Bank (Muslims, Christians and Jews).

The next question to ask is: what do the modern politico-religious movements in the Middle East have in common? A basic shared ingredient, as Sami Zubaida notes, is that they operate within a common historical context in which they are almost all contestants for power and influence within specific national political arenas defined by particular state borders.[4] This is not to deny that a number of the movements concerned have significant cross-border or international linkages, nor that some have attacked the very legitimacy of the modern state on theological grounds. What it does mean is that the vast majority of religio-political actors behave as though their primary aim was to influence policies and practices within one given system.

Two somewhat contradictory implications follow. One is the fact that, given their concern to obtain power and influence in a twentieth-century context, the religious actors share many of the same vocabularies and types of organisational structures with the more secular politicians within the same political arena. They speak of democracy, of civil society, of human rights and of governmental accountability. Above all, they share a general concern with nationalism and the national project, even when, like the founder of Egypt's Muslim Brotherhood, they take pains to underline the distance between their type of patriotism and love of country and that of their secular adversaries.[5] The second implication is that, for all their engagement with modernity, men with a basically religious world view find it difficult to translate their theological principles into concrete programmes for creating institutional structures markedly different from those of the secular nation state. Hence, for all the vast amount of religious literature devoted to questions of state power, no Islamic movement has been able to provide a satisfactory alternative to the existing politico-administrative structures made up of bureaucracies, judiciaries, parliaments and parties.[6] It follows that, on those rare occasions when a religious movement has been in a position to create a new political system, as in Iran in 1979, it simply put the existing institutions to its own use. However, it also follows that there is a general air of uncertainty about what a truly Muslim, or Jewish, polity would look like. And this in turn helps to explain some of the widespread opposition to movements which might conceivably seize state power without anyone being able to know in advance exactly how they would put it to use.

It is also important to ask what it was that caused so many groups of different religious persuasions to become very much more active in the period following the 1967 war. It certainly had something to do with the traumatic impact of the war itself, whether as a blow to Muslim self-confidence – and so a spur to greater religious activism – or as an apparent vindication of a Jewish right to live in, and to govern, all of Palestine. More generally, it can be ascribed to the perceived failures of the secular, developmentalist ideologies and strategies which had been used to legitimate most newly independent regimes. Lastly, it can be linked to the local impact of the stresses and strains posed by the world economic crisis of the 1970s, followed by the drive towards global economic integration in the 1980s, and its encouragement to what V.S. Naipaul has styled the 'awakening' to historical self-consciousness of all kinds of groups and communities which began to see themselves as others saw them – often as backward, marginal, obscurantist – and then responded by developing counter-movements of spirited self-assertion.[7] In an increasingly interconnected world, differences in belief are more directly visible and directly encountered, and so, in Clifford Geertz's words, 'ready for suspicion, worry, repugnance and dispute'.[8] It is these new conditions which, as much as anything else, generated that sense of being under threat, and that mood of urgency and impatience which was the hallmark of so much of the new religious politics.

The most vocal, the most militant and, as it happens, the smallest (numerically) of such groups were soon classified by western commentators under the general term of 'fundamentalist'. This was a very unsatisfactory notion in any number of ways. The concept was originally coined to describe the doctrines of certain Protestant denominations in the United States just after the First World War which were based on a belief in the absolute truth of the holy scriptures combined with a rejection of so-called 'modern' values and much of the rest of the modern world.[9] However, as has often been pointed out, the vast majority of Muslims are – and have always been – scripturalists with a faith based squarely on belief in the literal inerrancy of the Quran.[10] But, just as important, Islam, like the other major religions, is a lived tradition in which believers are surrounded by institutions and agencies (mosques, schools and preachers) for reminding them of its history and reinforcing certain types of correct religious practice.[11] Yet none of these institutions can stand still. And all take part in a constant reinterpretation of beliefs and practices in the light of contemporary conditions, a process which can also be made to yield political programmes and new political perspectives for anyone who wants to use them. In the case of Islam, at least, a better word to describe the religious politics of the 1970s and onwards is the one most of its practitioners use themselves: *tajdid* or 'renewal'.[12]

Two more valuable concepts for understanding the contemporary practice of religious politics are 'communalism' and 'protest'. The former springs directly from the use of religion as an ethnic marker defining one community against another. As Zubaida points out in the Islamic context, communal ideas do not necessarily entail any specific political ideas other than the inferiority of another religion.[13] However, they can, and have been used very successfully to mobilise large numbers of people behind movements calling for particular religious-based forms of self-assertion, for example by the NIF in Sudan or the heightened form of political self-awareness to be found among many Egyptian Copts from the 1970s on.

Protest, for its part, involves a resolve that the wrongs in society must immediately be put to right. As a concept it can be used to explain why certain social groups feel more discontented by the actual status quo than others.[14] It can also be used to describe a form of politics in which the protesters seek to delegitimate existing regimes by calling attention to their failure to maintain such core religious values as honesty and social justice as well as, in the Islamic case at least, their failure to implement vital parts of the *sharia* or religious law. The alternative is to be provided by Islam, presented as an instrument of social change. This can operate at the national level or as part of an attempt to create what Olivier Roy describes as 'Islamized spaces' in which local groups enforce their version of religious values over people living within relatively small and well-defined areas.[15]

Lastly, we should note an essential feature of most religious politics through the ages and that is the tension between the conversion of society at large, through teaching and preaching, and that of obtaining sufficient power to oversee the introduction of a religious way of life by the state itself. Both are such large and difficult projects that it is perhaps not surprising that, in a western historical experience at least, there have been only rare examples of theocracies in which day-to-day government was exercised by religious personnel. It can also be argued that, from at least the eighteenth century onwards, the notion of the division between church and state was devised to draw a hard and fast boundary between the two spheres, making religious influence over the executive and legislature ever more difficult. The existence of such a boundary also fitted well with the institutionalised experience of churches like the Roman Catholic, that direct involvement in the political arena was dangerous, divisive, and undermining of its eternal mission. As we shall see, something of the same debate about the proper relationship between religion and the state took place in Iran after the clerical take-over of 1979–80. It has also created a constant tension within the Muslim Brother organisations in Egypt and Sudan where the leadership has generally concentrated on winning converts, leaving it to smaller and more radical groups to argue for direct intervention in the general political process as a way of accelerating the achievement of their particular religious aims.

I will now try to elaborate on some of these themes by beginning with an examination of the Islamic context. It was there, during the last decades of the Ottoman Empire, that the modern division between church and state, religion and politics was first asserted, practised and contested, and where forms of communalism first became institutionalised in politically important ways. I will then move on to a discussion of the Iranian revolution, a significant example of a largely religiously-inspired movement which obtained the power needed to create an Islamic state. As a result, it exercised an immediate influence over many other types of religio-political movements in the Middle East, even if, over time, its impact on most Sunni Arab political groups was much reduced, and often heatedly denied.[16] I will look at Arab religio-political movements in the next section, and those involving Christians and then Jews in the last.

The Islamic context: an introduction

The first encounter with the modern world as far as the practice of an Islamic politics was concerned was the introduction of western commercial and penal codes into the Ottoman Empire in the mid-nineteenth century. Prior to this moment, although there had been two recognisable types of law, the religious (*sharia*) and the Sultan's (*qanun*), both had been administered by the same religious personnel and constituted, to all intents and purposes, a single, interlocking, mutually reinforcing system. However, with the spread of the new *nizamiye* (westernised) courts administered by a Ministry of Justice, not only was this uniformity broken but it also began to be possible to make the conceptual distinction between religion and state, something that was neither thinkable nor permissible before.[17] And this, in turn, became the basis for a new type of politics begun during the reign of Abdul-Hamid II (1876–1909), in which the Sultan and his advisers sought to instrumentalise Islam as a means of integrating the Muslim peoples more firmly into the Empire as well as to provide extra legitimacy for sultanic rule. Later, with the creation of the Turkish Republic in 1923, the notion of the division between politics and religion was used as the basis for a policy of secularisation (better described as laicisation) aimed at reducing the power of the religious establishment to influence state policy.

A second nineteenth-century innovation with important consequences for the future of religious politics stemmed from the Ottoman response to European pressure to grant legal equality to the Empire's Christian and Jewish subjects. This took the form of combining a general support for universalism with the creation of communal frameworks for peoples of different sects and religions in which they were allowed – even encouraged – to maintain their ethnic identity and language. Many of the same arrangements were carried over into the colonial period but with the further distinction that the Christians and Jews now represented 'minorities' which required special protection from the Muslim 'majority', yet another powerful modern notion. Much later, at the end of the twentieth century, such practices began to be seen by some thinkers as a possible model for a set of relationships to be established in any Arab Islamic state with a substantial non-Muslim population, for example in Sudan.

The response of most Middle Eastern Muslims to these developments took two particular forms, both based on the new notion of religion as something distinct from politics and the state. One was the attempt begun in Egypt and the Ottoman Empire to legitimise Islam in a modern context by finding counterparts in Islamic political theory to such powerful western concepts as 'democracy', 'constitutionalism' and 'popular sovereignty'. The other was to oppose the threat posed by secularism and western cultural invasion either by creating a protective umbrella of institutions within which a good Muslim could continue to practice his religious duties without outside interference or by pressuring the state to reverse its policies of pushing the *sharia* to the margins of the legal system. Undoubtedly the most powerful and influential organisation engaged in this latter type of politics was the Society of Muslim Brothers founded in Egypt in 1928 to which I will return later in the chapter.

Which Middle Eastern religio-political movement was the first to call explicitly for the creation of an Islamic state remains something of a moot point. Some argue that it was the Muslim Brothers in the 1930s, others that this development had to wait until well after the Second World War.[18] There is more consensus about what the key components of such a state were supposed to be. Thinking on the subject by Muslims tended to concentrate on two major points, to the exclusion of almost all else.[19] One was the question of leadership which involved specifying what type of person had the qualifications necessary to govern such a state and who his advisers should be. The second was the belief that an Islamic state had both to sustain, and to be guided by, Islamic Law conceived of as a set of God-given principles to guide conduct and to indicate what was good and what was not. Discussion of just how the *sharia* was to be implemented in its entirety, or how it could form the basis of a modern legal system, took up much less time. We can be reasonable sure that, as Talal Asad asserts, there has never been a Muslim society in which the *sharia* has 'governed more than a fragment of social life'.[20] Nevertheless, for the vast majority of Muslim political activists, disturbed by the extent to which their religion seemed to have been driven out of the public sphere, its application, either directly or as the basis for the entire legal system, became their major rallying cry and the touchstone of whether a state was to be considered properly Islamic or not. For them, the gap between religion and politics, religion and the state, impiously opened up by western interference, had to be closed without delay.

Religion and politics in the Islamic Republic of Iran

Shortly before the overthrow of the shah's regime in January 1979 the leadership of the revolutionary coalition adopted as its slogan: 'Independence, Freedom, Islamic Republic'.[21] This was a clear indication of the growing importance of the Ayatollah Khomeini and his clerical allies. However, they were, as yet, still only part of a much larger coalition of anti-shah forces containing groups with a wide variety of ideological positions and it was some years before the role of religion in the new power structure came to be more clearly defined. As I have given an account of the main outlines of the political history of the Iranian revolution in Chapters 5 and 6, I will now concentrate more directly on those issues which are basic to an understanding of the central project for establishing an Islamic state.

No sooner had the revolutionary leadership assembled in Teheran after the flight of the shah than it created a revolutionary council and a provisional government with responsibility for drawing up a new constitution and for organising elections to fill the major offices of state. This was followed, in March 1979, by a popular referendum containing the single question: Do you agree with the replacement of the Monarchy by an Islamic republic? The result was an overwhelming majority for the 'yes' vote. Although there is evidence of considerable pressure to toe the official line, Shaul Bakhash is surely correct to argue that the result did indeed represent the wishes of a considerable majority of the Iranian people.[22]

There was similar general agreement that the institutional structure of such a republic should be defined in a new constitutional document. Its first draft was drawn up by members of the provisional government and relied heavily on principles to be found in both the 1906 Iranian constitution and that of the Fifth French Republic. It is surprising now to discover how readily this was agreed to by Khomeini and his close colleagues who made only minimal amendments, even though the draft principles contained no mention of a privileged position for the clergy and provided its newly created Council of Guardians only limited veto power over legislation deemed to be un-Islamic.[23] Just why this was so remains unclear. However, it may well have had something to do with Khomeini's desire to set up the new governmental structure as quickly as possible so that it would be in place before his death which he then thought imminent.[24] Furthermore, he also seems to have been initially distrustful of the clergy's ability to govern on its own and so wanted a way of incorporating lay expertise.

Nevertheless, no sooner was this draft submitted for discussion by an elected assembly of experts with a large clerical majority than it was subject to significant revision. As a riposte to those on the left who accused it of making too many concessions to religion, the clerical party led by the Ayatollah Mohamad Beheshti now introduced the notion of rule by a just and wise expert in religious law – *velayet-e faqih* (the government of the Faqih or just jurist) – as the centre-piece of the whole constitutional structure, although only after an interesting debate which had revealed considerable misgivings on the part of some of the mullahs concerning the dangers to religion itself of clerical involvement in day-to-day politics. However, in the end, as Bakhash notes, it was the argument that the role of the Faqih was essential to the realisation of an Islamic state that won the day.[25] A second key amendment was one which provided the Council of Guardians with automatic scrutiny over parliamentary legislation, a power to review greatly in excess of that of the highest court in, say, France or the United States, and something which was to have major political consequences in the years to come.[26]

The promulgation of the new constitution paved the way not only for the election of a president and Majles (parliament) but also for a fierce struggle for power which pitted Beheshti's newly formed Islamic Republican Party (IRP) against an array of religious and secular forces which opposed what they soon identified as a blatant attempt to monopolise power. To begin with, the leaders of the party were very much on the defensive and unable to rely on the sustained support of the Faqih, the Ayatollah Khomeini himself. Nevertheless, as the months went by they began to obtain enough influence within the new revolutionary organisations, such as the revolutionary courts and revolutionary guards, as well as over important networks of provincial clergy, to support their sustained drive to create what was soon to become a virtual theocracy with mullah control over almost every aspect of government. Hence, although the IRP's candidate received only a small proportion of the votes in the presidential election of January 1980, its greater success in the Majles elections two months later gave it a platform from which to obtain most of the important posts in the cabinet in spite of fierce opposition from its most formidable opponent, the new President Abol Hasan Bani-Sadr.

The IRP's drive for power was supplemented, first by a so-called 'cultural revolution' designed to impose its own brand of Islamic orthodoxy on the universities and the media, then by a purge in which opponents within the bureaucracy were replaced by its own loyal supporters The only institution able to blunt its onslaught was the army, whose role in the defence of the country against the Iraqi invasion in September 1980 was too important to allow its efficiency to be undermined. But, even here, the IRP made considerable inroads by insisting that the army employ the revolutionary guards as a parallel military arm.

The role of the Ayatollah Khomeini in this whole process was not at all clear-cut. In Bakhash's account of the struggle between Bani-Sadr and his IRP ministers, he often sided with the president, at least in the early stages.[27] Over time, however, his reservations about the role of mullahs in government seem to have greatly diminished, while Bani-Sadr's own somewhat erratic performance did nothing to maintain his confidence in either the skill or the reliability of non-clerical experts. Meanwhile, he was inevitably influenced by the IRP's own drive for power and its success in subduing a fragmented and increasingly desperate opposition. As a result, when the Majles began impeachment proceedings against the president in June 1981, Khomeini seems to have felt that he had little option but to go along with the decision to remove Bani-Sadr and to replace him with the IRP's own candidate, Mohamed al-Raja'i. Two months later Raja'i himself was killed in the second of two huge bomb explosions directed against the IRP leadership by a coalition of radical Islamic and leftist groups led by the People's Mojahedin. He was succeeded by Ali Khamenei who was elected president in October 1981.

During the next two years the clergy associated with the IRP crushed what was left of the opposition and established the type of theocratic government and politics which has lasted until the present day. It is interesting to ask what role religion played in its institutional structures and practices as well as to address the larger question of what this might show us about the character of the Iranian version of an Islamic state.

These questions can be approached from two opposite perspectives. The first is to ask what Khomeini and his supporters thought about the matter. To judge from their own statements, they were in no doubt whatsoever that, given the existence of an Islamic constitution and the role of the Faqih, Iran was, by definition, an Islamic state. This can be seen, for example, in President Khamenei's speech on the eighth anniversary of the revolution in February 1987 in which he pointed out that:

the environment is now an Islamic environment, not the environment of western culture. It is a healthy environment. Parents are no longer worried about the morals of their children.[28]

If further proof was needed the leadership could have pointed to the Islamisation of the legal system, something to which Khomeini himself attached particular importance.[29] This involved the progressive elimination of all non-religiously trained judges as well as the re-writing of many of the laws to ensure that they conformed to Islamic precepts.

Looked at from the outside, and taking account of actual political practice, the picture appears somewhat different and the tension between the system's Islamic and modern features much more apparent. In Ali Banuazizi's apt summation, there was an inevitable contradiction between a modern bureaucratic state operating within a constitutional framework and a non-elected theocratic 'sovereign' (the Faqih) who is above all such accountability.[30] This contradiction informed politics at two levels. One was inside the clerical elite itself. To return to Banuazizi again: he observes that 'one of the most remarkable features of the rule of the Ayatollahs has been the degree to which this relatively small group of men, in spite of their many similarities in social origin and intellectual background, have disagreed on some of the most fundamental issues concerning an Islamic society and government'.[31] Even Khomeini himself, a man with a 'towering presence' and a uniquely powerful position within the constitutional structure was unable to impose his own views on his senior colleagues in many important instances, for example, in the on-going dispute between the Majles and the Council of Guardians over the role of private property in an Islamic state.[32] His successor, Ali Khamenei, a man with smaller religious learning and authority, made even less effort to stand above the various clerical factions, siding openly with the conservatives on most issues, and having to resort to simple political manoeuvrings if he was to have any hope of being able to exercise any influence over the rest.

Nevertheless, for all their internal debate, the mullahs of the clerical elite, managed to maintain enough of a common front to create a well-advertised boundary between what types of subject were and were not open to debate. They did this, in part, by making it clear that they would tolerate no criticism of the leader himself or of the government's ideological foundations. This was reinforced by their control over the Council of Guardians which had responsibility for vetting candidates hoping to stand for president or for the Majles elections. And if all else failed they had no compunction about arresting alleged opponents or sending members of the revolutionary guards to harass them or to beat them up. Power of this type placed considerable limits on the development of Islamic political thought, forcing liberal elements like President Khatami to keep his projection of a more pluralist, open Islam within the general ideological consensus and making life difficult for critics like the philosopher, Abdelkarim Soroush, who tried to promote a view of Islamic history as containing multiple traditions of thought and practice as opposed to the single orthodoxy stressed by the clerical regime.[33]

The second level was the one on which the clerical leadership had not only to coexist with the institutions of a modern state but also to devise policies to deal with the quotidian problems of the economy, rapid urbanisation and the management of a host of large state enterprises. Here the language of religion which was used to debate most issues at the highest level fitted uneasily with the technical vocabularies of the experts. Here too the mullahs were forced to recognise the constraints imposed by a constitution on, for example, the workings of the legal system which, although based on the *sharia*, was also enshrined in a written public law and overseen by persons chosen by the state rather than the religious establishment itself.[34] This was also the terrain in which the clergy had to negotiate with forces from the larger society about what was legitimate cultural activity and what constituted correct political behaviour. And, over time, it became the site for so many compromises between modern activities and religious norms – over women's employment, over music and entertainment, over sport, etc. – as to make Iranian daily life considerably less Islamic than that in many Muslim countries where the position of the *ulama*, or religious establishment, was very much less institutionalised.[35]

As for the underlying trends, close involvement in government and policy-making led to that loss of clerical legitimacy which critics had predicted at the time of the new revolutionary constitution in 1979. Furthermore, Olivier Roy is surely correct in his assertion that, if you start by creating an avowedly Islamic republic under religious guidance, further movement can only be one way: that is towards greater secularisation.[36] Nevertheless, as Roy also notes, by adopting a constitutional mode, the religious revolution has been able to buy itself time, finding what he calls a 'political space beyond Islamist and revolutionary rhetoric, that does not depend on the impossible virtue of its members but rather functions on the basis of institutions that survive in the absence of the divine world'.[37] It was this, more than anything else, that allowed the longevity of the clerical regime, its relative stability, its regular transfers of power and its on-going compromises between religious norms and the necessities of modern life.

Religious politics in the Arab countries

The Iranian revolution had a great impact in the Arabic countries, both on the local Shi'i populations who saw it as a means to improve their own, often marginalised, local status and many sections of the Sunni Muslim community, particularly those living under dictatorial or western-allied regimes. Coming as it did at the end of a decade of increasing religiosity and of religio-political activity, it was taken as proof of the fact that a popular movement could overthrow a tyrannical regime. 'For every pharaoh,' as the Iranian revolutionary slogan had it, 'there is a Moses'. Authoritarian regimes were already very much on the defensive from the 1967 Middle East war onwards. They now faced this fresh challenge from a whole variety of political actors who were rediscovering the vitality and mobilising power of an Islamic vocabulary particularly when it incorporated such powerful themes as nationalism and social justice. The fact that the mosque and its associated educational and welfare activities provided one of the few spaces that an authoritarian regime found difficult to control also helped the spread of a more activist message and the recruitment of more militant followers.

Of the various existing Sunni religious movements, the ones best placed to take advantage of the new mood were the Egyptian Muslim Brothers and their off-shoots in neighbouring Syria, Jordan, Palestine and Sudan. In Egypt, the Brotherhood had been founded in 1928 by a school teacher, Hasan al-Banna. To begin with it was just one among a large number of tiny religious organisations engaged in charity, education and mutual support.[38] However, the Brotherhood soon grew far beyond the others in membership and scope, and it is useful to ask why. One factor was certainly the organisational skill of its charismatic leader. This allowed him to create a loose structure by which an endless multiplication of self-sustaining local neighbourhood groups could be linked and directed at the national level by a high-profile leadership with access to newspapers and other forms of direct communication. Second, al-Banna developed what Nazih Ayubi calls a distinctive concept of the 'comprehensiveness of Islam' in which the construction of mosques, schools and clinics provided the framework in which an urban Muslim could live much of his life with little contact with the western and secular influences around him.[39]

Given these various strengths, the Muslim Brothers were able to recruit members at a rapid rate through the 1930s and were soon numerous enough to come into forceful contact with the major forces in the political arena. This had a number of important consequences. First, it encouraged the leadership to adapt its message so as to attract groups like workers or government employees who had previously been associated with the Wafd or one of the other more radical nationalist parties. Second, Hasan al-Banna and his lieutenants were alternately wooed and attacked by other politicians in such a way that it was necessary for them to try to define their political role more precisely. While al-Banna himself seems to have been content to act as the religious conscience of the nation, for example by writing letters to the king containing his views on matters of national importance, others began to prepare the movement for a more active role, first by taking steps to allow it to take part in elections, then, when they felt that the organisation and its assets were in danger of direct attack by its opponents, forming a 'secret apparatus' which began a series of pre-emptive assassinations against those thought to be its most dangerous enemies. Al-Banna's own role in these latter developments has been endlessly debated.[40] What is probably more important is the observation that there is a particular logic which informs the trajectory of such movements, endlessly forcing them to choose between activism and quietism in contexts complex enough to ensure that there will always be rival groups trying to push them in one direction or the other.

The subsequent history of the Muslim Brothers after the Second World War does much to bear this out. During the 1940s the organisation's efforts to take part in national politics combined an uneasy mixture of popular mobilisation and underground terrorism so threatening to the other politicians that it was not only placed under severe legal constraints but also lost Hasan al-Banna to assassination in 1949. Then, after a short period of being so close to the new revolutionary government of Nasser's Free Officers that one of its most important recruits, Sayyid Qutb, was appointed Secretary-General of the regime's Liberation Rally in 1953, relations deteriorated to such an extent that the Brothers themselves were proscribed and Qutb and most of the rest of the leadership put in jail after an unsuccessful attempt by one of their members on Nasser's life in 1954.[41] Qutb used his ten years in prison to produce a powerful re-working of Islamic history to support his argument that Egypt was no longer an Islamic country but in a state of *jahiliya* (religious ignorance) and that Muslims could not lead a properly religious life without a root and branch cleansing of the existing political order.[42] This formulation became widely known after Qutb's execution in 1966 and provided the inspiration for many of the small extremist groups which were formed in the 1970s.

President Sadat allowed the Brothers to re-establish their organisation as part of his struggle with the hard-core Nasserites and their leftist allies. While the bulk of its members contented themselves with building new clusters of mosques, schools and clinics, others took advantage of Sadat's economic liberalisation to start various types of Islamic investment and banking institutions, while a few activists broke away to participate in a shifting set of militant organisations which went under the general title of *Al-Jama'at al-Islamiyya* (The Islamic Groups). It was some of these same groups which sought the direct overthrow of the Sadat regime itself, a process which had only limited success until one of them managed to engineer the assassination of the president himself during an Army Day Parade in October 1981.

For the first decade or so of his rule, the new president, Hosni Mubarak, pursued a dual policy towards Egypt's religious movements, encouraging the Muslim Brothers to take part in the political process of parliament and elections (although never as an official party) while seeking to isolate its more radical offshoots through arrest and imprisonment. In these circumstances, the mainstream of the Brotherhood returned to its initial strategy of pressing for the piecemeal introduction of symbolically important parts of the *sharia* while building up the institutions of an alternative Islamic economic and social structure against the day when they could achieve real political power.

The situation then changed again as a result of the outbreak of religiously-motivated violence following the Gulf War when the Mubarak regime moved from a policy of confrontation with the militants to a more general attack on any religious organisation which it could not itself directly control. This turn of events posed a huge problem for the Brotherhood's increasingly weak and divided leadership. Some members gave discrete support to the militants. Others attempted to spread their influence into Egypt's many semi-official organisations

double fisted approach by Hosni

like the professional associations for doctors, lawyers, journalists, some of which they managed to control until driven out by government changes in their electoral rules. Others again participated in the intensified religio-cultural wars of the 1990s, attacking secular intellectuals and trying to exploit certain inconsistencies in the legal system to bring private suits based on the continued presence of bits and pieces of the *sharia* which still placed restraints on individual freedoms to marry or, in the case of women, to enjoy full equality before the law.[43] The regime fought back in some cases, for example outlawing the veiling of female school children, but gave way in others, creating a situation of uncertainty which imposed further strains on the Brotherhood itself. By and large, however, it stuck to an accommodationist role, even though many of its leaders continued to insist that it be given full party status so as to be able to operate freely and independently of the other political groups.[44]

Muslim Brother organisations elsewhere followed a similarly bumpy path. In Syria this took them from participation in the parliamentary life of the 1950s, to militant opposition to the Ba'thi state in the late 1970s and early 1980s and then back to an uneasy accommodation with the Asad regime. In Jordan they passed from a favoured position of alliance with the monarchy to become the majority group in the 1989–93 parliament and then to increasing confrontation with King Hussein. In Sudan they participated in parliamentary life, when allowed, from the 1960s onwards but came to power in 1989 only because of their close association with the new military government. And in Palestine they remained committed to educational and welfare work while providing the initial basis for the very much more activist Hamas (Islamic Resistance Movement) which promoted direct popular resistance to the Israeli occupation during the *Intifada* and after. I will comment briefly on the Sudanese and Jordanian movements as separate illustrations of the relationship between the Muslim Brothers and real political power.

It took several decades after independence for the Sudanese Muslim Brotherhood to develop into a mass movement. Initially, in the 1950s and 1960s, it had to operate in an arena already dominated by two large sectarian Islamic groupings, the Ansar and the Khatmiyya, both with their own associated political parties which obtained the bulk of the votes in all of the freely contested elections. Hence there was little scope for the Brothers' more openly ideological appeal and it was only with the return of Hasan al-Turabi to Sudan in 1964 that one section began to move towards a more activist position based on an increasing ideological independence from the Egyptian movement and a developing challenge to the democratic system favoured by the older parties.[45] Opportunity for a breakthrough came as the result of President Nimeiri's policy of reconciliation with his opposition in 1977, allowing the Turabi section, now organised as the National Islamic Front (NIF), to participate closely with the regime, to obtain important posts in the administrative and educational systems for its members and then to win a significant number of seats in the 1980 elections.[46] It was able to obtain further advantage from Nimeiri's own decision to introduce parts of the *sharia* in 1983.[47] This not only allowed the NIF to pose as the main implementers of the holy law but also to profit from the inevitable rise in tension between the Muslims and those millions of Sudanese Christians and animists who were now unwillingly subject to its provisions. As a further bonus, the application of *sharia* principles outlawing interest paved the way for an expansion of Islamic banking which provided the Front with a major source of funds.

National Islamic Front

The growing power of the NIF is well illustrated by the way its leaders were able to negotiate the rapidly changing political system as Nimeiri's power waned and then the old parliamentary system was revived. Winning nearly 20 per cent of the vote in the 1986 elections gave it sufficient power to block any move either to withdraw parts of the *sharia* or to adopt a more conciliatory attitude to the rebellion which had, once again, broken out in the south.[48] Finally, it was able to play an important behind-the-scenes role in the new military government that came to power in July 1989. Though not active participants in the coup itself, the NIF had much in common with General Bashir's new regime which was not only of an Islamist orientation but also shared the Front's general opposition to the old multi-party democratic system which both identified as an essential prop for their northern as well as their southern opponents.[49] Within months, Turabi had been adopted by the military as its main ideological guide.

It is from this new position of power that Turabi and his officer colleagues proceeded to try to Islamise Sudanese society. They began in much the same way as the Iranian revolutionaries by establishing Special Revolutionary Security Courts, purging supposed opponents from the judiciary, the universities and the civil service and by putting pressure on women to wear a more Islamic style of dress, although usually with no great success. Turabi then tried to institutionalise religious influence on the government by creating a new political party, The National Congress, of which he himself became the Secretary-General and to which, over time, most Sudanese ministers came to belong. Finally, he introduced what is best described as an Islamo-IMF style of economic management, cutting subsidies and imports in order to meet IMF targets, selling off parts of the public sector to his wealthy supporters and relying on financing investment projects with funds from the Islamic banks.[50]

The fact that Sudan seemed beset by enemies, both in the rebellious south and from large sections of the international community upset by its support for Iraq during the Gulf War, made the initial introduction of new policies in the name of Islam and national self-sufficiency that much more easy. However, over time, the continued lack of political freedom allied to a deteriorating economic performance heightened internal resistance to the regime, reducing Turabi's own influence and causing the army to rely more on a simple pragmatism underpinned by military force to survive.

The Jordanian Muslim Brothers obtained a privileged position in Jordan during the 1970s and 1980s as a result of their support for the monarchy and their joint opposition to the left and the secular Arab nationalists of the Nasserite variety. This put them in a good position to benefit from the return to parliamentary life in 1989, being far and away the best organised group within the kingdom even if, as yet, they were not permitted to organise themselves formally as a political party. They used their influence within parliament to elect one of their members as speaker in 1990, to obtain four cabinet posts and then to begin to push for the Islamisation of parts of Jordanian society, for example by an attempt to ban the sale of alcohol in public places and to divide the educational system into different schools for boys and girls. This was fiercely resisted by members of the establishment, already worried by the Brothers' participation in parliamentary hearings which had exposed considerable corruption by members of the pre-1989 ministry. It also disturbed the king himself who, in a well-published speech in late 1992, accused Jordan's Islamists of being 'proponents of backwardness and oppression'.[51]

In spite of changes in the electoral law, the Brothers, organised as the Islamic Action Front (IAF), won most seats in the 1993 elections. But then, after a further period of confrontation with the palace, they decided to boycott the next set of elections in 1997 on the grounds that the system was unfairly rigged against them. Confrontation also helped to create a familiar split between what Glenn Robinson styles the 'social' and the 'political' Islamists with the former concentrating on the more traditional policies for Islamising Jordanian society and the latter more concerned with such issues as economic and social justice, corruption and opposition to the peace treaty with Israel.[52] Both represented important constituencies which the king could not afford to ignore. The result was inevitably something of a stand-off in which the IAF, while posing no direct threat to either monarch or administration, still had sufficient power and influence to make its voice felt and its demands heeded. Like the Egyptian Muslim Brothers, who found themselves in a roughly similar situation outside government, its leadership tended to stress its support for the kind of democratic system which would secure its own independence as well as providing it with a platform from which to pursue its aim of reclaiming Islamic civilisation in a 'gradual' fashion.[53] It was this line of thinking which caused the IAF to agree to compete in the Municipal elections of July 1999, six months after King Abdullah's accession, getting 72 of its 100 candidates elected and winning the mayoral campaign in five of the larger towns. Thus encouraged, it announced that it would also be willing to take part in the 2001 general election provided the electoral law was amended to allow a fairer and more open contest.[54]

During the 1980s other Sunni movements were created which, though following the original strategy of the Muslim Brothers in building up grass-roots support, can be distinguished from them by their more populist politics, revolutionary slogans and their obvious impatience to gain power.[55] The two most prominent in the Arab world were the Nahda (originally the Mouvement de la Tendence Islamique/MTI) in Tunisia and the FIS in Algeria. The organisers of the former, notably its leader, Rachid al-Ghannouchi, tried to take advantage of the various liberal openings under President Bourguiba to form a political party. Denied this possibility they sought to extend the MTI's influence in two main ways. One was to set up a network of welfare programmes, free legal assistance and medical care. The second was to co-operate with other oppositional forces in support of various human rights and social issues. It was this latter activity which distinguished them most obviously from the Egyptian Muslim Brothers whom Ghannouchi accused of being simply concerned to exercise tutelage over society without trying to change it.[56] The MTI tried once again to enter the electoral process in 1989, this time under the rules laid down by the new president, Ben Ali, which forbade political parties from sponsoring an overtly religious agenda. Denied again, some members of the movement turned to an increasingly militant confrontation with the government, a process which culminated in Ghannouchi's voluntary exile followed quickly by a campaign of repression which saw three activists executed in 1991 and many of the rest tortured and put in jail.

The Algerian FIS followed something of the same trajectory although with much more dramatic ups and downs. Organising itself as a political party in order to contest the 1990 municipal elections it managed to obtain power in most of the country's major cities which it then used both to build up further local support for itself and to experiment with a programme of Islamisation aimed at such obvious targets as bars, nightclubs and mixed bathing beaches. It then moved even close to power through its victory in the first round of the national elections in December 1991. However, the militant statements of some of the FIS leadership, combined with its obvious popularity, was enough to arouse the fear of the military who moved in to cancel the second round of the election in January 1992, banning the organisation two months later and arresting thousands of its members.

Just who was responsible for the ensuing violence remains a much debated question. Certainly the FIS had already developed a military wing, the Mouvement Islamique Armée (MIA), which was responsible for some of the early atrocities. However, much of the violence was also the work of a more shadowy organisation, the Groupe Islamique Armée (GIA), with its extremist programme of killing or destroying anything and anyone connected with the state apparatus, inspired, it was widely believed, by the presence of a number of so-called 'Afghans' among its leaders, that is Algerians who had been trained by the CIA and Pakistan to fight against the Russians in Afghanistan. The army too must share a great deal of the blame, both because of its initial intervention and then, latterly, through its promotion of an increasing penetration of the militant movements by its own spies and agents, making responsibility for any particular massacre harder and harder for any outsider to determine.

The context in which militant Shi'i movements started to operate was quite different again. Historically the Shi'i communities had been forced to the margins of the Arab world by a long series of Sunni ruling dynasties, and tended to live in poor, mountainous or desert areas with access to few resources and only the poorest land. Their members were thus particularly responsive to late twentieth-century movements of communal self-assertion, whether expressed in religious or class terms. Another feature of Shi'i communal life was the role of the clergy and the influence on it of some of the new religio-political ideas learned during their period of study in the holy cities of Iraq and Iran. It was there, for instance, that many of its members went for study and became acquainted with the ideas of men like the Ayatollah Khomeini or Muhammad Baqir al-Sadr of Najaf, whose thinking had developed a very obvious political component combining a stress on clerical activism with an obvious engagement with the powerful vocabularies of Marxism and popular revolution espoused by some of their more politicised co-religionists, In these circumstances, the fact that the Iranian revolution took place in the most important country in the Shi'i world was bound to have a particularly potent effect, both on communal organisations seeking greater equality and the more ideologically-motivated movements committed to the overthrow of existing Arab regimes and the immediate establishment of an Islamic state.

Shi'i movements were particularly prominent in the Gulf during the 1980s, many of them receiving inspiration and sometimes direct assistance from members of the Iranian revolutionary government. The result of their growing assertiveness was a series of clashes with the Sunni rulers, notably in the eastern province of Saudi Arabia in 1979–80. But over time, such movements tended to be contained or dispersed by the local authorities while the leaders of some of them began to concentrate more on a political call for a greater democracy as a way of attending to some of their demands for better representation and greater equality. This brought some short-term gains in Saudi Arabia but not in Bahrain where pressure to revive the parliament, dissolved in 1974, was met by increasing government repression aimed at the Shi'i community as a whole.[57]

The Arab Shi'i movements which made the most impact on both the military and the political level were organised in Lebanon. Two were of particular importance: the Harakat al-Amal, founded as a militia in 1975, and the more militant Hizbollah which emerged from the radicalisation of the Shi'i population as a result of the Israeli invasion of June 1982. Both were supported by the Iranian government whose funds were used not only to buy arms but also to sustain a wide range of welfare and educational activities. However, only Hizbollah adopted the more extreme form of revolutionary activism promoted by Teheran in the early 1980s with the aim of converting Lebanon into an Islamic state. The situation then changed radically with the end of the civil war and the return to parliamentary life in 1992. Both movements took the opportunity to convert themselves into political parties in order to participate in the elections, even though this meant that the Hizbollah leadership was forced to abandon its revolutionary aims and to join Amal in its support for a democratic pluralism based on co-existence with the other Lebanese sects and communities. In the event Amal obtained four seats in the 108-seat parliament and Hizbollah eight seats.

Entry into parliament did not mean the end of Hizbollah's guerrilla activities against the Israelis in the south which continued to provide an important aid to recruitment and political mobilisation. However, it did mean a change in the ways it competed for the support of Lebanon's Shi'i population, moving from the armed clashes with Amal in the late 1980s to the pursuit of economic and social policies designed to improve the condition of the poorer members of the community. To begin with it seemed that Hizbollah had many important advantages over its rival. Nevertheless, as the economy failed to pick up, it was temporarily outflanked by one of its former leaders, Shaikh Subhi al-Tufayli, whose advocacy of a 'hunger revolution' on behalf of the poor and oppressed brought him into violent conflict with the government in 1998, forcing the mainstream movement to lose popular support when it failed to come to his assistance.[58] As must be the case with all such movements which abandon revolutionary rhetoric for the parliamentary path, there was an uncomfortable gap between the demands of political respectability and the aspirations of its more radical followers. Fortunately for the Hizbollah leadership, however, this problem was made somewhat easier by the fact that the Iranian government seemed to be following much the same path, from revolutionary fervour to President Khatami's emphasis on an Islamic democracy in which government is seen to depend on the assent of the governed.

assent of governed

Muslim politics: a brief conclusion

The forgoing analysis allows us to draw some lessons concerning the practise of Islamic politics in the Arab countries since the Second World War. Some of these will also apply to the two other Muslim countries, Iran and Turkey, although the religious revolution in the one, and institutionalised secularism in the other, make them somewhat special cases.

The obvious starting point is the observation that, with the exception of Lebanon, all the countries discussed have large Muslim majorities.[59] This provides a particular incentive for Islamic parties to participate in the democratic process particularly in so far as democracy is identified with majority rule. To this can be added the fact that such parties have proved to be better than almost all of their rivals at creating the grass-roots organisations necessary to get large numbers of people to the polls. Furthermore, they can always make the kind of claim made by Hasan al-Turabi that, although the NIF only obtained 20 per cent of the vote in the 1986 Sudanese elections, its 'influence was greater than [its] numbers because it represented Islam'.[60]

By the same token, of course, the electoral power of the Muslim parties was feared by the leaders of most Arab regimes, by well-entrenched institutions like the army and by their rivals in the political arena. They were also faced with the understandable concerns of those uncertain about how their generalised religious principles would translate into concrete economic, social, military and other policies if they came to power. The result was the creation of numerous barriers to religio-political activity, either by law or, more usually, by direct repression. And in cases where the movement in question had a military wing or a militant membership, this could lead quickly to a cycle of violence and counter-violence in which killings by one side were quickly avenged by the other. Meanwhile, for the rank and file, official repression did much to raise the cost of being an active member in terms of possible imprisonment, ouster from jobs and regular harassment by the police.

Faced with such barriers many movements were forced to adopt alternative strategies for promoting their goals. One was to engage in a type of general cultural warfare aimed at Islamising the media, the educational system, the law and the museums whenever openings presented themselves. The other was to seek to Islamise particular neighbourhoods and urban quarters wherever possible. In many cases regimes were prepared not only to tolerate such activities but even to encourage them as a way of reinforcing their own Islamic credentials. However, such short-term gains were often bought at the price of exacerbating the division between the social or accommodationist tendencies within the organisation and those with a more immediately political or economic programme requiring instant action and quick results.

In the Muslim Middle East all this became part of a process which could not be easily brought to a close before reaching some new, and generally acceptable, balance between religion and politics, state and society. We might also conclude that it required finding a place for politico-religious movements somewhere within the general system of decision-making, representation and allocation of values. While permitting religious parties to compete in elections is not a sufficient condition for promoting social stability and electoral democracy in the Arab countries it is certainly a necessary one.

The Christians between communalism and nationalism

Arab Christians were affected by many of the same processes as Arab Muslims, most notably the shock of the 1967 war and the atmosphere of heightened religiosity it engendered. However, as with the Muslims, their response was highly dependent on a context in which they found themselves, particularly their place within their own country's national movement and their relations with their non-Christian neighbours. I will illustrate these points by reference to Lebanon and to two states in which the Christians constituted a well-defined but small minority, Egypt and Israel-Palestine.

According to the only official census ever taken in modern Lebanon, in 1931, the Christians constituted a majority of the population and it was on this basis that they obtained the office of the presidency, the commander of the armed forces and the largest share of posts in government service. However, over time, some of their leaders began to fear for their ascendancy, observing the growing power of Arab nationalism beyond their borders and then, after 1967, the even more menacing increase of Palestinian power within. For a while they tried to use state power, including the army, to contain the PLO guerrillas. But when this proved ineffective, they began to place greater reliance on their own, sectarian, counter-power in the shape of Christian-based militias, a development which led directly to the first stage of fighting between them and the forces of the Palestinian/leftist alliance in 1975.

As the fighting intensified, and as individuals and then whole districts, became targeted simply in terms of their confessional allegiance, the role of religion as a marker assumed great salience. Nevertheless, the struggle is only explicable in communitarian, rather than purely religious, terms. While it is true that the majority of Lebanese Christians identified themselves as believers, or 'strong' believers, this in no way seems to have implied that they thought that they or their leaders should be fighting for a Christian state. Indeed, as Theodor Hanf's surveys made during the 1980s appear to indicate, the vast majority wanted a secular Lebanon.[61] Further proof of this same assertion comes from the fact that the leadership was provided almost exclusively by the old politicians and the newer militia leaders with only a minimal contribution from the church authorities such as the Maronite Patriarch. We must assume, therefore, that it was fear of communal extinction, rather than religion *per se*, which was the major reason for the bulk of the Christian communities to place themselves under the protection of what were essentially politico/military forces.

The behaviour of many of the smaller Christian communities elsewhere expresses the same concern with communal self-preservation. This is well-illustrated by the changes which took place in Egypt after the Nasser revolution. During the first decades after independence, the political leadership had great success in demonstrating that the Coptic community – no more than 6–7 per cent of the population according to all twentieth-century censuses – was an integral part of the Egyptian nation. This was most easily accomplished in the days of the Wafd Party which served as an important vehicle for Christian politicians. But with the abolition of the old parties in 1953, and the attack on the wealth of the rich landowning and industrial class which followed, concern for the well-being of the community was left largely to the clergy.[62] And it was they, under the energetic leadership of men like Pope Shenouda who was elected patriarch in 1971, who encouraged a process of Coptic self-assertion during the early Sadat period. This took the form of a communal mobilisation centred round the churches and the creation of many new benevolent associations often with funds from the Coptic immigrants abroad.[63]

Local stimulus for these developments was provided by a powerful sense that some of Sadat's initiatives were moving Egypt towards a more forceful assertion of its Islamic character, for example his invitation to the Muslim Brothers to participate in the discussions concerning the 1971 constitution. It was also fuelled by growing opposition from some of the more militant Islamic groups, beginning with a dispute over an attempt to convert a Coptic philanthropic association into a church in 1972 and culminating in a series of attacks on Christian property in Cairo and Upper Egypt in 1980.[64] President Sadat's efforts to restore peace included the arrest of hundreds of both Muslim and Christian activists in the summer of 1981, including Pope Shenouda himself.

The process of communal assertion continued in a more muted way under President Mubarak with further efforts to draw as many Copts as possible into church-led institutions and to participate openly in Coptic religious festivals like Christmas and Easter. Nevertheless, the leadership also made efforts to meet Muslim accusations of promoting separatism by stressing the importance of religious culture in Egyptian history and of the role of Copts as popular saints and heroes.[65] Meanwhile, Shenouda himself became one of Mubarak's most demonstrative supporters while resolutely denouncing any attempt to portray the Copts as a 'minority' in need of special protection.[66]

A third context was that of the Palestinian Christians under Israeli occupation. Lacking a state of their own, or even the possibility of creating national institutions, the maintenance of communal unity had to be the work of individuals and groups on the ground, assisted on occasions by the PLO leadership outside. Given such constraints it was inevitable that the main activity should be in the cultural field and it was here that strenuous efforts were made to popularise particular interpretations of Palestinianism and Palestinian history in which religion was seen as part of cultural tradition rather than as a mark of identity.[67] All this proved of great importance, first during the *Intifada*, and then after the establishment of the Palestinian National Authority in 1994, when Muslim groups like Hamas used their opposition to Israeli policies to promote the Islamisation of Palestine society. Over time, however, divisions between the two components of the community began to increase, occasionally breaking out into open conflict as in the case of the rival Muslim and Christian plans for the use of public space at the centre of Nazareth, the home of Jesus, as part of the latter's preparations for the millennium.

Religion and politics in a Jewish state

Ever since 1948 there has been an almost universal consensus among Israeli Jews that Israel should be a Jewish state. This found expression in 1949 in a series of compromises between Ben-Gurion's government and the newly created National Religious Party (NRP) in which agreement not to draw up a permanent constitution – in order to avoid the NRP's insistence that it be based on the *Halacha* (Religious Law) – was offset by the establishment of a ministry of religious affairs with formal jurisdiction over many aspects of Jewish life, including marriage and divorce. It was on this basis that the National Religious Party came to play a central role as mediators between the state and the majority of religiously observant Israelis.

The overwhelming victory over the Arab armies and the occupation of the West Bank (known historically to Jews as Judea and Samaria) called all these arrangements into question. The war was given a religious, often messianic, interpretation. It raised the possibility of new definitions of what it was to be an Israeli and a Jew. And it encouraged expressions of a very much more intense form of territorial and ethnic nationalism in which the religious obligation to settle the West Bank – and even to purge it of its non-Jewish inhabitants – was given increasing prominence. Hence, although the share of the vote going to purely religious parties remained more or less the same until the 1990s, the way was now open for activists to develop new forms of politics based on new combinations of religion, communalism, ethnicity and more extreme forms of Jewish nationalism.[68]

The first organisation to respond to the change in political environment was the NRP which, even before 1967, had contained a group advocating a more active use of religious tradition to inform a wide range of social and other issues. One immediate consequence was a strong focus on West Bank settlement where religious and nationalist issues were closely mixed. This, in turn, led to the creation by NRP members of the Gush Emunim (Block of the Faithful) in 1974 with a programme that combined pressure for new settlements with opposition to any territorial concessions to the Palestinians which might weaken Israeli control. The Gush was followed by the creation of other parties with politico-religious projects, including Kach founded by Meir Kahane who was temporarily elected to the Knesset in 1984 on a platform stressing the need to purge the Jewish Holy Land of the presence of all gentiles, only to get himself expelled by his fellow parliamentarians on the charge of spreading racialism and undermining the democratic character of the state.[69]

Meanwhile, other religious parties representing different sections of the Orthodox and Sephardic communities began to stand for election. Such parties had only to obtain a handful of seats in order to be considered potential coalition partners in the complex negotiations which preceeded the formation of any new government in the 1980s and 1990s. And this in turn allowed them to bargain for ministerial posts as well as for the government funds needed to expand their associated schools, clinics and other welfare activities. Helped by the demographic increase among the Oriental and ultra-orthodox communities, and by their success in obtaining more and more concessions for their members at a time when state welfare provisions were being much reduced, the three main religious parties increased their representation from sixteen Knesset seats in 1992 to twenty-three in 1996. Further strength accrued from the fact that, over time, the ideological differences between them began to diminish as all moved towards a new combination of nationalism, Orthodoxy and general religious zeal. The result was the creation of a formidable bloc within the Knesset in support of a united agenda to Judaise both state and society and, in so doing, to change Israel's Jewish identity from one defined in national to one defined in religious terms.[70] In such a campaign, both parliamentary and extra-parliamentary methods were used to challenge existing laws and institutional practices which were seen to stand in the way of Orthodox control over religious and social life. The state, for its part, tried to hold the ring between the interests of the different social groups but with a tendency to give way to religious pressure when this was exerted with sufficient political skill and determination.

Notes

1 Dale Eickelman and James Piscatori, *Muslim Politics* (Princeton, NJ: Princeton University Press, 1996), p. 4.
2 I take this formulation from Harvey G. Cox, 'The myth of the twentieth century: The rise and fall of secularization', *Harvard Divinity Bulletin*, 28/2/3 (1999), p. 8.
3 This point is well covered by Clifford Geertz in his William James Lecture, 'The pinch of destiny: Religion as experience, meaning, identity, power', given at Harvard

University in 1998 and reproduced in the *Harvard Divinity Bulletin*, 27/4 (1998), pp. 7–12.

4   See Sami Zubaida, 'Reading history backwards', *MERIP*, 19/5, 160, (September/October 1989), pp. 39–41; also his *Islam, the People and the State*, pp. 152–5.

5   For example, Charles Wendell (ed. and trans.), *Five Tracts of Hasan Al-Banna' (1906–1949)* (Berkeley, CA: University of California Press, 1978), pp. 40–65.

6   This point is forcefully underlined by Olivier Roy, *The Failure of Political Islam*, trans. (Cambridge, MA: Harvard University Press, 1994), particularly Chapter 4.

7   V.S. Naipul, 'The shadow of the Guru', *New York Review of Books*, 20 November 1990, p. 69.

8   Geertz, 'The pinch of destiny', p. 10.

9   For example, Roger Savory, 'Ex Oriente Nebula: An inquiry into the nature of Khomeini's ideology', in Peter J. Chelkowski and Robert J. Pranger (eds), *Ideology and Power in the Middle East* (Durham, NC and London: Duke University Press, 1988), p. 340.

10 For example, ibid., p. 341.

11 I have drawn on ideas to be found in Talal Asad, *The Idea of an Anthropology of Islam* (Washington, DC: Center for Contemporary Arab Studies, Georgetown University, Occasional Papers, March 1986), pp. 14–15.

12 See, for example, Richard T. Antoun and Mary Elaine Hegland (eds), *Religious Resurgence: Contemporary Cases in Islam, Christianity and Judaism* (Syracuse: Syracuse University Press, 1987), p. 259.

13 Zubaida, *Islam, the People and the State*, pp. 152–4.

14 For example, Eickelman and Piscatori, *Muslim Politics*, p. 109.

15 Olivier Roy, *Failure of Political Islam*, pp. 80–1.

16 See, for example, the statement by the leader of the Jordanian Islamic Action Front, Ishaq Farhan, to the effect that he does not see Iran as a 'model' Islamic state. Quoted in Glenn E. Robinson, 'Can Islamists be democrats? The case of Jordan', *Middle East Journal*, 51/3 (Summer, 1997), pp. 318–19.

17 I have borrowed these ideas from Professor Huricehan Inan. See also Roderic H. Davison, *Reform in the Ottoman Empire 1856–1876* (Princeton, NJ: Princeton University Press, 1963), pp. 251–6.

18 See, for example, Nazih Ayubi, *Political Islam: Religion and Politics in the Arab World* (London and New York: Routledge, 1991), p. 131.

19 No less a person than the president of the Islamic Republic, Mohammad Khatami, makes the point that Islamic thought, though rich in conceptions of theology and jurisprudence, is deficient in those of government and principles for the management of society. See Shaul Bakhash's review of Khatami's, *From the World of the City to the City of the World: A Survey of Western Political Thought*, in *New York Review of Books* (5 November 1998), pp. 47–51.

20 Asad, *The Idea of an Anthropology of Islam*, p.13.

21 Fred Halliday, 'The Iranian revolution and religious populism', *Journal of International Relations*, 36/2 (Fall/Winter, 1982/83), p. 197.

22 Shaul Bakhash, *The Reign of the Ayatollahs: Iran and the Islamic Revolution* (London: I.B. Tauris, 1985), p. 73.

23 Ibid., p. 74.

24 This is the personal suggestion made to me by a member of the Revolutionary Council at the time.

25 Bakhash, *Reign of the Ayatollahs*, pp. 84–5.

26 Chibli Mallat, *The Renewal of Islamic Law: Muhammad Baqer as-Sadr, Najaf and the Shi'i International* (Cambridge: Cambridge University Press, 1993), p. 80.

27 Bakhash, *Reign of the Ayatollahs*, pp. 99–110 and Chapter 6.

28 BBC, *SWB*, 2nd series, ME/8491 (13 February 1987), A/3.

29 Bakhash, *Reign of the Ayatollahs*, pp. 227, 241.
30 'Iran's revolutionary impasse: Political factionalism and societal resistance', *Middle East Report*, 24/6, 191 (November/December 1994), p. 5.
31 Ibid., p. 2.
32 The phrase comes from Bakhash, *Reign of the Ayatollahs*, pp. 241–2. For the dispute about whether Islam did or did not protect private property see, ibid., pp. 204–11; and Asghar Schirazi, *Islamic Development Policy: The Agrarian Question in Iran* (Boulder CO and London: Lynne Rienner, 1993), Chapter 9.
33 See Ahmed Sadri and Mahmoud Sadri (eds), *Reason, Freedom and Democracy in Islam: Essential Writings of Abdelkarim Soroush* (Oxford: Oxford University Press, 1999).
34 Roy, *Failure of Political Islam*, pp. 177–8.
35 This point is made in ibid., p.181.
36 Ibid.
37 Ibid., p. 177.
38 Al-Banna himself had previously belonged to a number of similar organisations with names like the Society for Moral Behaviour and the Society for the Prevention of the Forbidden. R.P. Mitchell, *The Society of Muslim Brothers* (Oxford: Oxford University Press, 1969), p. 2.
39 Ayubi, *Political Islam*, p. 131.
40 For example, Mitchell, *Society of Muslim Brothers*, pp. 30–2, 54–7, 62, 73, 88.
41 Ayubi, *Political Islam*, p. 138.
42 See, for example, Zubaida, *Islam, the People and the State*, pp. 51–3.
43 See for example the successful prosecution of a case in which a Professor at Cairo University was ordered to divorce his wife on the grounds of his own apostasy in George M. Sfeir, 'Basic freedoms in a fractured legal culture: Egypt and the case of Nasr Hamid Abu Zayd', *Middle East Journal*, 52/3 (Summer, 1988), pp. 402–14.
44 Sana Abed-Kotob, 'The accommodationists speak: Goals and strategies of the Muslim Brothers in Egypt', *International Journal of Middle Eastern Studies*, 27/3 (August 1995), pp. 326, 329.
45 John L. Esposito and John O. Voll, *Islam and Democracy* (New York and Oxford: Oxford University Press, 1996).
46 Alexander L. Cudsi, 'Islam and politics in Sudan', in James Piscatori (ed.), *Islam in the Political Process* (Cambridge: Cambridge University Press, 1983), pp. 48–53. The NIF broke officially with the rump of the Muslim Brothers in 1985.
47 Esposito and Voll argue that the decision to return to the *sharia* was taken by Nimeiri on his own without any influence from Hasan al-Turabi, then his Attorney-General. See their *Islam and Democracy*, pp. 92–3.
48 Ayubi, *Political Islam*, pp. 108–12.
49 Esposito and Voll, *Islam and Democracy*, pp. 94–5.
50 For example, Banaiah Yongo-Bure, 'Sudan's deepening crisis', *Middle East Report*, 21/5, 172 (September/October 1991), p. 12. This view is supported by Hasan al-Turabi himself at a Round Table organised in May 1992 and quoted in Arthur L. Lowrie (ed.), *Islam, Democracy and the West* (Tampa, FL: The World and Islam Studies Enterprise, 1993), pp. 49–51.
51 Robinson, 'Can Islamists be democrats?', p. 382.
52 Robinson, 'Defensive democratization in Jordan', pp. 403–4, in *International Journal of Middle Eastern Studies*, 30/1 (Aug. 1998).
53 Robinson, 'Can Islamists be democrats?', p. 377.
54 Sana Kamal, 'Jordan: democratics tests', *Middle East International*, 30 July 1999, pp. 14–15.
55 Olivier Roy makes this point but pushes the differences too far by referring to these new movements as neofundamentalist, *Failure of Political Islam*, Chapter 5. Hasan al-Turabi makes a somewhat different distinction between the elitism of the mainstream

Muslim Brothers and the much greater engagement with popular life of the new. Lowrie (ed.), *Islam, Democracy and the West*, p. 16.

56 Ayubi, *Political Islam*, p. 115.
57 For example, Madawi Al-Rasheed, 'The Shi'a of Saudi Arabia: a minority in search of cultural authenticity', *British Journal of Middle Eastern Studies*, 25/1 (May 1998), pp. 136–8.
58 For example, Reinoud Leenders, 'Hizbullah's Baalbek reversal', *Middle East International*, 19 June 1998, pp. 8–9.
59 Lebanon in the 1990s had a substantial Muslim majority but this could not be statistically confirmed due to the fact that there has been no agreed census since 1931.
60 Quoted in Lowrie, (ed.), *Islam, Democracy and the West*, p. 22.
61 Theodor Hanf, *Coexistence in Wartime Lebanon: Decline of a State and Rise of a Nation* (London: I.B. Tauris, 1993), pp. 480–2, 513.
62 It is significant that no Copt was elected to any of the national assemblies created by Nasser and Sadat.
63 Hamied Ansari, 'Sectarian conflict in Egypt and the political expediency of religion', *Middle East Journal*, 38/3 (Summer, 1984), pp. 398–400.
64 Ibid., pp. 408–15.
65 For example, William Suliman Kilada, 'Christian-Muslim relations in Egypt', in Kail C. Ellis (ed.), *The Vatican, Islam and the Middle East* (Syracuse, NY: Syracuse University Press, 1987), pp. 258–9.
66 See *Civil Society* (Cairo), III/30 (June 1994), pp. 28–33.
67 Glenn Bowman, 'Nationalizing the sacred: Shrines and shifting identities in the Israeli-occupied territories', *Man*, XXVIII/3 (September 1993), pp. 431–60.
68 Itzhak Galnoor, 'The 1984 elections in Israel: Political results and open questions', *Middle East Review*, XVIII/4 (Summer, 1986), p. 54.
69 Aviezer Ravitsky, 'Religious radicalism and political Messianism in Israel', in Emmanuel Sivan and Menachem Freidman (eds), *Religious Radicalism and Politics in the Middle East* (Albany, NY: State University of New York Press, 1990), pp. 33–7.
70 Avishai Ehrlich, 'For land and God: Israel under Netanyahu', *Israel and Palestine*, 203 (n.d.: 1998?), p. 17.

10 The military in and out of politics

Theoretical approaches to the study of the military's political role

Most studies of the political role of Middle Eastern armies have been written from one of two perspectives. The first is concerned to find an explanation for the frequent occurrence of military 'coups'; the second to address the larger question of the role of the army in the general process of state or nation building. This is perhaps understandable given the salience of military interventions in the recent history of the region but it has yielded little insight. By and large, writers on Middle Eastern coups have tended to base their explanations on the simple premise that an army's only way to exercise political power is by means of the overthrow of a civilian regime. They have also been prone to attach too much importance to specifically local factors, such as the allegedly militaristic nature of Islam or of Arab culture, as reasons for military intervention.[1] However, officers in barracks can be just as influential as officers in government. And coups and military regimes are such a common feature of the post-colonial world that their occurrence must be due in large part to international, rather than simply Middle Eastern, factors. Notions such as the one that seeks to define the nation building role of the officer corps as that of the 'middle class in uniform' have proved equally unhelpful.[2] Armies have their own institutional imperatives which mean that their technological, educational or administrative resources are not simply available to the rest of society for whatever civilian purpose they may happen to be needed.

Given the unsatisfactory nature of such simplistic approaches, it is more helpful to examine the role of the army within a much larger frame of reference; one that seeks to identify its place within both state and society. Following the work of Maurice Janowitz, Robin Luckham and others, this involves concentration on three specific features.[3] The first is the notion of an army as a special type of organisation, with its own particular form of hierarchy, its own well-defined boundaries and its own type of professionalism, features that are more or less common to all military formations everywhere. Typically, armies will want complete control over the way they recruit, train and then promote their own officers. And they will generally try to protect themselves from any influence that threatens their institutional integrity, for example, the accelerated promotion of politically favoured officers or the politicisation of its other ranks. All such structural necessities can be observed in a Middle Eastern context as well. Unfortunately, with the exception of two books on the Turkish army and a few on the Israeli, the cult of military secrecy has prevented any proper research on the way they operate in actual practice.[4]

A second area of examination involves the international sphere. Most Third World armies were originally modelled on the European military organisations used to fight colonial wars with European weapons and tactics. Later, new types of dependencies were created as a result of the gifts or purchases of complex modern weapons systems that largely dictated the type of organisational structure and tactics required to make best use of them as well as requiring the skills, spare parts and a general technical training only found abroad. Furthermore, local staff officers have usually to take whatever armaments their suppliers choose to give them. Meanwhile, efforts to establish a domestic arms industry have been subject to even greater reliance on outside assistance. In a Middle Eastern context, only the Israeli army has managed to free itself to any degree from such dependencies by means of the quality of its technical know-how and its close co-operation, first with the French military, then with the Americans.

The third, and final, feature that requires examination is the relationship of an army to the state of which it forms a part. This is another extremely complex subject. For one thing, any such relationship depends on the structure of that society itself, on the level of development of the economy and on difficult calculations concerning the likelihood of war breaking out with its immediate neighbours.[5] In addition, there are also certain Middle Eastern examples of what might be termed 'warfare' states, that is states which are so preoccupied with military preparation that it permeates almost all levels of the economy, the society and the culture. Israel from its inception, and Syria from the 1970s, are examples which come immediately to mind. For another, the subject requires detailed analysis of the way in which relations between the military and society are mediated in institutional terms, starting with the association between the president or prime minister and the minister of defence, who in many Arab countries has often been the commander-in-chief as well. Typically an army will want to maintain maximum control over its own internal affairs while the civilians will try to prevent the military from seeking political allies beyond the cabinet. Beyond this, both sides will seek to influence a whole variety of working practices governing their relationship, for example, the methods by which budgets are drawn up, resources allocated and roles established. In most systems, the final results are a matter of hard bargaining in which the relative strengths of the military *vis-à-vis* the politicians can be judged by its success in getting its way in a number of key areas such as its share of the annual budget, the size of the defence industry or the often vexed question of whether an army should share internal security duties with paramilitary forces over which it has no control.

What determines their relative strengths? Here a whole host of other factors come into play, including the prestige of the army itself, its ability to overawe or simply to by-pass the decisions of a civilian cabinet, the cohesiveness of its senior officers and, perhaps most important of all, the degree to which the country is perceived to be in pressing military danger. Viewed from these perspectives, the position of an army within a state and the larger society is unlikely ever to be a fixed or a stable one and will, necessarily, change over time. Chiefs of staff will continually struggle for scarce resources or to be allowed to define their own role in the maintenance of national security. Politicians, whether civilians or retired officers, will seek to keep military activity under some sort of control. Both sides will manipulate public opinion, look for allies, try to win over or divide key opponents. Rules establishing their relationship will be agreed to, challenged and then sometimes broken. Temporary balances will be reached, only to be quickly upset. This is the essence of civil–military relations in the Middle East, as elsewhere, and I will now go on to say something about it in detail within several different types of institutional and historical contexts.

The growth of large armies within relatively strong Arab states: the case of Egypt, Syria and Iraq

The modern Egyptian, Syrian and Iraqi armies were all created, completely anew, by the British and the French colonial powers after the disbandment of previous military formations. They were kept small, unless needed in an external role (for example, in Iraq at the time of the Turkish threat in the mid-1920s), given only simple weapons, and usually required to coexist with a paramilitary police. Real growth only began after independence, and led to a considerable expansion in the number of young officers accepted for training. As in the colonial period, an army's main role was one of maintaining internal security, for which it generally managed to obtain control over all other armed units. As in the colonial period, too, there was a continued emphasis on the need for officers to obey their civilian masters and to keep out of politics. However, such practices were now much more difficult to maintain as armies found themselves closely involved in highly politicised activities, such as putting down strikes and regional revolts, and as their officers became the target of recruitment by small, radical, nationalist groups which sought to increase their limited political strength with military support.

The first coups, in Iraq in 1936, in Syria in 1949 and in Egypt in 1952, can be explained in terms of a combination of institutional and political factors. In the case of Iraq, the army was large enough, and had obtained sufficient prestige from its role in putting down internal rebellion, for its commander-in-chief, General Bakr Sidqi, to be quite easily persuaded to join the coup planned by certain frustrated politicians.[6] In Syria, just over a decade later, the main incentive for another commander-in-chief, General Husni Zaim, to take over was to defend the army's honour in the midst of an acrid dispute between the military and civilian politicians over responsibility for its poor showing in the

Palestine war. However, in both cases, lack of unity among the senior officers about what to do with the power they had seized, led to serious internal disputes, marked by, among other things, the killing of Generals Bakr and Zaim only a few months after their respective coups, followed by a period of divided power in which the Iraqi and Syrian armies were able to dominate civilian cabinets without being strong enough to replace them.

Zaim's overthrow by a colonel later in 1949 can be said to mark a new era of military intervention in which coups were led by young officers who had first to by-pass their own generals before going on to establish a new regime. Such men had often become radical nationalists while at the Military Academy. They were also well placed to organise coups as, in most military structures, colonels are the most senior officers with direct command over troops in barracks. Colonel Nasser's well-planned take-over of the key installations in Cairo in July 1952 is a perfect example of this new type of intervention.

Nevertheless, even when they had complete control over the army and the civil administration, the new military regimes still had to face the problem of maintaining unity inside the officer corps itself. In the case of Egypt, for example, the problem of creating a new balance between the army, on the one hand, and the military-dominated cabinet, on the other, was only solved by giving the commander-in-chief, Field Marshal Abd al-Hakim Amr, an increasingly free rein to manage military affairs as he chose. Elsewhere, when coups by officers below the rank of general recommenced in Iraq in 1958 and in Syria in the early 1960s, the new rulers also found it extremely difficult to institutionalise their relationship with the army, given the fact that the whole officer corps was now so highly politicised. By the same token, military commanders became too closely involved in domestic affairs to be able to ensure that their armies remained efficient fighting machines, certainly one of the many reasons for their poor performance in the 1967 war with Israel.

The 1967 defeat, followed so closely by the establishment of new military-led regimes in Iraq in 1968 and Syria in 1970, as well as the succession of President Sadat in Egypt, paved the way for yet another shift in the balance between the army and the state. First, the three armies were enlarged, re-equipped with more sophisticated Russian weapons, given better educated recruits and, in general, turned into more professional organisations whose main purpose was stated, very clearly, as that of defending the country against its external enemies. The success of this new policy can be seen in the improved performance of all three formations in the next war against Israel, in 1973. Second, various types of other, paramilitary, organisation were developed to take over the major responsibility for internal security. In Egypt this was the Central Security Police, in Syria the Defence Companies commanded by the president's brother, Rifaat al-Asad. Third, each of the three regimes paid much more attention to establishing their control over the military, sometimes by old and tried methods such as Sadat's repeated changes of minister of defence and chief of staff, sometimes by new ones like the use of the Iraqi Ba'th as a kind of watchdog over the army. As the report of its Eighth Congress in 1974 put it, one of its main goals was to 'subsume the military under party control'.[7] In the event, this was achieved by a combination of the party itself, which oversaw officer recruitment and general ideological indoctrination, various intelligence and security organisations and the kinship networks and tribal alliances which Saddam Hussein used as an additional monitor of military loyalty.[8] The Syrian system was different again with President Asad relying more on the use of overlapping intelligence agencies than on the Ba'th itself. The final result of all such measures was to make the larger Arab regimes more or less coup-proof.

Another result was that the Syrian, Egyptian and Iraqi armies became so large and important that they occupied a salient position within state and economy (see Table 10.1) There are no accurate figures but it would seem that, by the early to mid-1980s, the Syrian armed forces, heavily committed in Lebanon and facing possible war with Israel, had grown to approximately 400,000 men. This represented some 5 per cent of the total population and over 20 per cent of the country's labour force.[9] At the same time, military expenditures took up at least 40 per cent of the annual budget and were the equivalent of 15 to 16 per cent of the national product.[10] The long war with Iran meant that the Iraqi armed forces had grown even larger, with perhaps one million men in the mid-1980s.

In these circumstances, the size and general salience of the army as an institution was bound to have a significant impact on national policies of all kinds. A good example of this is the way in which the Syrian and Iraqi armies were encouraged to use their own resources to develop the factories and the repair shops needed to maintain their huge arsenals of modern weapons and, where possible, to reduce their dependence on imports by making as much of their equipment as they could themselves. This was accompanied by a tendency to move into certain areas of non-military activity, pioneered in Syria by the military-run contracting firms, the Establishment for the Execution of Military Construction (1972) and the Military Housing Establishment (1975), which, by the mid-1980s, had become the country's two largest business enterprises.[11] A similar role was played by the powerful ministry of military industry in Iraq.[12]

Table 10.1   The armed forces in relation to population and national income in Egypt, Iraq and Syria, 1989

	Armed forces	*Population (million)*	*Defence expenditure ($bn)*	*GDP ($bn)*
Egypt	450,000	54.774	6.81	102.01
Iraq	1,000,000	19.086	12.87 (1988)	46.09 (1988)
Syria	400,000	12.983	2.49	20.26

Source: International Institute for Strategic Studies, *The Ministry Balance 1990–1991* (London: Brassey's, 1990).

Developments in Egypt followed a somewhat different trajectory. There, President Sadat took advantage of the peace agreement with Israel to make drastic reductions in the size of the army and to redefine its role now that it was no longer expected to have to confront its former enemy. Both initiatives had a deleterious effect on army morale, however, and were blamed by some influential Egyptians for the fact that the president was himself assassinated by disgruntled soldiers. In contrast, the new president, Hosni Mubarak, who was much more of a military man than his predecessor, sought to reverse the process, building up the size of the army again, replacing its ageing Russian equipment with new weapons from the United States and providing its officers with numerous extra privileges. In this he was greatly assisted by his minister of defence and general commander of the armed forces, Field Marshal Abu Ghazzaleh.

Nevertheless, within a few years Abu Ghazzaleh had expanded the role of the military into so many new areas of Egyptian life that obvious tensions developed between him and the president, causing many commentators to compare their uneasy relationship to the one that had developed between President Nasser and Field Marshal Amr in the mid-1960s.[13] Such comparisons generally tend to blur important distinctions between different historical contexts. In this case, however, it does have the advantage of raising a number of questions about a situation in which an army is able to obtain more or less what it wants in the way of autonomy and access to national resources; but only at the expense of increasing friction with different civilian groups and the risk of a sharp decrease in military cohesion and operational effectiveness. I will now examine the politics of this process in somewhat greater detail.

The expansion of the role of the Egyptian army after 1981 affected three major areas. The first was that of internal security, where it was able to establish its control over the major paramilitary force, the Central Security Police, after many of its Cairo units had rioted over their low pay in February 1986. As Field Marshal Abu Ghazzaleh was to define the new relationship later the same year:

> The role of the police and the army are complementary and cannot be separated. To both of them falls a unique task: to guarantee the security of Egypt both internally and externally.[14]

The army's domestic presence was also maintained through the continued use of military courts to try civilians, particularly Islamic fundamentalists, accused of plots against the state. A second area was that of military industry, where the army used its control over the National Organisation for Military Production and the Arab Organisation for Industry to launch an ambitious programme of manufacturing and rebuilding equipment, either for its own use or for export. To do this, the army was able to take advantage of the fact that Egypt had the most advanced technological facilities to be found in the Arab world, as well as long experience with the Russian weapons systems used by many of its neighbours. The third, and last, area of expansion was into public works, through the National Service Products Organisation founded in 1979, and then into numerous other sectors of the economy, most notably those concerned with land reclamation and food production.

All these activities created new sets of tensions. In the case of security, for example, the expanded role of the army led to a competition between the military, on the one hand, and the police and civilian intelligence agencies, on the other, as to which was best able to apprehend plotters and to keep the peace. Meanwhile, the development of a military industrial complex outside the control of the government's general accounting organisation, and run by men powerful enough to negotiate joint ventures with foreign companies and to make their own arrangements for the sale of their products to other Arab regimes, automatically brought the army into competition, and potential conflict, with a wide variety of civilian ministries involved in planning, the economy and foreign relations.

By 1986 the role of the army had grown so large and had begun to affect Egyptian life in so many ways that it could no longer hide itself from public criticism, particularly in the opposition press. It is also possible that President Mubarak was happy to use the greater freedom associated with multi-party activity to allow this to happen as part of a campaign designed to bring the situation back more under his control. The army countered with a public relations campaign in which it presented itself as an efficient, well-managed organisation vitally concerned to promote the national welfare. The result was an ongoing debate in which, for a few years, it was possible to engage in open discussion on the proper role of the army within Egyptian society.[15] This had some advantages for Abu Ghazzaleh, allowing him to make a case for enlarging the military budget at a time when the country lacked any powerful enemy. Nevertheless, the debate also highlighted certain difficult problems that demanded immediate solution. As far as the army itself was concerned, some of the most pressing were the accusations that its emphasis on economic activity had reduced its military efficiency, that its factories were not cost effective, that the Armed Forces Cooperatives were exempt from taxation and that the close links between officers and civilian businessmen were a breeding ground for corruption.[16]

It has been a central feature of this analysis that the role of the military is a continually shifting one and in constant need of adjudication and renegotiation. A good example of this took place in Egypt with the dismissal of Abu Ghazzaleh in April 1990 after he had lost American support due to his association with an attempt to smuggle rocket parts to Egypt. One result was that President Mubarak was able to reassert greater control over the military budget and arms purchases from the United States. More generally, he used his authority to promote a process of what Robert Springborg has called 'enclavization', that is the retreat of the armed forces into areas which are largely cut off from ordinary civilian life, with their own hotels, sports facilities and retirement villas.[17] Even so, this still left them with considerable resources of military-controlled land, cheap labour and a significant manufacturing capacity, all of which is largely protected from criticism by either parliament or the press.[18] Just as important, the army remained the regime's defender of last resort and was generally expected to play an important role when it came to the choice of President Mubarak's successor.

The situation in Syria and Iraq in the 1980s was made very different by the fact that both were engaged in major military confrontations. The result was not only a huge increase in the size of the armed forces and in the resources required to sustain them but also a modification in the relationship between the president and his senior officers, particularly in Iraq. On the one hand, Saddam Hussein needed efficient military commanders in the war against Iran and then later in Kuwait; on the other, he had to ensure that they continued to obey his orders and were not moved by either great victories or great defeats to seek his replacement. President Saddam Hussein managed this difficult situation by a policy of rotating his generals rapidly from post to post so that none could build up a personal following, firing or executing those responsible for battlefield failures and taking the credit for any victories himself.[19] This worked well enough until the period of demoralisation following the army's expulsion from Kuwait in 1991 after which there is evidence of at least three attempted coups, the last by members of the elite Republican Guard in 1996.[20] At this stage, according to Amatzia Baram, Hussein's control over the Iraqi officer corps was exercised simply by fear and the knowledge that any signs of disaffection would immediately be followed by torture and death.[21]

President Asad also had problems with the commanders of some of his own paramilitary forces as they competed with one other to dominate the streets of Damascus during the succession crisis brought on by his serious illness in the summer of 1984. Once he had exiled several of the commanders in question, including his brother Rifaat, he then seems to have incorporated some of the defence companies they controlled into the regular army.[22] Meanwhile, senior officers were given considerable opportunities to make money on their own account through partnership with the civilian business or a kind of licensed smuggling from Syrian-controlled Lebanon. Indeed, one of the president's main problems in the 1990s was the fact that many of the senior generals had become 'military barons', exercising power over large economic fiefdoms which made them unwilling to retire at the appointed age.

The role of the military in the smaller Arab states

None of the other Arab states possessed a military establishment of anything like the same size as Egypt, Syria and Iraq. In the mid-1980s, for example, the only other two armies with over 100,000 men were the Moroccan army, swollen since the 1970s by the need to confront the Polisario guerrillas in the Sahara, and the Algerian one (see Table 10.2). Nevertheless, there are a number of countries in which even a relatively small military organisation played a vital role in the political process, most notably by ensuring regime survival or its replacement by a military-backed government.

Table 10.2   Middle East defence expenditure and size of armed forces, 1985 and 1997
(1997 constant prices)

	Defence Expenditure Total US$m		Defence Expenditure Numbers in % of GDP		Armed Forces Total (000)	
	1985	1997	1985	1997	1985	1997
North Africa:						
Algeria	1,357	2,114	1.7	4.6	170.0	124.0
Libya	1,923	1,250	6.2	4.7	73.0	65.0
Morocco	913	1,386	5.4	4.2	149.0	150.0
Tunisia	594	334	5.0	1.8	35.1	35.0
Levant:						
Egypt	3,679	2,743	7.2	4.3	445.0	450.0
Israel	7,196	11,143	21.2	11.5	142.0	175.0
Jordan	857	496	15.9	6.4	70.3	104.1
Lebanon	285	676	9.0	4.5	17.4	55.1
Syria	4,961	2,217	16.4	6.3	402.5	320.0
Turkey	3,268	8,110	4.5	4.2	630.0	639.0
Arabian Peninsula and Gulf:						
Bahrain	215	364	3.5	6.5	2.8	11.0
Iran	20,258	4,695	36.0	6.6	305.0	518.0
Iraq	18,328	1,250	25.9	7.4	520.0	387.5
Kuwait	2,558	3,618	9.1	11.4	12.0	15.3
Oman	3,072	1,815	20.8	10.9	2.5	43.5
Qatar	427	1,346	6.0	13.7	6.0	11.8
Saudi Arabia	25,585	18,151	19.6	12.4	62.5	162.5
UAE	2,910	2,424	7.6	5.6	43.0	64.5
Yemen	696	403	9.9	7.0	64.1	66.3

Source: International Institute for Strategic Studies, *The Military Balance 1998/99*
(Oxford: Oxford University Press, 1998), pp. 294, 296.

In very general terms, the smaller Arab armies can be divided into a number of types. These include: the modern professional (for example, Algeria, Jordan, Morocco, Sudan, Tunisia and the former North Yemen); the modern professional that coexists with tribal-based military organisations (Saudi Arabia and Oman); the modern confessional (Lebanon); and the guerrilla (the Palestinian resistance). I will now examine the political salience of a few armies from each of these types except the last.

The two Middle Eastern regimes that relied most heavily on the support of a professional army for survival are the monarchies in Jordan and Morocco. Both have much in common. In each case their army was very largely the creation of the former colonial power and continued to be commanded and largely controlled by foreign officers for the first few years after independence. In each case too, the process of 'nativising' an enlarged officer corps proved difficult and led to attempted coups which were only with difficulty put down. Finally, both King Hussein of Jordan and King Hassan of Morocco came up with much the same formula for securing the loyalty of their armed forces: a combination of the monarch's day-to-day attention to the needs of the military in his role as commander-in-chief, and the creation of a well-paid, prestigious career for men drawn largely from the more conservative, tribal, areas with plenty of opportunities for going into business or government service after retirement. Once this was achieved, the monarchs possessed an efficient, reliable fighting force which performed well in battle and could also be used to maintain internal security, helped by the fact that it was allowed a large measure of control over the state's paramilitary forces as well.

As far as Jordan was concerned, the basis of the army was the British-officered Arab Legion drawn mainly from members of the smaller tribes in the south. The Legion was expanded rapidly in the late 1940s and early 1950s and experienced its first major crisis when, under newly-appointed Jordanian officers, it became directly involved in the radical Palestinian and Arab nationalist politics of the period just following the 1956 Anglo-French and Israeli attack and invasion of Egypt which raised President Nasser's prestige to great heights. King Hussein only just managed to save himself by rallying officers loyal to himself, pre-empting a possible military coup in April 1957, purging unreliable elements and then reorganising the army on a more secure basis.[23] This included reducing the importance of the better-educated, more politicised Palestinian soldiers by confining them to the technical arms, and then recruiting large numbers of men from the tribes, who were given control over the tank and infantry units that could be expected to play the major role in any future conflict. This was enough to ensure that the bulk of the army remained loyal to the king throughout the troubled period running from the defeat by the Israelis on the West Bank during the June war of 1967 to the fierce fighting against the guerrilla forces of the Palestinian resistance in Amman and in the north in 1970/1. However, the cost of maintaining such a force was high, requiring large amounts of foreign aid and taking up a considerable proportion of the local budget (see Table 10.2).

The core of the modern Moroccan army, which officially came into existence in May 1956, was provided by Moroccans, mostly Berbers from the south, who had served with French and Spanish units in the colonial period. Until 1960 it relied heavily on French officers and non-commissioned officers (NCOs) for leadership and training. Its first chief of staff was the king's son, Prince Hassan, who devoted great attention to it both before and after he succeeded his father in 1961. This automatically raised questions concerning control over the army during the initial struggles with nationalist politicians anxious to reduce the royal prerogatives. By and large the officer corps remained loyal to the king, although there were isolated military-led attempts to assassinate him in 1971 and 1972. Since then a purged and reorganised army remained the major bulwark of the king's power, controlling internal security by providing officers for the various paramilitary police forces and playing an important role in King Hassan's forcible take-over of the Spanish Sahara.

Two other of the modern armies played a more overtly political role, those of Algeria and Sudan. It was the Algerian army which intervened to pre-empt a FIS-led government in January 1992 and to install itself in power instead. The exact reasons for this remain uncertain but must certainly have had something to do with the wild talk of one of the FIS's two main leaders, Ali Bel Hadj, to the effect that the military would have to be purged and brought directly under the control of the future Islamic regime. Thereafter, it was the army, acting through a military president, Lamine Zerouel, which took the lead in trying both to contain the religious violence and then to re-shape the Algerian political system by means of managed elections and the constant manipulation of a variety of parties, new and old.

The Sudanese military was drawn back into politics in 1989 for quite different reasons. It was engaged in a long drawn-out fight with the southern rebels which had badly damaged morale of both officers and men. It distrusted the use being made of it by the civilian government under the prime minister, Sadia al-Mahdi. And it contained a significant number of Islamist officers who were worried about the possible abrogation of the *sharia* in the interests of a compromise peace with the Christian south.[24] Whether or not they also acted to seize power in association with the NIF remains an open question. However, there is no doubt that many officers were responsive to its message and shared its distrust of the old civilian politicians. Thereafter officers and NIF united to form a joint regime, although one in which, over time, there were signs of increasing friction. One bone of contention was the Front's own security apparatus, the *Amm al-Thawra*. Others included NIF pressures to purge officers accused of disloyalty and its attempt to use civilian volunteers, organised into a para-military People's Defence Force, to defend its own organisational interests as well as to fight in the south.[25] This led to an obvious shift in real power back to President Bashir and his more pragmatic military colleagues, even though discontent within the officer corps remained rife.[26] An army in government has much more difficulty in maintaining its own institutional integrity than one in barracks, the more so if it is allied with a religious movement with its own appeal to military loyalty. Yoked together in uneasy partnership, the army and the NIF reorganised as the National Congress, each sought different ways to bring the increasingly unpopular war in the south to an end.

The best example of the second type of military organisation, the one that combines tribal forces with a small professional army, is Saudi Arabia. In the first decades of the state's existence the ruling family relied exclusively on the tribes for armed men, persuading some to settle permanently in important strategic locations and calling up others whenever the occasion demanded. Such a policy proved entirely satisfactory in an era when the presence of the British at so many places round the Arabian peninsula provided the Saudis with a shield against any more modern force that might have tried to overthrow them. There was also little money for military expenses, and a justifiable fear that the existence of a professional officer corps might create a basis for political opposition. Nevertheless, there were pressures for the creation of a more permanent force, particularly after the export of the first oil, which not only provided the cash but also gave the Saudis valuable installations to defend. The result was the recruitment of a small royal guard and then of the nucleus of a professional army trained by the United States.

A further stimulus to military expansion came in 1962 with the overthrow of Imam Ahmad's regime in North Yemen by a group of Nasserite officers, followed by a civil war in which the Saudi-backed royalists were faced by a republican regime supported by an increasingly large, and hostile, Egyptian expeditionary force which at one time numbered some 70,000 men. Nevertheless, the Saudi royal family proceeded with its usual care, aware of the importance of great caution at a time when the presence of Nasser's army so close to its border had encouraged at least two serious military plots against it. Its formula for control had the following features: the use of royal princes as senior commanders; the allocation of internal security duties to a separate national guard formed largely of loyal tribal elements; and the employment of foreign officers to provide technical advice as well as a further defence against possible coups. In addition, the family was prepared to spend huge sums of money, not just on new weapons but also on barracks, housing and military hospitals. The results seem to have been the creation of a reliable but highly privileged officer class, which, with the exception of pilots in the air force, spent little time on training or manoeuvres and could not be expected to fight with any great effectiveness in battle as events at the beginning of the Gulf War proved only too well.[27]

Meanwhile, much the same model was followed by Saudi Arabia's small Gulf neighbours, all of whom built small, expensively equipped, armies, trained by foreign experts and commanded by members of their own ruling families. Their weakness as an effective fighting force was also cruelly exposed at the time of the Iraqi invasion of Kuwait in August 1990.

The last type of Arab army, the modern confessional, is peculiar to Lebanon. It owed its special form of organisation and its role within the political system to two main factors One was the way in which the sectarian balance was reflected not only in the attempt to recruit roughly equal numbers of Christians and Muslims but also in the division of the army into units composed largely of one sect or another. The second was the consensus among most of the leading politicians that the army should be kept small. This was supposed to prevent the it from becoming involved in domestic politics, as well as to inhibit the country from being drawn into military conflicts with its neighbours, especially Israel. The result was that, in the first years after independence in 1943, the army remained little more than a gendarmerie with limited powers to keep the peace and to ensure the proper conduct of elections. Nevertheless, just because it could act as a neutral force so long as it remained united, the army, under its first commander-in-chief, Fouad Chehab, soon began to play an increasingly important political role. This happened first in 1952 when General Chehab refused to intervene to put down the protests against President Beshara al-Khouri's attempt to change the constitution, and then acted for a few days as caretaker president himself to ease the transition to the next president, Camille Chamoun. It happened once more in 1958 when Chehab again kept his troops out of the fighting between pro- and anti-Chamoun elements and was finally elected president himself.

Given the fact that the new president deliberately began to use the army in support of his efforts at political and administrative reform, the stage could have been set for the establishment of yet another Arab military government. This was certainly what many officers and some civilian politicians believed. Nevertheless, Chehab himself soon stepped back from this particular course, threatened to resign as a way of getting his way with his military supporters and then attempted to create a new relationship between the army and the state in which the former would back his efforts strongly but from behind the scenes. The result was not stability, however, but a situation in which an increasing number of politicians came to fear and to resent military interference, particularly that of the army's intelligence organisation, the Deuxième Bureau.

This process reached its culmination in the 1970 presidential elections when an anti-Chehabist majority elected Sulieman Franjieh with a clear mandate to reduce the ability of the military to interfere in the political process. In these circumstances the army was unable to play a positive role in the growing crisis that led up to the outbreak of the civil war in 1975, and it was left to other forces, notably the Christian and leftist militias, aided by the Palestinian guerrillas, to fight it out between themselves. General Aziz al-Ahdab's attempt at a military coup in February 1976 was the last effort by an officer to use the army as a neutral force. However, the army was now far too weak and divided to play such a role and, only a few days later, a small mutiny led by a young Muslim officer began a process of disintegration that led Christian and Muslim soldiers either to desert or to regroup in sectarian units loosely attached to the major militias.

What was left of the army played a somewhat paradoxical role in the events surrounding the Taif Accord of 1989 and reconstitution of Lebanon's national government at the end of the Civil War. Its Christian commander, General Michel Awn, declared himself president in November 1989, and placed himself and his forces at the head of a movement of opposition to the Accord. This involved him in heavy fighting not only with elements of the Syrian army but also with the most powerful of the Christian militias whose own commander had opted to join the putative national government. It only came to an end in October 1990 when Awn could no longer obtain military equipment from Iraq following its own invasion of Kuwait, and was forced to take refuge in the French Embassy in Beirut. Thereafter the Lebanese army was reunited under new command, General Emile Lahoud, and played a significant role in finding employment for many thousands of the now demobilised sectarian militiamen.[28] As confidence in its national character grew, it was used to maintain local security, particularly during elections and, more controversially, to support the government's decision to ban the demonstrations organised by the General

Confederation of Lebanese Workers in February 1996.[29] This, in turn, provided a platform for General Lahoud's election as the country's president in 1998.

The military and politics in Turkey, Iran and Israel

While observers are united in acknowledging that the military has an unusually salient role in Turkey, there is no general agreement as to how this is to be explained. One factor that is often mentioned is the long continuity in the importance attached to the army, from Ottoman Empire times and then through the creation of the republic in 1923. However, just as significant would seem to be the ability of the military to control its own processes of recruitment, training and promotion, which have given it a particular ability to mould its officer cadets and to create a specific military culture representing the army's own view of its role within Turkish society. This is well illustrated in Mehmet Ali Birand's account of the way in which the army recruits young men from all over Anatolia at the age of twelve and subjects them to a long process of discipline and training clearly designed to distance them from all their civilian loyalties and attachments.[30] The result is an organisation which is difficult to manipulate for political purposes from outside and which has shown a remarkable ability to maintain its cohesion and organisational integrity at times when Turkish society itself was fragmented into competing classes, ethnic and religious groups and factions. This, in turn, has produced a useful basis for the position which has been developed with increasing skill since the 1950s: that of the army as being the true guardian of national values, standing over and above the day-to-day politics of the parties and the politicians.

The first major challenge to redefine the place of the army within the state in the modern period came in 1950 with the replacement of the Republican People's Party (RPP) in government by the Democrat Party led by Adnan Menderes. This at once deprived the military of its long-time political partner, as well as encouraging Menderes to try to ensure its uncertain loyalty by interfering in senior promotions. Another change came when Turkey joined NATO in 1952, an event which, although welcome to the bulk of the officer corps, forced them to realise just how ill-trained and ill-equipped they had become in comparison with the armies of the major European states. The resulting dissatisfactions came to a head in 1960 when the increasingly dictatorial behaviour of the Democrats sparked off a military revolt by a group of younger officers, only to have their initiative seized from them by a group of more senior officers who controlled the rest of the coup through the creation of a National Unity Committee (NUC). This provided just enough cohesion to allow agreement that the army should hand back power after the promulgation of a new constitution and the holding of new elections. However, it took much longer to work out the terms on which the military would co-operate with civilian governments in future. The problem was only resolved by the creation of a new permanent body, the National Security Council, with a constitutional role that allowed it to make 'recommendations' about military matters to the cabinet, and by the tacit alliance that developed between the senior officers and Suleyman Demirel, the leader of the Justice Party, which had emerged as the electorally successful successor to the banned Democrats.[31]

The second intervention in 1971 had many of the same characteristics as the first. Once again it came at a time of growing economic difficulty, highlighted on this occasion by considerable political violence, mainly from the left. It also had all the hallmarks of having been forced on the generals by fear of yet another junior officers' coup. Perhaps because of this, the coup's leaders were significantly more divided than they were ten years before and could agree on little more than the installation of a new civilian government with a mandate to introduce a few constitutional amendments restricting political freedom in a number of areas. Military division was also used by the politicians to prevent the election of the generals' own candidate for president, the former chief of staff, General Sunay. This failure then opened the way for a clear return to civilian rule after the national elections held in October 1973.

There is good reason to suppose that the army drew enough lessons from the 1971–3 episode to ensure that its next intervention, in 1980, was of quite a different character.[32] On this occasion there was clearly a great deal of prior planning, combined with a general determination to keep the army as united as possible while a new constitution and a new political structure, purged of the old politicians, was introduced.[33] Nevertheless, we must always be careful before accepting a military's explanation of its own motives at face value, particularly when it is accompanied by a concerted public relations campaign designed to present the army as a neutral arbiter and servant of the national interest, forced, unwillingly, to intervene in a situation of social chaos and total administrative breakdown.[34] While it is certainly true that the political and sectarian violence had begun to degenerate into civil war at the end of the 1970s, there were also pressing military reasons for intervention as well These included fears that the conflict would spill over into the barracks, and a concern that the deteriorating economic and social environment was harmful to the military's interest in terms of recruitment, arms production and the activities of the huge Armed Forces Assistance Fund (OYAK) set up to manage military pensions in 1961.[35] There was a similar military interest in getting out of the political scene as quickly as possible, as witnessed by a speech made by General Evren to some cadets at the War Academy just twelve days after the September 1980 coup:

> Whenever the army entered into politics it began to lose its discipline and, gradually, it was led into corruption. … Therefore I demand you once again not to take our present operation as an example to yourselves and never to get involved in politics. We had to implement this operation within a chain of command and orders to save the army from politics and to cleanse it from political dirt.[36]

The military's efforts to restructure Turkey's political system and to sanitise it from what it regarded as harmful political influences have already been discussed elsewhere (see Chapter 5). However, at a more general level, they raise important questions about the officers' analysis of what had gone wrong in Turkey and how it ought best to be put right. Seen from their perspective, the problems caused by several decades of rapid economic and social change were either not tackled properly by power-hungry and narrow-minded politicians or were deliberately exacerbated by misguided Turks under the influence of dangerous foreign ideologies. And this led them to conclude that the way ahead was to create a structure in which new national parties led by public-spirited persons could develop constructive policies in isolation from the harmful influences of class or interest groups located in the wider society. No doubt officers in many other armies would agree. However, such thinking runs counter to the fact that the political life of an industrialised, highly urbanised society cannot so easily be forced into this or that narrow channel. And that even the most passive of new parties would sooner or later be forced to link up with existing socio-economic interests or face electoral extinction.

After the elections that brought Turgut Ozal's Motherland Party to power in 1983, Turkish political life began slowly to move towards a new balance between the military and the civilian. On the one hand, neither the military president, General Evren, nor the members of the National Security Council, for all their great powers, were able to find a mechanism for influencing the civilian government on a day-to-day basis once they had abandoned recourse to regular diktats. On the other, even under the new constitution, the elected prime minister had sufficient authority to begin to make his own policies and then, when confident enough, even to challenge the military on part of its own ground, for example, by seeking to influence senior promotions. Other factors strengthening the position of the civilians against the military were the stability provided by the Motherland Party government for most of the 1980s and its decision to apply for membership of the European Community in April 1987. The result was something of an implicit division of political labour, with the military nearly doubling its share of the national budget between 1980 and 1985 and playing a major rôle in internal security but leaving most other areas of policy-making to the civilian government.[37]

There was a brief moment during Turgut Ozal's presidency beginning in 1989 when it looked as though civilian control over the top echelons of the military might even be put on a permanent basis.[38] But during the early 1990s the balance began to shift the other way again as a result of a combination of weak civilian governments and the army's growing involvement in putting down Kurdish rebel activity in the east. Relations were then further exacerbated during the brief government led by Necmettin Erbekan, the head of the Refah party, which many of the senior generals interpreted as the prelude to a full-scale assault on Turkey's secular institutions by way of the Islamisation of both Turkish society and Turkish foreign policy. The result was a series of confrontations in which the generals used their presence in the National Security Council to pressure the prime minister into ratifying a defence and intelligence treaty with Israel, which he had previously opposed, and to pay heed to a list of eighteen recommendations designed to curb the power of the Islamists throughout government. Then, when he proved slow to implement these measures, he was forced to resign in what many commentators have termed a 'silent' coup designed to exert a powerful military influence while still preserving the trappings of civilian democracy.[39]

Military pressure appeared to intensify under Erbekan's successor, Mesut Yilmaz, leading to a hardening of positions on both sides. While Yilmaz and his deputy, Bulent Ecevit, did their best to assert that it was the government, not the military, which had the duty to lead the fight against the Islamists, the army in the shape of General Cevik Bir, a deputy to the commander-in-chief, countered with a series of strong statements to the effect that the army had a 'legal obligation to protect the present constitutional order from Islamic agitation', followed by the even more blunt assertion that 'we founded this republic and we are going to protect it'.[40] Just as telling was the army's drumming up of popular support for its position in repeated news conferences and other forums reinforced, on at least one occasion, by the use of a specially commissioned poll which claimed to have found that the Islamists still dominated the political scene whatever the civilian politicians might say.[41] This left these same politicians to make whatever they could of the argument that it was they who had been elected by the people to govern Turkey and who remained the representatives of its democratic tradition.

In spite of the many similarities between Ataturk's policies in Turkey and those of Reza Shah in Iran, the role of the military developed in quite different directions in the two countries. Perhaps the most important reason for this is that, in Iran, the army always remained firmly under the control of the monarch and was never allowed to develop its own institutional identity or its own view of its place within the nation. Both shahs were obsessed with the loyalty of the officer corps, and went to great lengths to demonstrate their personal authority by preventing their generals from exercising any freedom of action and by presiding over a system of licensed corruption in which individual officers were able to make large sums of money but only at the risk of being tried and punished if the ruler should turn against them. In these circumstances, for all the size of the army and the large share of the budget devoted to it, it played little role in policy-making. It also remained the single recipient of the huge quantities of advanced American weapons it received without having any real say about how they were to be used or against what potential enemy. The great advantage to the shah of this system was shown during the popular demonstrations that marked the final stages of the revolution in 1978, when there were no mutinies and the army remained entirely loyal until after he had actually left the country. Paradoxically, however, the huge power of the military could never be consistently deployed against the opposition as it relied entirely on its vacillating, moody, royal commander-in-chief for its orders.[42]

In the event, the army fragmented as soon as the shah was forced to leave Iran, providing a vacuum which the new leadership was quick to fill with the creation of the paramilitary revolutionary guards. This also allowed time for a thorough purge of the shah's senior officers and their replacement by men with better revolutionary credentials.[43] Meanwhile, a shadowy organisation, known as the Ideological/Political Directorate, was created in October 1980 to provide loyal personnel, mostly mullahs, to indoctrinate the officers and men and to monitor their activities.[44]

It was soon after this that the Iraqis, over-estimating the demoralisation of the Iranian army, chose to invade south-western Iran, forcing the new Islamic republic to rebuild its military forces in order to meet the threat. Its answer was to combine the use of regular units with revolutionary guards as a precaution lest the still distrusted officer corps be tempted to take advantage of any victory it gained on its own to effect a counter-revolution. Both forces worked sufficiently well together to drive the invaders back across the border and then to capture significant amounts of territory in southern Iraq itself. Nevertheless, as the war dragged on, their military effectiveness became seriously undermined producing a widespread collapse of morale in the spring of 1988, due in large measure to the loss of huge numbers of officers and NCOs in earlier mass attacks and the great difficulty in obtaining the new recruits needed to keep the revolutionary guards at anything like full strength.

Given the fact that the decision to end the war in 1988 came after a string of Iraqi victories it might be supposed that the Iranian military might have turned round to pose difficulties for the civilian/clerical leadership. But this was not the case. The leadership has remained remarkably successful at keeping the army out of politics, partly through close control and observation, partly by continuing the basic division between the army and the Revolutionary Guard, now transformed into something approaching a regular army with its own military academy and a force which, by 1994, numbered some 150,000.[45]

Analysis of the role of the Israeli military in state and society presents other kinds of problems. To begin with, it is a very unusual form of organisation, established in 1949 on the assumption that, as the country did not possess the resources to maintain a large standing army, what was required was 'a militia of civilians trained and equipped for combat and capable of being mobilized at very short notice'.[46] The result was the creation of something that many observers have chosen to call a 'citizens' army' with its strength based largely on reserve formations. This had important consequences as far as civil/military relations were concerned, producing what Dan Horowitz has characterised as a 'civilianized military in a partially militarized society'.[47] The weakness of such a characterisation is that it tends to obscure the equally important facts that, in order to maintain such an army, it is also necessary to have a core of long-service professionals to ensure its capability between campaigns, and that this puts them in a position to play a major role in influencing such highly important matters as the size of the military budget and even, on occasions, the resort to war itself.[48] Indeed, a better sense of the relationship is provided by the theory generated by the notion of a 'nation in arms', where preparation for war becomes a central part of the national project, where the boundaries between the military and the civil are rendered indistinct in certain areas and where the military and civilian elite work together to define what threats the nation faces and how it can best be protected.[49]

In terms of military policy, the key actors have been the prime minister, the minister of defence and the chief of staff. For the period 1948–52, and again from 1955–1967, two prime ministers, David Ben-Gurion and then Levi Eshkol, served as their own ministers of defence, an arrangement that could, in principle, have given the cabinet considerable control over the military. But this was not usually the case. Ben-Gurion's strongly-held belief in the over-riding importance of national security led him to hide many matters from his civilian colleagues. And after his retirement in 1961, his successor lacked the authority to prevent a strong chief of staff from going his own way. Hence in the crisis leading up to the June war of 1967 it was the military, not the prime minister, that began to make the important decisions, particularly after it had pressured Eshkol into surrendering the defence portfolio to General Moshe Dayan. General Dayan stayed on as minister until 1974 and was succeeded, first by Shimon Peres and then, after 1977, by another strong personality, General Ezer Weizman. But certainly the minister with the greatest ability to dominate a cabinet was General Ariel Sharon, 1980–3, who used the post to become what Horowitz called a 'super commander-in-chief'; that is, someone who was strong enough to use his control over the whole defence establishment to force major decisions involving peace and war, most notably his exploitation of the 1982 invasion of Lebanon to try to alter the whole balance of political power between Israel and its Arab neighbours.[50]

Yoram Peri's attempt to define four different types of relationship between the prime minister, the minister of defence and the chief of staff is too rigid, and does not take account of the great importance of personality.[51] More to the point is his argument that, in many important areas of national life, the boundaries between the military and the civil have expanded to the military's advantage. This he explains in terms of a number of factors, including the highly political role of the military as rulers of the West Bank and Gaza after its occupation in 1967; the increasing entry of senior reserve officers like Generals Rabin, Eytan and Sharon into politics; and, perhaps most important of all, the fact that relations between the civil and the military have developed more as a partnership than as a system by which the former can maintain regular control over the latter.[52] He also points to the fact that the two attempts made in 1968 and 1975 to define their respective responsibilities in terms of the constitution did not prove satisfactory.[53] And the same was also true of the third effort in this direction, the Kahan Commission of 1983, which, although effecting the removal of General Sharon for misleading the cabinet, did not introduce any new machinery for preventing similar situations in the future.

The army's role was then much affected by two developments during the late 1980s. One was the impact of its role in putting down the Palestinian uprising, or *Intifada*, that broke out in December 1987. The second was the substantial reorganisation carried out by the army itself, the result not only of a large reduction in the budget but also a deliberate attempt to create a smaller, more efficient, military to meet the new needs of the post-Cold War age.[54] One important consequence was the appearance of greater friction, not only between the generals and the politicians but also between the military and society at large As far as the former is concerned, Israel's participation in the peace process, and then in a limited withdrawal from the West Bank and Gaza, sometimes involved decisions where the civilian leadership overrode strong military objections. As for the latter, the army was subject to unprecedented popular criticism from the Lebanese war onwards.[55] Nevertheless, service in the military continued to provide an entry point into civilian politics as one ex-general, Ehud Barak, became leader of the Labour Party in 1997 and two others, Yitzhak Mordechai and Amnon Lipkin-Shahak, stood for the post of prime minister until persuaded to stand down just before the vote in May 1998.

Conclusion: the Middle Eastern military after the Cold War

Given the problems faced by most Middle Eastern states after independence, it is easy to see why regimes felt that they needed to create a substantial military force to enhance both internal and external security. Moreover, they were greatly assisted in this aim by the fact that the region's role in the Cold War provided them with superpower patrons willing to supply them with military aid and modern weaponry. Oil money too was an important factor from the 1970s onwards. By the same token it is also easy to see why military personnel became so salient in the administration and politics of many Middle Eastern states, posing particularly difficult problems for civilian control and leading to endless competition over the management of state power and the allocation of national resources.

How, if at all, was this particular situation altered by the end of the Cold War? In the developed world the 1990s saw both a general reduction in military budgets and in the prestige of the professional soldier. But in the non-European world at large, although there were signs that some of the same budgetary pressures were at work, regimes with weak legitimacy, ruling countries with restive populations and with unresolved disputes with their neighbours, could not afford to allow the process of military downsizing to go too far.[56] This was especially true of the Middle East where, apart from the two areas of major tension in and around Israel/Palestine and the Gulf, there were also any number of violent internal conflicts, most notably those in Algeria, Sudan and Eastern Turkey. Indeed, in all three of these latter countries, the intensity of the conflict itself was enough to ensure that the generals either ran the government directly or managed it forcefully from behind the scenes.

With armies so closely involved in both government and with the existence of still pressing problems of national security, it is not surprising that information about their size, their budgets and their control over national resources remains a closely guarded secret. This, in itself, is sufficient to make analysis of either their present position, or of their possible future position, particularly difficult.

All that can be said with confidence is that, over time, they are likely to be forced to come to terms with the general trend towards global liberalisation which will demand that they – just like the Chinese army – give up their privileged position with respect to their lack of accountability, their industrial holdings and their day-to-day role in internal security. However, this will depend on the peaceful settlement of regional disputes, as well as progress towards closer association with other regional organisations such as the European Union. Until then, it is quite easy to imagine the Middle Eastern army remaining part of the powerful coalition of forces which opposes privatisation, the retreat of the state and the further introduction of court-based rules of law.

Notes

1 For example, Eliezer Be'eri, *Army Officers in Arab Politics and Society*, trans. (New York: Praeger, 1969), Part 3.
2 For example, Manfred Halpern, 'The Middle East armies and the new middle class', in J. Johnson (ed.), *The Role of the Military in Underdeveloped Countries* (Princeton, NJ: Princeton University Press, 1962).
3 For example, Maurice Janowitz, *The Military in the Political Development of New Nations* (Chicago, IL: Chicago University Press, 1964); Robin Luckham, *The Nigerian Military: A Sociological Analysis of Authority and Revolt* (Cambridge: Cambridge University Press, 1971).
4 For Turkey, see Mehmet Ali Birand, *Emret Kapitan* (translated as *Shirts of Steel: An Anatomy of the Turkish Army*) (London: I.B. Tauris, 1991). For Israel, see Peri, *Between Battles and Ballots*.
5 For an introduction to some of the methodological issues involved, see Paul A.C. Kostinen, *Mobilizing for Modern War: The Political Economy of Modern American Warfare, 1865–1919* (Kansas: Kansas University Press, 1997).
6 Mohammad A. Tarbush, *The Role of the Military in Politics: A Case Study of Iraq to 1941* (London and New York: Kegan Paul International, 1985), pp. 123–33.
7 Quoted in Jabar, Shikara and Sakai, 'From storm to thunder: Unfinished showdown between Iraq and US', p. 17.
8 Ibid., p. 9. See also Baram, *Building Towards Crisis*, p. 46.
9 Brig. Gen. (Res.) Aharon Levran, 'Syria's military strength and capability', *Middle East Review*, 19 (Spring, 1987), p. 8.
10 Volke Perthes, *The Political Economy of Syria under Asad* (London and New York: I.B. Tauris, 1995), pp. 31–2.
11 Elizabeth Picard, 'Arab military in politics: From the revolutionary plot to the authoritarian state', in Dawisha and Zartman (eds), *Beyond Coercion*, p. 139.
12 Peter Sluglett and Marion Farouk-Sluglett, 'Iraq since 1986: The strengthening of Saddam', *Middle East Report*, 20/6, 167 (November/December 1990), p. 21.
13 Robert Springborg, *Mubarak's Egypt: Fragmentation of the Political Order* (Boulder, CO: Westview Press, 1989), p. 98 . See also Ahmed T. Zohny, 'Towards an apolitical role for the Egyptian military in the management of development', *Orient*, 28/4 (December 1987), p. 551.
14 Quoted in *Al-Yassar al-Arabi/L'Egypte Gauche* (Paris), 79 (December 1986), p. 13.
15 Springborg, *Mubarak's Egypt*, pp. 118–23.
16 For example, Zohny, 'Towards an apolitical role', pp. 554–5.
17 Robert Springborg, 'Military elites and the polity in the Arab states', *Development Associates Occasional Paper*, 2 (Arlington, VA, September 1998), p. 4.
18 Ibid., pp. 4–8.
19 Baram, *Building Towards a Crisis*, pp. 44–5.

20 Ibid., pp. 48–51.

21 Ibid., pp. 46–7.

22 Alastair Drysdale, 'The succession question in Syria', *Middle East Journal*, 39/2 (Spring, 1985), p. 252; Batatu, *Syria's Peasantry*, pp. 232–6.

23 P.J. Vatikiotis, *Politics and the Military in Jordan: A Study of the Arab Legion 1921–1957* (London: Frank Cass, 1967); Uriel Dann, *King Hussein and the Challenge of Arab Radicalism: Jordan 1955–1967* (Oxford: Oxford University Press, 1989), pp. 55–67.

24 These arguments are well presented by Abdou Maliqalim Simone, *In Whose Image?*, pp. 62–3, *Political Islam and Urban Practices in Sudan* (Chicago: University of Chicago Press, 1994).

25 Ibid., p. 64. Michaela Wong, 'Years of civil war sap Sudan's youth and stoke army discontent', *Financial Times*, 6 July 1998.

26 Mark Husband, 'International hostility stiffens the resolve of Sudan's rulers', *Financial Times*, 18 June 1997.

27 For a spirited defence of the Saudi army's fighting ability, see HRH General Khalid bin Sultan, *Desert Warrior: A Personal View of the Gulf War by the Joint Forces Commander* (New York: Harper Collins, 1995), pp. 361–90.

28 Elizabeth Picard, 'The military and political reconstruction' (Paper prepared for the IISS Conference on 'Armed Forces and Society in the Middle East', Beirut, 27–29 September 1998), p. 5.

29 Ibid., p.12.

30 Mehmet Ali Birand, *Shirts of Steel*, Chapter 1.

31 Ahmad, *Making of Modern Turkey*, pp. 129–30, 137–8.

32 Mehmet Ali Birand, *The Generals' Coup in Turkey: An Inside Story of 12 September 1980* (London: Brassey's, 1987), pp. 137–8, 198–208; William Hale, 'Transition to civilian governments in Turkey: The military perspective', in Metin Heper and Ahmet Evin (eds), *State, Democracy and the Military in Turkey in the 1980s* (Berlin and New York: Walter de Gruyter, 1988), pp. 163–6.

33 For example, Feroz Ahmad, 'Military intervention and the crisis in Turkey', *MERIP*, 11/1, 93 (January 1981), p. 56.

34 Ibid., p.67.

35 Alan Richards and John Waterbury, *A Political Economy of the Middle East: Class and Economic Development* (Boulder, CO: Westview Press, 1990), pp. 365–6.

36 Hale, 'Transition to civilian governments', p. 163.

37 Metin Heper, 'The state, the military, and democracy in Turkey', *Jerusalem Journal of International Relations*, 9/3 (1987), p. 613. Figures from Office of Joint Chiefs of Staff, *Milliyet* (2 May 1986).

38 This was most obviously manifest in the resignation of the army commander-in-chief, General Toromtay, in December 1990 over what seems to have been a major dispute with the president over the nature of Turkey's contribution to the Gulf War alliance.

39 For example, Michael M. Gunter, 'The silent coup: The secularist/Islamist struggle in Turkey', *Journal of South Asian and Middle Eastern Studies*, XXI/3 (Spring, 1990), pp. 1–12

40 John Barnham, 'Turkish ministers bow to generals', *Financial Times*, 8 July 1998.

41 Nicole Pope, 'Expanding ties with Israel', *Middle East International*, 17 June 1998, p. 12.

42 Bakhash, *Reign of the Ayatollahs*, pp. 161–8.

43 Zabih, *The Iranian Military in Revolution and War* (London and New York: Routledge, 1988), Chapter 5.

44 Rebecca Cann and Constantine P., Danopoulos, 'The military and politics in a theocratic state: Iran as a case study', *Armed Forces and Society*, 24/2 (Winter, 1997), p. 272.

45 Ibid., pp. 271, 276.

46 Edward Luttwak and Dan Horowitz, *The Israeli Army* (London: Allen Lane, 1975), p. 76; Ze'ev Schiff, 'Fifty years of Israeli security: The central role of the defense system', *Middle East Journal*, 53/3 (Summer, 1999), pp. 434–2.

47 'The Israeli Defence Forces: A civilianized military in a partially militarized society', in R. Kolkowicz and A. Korbanski (eds), *Soldiers, Peasants and Bureaucrats* (London: Allen and Unwin, 1982).

48 Peri, *Between Battles and Ballots*, Chapter 7.

49 This argument is made by Uri Ben-Eliezer, 'Is a military coup possible in Israel? Israel and French-Algeria in historical-sociological perspective', *Theory and Society*, 27 (1998), particularly pp. 318–23.

50 Dan Horowitz, 'Changing patterns of civil/military relations in Israel' (lecture), Oxford, 26 October 1982.

51 Peri, *Between Battles and Ballots*, Chapter 7.

52 Ibid., pp. 172–4.

53 Ibid., pp. 131–43.

54 Ben-Eliezer, 'Is a military coup possible?', pp. 326–8.

55 Ibid., p. 327; Schiff, 'Fifty years of Israeli security', pp. 441–2.

56 For a good discussion of this subject, see Michael Barnett, 'Foreign policy change and its impact on the military's status' (Paper prepared for the IISS Conference on 'Armed forces and society in the Middle East', Beirut, 27–29 September 1998).

11 Some important non-state actors

Introduction

This book so far has viewed Middle Eastern politics from an almost entirely state-centred perspective. It has also been based on the proposition that in an authoritarian, or authoritarian/rentier, state there are few individuals or groups who can act independently of the state within the domestic political arena. Clearly, it was not always the case. In the late colonial and early independence period there was scope for such a type of political activity either in those regions which the state had only just begun to penetrate or by groups which had sources of wealth and power largely outside state control, such as rural landed property or privately owned economic enterprises. And at the end of the twentieth century, after a decade or two of structural adjustment and economic reform, there were many social analysts who seemed to believe that non-state acting could begin to flourish once again under the general rubric of a return to, or promotion of, what is widely called 'civil society'.

As is well known, the notion of civil society has been in existence since at least the eighteenth century and lives on in a wide variety of political vocabularies, including the liberal, the Hegelian and the Marxist, without there ever having been any generally-held consensus about how to define it and what it might really mean.[1] Nevertheless, one particular interpretation began to gain widespread support as a result of the apparent success of various non-party institutions in challenging the role of the communist parties in Eastern Europe in the 1980s. This stresses the role which vibrant civic associations can play in curbing state power and has been widely used as a prescription for democracy in the states of the non-European world undergoing something of the same transition from one-party statism to a more plural political and economic system. Although exact usage varies, the main thrust concerns the importance of encouraging the emergence of a melange of interest groups, social clubs and political parties to occupy the space between the individual and the state.[2] Religious associations are sometimes included in such a definition, but not always.[3] Most of the groups identified as part of civil society usually get defined as NGOs (Non-governmental organisations). Their exponential growth in number is conventionally taken as an index of the increasing vibrancy of non-state associational life.

Meanwhile, the concept of civil society has also become very much part of the Middle Eastern political vocabulary itself, both as a means to criticise authoritarian government in the name of social justice and human rights, and as a way of mobilising people towards alternative forms of political action. This is possible, as Eva Bellin argues, because the term remains 'sufficiently elastic' to suit all forms of oppositional activity from the far left to the far right.[4] And here lies the problem. Both in its original European form, and in its present political usage, the term remains too slippery and ambiguous to be of any help as a tool for the analysis of the political process. To make matters worse, it often tends to obscure the fact that many so-called NGOs are in fact instruments of government themselves. Moreover, as Sami Zubaida notes, civil society has never been a 'single sphere' but a number of islands of independent, or quasi-independent, endeavour, heavily dependent on the state itself to provide the 'clear legislation and institutional mechanisms' which alone can guarantee their autonomy.[5] And, as he also observes, the fact that such legislation rarely exists in the contemporary Middle East, and is even more rarely implemented in a regular and predictable manner, further accentuates this dependence, by forcing the managers of such associations into endless negotiation with the state officials called upon to enforce an imprecise and unsatisfactory set of rules and regulations.[6]

For all these reasons I prefer the notion of 'informal' politics to civil society. Rather than suggesting a total divorce from formal state activity, it suggests the possibility of different degrees of separation and association between state and society and so of different strategies which the informal – or non-state – political actor may be forced to adopt. I will examine this situation as it relates to two sets of groups, workers and women. However, first I will look at one field of non-state activity: that practised in some of the rural areas before land reform and state control. Lastly, I will conclude with a brief examination of the situation of the Palestinians of the West Bank and Gaza since 1967 who were clearly non-state actors as far as their relations with the Israelis were concerned but something more ambiguous when it came to their growing incorporation into the state-like institutions created by the Palestinian Liberation Organisation (PLO).

The self-contained world of rural politics

For most of the twentieth century the majority of Middle Eastern peoples lived in rural areas at some distance from the main centres of urban power. And for most of them, their local politics tended to be dominated by the owners of large agricultural estates until these same estates began to be broken up by the land reforms which took place in the Arab countries and Iran beginning in the 1950s. However, even then, the power of those medium landowners who remained in the villages continued to be important given that they were well placed to play a leading role in the co-operatives, local councils and other institutional mechanisms introduced by an expansionist state. By the same token, the owners of medium-sized properties tended to stand a better chance of getting elected to the assemblies established by the new authoritarian regimes.[7]

In the era before the land reforms, the rural populations lived largely in isolation from the politics of the capital city, their daily concerns centred mainly on such immediate interests as the struggle for control over land, labour and access to water. This, in turn, generated its own form of local politics in terms of the overwhelming importance attached to the settlement of the inevitable disputes over the use of such resources, either by a direct exercise of landlord influence or through more communal methods of conflict resolution. Meanwhile, the marked disparities in rural wealth and power also generated a constant struggle between landlord control and peasant resistance in which violence and the use of force was an ever present possibility.

This is a huge subject and it is only possible to illustrate a few of its many forms. I will concentrate on three instances where historically-minded social anthropologists have done sufficient research to lay bare some of the most important local dynamics at work, in Egypt, Iraq and Lebanon.

Before the beginnings of the Nasser-period land reform, a third of Egypt's agricultural land was concentrated in some 12,000 large estates.[8] The majority of these consisted as what was known as an *izba*, a word which meant both a concentration of central buildings containing the landlord's own house, the stores and so on, and a system of land management combining the use of service tenants who lived on the estate and day labourers recruited from outside.[9] A small proportion of these owners were foreign, but the majority were Egyptians who were able to represent the local power of the state. As Reem Saad writes of the *izba* village she studied south of Cairo, the estate there was bought in 1947 by a politician from the capital who used the police as his agents and became 'the government' as far as the local people were concerned.[10] Indeed, he had so much coercive power at his disposal, supplemented by his direct control over wages, the allocation of land, and the provision of food for his tenants, that overt resistance was rarely possible, leaving his peasants with only the traditional weapons of the weak such as stealing, time-wasting and other petty acts of defiance. Hence, politics, both inside the *izba* and in the surrounding, area was largely disjoined from national politics: with the landowner simply ordering his tenants to vote according to his wishes in any general election and monopolising all the other links between state and *izba* through his own position in Egypt's parliament. Only with land reform was the era of Pasha domination brought to an end, a moment of such significance for Reem Saad's peasant interlocutors that they structured their entire view of village history in terms of the bad old days before the reform and the good period that followed.[11]

Parts of southern Iraq shared many of the same characteristics before the beginnings of land redistribution in 1958. Agriculture was characterised by the existence of large estates directed by the agents of mainly absentee owners powerful enough to ensure that the local government administrators were almost entirely under their direction.[12] However, in other areas, like the one studied by

Robert Fernea on the Middle Euphrates, there was a more complex pattern of interests involving settled tribesmen (working for both absentee and local landlords), merchants in the local market town of Dhaghara and a hundred or so government officials of whom far and away the most important was the irrigation engineer who had the last word in the allocation of water.[13] The state was also present in the form of the police and a number of residents who were required to assist them in their duties.

The result was a set of two interlocking circles of local politics. One involved the tribesmen who settled their disputes on the basis of their shared understanding of tribal knowledge and practice. The other was administered by the police who enforced the law on the basis of a notion of individual responsibility, often with considerable brutality and the regular use of mass imprisonment and torture in order to obtain a confession for a single crime or misdemeanour. The tribal shaikh studied by Fernea moved between both worlds in his role as leader, landowner and senator in the Baghdad parliament, settling disputes by an exercise of influence and by his ability to mediate between state power and local social norms.[14] However, it was also possible for Fernea to identify a tendency in which the need for government officials to manage the irrigation system was promoting a shift in the balance of power towards the centre, leaving less room for local initiative and causing more and more disputes to be addressed directly by the representatives of the state.[15]

Lebanon's large estates were concentrated in those areas to the north, south and east of the central mountain range which had been added by the French after the First World War. In the part of the northern Akkar plain studied by Michael Gilsenan, the dominant political figures were the beys who had built up their power as landlords during the French mandate. They used their position to control their estates and the peasant population needed to farm them, partly through the use of local agents, partly through an ostentatious exercise of social superiority, the deliberate creation of an atmosphere of fear and an unceasing series of manoeuvres and manipulations based on their intimate knowledge of the local population and its history of family feuds. As Gilsenan describes it, there was a constant sense of threatened violence so powerful as to ensure that it rarely needed to be actually used. Local politics were linked to the larger world of national politics through the competition of the beys for land, labour and votes, as well as by the ability of individual beys to use their election to parliament to secure cabinet office. However, they were also unwilling to share whatever political resources they possessed, deliberately keeping the Akkar backward as a means of preventing government intervention in the lives of those whose well-being they controlled.[16]

The three examples just given illustrate a context in which politics appears at its most basic, as a day-to-day competition for control over resources, with little room for organised alliances or ideology. It involves face-to-face – one is tempted to say, 'in your face' – contacts. Nevertheless, to those outside observers who attempted to understand its essential dynamic, it was also beginning to change from about mid-century on, first with the growing intrusion of the state, then with the direct attack on landlord power in Egypt and Iraq in the 1950s. This process was then accelerated by the appearance within the closed world of the village of other actors and, later, other options, including direct involvement with the state apparatus or urban migration or working abroad.

Organised labour and the limits of political action

An important feature of twentieth-century urban life has been the role played by organised labour using strikes and demonstrations in pursuit of political as well as economic ends. The Middle East has been no exception. However, the links between trade unions and other forms of workers' associations has followed its own particular trajectory, being intimately associated with colonialism, nationalism and the process of state building. In what follows I will look briefly at this trajectory, first in terms of the Arab countries, then of Iran, Israel and Turkey. In each case I will try to identify those moments when the intervention of workers' movements played a significant role in the larger politics of the day.

Arab workers' associations of a modern type tended to be first formed in the colonial period, either in enterprises owned and managed by foreigner companies (for example, the tramways in Egypt) or by the colonial state (for example, the port and railway workers in Iraq, Palestine and Sudan). In some cases they were also organised directly by trade unions active in the metropolis, as in North Africa where the first unions were set up by the French Confédération Générale du Travail (CGT). Unionism then received further encouragement as part of the Allied efforts to manage the Middle Eastern economies during the Second World War.

Given their ability to bring key workers out on strike in the major urban centres, the first unions proved useful allies to the local nationalists, although usually as part of a wider coalition of forces which included students as well. However, once independence had been achieved, the regimes which controlled the new states grew increasingly fearful of union power, the more so as leadership often seems to have been concentrated in the hands of left-wing activists. Hence they moved quickly to restrict their freedom of action by new laws and to incorporate their leaders more directly within the state apparatus. In other cases, for example Saudi Arabia in the 1950s, strikes were simply outlawed and all forms of unionism banned.

Incorporation was particularly popular with those authoritarian regimes like the Egyptian or the Algerian ones which based their own legitimacy on an appeal to national unity as an instrument of rapid economic and social development. To many analysts such a strategy suggested a Middle Eastern variation of the types of corporatism identified with, say, Mussolini's Italy, where working-class activism was contained by means of a kind of social contract in which the state undertook to look after workers' economic interests, including wages, welfare benefits and job security, in return for a commitment not to strike or to engage in any form of political activity.[17] Such policies also had the added benefit of creating a sharp division between those public sector workers organised in state-managed labour federations, who tended to form an aristocracy of labour in terms of pay and conditions, and those in what remained of the private sector who were left without protection of any kind.

Nevertheless, Middle Eastern corporatism was rarely successful enough to prevent a variety of unofficial strikes, demonstrations and sit-ins which remained the most common method of expressing deep-rooted discontents. As a rule, these were largely deployed defensively, in order to protect existing rights under threat by individual factory management.[18] However, on occasions, they also played a much larger political role, as in Egypt in February 1968 and again in January 1977. On the first occasion, a protest initiated by the workers in the military aircraft factory at Helwan just south of Cairo, against the lenient sentences imposed on the airforce commanders on trial for failing to protect the country from Israel's surprise attack at the beginning of the June 1967 war, became the catalyst for a huge march through the capital by unionists, students and others which was widely interpreted as a demonstration of serious popular dissatisfaction with many aspects of the Nasser regime. President Nasser, who was described by close associates as both 'frightened and fascinated' by this event, hurried off to address the workers at Helwan where he was met by cries of 'ghair, ghair, Ya Gamal' ('Change, Change, O Gamal') even as he was announcing that the commanders' light sentences would be reviewed.[19] He also made a promise of greater democracy, one of the demonstrators' key demands. Nevertheless, although this led to something known as the March 30th Declaration which promised to address the question of basic political reform, Nasser himself proved unable to introduce more than minimal change, and it was left to his successor, Anwar Sadat, to use the widespread desire for greater freedom as the basis for his own new policy of *infitah* first announced in 1971.

In the event, Sadat's own policies came under huge popular challenge in January 1977 when a period of economic hardship promoted by the first wave of economic liberalisation came to a head with two days of country-wide demonstrations and attacks on the police triggered off by the announcement that the government subsidy on flour and other necessities was about to be cut by up to 50 per cent. Once again, it was groups of workers, in both Alexandra and Helwan who acted as the catalyst.[20] And even though the protests were quickly brought to an end by military intervention supported by a general curfew forcing people off the streets, it was enough to cause the cuts to be rescinded. Furthermore, in the longer run, the popular outburst was enough to convince both the Sadat regime and the international financial community represented by the IMF that efforts to impose a tight programme of austerity on Egypt were likely to arouse such popular protest as to be essentially counter-productive.

The history of worker activity in Iran bears some resemblance to that of the Arab states, at least until the Revolution. A period of intense trade union activity in the 1940s and early 1950s was brought to an end by sustained pressure from the shah and his security forces on the left-wing parties like the Tudeh which had been most active in encouraging, and then channelling, working-class militancy. This was followed by nearly two decades, 1963–78, in which, in Habib

Ladjervardi's words, 'the government's official but un-stated labour policy was that if the workers remained silent and a-political, then [it] would protect the security of their jobs by pressuring employers to refrain from discharging their workers'.[21] This policy was successful enough that labour militancy did not become an important factor until the summer of 1978, well after the start of the revolutionary movement by middle-class activists followed closely by sustained pressure from the religious establishment.[22] But having finally entered the political fray, it was workers' groups which played a significant role in paralysing the economy and in bringing the shah's government to a halt. They did this by engaging in what Ervand Abrahamian has characterised as 'in effect, a general strike' in which government offices, the oil industry, government television and radio and many of the banks and large factories largely stopped functioning as a result of mass absenteeism.[23]

Labour militancy also played an important role in the first years of the Islamic Republic, proceeding, in Assef Bayat's analysis, in three stages.[24] In the first, the workers stepped into the vacuum created by the flight of many of the former factory owners and most senior management, running the enterprises through a variety of different types of workers' councils while pressuring the government to nationalise more and more of the establishments as state property. Then, beginning in the autumn of 1979, the new government began to assert its own authority by reintroducing 'management from above', purging the councils of their more radical members and promoting Islamic associations as a counter to leftist militancy. Finally, starting in the summer of 1981, complete government hegemony was achieved as the Islamic associations were encouraged to complete the rout of their rivals leaving them in sole control of a now thoroughly tamed labour force. Nevertheless, one important legacy from the earlier period remained: a large and unwieldy public sector which, to this day, stands in the way of efficiency and reform.

The labour history of Israel also contains a number of unusual features. For one thing, the main representative of workers' interests, the Histadrut (the General Organisation of Jewish Workers), has always combined two other functions: that of the owner of a large economic empire including the largest bank and industrial conglomerate, and, until the 1990s, the provider of the bulk of the country's health and pension services. For another, from its inception in 1920 the Histadrut had been in intimate partnership with the Zionist movement, with its primary task that of assisting the creation of a Jewish state in Palestine and then Israel.[25] As a result its representation of labour interests was always subordinate to this larger task of co-operating with the government after 1948. One significant example is the Histadrut's support for policies of wage restraint, whenever these were deemed necessary, even going so far as to endorse the cabinet's deliberate creation of extra unemployment during the economic recession that preceded the 1967 war. However, such ambiguity was sufficient to persuade important groups of workers that the organisation was unwilling to protect their interests and so helped to encourage the wave of unofficial strikes and extra-parliamentary actions in the late 1960s and early 1970s that Michael

Shalev styles a 'rank and file revolt'.[26] This, in turn, was one of a number of factors undermining the Labour Party's hegemony and so paving the way for the Likud victory in the 1977 election.

Turkish labour militancy also played an important political role, for example by helping to create the conditions which led to the military intervention of March 1971. Until 1967, workers' interests were represented by one large Confederation of Turkish Workers' Unions (Turk-Is), an organisation with only economic aims and a largely apolitical leadership. But in that year a rival Confederation of Revolutionary Workers Unions (DISK) was founded by a break-away faction interested in a more activist stance and the forging of close links with the newly created Turkish Workers Party.[27] This in turn so alarmed both the political and military establishment that an amendment to the Trade Union Law of 1963 was passed in June 1970 with the aim of making it more difficult for DISK to recruit private sector members. DISK's response was a series of strikes which totally paralysed the Istanbul/Marmora region for several days, followed by enough further militancy to alarm the generals into making their second intervention.[28] From then on, both the military and their civilian allies sought ways to limit unionism and to prevent links between unions and political parties, a process which culminated during the third military intervention, 1980–3, in the closure of DISK, the arrest and imprisonment of its leaders and an article in the 1982 constitution explicitly preventing parties from having any institutional ties with economic interest groups of any kind. These actions were sufficient to cow labour activism until the late 1980s when a series of unofficial strikes were instrumental in allowing many workers to obtain the increases necessary to bring the real value of their wages back to those of a decade earlier.

Looking at the Middle East as a whole, the almost universal implementation of policies during the 1990s designed to encourage private sector activity by, among other things, selling off state assets, posed new problems both for regimes anxious to create market economies and for the workers themselves. In many cases, efforts to privatise were blocked, for shorter or longer periods, by strikes, demonstrations and other forms of political activity by those who feared loss of jobs or changed conditions of service. At the same time, labour became a partner in the negotiations to draw up the new laws necessary to redefine industrial relations for the new era, for example in Egypt where it was involved in a lengthy process of bargaining in which it sought, unsuccessfully as it turned out, to ensure that an unfettered right to strike was included in the proposed legislation.[29] One lesson learned from such negotiations was that the country could well be moving towards a situation in which employers and employees would themselves bargain over conditions of work free from the tight system of government supervision which had been such a feature of the post-independence decades.

Women in the political process

Women's main role in the Middle Eastern political process has been as actors in the larger national politics, first as participants of the anti-colonial struggle, then as members of political parties, as voters and as grass-roots activists. They received the vote in Turkey in 1934, in Syria and Lebanon in 1953, Egypt in 1956 and in Jordan in 1974. They have also provided a number of the cabinet ministers and members of parliament, although, as the United Nations *Human Development Report (1998)* points out, the proportion of Arab women in national assemblies, 3 per cent, is the smallest of any region in the world.[30] Even in Israel, women's representation in the Knesset has always been under 10 per cent.[31] This lack of public presence has then generated a variety of movements aimed either at expanding women's participation or, as in the case of Kuwait and Bahrain, at obtaining the vote for the first time.

Beyond this, there is also a distinctive form of activity which can be called 'women's politics'. This involves a range of interventions from those that are of specific interest to women, such as the laws of marriage, divorce and inheritance, to the larger debates arising from their role in wars, revolutions and national uprising and as citizens of the new Middle Eastern states. In ways which are now widely discussed, women are seen as bearers of a cultural identity that stands in a problematic relationship to their emergence as 'full-fledged' citizens.[32] This, in turn, has given rise to the notion of 'state-feminism' where women find themselves co-opted by the state in support of regime definitions of their national and social role.

While it can be argued, with good reason, that women do not constitute a single unit for analysis, and that they are divided by class, religion and culture, the fact that, for certain purposes, they appear on the public stage as an undifferentiated category of persons defined only by their gender, has come to make the notion of a women's politics a particularly highly-charged and contested one. It is subject to a variety of strongly held opinions, both religious and secular. It is also greatly influenced by a growing consciousness that most of the present definitions of women's roles are the work of men and so open to challenge for the way that they generally seek to reduce women's ability to change their personal circumstances or, ultimately, to shape the public positions assigned to them as citizens.

One particular area of contention has concerned the contrast between the valued participation of women in various kinds of national struggle and then their relegation to a more passive role thereafter. In the Arab world this phenomenon was first observed, and subject to challenge, in Algeria where, as one account put it, Algerian women had fought against the French 'like men'.[33] Later, however, the draft Family Code introduced in 1972 was subject to strong opposition from various women's groups led by the *mujahedate* (women fighters in the War of Liberation) and others who were particularly incensed by the notion of male guardianship over women which it contained. They organised demonstrations outside government buildings under banners containing such slogans as 'We want full citizenship' and references to the fact that they had borne arms and sacrifices 'like men'. Their protest achieved temporary success. Nevertheless, many of the objectionable clauses later reappeared in the new Family Code of 1984 which did pass into law.[34] Arguments of much the same kind have been expressed by Israeli and Iranian women concerning their participation in war, Palestinian women concerning their role in the *Intifada* and Kuwaiti women concerning their opposition to the Iraqi occupation of 1990/1.

Another arena was opened up by the central emphasis given to women's participation in an expanded civil society. This provided the ideological framework for the explosion of women's associations and NGOs in the Middle East during the 1990s. Often employing the notion of women's empowerment, these new organisations tended to address such issues as the alleviation of poverty via the promotion of income-generating activity for women and education about their legal rights. If measured simply in terms of numbers of groups formed, this movement is often considered to be a success. However, statistics alone tend to mask the fact that most of the new groups tend to be run by English-speaking, middle- or, in the Gulf, upper-class women, and that they rarely address the structural problems that define women's place within society and so are easily co-opted by the various Arab regimes in a way that makes their official designation as 'non-governmental' organisations something of a misnomer. One extreme form can be found in Kuwait where women's groups, like all other associations, are controlled and funded through the Ministry of Social Affairs.[35]

Nevertheless, there are other ways in which women take a more active, and more challenging, part in politics. I would like to mention three. The first is the conscious assertion of their gender in a public space in which they use the body and associated symbols to make particular statements concerning such issues as their opposition to war and violence or the fate of some of their relatives. One example is the group known as the 'Saturday Mothers' who met every week in central Istanbul in the mid-1990s to protest the disappearance of husbands, children and other relatives. Another is the Israeli 'Women in Black' who made Friday night vigils near important crossroads in Tel Aviv at which they called for the withdrawal of Israel's troops from the Occupied Territories during the Palestinian *Intifada*.

A second form of use of public space involves the women's networks which operate in the poorer quarters of many Middle Eastern cities as a form of mutual support. Although their primary purpose is to help to protect and sustain women and their families in their day-to-day struggle for economic survival, they also play a role in providing useful information about how to cope with, or to circumvent, local state officials or to make contact with representatives of national or municipal parties. In this way, they encourage a form of collective action which can be used on a regular basis both to make demands on the government and to protect or expand the space in which to practise a local and more informal type of politics.[36]

In Turkey, in particular, many such networks were also run by women Islamic activists connected first with the Refah party, then with its successor, the

Fazilet (Virtue) party. Not only did they provide a mechanism for helping local members in difficulty and for getting them out to vote, but they also allowed large numbers of women to be mobilised around certain issues which have to be contested at the national level, for example the frequent demonstrations which took place in the late 1990s against the government's ban on head scarves in schools, universities and public offices.[37]

A third example of the use of public space is provided by the debates inside the Islamic Republic of Iran about such central issues as women's right to work. As Homa Hoodfar notes, large numbers of women who had been politicised during the first stages of the Iranian Revolution remained in the political arena where, over time, they learned how to extract concessions from the senior members of the regime.[38] One issue concerned the problem of the widows of Iranian soldiers killed in the war with Iraq who then lost the custody of their children to their husband's male relatives, such as their fathers-in-law. Hearing their protests, their case was taken up by the media and the Martyr's Foundation which were able to embarrass the regime to such an extent that the Ayatollah Khomeini himself was led to issue a statement allowing them custody of their children (although not 'guardianship') even if they remarried. Taking this as a precedent, many women were emboldened to flood the press with letters about their harsh treatment at the hands of the Islamic courts, encouraging the government to modify the marriage contract with respect to such matters as the need for an equal division of the property accumulated by both parties in the case of divorce. A last example concerns the lobbying done by women activists which secured the passage of a 'wages for housework' law in 1991 which could now be claimed by a divorced wife provided she was deemed to have performed her wifely duties during the marriage.[39]

Women's politics in Iran also involves a number of issues on which Islamic activists could be found on both sides of such key debates as those concerning women's employment. Some female members of the regime supported the official discrimination against women leaving home to work, for example the woman appointed in the early 1990s as the first Presidential Adviser on Women's Affairs. Others opposed it so vigorously that they were able to persuade the Higher Council of the Cultural Revolution to formulate what was described as an Islamic female employment policy in 1992, which, though still asserting that a woman's first priority was to the home, also argued that Islam offered women the opportunity to develop their full potential through work and that the state had a duty to encourage this.[40]

Palestinians: between rejecting one state and becoming citizens of another

Having had no state of their own, Palestinians can be defined as the quintessential non-state actors except where they have been incorporated, either as individuals or en bloc, into some new state, for example Jordan. And, in the case of those living in the West Bank and the Gaza Strip, they stood in clear opposition to the states which controlled them, first Egypt and Jordan, then Israel.

Nevertheless, their case is not quite so simple if we allow that the PLO had statist aspirations of its own, first as it built up its strength in Lebanon and Tunis and then, even more intensely, after Yasser Arafat's return to Gaza in 1994 and the creation of the Palestine National Authority (PNA). All movements of national liberation aspire to create a state. But in Yezid Sayigh's compelling argument, the PLO, from its inception in 1964, began to shape itself into the form of a non-territorial equivalent of a state, as if in anticipation of its eventual success.[41] This included forging a relationship with Palestinian society which allowed it to stand above it, to control it and to shape its nationalist agenda. To do so it encouraged what Sayigh calls the formation of a 'durable bureaucratic elite' to manage its day-to-day operations.[42] Its autonomous character was further encouraged by the receipt of large funds from Arab and other sources which not only assured its independence from its own popular base but also allowed it to keep considerable numbers of Palestinians on its payroll, as well as to provide social welfare and other collective services to its people. Lastly, it either created or co-opted the various mass organisations which it used to represent, and also to mobilise, the various segments of the Palestinian population such as students, workers and women.[43]

During the 1970s, after the failure of its initial attempt to wear down the Israelis by means of armed struggle, the PLO began to create a relationship with what was increasingly recognised as its 'vital constituency', the people who lived on the ground in the West Bank and Gaza where the eventual Palestinian state was supposed to be formed.[44] This meant, in essence, the creation of mechanisms designed to monopolise and control. However, in so doing, it was forced to interact with a population whose opposition to Israeli rule had begun to develop a dynamic of its own. Moreover, it had to do it at a distance and in direct competition, not only with Jordan and Israel, but also with the efforts of a whole variety of international aid agencies which had begun to direct their attention to the peoples of Israel's Occupied Territories.

In these circumstances, what emerged in the West Bank and Gaza was a distinct political culture of accommodation and resistance with a number of interesting features of its own. Of primary importance was the emergence after 1967 of different groups of grass-roots activists with agendas and organisational experience quite different from that of the traditional notable families whose leadership they began to replace. One component consisted of students either newly returned from universities abroad or the graduates of the three West Bank universities established in the early 1970s at Bir Zeit, Bethlehem and Nablus. A second came from the ranks of the trade unions which represented the growing number of men finding work either in the burgeoning Palestinian economy or in Israel. And a third, which overlapped with the first two, was made up of those Palestinians who had passed through Israeli prisons where interaction with their fellow prisoners had increased their nationalist consciousness while allowing the creation of activist networks as they were selectively released. According to one estimate quoted by Yezid Sayigh, some 230–250,000 Palestinians had passed through Israeli interrogation centres and experienced at least 24 hours of detention by 1981.[45] This was enough not only to create a militant leadership but also a plentiful supply of second and third rank activists ready to take their leaders' places should they be killed or re-arrested.[46]

Two other features of Palestinian society under occupation were also important. One was the competition between the various component factions within the PLO – most notably Fatah and the Popular and Democratic Fronts – to mobilise, and so to politicise, ever larger numbers of the local population through the creation of a whole variety of new associations, charities and clubs. In this they were also joined by the Palestinian Communist Party which was finally admitted into the PLO in 1987. If the result was often the existence of four rival organisations, for example for women or for students, the competition itself was a powerful force driving the process along. The second feature was the constant process of interaction not only with the forces of the Occupation but also with the larger Israeli society which lived so close. Israeli policy encouraged an endless series of responses and adaptations, for example by regularly allowing new possibilities for political action while shutting off others. Hence, it helped to create one kind of leadership by permitting mayoral elections in twelve West Bank towns in 1976, and quite another after 1982 when its closure of the Palestinian National Guidance Council encouraged the emergence of a much more localised form of political mobilisation. Meanwhile, Israel's own experience of both pre- and post-state political life provided a repertoire of models which Palestinians could adapt and use for their own purposes.

Out of this mix came two significantly different movements of action, organisation and protest in the 1980s. The first focused on the creation of a variety of politically-motivated associations designed to promote self-sufficiency and new forms of resistance. While the second was the mass uprising known as the *Intifada* which began in December 1987. I will discuss each in turn.

The first movement was very much a reaction to policies imposed on Palestinians from outside. As the Israeli occupation began to assume permanence, both the Jordanians and the PLO encouraged the rather passive policy known as *sumud* (steadfastness) in which what was required of the West Bank population was simply to stay put. To this end they were provided with outside funds to prevent them from being turned into economic refugees, but without any emphasis on more than passive resistance. To this was then added a veritable invasion of foreign charities which, for a while, also seemed to be setting the local agenda as to what Palestinians should and should not do. In reaction to this, and also to the increasing Israeli settlement of the West Bank after the Likud electoral victory of 1977 and to the shock of Egypt's separate peace with Israel in 1979, many community leaders began to look for ways in which they could create institutional mechanisms which would assert activism and independence rather than passive dependence.

It is generally believed that the first of the new-style movements was the committee of doctors formed in the late 1970s to organise visits to villages at some remove from towns and hospitals. This was quickly followed by the Women's Work Committee founded in Ramallah in 1978 and then three others of the same type representing rival political groups. All were designed to mobilise women behind the national cause, to generate political consciousness and to engage in such 'national' tasks as providing aid to the families of imprisoned activists.[47] And although most were founded by people who were connected, in one way or another, with the PLO, all were critical of its policies and, particularly after its expulsion from Lebanon to Tunis in 1982, worried whether it could continue to exercise its leadership role.

The new associations proved adept at obtaining funds from international agencies but without having to surrender their own independence and freedom of action. Indeed, at least one of these agencies, Oxfam (UK), began to see them as a model for grass-roots organisation throughout the rest of the Middle East and promoted several conferences and workshops to draw attention to their role as a focus for non-state self-empowerment. However, from a Palestinian point of view, their historical importance derives more from their search for a radical political agenda, their development of new modes of political actions and their inherent populism which sought to include all sections of local society.[48] As such, they also provided one of the main organisational foundations of the next act of sustained resistance, the *Intifada*.

The outbreak of the uprising is conventionally related directly to an incident in December 1987 when an Israeli farm vehicle drove into two cars carrying Palestinian workers in Gaza, killing four. However, it is also important to note that it was the culmination of a period of ever more militant activism underlined in Meron Benvenisti's West Bank Data Project's 1987 report published just before. '[Palestinian] Violence,' he wrote, 'is largely carried out in broad daylight by individuals who spontaneously express their feelings, undeterred by the consequences'.[49] As for the *Intifada* itself, it soon became a general confrontation with the Israeli occupation on many fronts, involving novel forms of organisation and resistance. These included street demonstrations, strikes and boycotts as well as co-ordinated stone-throwing attacks on Israeli patrols, increasingly encouraged and supported by local action committees and under a loose system of general guidance exercised by the United National Leadership (UNL) formed in January 1988 and consisting of representatives from the main political organisations including the Palestine Communist Party.[50]

It was the leaflets and other instructions issued periodically by the UNL which provided official direction, practical advice and a programme of co-ordinated strikes and boycotts aimed, so it was hoped, at encouraging the withdrawal of Palestinian society from Israeli control. The local committees organised in the towns, villages and refugee camps, as well as among students, workers and women, would then try to carry out these instructions as best they could but always with a great deal of local initiative. Women, for example, played a significant role in organising demonstrations, marches and sit-ins on a daily basis.[51] Altogether, it was this particular combination of central direction and local input which first allowed the uprising to spread so fast, and then sustained it through months of activism and harsh repression. However, in the end, it was insufficient on its own to effect a change of status on the ground. As in all similar struggles, widespread violent or passive resistance is rarely able to end an occupation by itself. What it can do, though, is to raise the cost to such an extent as to pave the way for a political or diplomatic solution.

Another important factor was the Israeli response. The almost immediate use of various forms of collective punishment, like curfews and mass arrests, which affected more and more of the Palestinian population helped to spread the uprising to practically all sections of Palestinian society. For example, Hunter cites a report which suggests that there were some 1,600 curfews imposed in the first year of the *Intifada*, 400 of them for between three and forty days.[52] Another was the way in which the Israeli military desired to obliterate every manifestation of Palestinian nationalism, including graffiti and the use of the national flag, thus provoking seemingly endless cycles of repression and resistance. A good example is the way a village or a quarter of a camp would proclaim its own independence by raising a Palestinian flag, wait for an Israeli patrol to come and tear it down and then raise it once again after the patrol had left.[53]

One significant group of recruits were the members of the Muslim Brothers whose formerly quietist attitude to the occupation changed almost immediately the *Intifada* began with the formation of its militant wing, Hamas, in December 1987. Another was a group of moderate notables, generally from old Palestinian families, who acted as the public face of the *Intifada* by holding news conferences and organising tours for foreign journalists and visiting diplomats. All shared the general aim of the uprising as well as the importance of using only stones as weapons rather than firearms. But, over time, they became the focus for important differences over strategy with some emphasising violence and others negotiation and discussion with Israel.

The uprising was at its most intense during its first year, 1988. And it was then that it achieved its most important results, notably King Hussein's decision to renounce all Jordanian claims to the West Bank in July. However, even though it was able to become what Hunter calls a 'way of life' for Palestinians, there was an inevitable loss of energy and direction over time in the face of continuing Israeli collective punishment and the growing economic deprivations endured by a weary population.[54] One result was a growing division over strategy with those in favour of a negotiated settlement gaining strength against those who were unwilling to give up the struggle on the ground even when it was clear that the drive towards a mass campaign of civil disobedience had faltered. Another was a reduction in the level of activity with smaller groups involved in day-to-day confrontations with Israeli troops. There were also signs of growing frustration marked by tensions between the activist local committees and the people they attempted to mobilise, by angry attacks on Palestinians accused of being collaborators and by an increasing tendency to the use of guns.

Nevertheless, the *Intifada* was able to continue to generate sporadic resistance until the whole situation was changed, first by the Iraqi invasion of Kuwait, then by the renewed international effort towards a Palestinian/Israeli settlement which followed. These years also saw a sustained effort by the PLO to regain its control over the Palestinian population at large, an effort that became ever more intense after the Oslo Agreement paved the way for Arafat's return and the establishment of a national authority on the West Bank and Gaza. With the population exhausted by the effort of prolonged resistance, and with much of its local leadership in Israeli prisons, it proved relatively easy to find Arafat loyalists willing to exercise influence and control.[55]

The PLO's position was further solidified in the months just before Arafat's return when it was able to persuade international donors to transfer the funds they had previously used to support local Palestinian welfare societies to the PNA's own embryonic ministries of health and education.[56] Finally, the Israeli handover of responsibility for taxation, justice and welfare to the PNA in 1994, paved the way for the creation of a new set of relations between the Authority and the people of the West Bank and Gaza largely analogous to that between a state and its citizens.[57] This could, in theory, have taken a pluralist form, as many hoped, with a great deal of space for civic activities independent of statist control. However, it was not to be. The state-building model pursued by the PLO in exile turned out to have a marked similarity with that pursued in the neighbouring Arab states, with its own version of authoritarianism and central control.[58] Israeli pressure to clamp down on all signs of anti-Israeli protest only made things worse. Hence the freedom of the Palestinian media and of the universities was gradually whittled away and the decisions of the Supreme Court and the elected Legislative Council largely ignored, leaving the population with little protection against the heavy-handed actions of the security forces and the PNA bureaucracy. Having struggled for years to resist control by one state – the Israeli – the Palestinian people now found themselves with little redress against the arbitrary actions of another: their own.

Notes

1 For a useful overview, see John Keane, 'Despotism and democracy', in John Keane (ed.), *Civil Society and the State; New European Perspectives* (London: Verso, 1988), especially pp. 35–9.
2 Eva Bellin, 'Civil society and state formation in Tunisia', in Richard Augustus Norton (ed.), *Civil Society in the Middle East*, I (Leiden: E.J. Brill, 1995), p. 125.
3 For example, religious groups are excluded from the definition in Saad Eddine Ibrahim's, 'Civil society and the prospects for democratization in the Arab world', in Norton *Civil Society*, I, p. 28.
4 Bellin, 'Civil society and state formation in Tunisia', p. 121.
5 Sami Zubaida, 'Islam, the state and democracy: Contrasting opinions of society in Egypt', *Middle East Report*, 22/6, 179 (November/December 1992), pp. 2–3.
6 Ibid.
7 For example, Leonard Binder, *In a Moment of Enthusiasm: Political Power and the Second Stratum in Egypt* (Chicago, IL and London: University of Chicago Press, 1978), Chapter 9; Raymond Hinnebusch, *Peasant and Bureaucracy in Ba'thist Syria: The Political Economy of Rural Development* (Boulder, CO: Westview Press, 1989), pp. 107–16.
8 Gabriel Baer, *A History of Landownership in Modern Egypt* (London: Oxford University Press, 1962), Appendix I; Ansari, *Egypt*, p.73.

9 For example, Roger Owen, 'The development of agricultural production in nineteenth-century Egypt – capitalism of what type?', in A.L. Udovitch (ed.), *The Islamic Middle East 700–1900: Studies in Economic and Social History* (Princeton, NJ: The Darwin Press, 1981), pp. 521–46 and Alan Richards, *Egypt's Agricultural Development, 1800–1980: Technical and Social Change* (Boulder, CO: Westview Press, 1982), pp. 523–31.

10 Reem Saad, 'Social history of an agrarian reform community in Egypt', *Cairo Papers in Social Science*, 11, monograph 4 (Winter, 1988) pp. 43, 46.

11 Ibid., Chapter 5.

12 This was true, for example, of the Kut/Amara region on the Tigris just south of Baghdad. See Robert A. Fernea, 'State and tribe in Southern Iraq: The struggle for hegemony before the 1958 Revolution', in Robert A. Fernea and Wm. Roger Louis (eds), *The Iraqi Revolution of 1958: The Old Social Classes Revisited* (London and New York: I.B. Tauris, 1991), p. 146.

13 Ibid., p. 147; Robert A. Fernea, *Shaykh and Effendi: Changing Patterns of Authority Among the El Shabana of Southern Iraq* (Cambridge, MA: Harvard University Press, 1970), Chapter 4.

14 Fernea, 'State and tribe', pp. 145–51.

15 Ibid., p. 152.

16 Michael Gilsenan, *Lords of the Lebanese Marches: Violence and Narrative in an Arab Society* (Berkeley and Los Angeles: University of California Press, 1996), Part I.

17 For example, Robert Bianchi, 'The corporatization of the Egyptian labor movement', *Middle East Journal*, 4/3 (Summer, 1986), pp. 429–44; Alan Richards and John Waterbury, *A Political Economy of the Middle East* (2nd edn, Boulder, CO and Oxford: Westview Press, 1996), pp. 316–17.

18 Examples of such defensive activity can be found, *inter alia*, in Marsha Pripstein Posusney, *Labor and the State in Egypt: Workers, Unions and Economic Restructuring* (New York: Columbia University Press, 1997), Chapter 3.

19 Kirk J. Beattie, *Egypt During the Nasser Years: Ideology, Politics and Civil Society* (Boulder, CO and Oxford: Westview Press, 1994), p. 215.

20 Raymond Hinnebusch, *Egyptian Politics Under Sadat* (Cambridge: Cambridge University Press, 1985), p. 71; David Hirst and Irene Beeson, *Sadat* (London: Faber and Faber, 1981), p. 242.

21 Habib Ladjervardi, *Labor Unions and Autocracy in Iran* (Syracuse: Syracuse University Press, 1985), p. 234.

22 Abrahamian, *Iran Between Two Revolutions*, pp. 510–12.

23 Ibid., p. 517–18. Bakhash, *Reign of the Ayatollahs*, p. 16.

24 Assef Bayat, 'Workers' control after the Revolution', *MERIP*, 13/3, 113 (March/April 1983), pp. 19–20.

25 Here I follow the argument of Michael Shalev, 'The labor movement in Israel: Ideology and political economy', in Ellis Jay Goldberg (ed.), *The Social History of Labor in the Middle East* (Boulder, CO and Oxford: Westview Press, 1996), pp. 138–45.

26 Ibid., pp. 151–2.

27 Gunseli Berik and Cihan Bilginsoy, 'The labor movement in Turkey: Labor pains, maturity, metamorphosis', in ibid., pp. 47–8.

28 Ahmed, *Making of Modern Turkey*, pp. 146–7.

29 For example, Gamal Essan El-Din, 'Liberalization bills in the offing', *Al-Ahram Weekly*, 19/25 November 1998.

30 United Nations Development Program, *Human Development Report 1998* (New York and Oxford: Oxford University Press, 1998), Table 18.

31 Tamar Hermann and Gila Kurtz, 'Prospects for democratizing foreign policy making: The gradual improvement in Israel women', *Middle East Journal*, 49/3 (Summer, 1993), Table 1, p. 451.

32 For example, Georgina Waylen, 'Analyzing women in the politics of the Third World', in Haleh Afshar (ed.), *Women and Politics in the Third World* (London and New York: Routledge, 1996), pp. 14–16.

33 Baya Gacemi, 'Algeria in the grip of terror: Hopes and lost illusions', *Le Monde Diplomatique* (September 1998), p. 10.

34 Ibid.

35 Haya al-Mughni, 'Women's organizations in Kuwait', *Middle East Report*, 26/1, 198 (January–March 1996), p. 32.

36 For example, Diane Singerman, *Avenues of Participation: Family, Politics and Networks in Urban Quarters of Cairo* (Princeton, NJ: Princeton University Press, 1995), pp. 71–3, 132–8, 255–68.

37 Yesim Arat, 'On gender and citizenship in Turkey', *Middle East Report*, 26/1, 198 (January–March 1996), p. 30.

38 Homa Hoodfar, 'Women and personal status law in Iran', *Middle East Report*, 26/1 198 (January–March 1996), p.36.

39 Ibid., pp. 36–7.

40 Haleh Afshar, 'Women and political fundamentalism in Iran', in Afshar (ed.), *Women and Politics*, pp. 127–30.

41 Yezid Sayigh, *Armed Struggle and the Search for a State: The Palestinian National Movement, 1949–1993* (Oxford: Clarendon Press, 1997), p. viii.

42 Ibid., p. x.

43 Ibid.

44 Ibid., pp. 464–5.

45 Ibid., p. 478.

46 For the importance of prison experience in creating a militant local leadership, see also Glenn E. Robinson, *Building a Palestinian State: The Incomplete Revolution* (Bloomington, IN: Indiana University Press, 1997), pp. 22, 37.

47 Hamida Kazi, 'Palestinian women and the national liberation movement: A social perspective', Khamsin, 13, *Women in the Middle East* (London: Zed Press, 1987), p. 34.

48 For example, Sayigh, *Armed Struggle*, pp. 612–13.

49 Meron Benvenisti, *1987 Report: Demographic, Economic, Legal, Social and Political Developments in the West Bank* (Jerusalem: West Bank Data Project, 1987), p. 28, quoted in F. Robert Hunter, *The Palestinian Uprising: War by Other Means* (London and New York: I.B. Tauris, 1991), p. 36.

50 Among the numerous detailed studies of the *Intifada*, two of the best are Hunter, *The Palestinian Uprising*, ibid., and Ze'ev Schiff and Ehud Ta'ari, *Intifada: The Palestinian Uprising – Israel's Third Front* (New York: Simon and Schuster, 1989).

51 Quoted in Maria Holt, 'Palestinian women and the Intifada', in Afshar (ed.), *Women and Politics*, p. 194.

52 Report by the Palestinian human rights organisation, Al-Haq, quoted in Hunter, *The Palestinian Uprising*, p. 96.

53 This process is well described in ibid., p. 141.

54 Ibid., pp. 182–215.

55 Sayigh, *Armed Struggle*, p. 636.

56 Graham Usher, *Palestine in Crisis: The Struggle for Peace and Independence after Oslo* (London and East Haven, CT: Pluto Press, 1995), pp. 46–7.

57 Rita Giacamen, Islah Jad and Penny Johnson, 'For the public good: gender and social citizenship in Palestine', *Middle East Report*, 26/1, 198 (January–March 1996), p. 11.

58 This is a central argument of Sayigh, *Armed Struggle*, Conclusion and particularly pp. 667–79.

Conclusion
The Middle East at the end of the twentieth century

Any account of the making, and then the re-making, of the political systems in the Middle East during the twentieth century must focus on both the general and the particular features of the process. As far as the former are concerned, I have described what might be considered a typical Third World passage for the major Arab countries: from the colonial state, through nationalism and independence, to the creation of an authoritarian system legitimised by an emphasis on both security and development, and then, finally, to the tempering of this authoritarianism by the opening up of space for independent and even oppositional forces. In each case, much of what happened has to be explained in terms of the global forces which were shaping much of the rest of the non-European world at the same time. These included colonialism, the two world wars, the general emphasis on state building and development, and, finally, the trend towards more liberal economic policies beginning in the 1970s and 1980s.

The other Middle Eastern states followed somewhat different trajectories in which local factors often played a more powerful role. The small oil states are one good example, with the development of their political system shaped largely by their own particular combination of great wealth and family rule. Lebanon, too, managed to follow its own path, beginning with a weak government dominated by stronger political forces, only for the system to break down during the long civil war of the 1970s and 1980s, and then having to be painfully rebuilt under Syrian supervision. As for the non-Arab states, both Turkey and Iran managed to avoid direct colonial control as a result of strong leadership from men like Ataturk and Reza Shah. However, they too went through a period of authoritarianism before, in the Turkish case, developing a more open political system tempered by repeated military intervention. Iran experienced an even more difficult passage involving revolution and then a series of experiments designed to find a new way of combining religious and political elements within a single governing structure. Finally, Israel emerged from colonial Palestine as a Jewish state with institutions profoundly shaped by its particular mix of party politics, money from abroad and continuing tension with its Arab neighbours.

What also needs to be kept in mind is that all the Middle Eastern states not only shared the same geographical space but one that was also defined and delimited by the world powers in terms of their own security interests. It was this which helped to ensure that the military campaigns conducted during the two world wars would impinge so directly on these states' politics and populations, with the war-related loss of civilian life in the Syrian provinces and Anatolia during the first of these world wars at least as great as in any part of Europe. It was this too which ensured that the Middle East became the scene of intense superpower rivalry during the Cold War. One result was the provision of military aid to the local allies of both sides, a process which fuelled a Middle Eastern arms race and so helped to make the major wars between Israel and its Arab neighbours, as well as the eight-year conflict between Iraq and Iran in the 1980s, more intense and destructive than they might otherwise have been. Meanwhile, European and then American efforts to organise either the self-defence or the economic development of the Middle East as a single unit inevitably foundered on the rocks of Arab/Israeli hostility or various types of anti-colonial or anti-western nationalisms, often reinforcing the very divisions such plans were supposed to overcome.

Arab efforts towards unity fared little better. In spite of the fact that the Arab peoples themselves felt considerable enthusiasm for pan-Arab causes, the individual regimes were never able to agree on what kind of unity they should strive for and on what type of institutional structures it should be based. Hence, despite some apparent early successes – from the creation of the League of Arab States to the series of summit meetings held by the Arab leaders in the 1960s – neither political nor economic union could be achieved. The same divisive processes were at work in the oil era as well. No matter that there seemed to be the makings of a profitable exchange in which the oil-rich states might trade revenues for much needed labor and military assistance from their stronger but poorer neighbours, the former choose to go it alone, preferring to buy protection from the United States and its allies rather than, say, from Egypt and Syria. Indeed, the fears felt by individual Arab regimes concerning the very real possibility of interference from other Arab regimes, usually outweighed any perception they might have had about the advantages of mutual co-operation, making all schemes for Arab unity seem very much a two-edged sword.

These were not conditions in which the fledgling democratic institutions which some states inherited from the colonial period could easily flourish. In a Middle East struggling to develop its own resources while also protecting itself from external threat, it was perhaps inevitable that the goals of national security, self-defence and rapid industrialisation should take precedence over those of political pluralism and individual rights. Then too, like developing states in other parts of the non-European world, local regimes had to cope with the pressing social problems associated with poverty, illiteracy, health, housing and rapid urbanisation, as well as with an urgent desire to catch up, economically, with the industrialised world. In such circumstances most opted for authoritarian systems which placed great emphasis on management, supervision and control. Meanwhile, those few which attempted the democratic path were sometimes simply overwhelmed by their own problems, like Lebanon; or, like Turkey, experienced considerable difficulty in creating political institutions flexible enough to meet the huge number of demands placed upon them. And even in Israel, the rights of its Arab citizens, as well as some of those of its Jewish ones, were regularly sacrificed to the general goals of Zionism and national security.

In almost every Middle Eastern state great importance was attached to the creation of national consensus. However, given the general absence of democratic institutions, such a consensus was more likely to be simply imposed rather than emerging out of general public discussion and debate. To begin with, in the major Arab states at least, the usual formula involved that combination of nationalism, anti-colonialism and socialism (interpreted to mean populism, public ownership and the local version of the welfare state) first specified by the Ba'th party intellectuals in Syria and then repackaged as Arab Socialism by the Nasser regime in Egypt. Later, the nationalist component tended to place greater emphasis on a kind of local territorial patriotism in which the notion of specific Arab peoples living in specific Middle Eastern localities took precedence over loyalty to a larger Arab nation. Meanwhile, in the Gulf states, the stress was placed on the legitimacy of the ruling families combined with a concept of a loyal citizenry, with notions of religion, kinship, proper behaviour and economic welfare taking precedence over the importance of political rights.

Over time, however, it became apparent that the more a consensus was imposed on the people by the state, the more it forced opponents to find ways to mobilise a counter-power based on such alternatives as an appeal to regional or communitarian loyalties, or to a rival interpretation of the proper role of religion and religious leadership in an Islamic state. The most obvious example of a root and branch challenge to the existing structure of power and its sources of legitimation came in Iran in the late 1970s. Other significant, but ultimately less successful, examples can be found throughout the Arab world. Even Israel and Turkey, with their more homogenous populations and more open public debate, were not immune to powerful challenges from groups which believed passionately that the whole apparatus of law and government was based on illegitimate, because non-divine, foundations.

To make matters more complex still, the end of the Cold War, and the perceived triumph of liberal capitalism within its new global framework, introduced new forces, new challenges and new opportunities for the governments and societies of the Middle East. However, the response to these same forces has not been going on for long enough to be able to predict with confidence how the various components of this 'liberal' experiment will work out over the first decades of the twenty-first century. Hence the best that can be done from the vantage point of someone writing in 1999 is simply to describe the changes which have taken place so far, together with the issues, both short- and long-term, which they already have begun to raise for future attention.

The regional context

The Middle East remains a single unit from an international security point of view, just as it was a century ago. This is how it is seen by the regimes themselves which continue to act as though all military developments in the area between Iran in the east and Morocco in the west have a special salience which does not extend, say, to neighbouring regions like the Balkans or the Indian sub-continent. One example is the Arab and Iranian response to the Turkish/Israeli military alliance of the mid-1990s which they saw as immediately threatening to their security interests, squeezing Syria and making it much easier for Israeli war planes, now based in eastern Anatolia, to threaten Teheran. A second is the perception shared by Israel and the United States that the development of a nuclear capacity anywhere in the Middle East – Iraq, Iran and Libya have been seen as the most likely candidates – would have to be dealt with either directly or, in more ideal circumstances, by the institution of a region-wide anti-nuclear proliferation programme.

It is for this reason that the Israeli–Arab peace process which developed from the Madrid Conference of 1991 through the Oslo Accords and the 1994 Israeli–Jordanian treaty was seen as holding the key both to region-wide disarmament and to the integration of Israel into a larger, pan-Middle Eastern network of economic institutions designed to promote local trade and investment. By the same token, the obvious disinterest in pursuing the process during Israel's Netanyahu government, 1996–9, also had region-wide repercussions. On the one hand, it provided an opportunity for the settlement of a number of inter-Arab disputes as well as the establishment of a working alliance between Saudi Arabia and Iran. The regimes in Jordan and Egypt were no longer constrained by their treaties with Israel when it came to improving their relations with their neighbours. Arabs and Iranians shared a new sense of menace from Israel's military superiority. On the other, it exacerbated a number of existing tensions, notably those in south Lebanon between the Hizbollah guerrillas and the Israeli army in and around the Israeli security zone and between the pro- and the anti-Arafat factions within the large Palestinian refugee camps.

The revival of the peace process under Israel's Prime Minister Ehud Barak thus provided an opportunity not only to establish (or, in the case of Jordan and Egypt, to re-establish) good relations between Israel and its neighbours but also to return to the question of a new economic architecture for the Middle East. It is true that, in the interim, more than usually serious efforts had been made to push on with the establishment of an Arab common market overlapping with a somewhat larger Arab free trade area. However, whether the peace process flourished or not, any pan-Arab arrangement would always have to compete with the counter-attractions provided by such sub-regional arrangements as the Gulf Cooperation Council, as well as, for some, the obvious advantages of the close links with Europe provided by accession to the Euro-Mediterranean scheme. Another alternative available to Jordan, Lebanon and Egypt is the exploitation of what might be called the 'geographic' economies of scale between them and Israel – for example, by linked transport, tourist arrangements and power grids – which offered many possibilities for short-term gains.

Nevertheless, even if there could be peace and co-operation at the eastern end of the Mediterranean, two major regional problems would still remain. One is the political future of Iraq and its possible re-integration into the Arab world. The second is the existence of a number of internal insurrections with dangerous external implications for neighbouring states. The Kurdish movement in Iraq, and possibly Iran and Turkey, is one such candidate. The ramifications of the on-going Sudanese civil war is another. It is also possible to imagine a scenario in which, even after the negotiated establishment of a Palestinian mini-state, the ensuing tensions between Palestinians and the Israeli West Bank settlements, as well as between the Palestine National Authority (PNA) regime and its own people, would pose significant problems, not only for those immediately concerned but also for the Lebanese, Syrians, Jordanians and Egyptians just across the border.

The domestic political context

It is not difficult to argue that, during the 1990s, it was the process of economic liberalisation which was the driving political force as far as the major Arab non-oil states were concerned. Programmes involving privatisation, the opening up of the banking industry to private capital, the expanding role of stock markets and the signature of a web of trade agreements with international institutions were beginning to have a major impact on the relations between government and business and the state and private sectors of the economy. In some countries at least, there was also evidence of a change in the balance between public and private consumption and of a reduction in the size of the public sector work force. More generally, it can be argued that the change in economic direction had led to the replacement of the developmentalist state by one much more concerned to manage relations between the public and the private sectors, with the latter now supposed to take the lion's share of new investment.

However, as I have argued in the second section of this book, these changes did not have quite the effect on political life that was originally expected. Instead of encouraging a more plural political system, the Arab regimes in question preferred not to risk their economic achievements by permitting free and open discussion or by encouraging the emergence of parties representing sectional interests such as capital and labour. Hence, business influence tended to be channelled towards the single government party while the necessary process of passing new laws to regulate labour relations, company formation, the dissemination of information and the activities of NGOs and the press tended to assume the form of a re-regulation in which much the same level of control was maintained but in some new form.

The result was a situation in which links between government and business were strengthened rather than reduced, producing an Egyptian or Tunisian or Jordanian version of 'crony-capitalism' in which competition was stifled and entrepreneurs with close connections with the regime were able to obtain most of the major contracts, as well as to bend or break planning laws and other legal restraints when it suited them. What they had to put up with, in turn, was a great deal of bullying from the regime itself which showed no compunction in forcing each country's leading businessmen to invest in its favourite business or welfare projects as a quid pro quo. Meanwhile, organised labor remained largely on the defensive, focused almost entirely on the protection of the jobs of its members in the public sector with little or no ability to shape legislation concerning working conditions in general.

How long such a state of affairs can be expected to continue is another matter. Given the world community's stress on general notions of proper business practice, it would seem reasonable to assume that, over time, Arab businessmen will seek to protect their affairs both from government interference and from regulatory unpredictability by making use of the kind of international leverage based on international treaties and organisations like the Washington-based International Center for the Settlement of Investment Disputes (ICSID) affiliated to the World Bank. They may also positively welcome certain kinds of foreign investment, for example the arrival of multinational banks which can more easily make their way through the uncertain legal environment allowing local concerns to follow. Others may make use of the powerful global currents concerning the environment, intellectual copyright and the sanctity of private property to advance their own interests against interfering bureaucrats and greedy politicians.

Relations between regimes and the main religious groups were generally much more conflictual than those involving local private business. Whether there was a period of armed opposition by militants, as in Egypt and Algeria, or not, ruling groups remained wary of allowing the formation of Islamic parties, preferring instead to deal with religious issues on a piecemeal basis. In this they were helped by the fact that, as the 1990s progressed, most of the more radical groups were coming to the conclusion that they would gain more by trying to work within the system than by opposing it from outside. One significant result was their switch from the type of single issue appeal that had animated their armed struggle – essentially a call for the return of the *sharia* – to the more general economic, social and moral agenda which had been the hallmark of the Muslim Brothers in the early independence period. This in turn began to suggest new types of divisions inside the religious camps. Instead of the old split between the accommodationists and those urging confrontation, there was now, for example, one between those whose main focus was on cultural rather than political activism and another between the economic liberals and the social conservatives.

The new emphasis on civil society and human rights often brought some of those in the religious movements into close relations with the secular NGOs and human rights activists who were emerging in Egypt and elsewhere as much more active critics of regime policies than most of the so-called 'official opposition' parties which had been more or less marginalised by their divisions and lack of electoral success. With funds from abroad, and a proved ability to publicise local human rights abuses in the foreign press, such groups were becoming a major irritant to Arab governments and subject to increasing harassment in return.

As for the military in the non-oil states, it continued to play a major role behind the scenes. Armies could impact directly on the political process, as in Algeria, making and breaking civilian governments, or they could choose to remain behind the scenes as a powerful factor in the calculations of any ruling elite when it came to assessing support for a king or president or the choice of his successor. This gave the military a privileged position which it was generally able to exploit to the full, first in terms of the construction of separate compounds and vacation facilities for its officers, then by developing its own sector of the economy which, in Egypt at least, went far beyond the need for locally-made weapons to include industrial goods and foodstuff for general consumption. The fact that armies had a whole host of cheap resources at their disposal, from labor to land, gave them yet more of an advantage, although also raising the general question of how their monopoly over various parts of the economy could be reconciled either with transparency and public accountability or with the promises contained in the many international treaties concerning open access to all areas of economic life.

Given the lack of real progress towards greater political pluralism in the 1990s, elite concern was focused on quite a narrow range of significant issues, most notably the presidential succession, the manipulation of elections, the control of information, and the activities of NGOs, human rights organisations and religious groups. The importance of the role of ruler was amply highlighted in 1999, for example, by the attention given to five presidential elections – in Syria, Egypt, Yemen, Tunisia and Algeria – as well as to the uncontested replacement of King Hussein of Jordan and King Hassan of Morocco by their eldest sons. Given the fact that in the first four cases, the incumbent presidents, Asad, Mubarak, Abdullah Salih and Ben Ali, had already been in power for several terms, their renewal in office for another five or more years had a number of important, and obvious, implications. It meant that the general direction of policy and political management would remain more or less the same. It also highlighted the great importance of their own choice of successor whenever it became clear that their own time was coming to an end. In such systems, where elections for president are more like plebiscites than real contests, and where prospects for real change are believed to await the arrival in office of a new, and much younger, man, stability becomes more important than competition between ideas and interests. What follows is a species of political inertia, with little tolerance for criticism even while there is more and more to criticise, and with the overthrow of the regime itself the only option for those who are harmed by its policies.

What also follows is that general elections become much like plebiscites too, with the results manipulated in advance to suit the purposes of the ruling party, and with the appearance of sufficient token opposition to give the whole process enough legitimacy to head off serious criticism from Europe or the United States. Meanwhile, the main task of criticising the regime and of trying to make it accountable for its acts falls to a combination of human rights and religious activists. Nevertheless, although both groups are able to make common cause round certain issues, the fact that they tend to hold radically different views about the type of society and political system they want, makes it relatively easy for governments to drive wedges between them in such a way that, whatever small victories may be gained for openness and freedom, are generally offset by the sops given to the religious component of the coalition in favour of greater censorship and interference in the individual right to choose.

How long such systems can continue is another matter. In a global economy, with a well-educated middle class and virtually open access to information from abroad, it does not seem likely that the present stick and carrot approach to political management can be maintained indefinitely. Sooner or later, issues which have always been implicit in both religious and secular discourse will be made increasingly explicit. These include notions of citizenship, the rule of law, religious toleration and a regime legitimacy that comes not from appeals to security, ideology or achievement but from popular representation and a consensus among the nation at large. There will also have to be reconsideration of the notion of civil society and the ways in which it has to be seen, not as a single-minded opponent of authoritarian government, which it can never be, but as a series of independent spaces which require new and better laws for their own proper protection.

Many of the same general considerations apply to the oil states and to Lebanon. They too live in the same global economy and are subject to the same pressure to liberalise their economies as well as to conform to international ideas of openness, individual rights and good government. As a result they too may be increasingly limited in their ability to base legitimating formulas and political structures on an appeal to traditional notions of family rule, confessionalism or on an endlessly managed consensus. They may also begin to face real choices involving such vital issues as whether to introduce direct taxes to cover their increasing budget deficits or how far to allow private capital to compete with both state and ruling family enterprises. And all this at a time when, by and large, their own legitimacy remains under assault not only for their failures of management up to, and during, the Gulf War but also, and even more seriously, on the grounds that they are improper guardians of their people's Islamic faith.

Some of these pressures were already apparent in the 1990s which marked a proliferation of consultative bodies, an increasing use of the electoral principle (including in Qatar and Oman, women electors), and, in the case of Saudi Arabia, the promulgation of a type of constitution which would have been unthinkable in the days of Abd al-Aziz Ibn Saud. However, as elsewhere in the Arab world, most political attention continued to be focused on the person of the ruler, with the appearance of a new one still the most likely stimulus to change, as in Saudi Arabia with the transfer of power from King Fahd to Crown Prince Abdullah, or in Qatar and Bahrain from father to son. For the rest, the practice of consultation was teaching its own lessons in terms of how far it might be possible to discuss, and then to criticise, governments still dominated by ruling family members, with the most progress, as always, in Kuwait, even if the al-

Sabahs still continued to use the threat of new elections in order to try to keep their parliamentary opponents in line.

The situation in Lebanon was different again. Even though the civil war had come to an end through a process of mutual exhaustion, it was only as a result of outside, and largely Syrian, intervention that the warring parties came together in Taif in 1989 to agree to what was in effect a second national pact laying down the ground rules for a reconstituted political life. This formula was enough to revive the parliament as a political market place in such a way that, over time, almost all the confessional leaders, including the Shi'i militants and the Maronite Christian hard-liners, were drawn back into the political process and so obtain access to the resources needed to satisfy their own clientele. Nevertheless, a combination of the Syrian security presence and continuing economic difficulty, including a large internal and external debt, put limits on the ability of the local politicians to meet all the demands made upon them, particularly by their poorer constituents. Search for a scapegoat led to the removal of Prime Minister Rafia Harriri amidst the usual accusations of favouritism and corruption. Yet his replacement by a government put in place by the president elected in 1998, General Emile Lahoud, did not promise any root and branch improvement. As in the case of General Shehab's reforming presidency after the 1958 civil war, the new executive was faced with the stark choice between working with what it considered a corrupt system dominated by old-style confessional politicians, or trying to introduce a new one for which there was no obvious popular support beyond its own narrow technocratic base.

Of all the countries with predominantly Muslim populations it was Iran which embarked on the most radical political experiment during the 1990s. Initially, under President Rafsanjani, this consisted of what might be considered the conventional programme of economy-driven liberalisation. But under his successor, Mohammed Khatami, it assumed a more purely political dimension, aiming at no less than the transformation of the country's monolithic system of authoritarian government in the direction of a much more open and pluralistic one. Backed by continued electoral success, the reformers were able to use their popular legitimacy to roll back the power of the conservatives who had previously dominated most of the important institutions of state. Indeed, by the end of the century they had succeeded so well that they now faced the extra challenge of keeping their large and unwieldy reform coalition, including the militant students, together long enough for it to generate the set of new political parties which were supposed to contest the year 2000 general elections. But, whatever the outcome, President Khatami has already raised the political stakes to a very high level, involving nothing less than the ability of an Islamic revolutionary regime to effect the peaceful transformation from one type of system to another. It was clear to all that huge problems remained ahead, not only in maintaining the drive towards political reform but also providing answers to the country's many economic difficulties, an area which Khatami himself had almost entirely ignored.

The two non-Arab democracies, Israel and Turkey, experienced quite a different mix of problems during the 1990s from their neighbours. These stemmed in part from their greater degree of interconnectedness with the global economy which, interacting with their own, more open, political systems, produced some of the same effects as those to be found in Europe and the United States. These included a further reduction in the ideological divisions between the major secular parties, an emphasis on the personalities of the leaders rather than their policies and the introduction of new, and largely western, methods of political mobilisation at election time via advertising and an appeal to individual life-style issues. To complicate the picture, however, the politics of both countries was also heavily affected by more parochial, Middle Eastern issues involving nationalism, religion and future relations with significant minorities, the Kurds in one case, the Palestinians in the other. This was enough to introduce a high degree of volatility in both systems with, on occasions like both the Turkish and the Israeli elections of 1999, considerable swings of support between both leaders and parties. However, the fact that these same elections allowed the creation of what looked like large, and relatively stable, parliamentary coalitions did hold out the hope that, for a few years at least, there would be governments with sufficient strength and authority to tackle the accumulation of difficult issues which their weaker predecessors had simply pushed to one side.

Twentieth-century legacy

Centuries are arbitrary ways to divide up historical experience as everyone knows. Nevertheless, it is possible to make the case that, in the Middle East at least, the period between the years 1900 and 2000 has a certain consistency, as well as a certain character, all of its own. The period began with the drive towards the final division of the region into separate zones of influence by the great powers. Later, after the First World War, these zones crystallised into states with only a few countries able to withstand outside pressure long enough to create independent polities of their own. Later still, after the Second World War, the British colony of Palestine became the site of the Jewish state of Israel, while oil was found in sufficient quantities in most of the smaller Gulf shaikhdoms to ensure that they began to protect themselves by developing state-like structures of their own. Meanwhile, all projects for voluntary Arab union, the Yemens apart, proved unsuccessful. So too did the occasional attempts to take over a neighbouring state, as the frustration of Iraqi claims to Kuwait well proved. And it was these same states which continued to form the basic units of the Middle Eastern regional system at the century's end.

What happened inside their state structures was another matter. Political institution-building, as well as political trajectories, varied greatly. However, I have suggested that, by and large, these developments can be subsumed under the general rubric of 'making and re-making', with the bulk of the century devoted to the former and the latter the work of just its last decade. 'Making' has been defined largely in terms of the creation of authoritarian systems while 're-making' is seen in terms of such tendencies as the liberalisation projects in many of the Arab countries, the mutation of the Islamic revolutionary institutions in Iran and the more pragmatic adaptation to both global change and nationalism and religious revival which took place in Israel and Turkey. The last decade of the century also promised, without being fully able to deliver, the hope that after years of open or expected inter-state conflict, the Middle Eastern countries would be able to co-exist in a relatively conflict-free regional environment. It is for reasons such as these that the tentative process of re-making looks set to continue well into the twenty-first century.

As for the peoples themselves, the twentieth century produced very mixed blessings. Materially there is no doubt that the vast majority were much better off than their grandparents. There were significant improvements in health, life expectancy, educational attainments and income from the mid-century on. But against this must be set the effects of wars, forced migration and external events such as the Holocaust, which can have left few Middle Eastern families untouched by one disaster or another. If we add to this the ways in which the hopes raised by nationalism and independence were so often dashed, with promised freedoms so often ending in dictatorship, a loss of all political rights, censorship and police control, then this is more than enough to account for the general tone of bitterness and despair to be found in so much of the Arabic, Turkish, Iranian and Hebrew literature of the period. And yet, at the century's end, there were as always some countervailing factors as well: good prospects for regional peace, somewhat less good prospects for greater political participation, and for those with access to the opportunities provided by global economic expansion, what seemed like endless prospects for individual self-advancement.

Select bibliography

Chapter 1   The end of empires: the emergence of the modern Middle Eastern states

Albert Hourani, *A History of the Arab Peoples* (London: Faber and and Faber; Cambridge, MA: Belknap/Harvard University Press, 1991).

Issa Khalaf, *Politics in Palestine: Arab Factionalism and Social Disintegration 1939–1948* (Albany, NY: State University of New York Press, 1991).

Philip S. Khoury, *Syria and the French Mandate: The Politics of Arab Nationalism 1920–1945* (Princeton, NJ: Princeton University Press; London: I.B. Tauris, 1987).

Elizabeth Monroe, *Britain's Moment in the Middle East 1914–1956* (London: Chatto and Windus, 1963).

Clement Henry Moore, *The Politics of North Africa: Algeria, Morocco and Tunisia* (Boston, MA: Little Brown, 1970).

M.E. Yapp, *The Near East Since the First World War* (London and New York: Longman, 1991).

Sami Zubaida, *Islam, the People and the State* (London: I.B. Tauris, 1995).

Chapter 2   The growth of state power in the Arab world: the single-party regimes

Nazih N. Ayubi, *Over-stating the Arab State: Politics and Society in the Middle East* (London: I.B. Tauris, 1996).

Hanna Batatu, *Syria's Peasantry, the Descendants of its Lesser Rural Notables and Their Politics* (Princeton, NJ: Princeton University Press, 1999).

Kirk J. Beattie, *Egypt During the Nasser Years: Ideology, Politics and Civil Society* (Boulder, CO: Westview Press, 1994).

Samir Al Khalil, *The Republic of Fear: The Politics of Modern Iraq* (Berkeley, CA: University of California Press, 1990).

Joel S. Migdal, *Weak States and Strong Societies: State-Society Relations and State Capabilities in the Third World* (Princeton, NJ: Princeton Univerity Press, 1988).

C.H. Moore, 'Authoritarian politics in unincorporated society', *Comparative Politics*, 6/2 (January 1974), pp. 193–218.

John Waterbury, *The Egypt of Nasser and Sadat: The Political Economy of Two Regimes* (Princeton, NJ: Princeton University Press, 1983).

Lisa Wedeen, *Ambiguities of Domination: Politics, Rhetoric, and Symbols in Contemporary Syria* (Chicago, IL and London: Chicago University Press, 1999).

Chapter 3   The growth of state power in the Arab world under family rule, and the Libyan alternative

Nathan Alexander, 'Libya: The continuous revolution', *Middle Eastern Studies*, 17/2 (April 1981), pp. 210–27.
Kiren Aziz Chaudhry, *The Price of Wealth: Economies and Institutions in the Middle East* (Ithaca and London: Cornell University Press, 1997).
Giacomo Luciani (ed.), *The Arab State* (London: Routledge, 1990).
Samir A. Mutawi, *Jordan in the 1967 War* (Cambridge: Cambridge University Press, 1987).
G.S. Samore, *Royal Family Politics in Saudi Arabia (1953–1982)*, Harvard University, unpublished Ph.D., 1984 (University Microfilms).
Dick Vandewalle (ed.), *Qadhafi's Libya 1969–1994* (New York: St. Martin's Press, 1995).
Alexei Vassiliev, *The History of Saudi Arabia (1745–1994)* (London: Saki Books, 1997).
John Waterbury, *The Commander of the Faithful: The Moroccan Political Elite: A Study of Segmented Politics* (London: Weidenfeld and Nicolson, 1970).
Rosemary Said Zahlan, *The Making of the Modern Gulf States: Kuwait, Bahrain, Qatar, the United Arab Emirates and Oman* (Reading: Ithaca Press, 1998).

Chapter 4: Arab nationalism, Arab unity and the practice of intra-Arab state relations

Benedict Anderson, *Imagined Communities: Reflections on the Origins and Spread of Nationalism* (London and New York: Verso, 1991).
Amatzia Baram, *Culture, History and Ideology in the Formation of Ba'thist Iraq, 1968–89* (Basingstoke and London: Macmillan/St Antony's, 1991).
C. Ernest Dawn, *From Ottomanism to Arabism: Essays on the Origins of Arab Nationalism* (Urbana, IL: University of Illinois Press, 1973).
Ernest Gellner, *Nations and Nationalism* (Oxford: Basil Blackwell, 1983).
Ahmed M. Gomaa, *The Foundations of the League of Arab States: Wartime Diplomacy and Inter-Arab Politics 1941 to 1945* (London and New York: Longman, 1977).
Sylvia Haim (ed.), *Arab Nationalism: An Anthology* (Los Angeles, CA: University of California Press, 1976).
Malcolm Kerr, *The Arab Cold War 1958–1967: A Study of Ideology in Politics* (London: Oxford University Press for R.I.I.A., 1967).
Eberhard Kienle, *Ba'th versus Ba'th: The Conflict Between Syria and Iraq* (London: I.B. Tauris, 1990).
Malik Mufti, *Sovereign Creations: Pan-Arabism and Political Order in Syria and Iraq* (Ithaca and London: Cornell University Press, 1996).
Patrick Seale, *The Struggle for Syria: A Study of Post-war Arab Politics 1945–1958* (London: I.B. Tauris, 1986).

Chapter 5   State and politics in Israel, Iran and Turkey from the Second World War

Ervand Abrahamian, *Iran Between Two Revolutions* (Princeton, NJ: Princeton University Press, 1982).

Feroz Ahmad, *The Making of Modern Turkey* (London: HarperCollins, 1991).

Fahkrddin Azimi, *Iran: The Crisis of Democracy 1941–1953* (London: I.B. Tauris, 1989).

Shaul Bakhash, *The Reign of the Ayatollahs: Iran and the Islamic Revolution* (London: I.B. Tauris, 1985).

Metin Heper and Ahmet Evin (eds), *State, Democracy and the Military: Turkey in the 1980s* (Berlin and New York: Walter de Gruyter, 1988).

Arthur Herzberg (ed.), *The Zionist Idea: A Historical Analysis and Reader* (New York: Atheneum, 1986).

Dan Horowitz and Moshe Lissak, *Trouble in Utopia: The Overburdened Polity of Israel* (Albany: State University of New York Press, 1989).

Caglar Keyder, *State and Class: A Study of Capitalist Development* (London and New York: Verso, 1987).

Don Peretz, *The Government and Politics of Israel*, 2nd edn (Boulder, CO: Westview Press, 1983).

Asghar Schirazi, *The Constitution of Iran: Politics and the State in the Islamic Republic*, trans. (London and New York: I.B. Tauris, 1997).

S. Ilan Troen and Noah Lucas (eds), *Israel: The First Decade of Independence* (Albany, NY: State University of New York Press, 1995).

Chapter 6   The remaking of the Middle Eastern political environment after the Gulf War

Adnan Abu-Odeh, *Jordanians, Palestinians and the Hashemite Kingdom in the Peace Process* (Washington, DC: United States Institute of Peace Press, 1999).

Fouad Ajami, 'The summer of Arab discontent', *Foreign Affairs*, 69/5 (Winter, 1990/1), pp. 1–20.

Muhammad Faour, *The Arab World After Desert Storm* (Washington, DC: United States Institute of Peace Press, 1993).

Mohammad Khatami, *Islam, Liberty and Development*, trans. (Binghamton, NY: Institute of Global Cultural Studies, Binghamton University, 1998).

Eberhard Kienle, *Contemporary Syria: Liberalization Between Cold War and Peace* (London: I.B. Tauris, 1997).

Graham Usher, *Palestine in Crisis The Struggle for Political Independence After Oslo* (London and New Haven, CT: Pluto Press, 1995).

Chapter 7   The politics of economic restructuring

Tosun Aricanli and Dani Rodrick (eds), *The Political Economy of Turkey: Adjustment and Sustainability* (London: Macmillan, 1990).

Hiba Handoussa and Gillian Potter (eds), *Employment and Structural Adjustment in Egypt in the 1990s* (Cairo: American University of Cairo Press, 1991).

Cameron Khosroshahi, 'Privatization in Morocco: The politics of development', *Middle East Journal*, 51/1 (Spring, 1997), pp. 242–55.

Hans Loftgren, 'Economic policy in Egypt: A breakdown of reform resistance?', *International Journal of Middle Eastern Studies*, 25/3 (August 1993), pp. 407–21.

S. El. Naggar, *Privatization and Structural Adjustment in the Arab Countries* (Washington: International Monetary Fund, 1989).

Roger Owen and Sevket Pamuk, *A History of the Middle East Economies in the Twentieth Century* (London: I.B. Tauris, 1998; Cambridge, MA: Harvard University Press, 1999).

Saeed Rahnama and Sohrab Behdad (eds), *Iran After the Revolution: Crisis of an Islamic State* (London and New York: I.B. Tauris, 1995).

Alan Richards and John Waterbury, *A Political Economy of the Middle East*, 2nd edn (Boulder, CO: Westview Press, 1996).

Nemat Shafik (ed.), *Economic Challenges Facing Middle Eastern and North African Countries* (Houndmills, Basingstoke: The Macmillan Press; New York: St. Martin's Press, 1997).

Michael Shalev, 'Contradictions of economic reform in Israel, *Middle East Review*, 28/2, 207 (Summer, 1998), pp. 31–3, 41.

Chapter 8   Parties, elections and the vexed question of democracy in the Arab world

Baaklini, Abdo, Guilain Denoeux and Robert Springborg (eds), *Legislative Politics in the Arab World: The Resurgence of Democratic Institutions* (Boulder, CO: Lynne Rienner, 1999).

F. Gregory Gause III, *Oil Monarchies: Domestic and Security Challenges in the Arab Gulf States* (New York: Council on Foreign Relations, 1994).

Guy Hermet, Richard Rose and Alain Rouquié (eds), *Elections Without Choices* (Basingstoke and London: The Macmillan Press, 1978).

Michael Hudson, *The Precarious Republic: Political Modernization in Lebanon* (New York: Random House, 1968).

Eberhard Kienle, 'More than a response to Islamism: The political deliberalization of Egypt in the 1990s', *Middle East Journal*, 52/2 (Spring, 1998), pp. 219–35.

Clement Henry Moore, *Tunisia Since Independence: The Dynamics of One Party Government* (Berkeley, CA: University of California Press, 1965).

Hugh Roberts, 'The politics of Algerian socialism', in R.I. Lawless and Allan M. Findley (eds), *North Africa: Contemporary Politics and Economic Development* (London: Croom Helm, 1984).

Ghassan Salamé (ed.), *Democracy Without Democrats?: The Renewal of Politics in the Muslim World* (London: I.B. Tauris, 1995).

Dirk Vandewalle (ed.), *North Africa: Development and Reform in a Changing Global Economy* (New York: St. Martin's Press, 1996).

Chapter 9   The politics of religious revival

Ervand Abrahamian, *Khomeinism: Essays on the Islamic Republic* (Berkeley, CA: University of California Press, 1993).

Richard T. Antoun and Mary Hegland (eds), *Religious Resurgence: Contemporary Cases in Islam, Christianity and Judaism* (Syracuse, NY: Syracuse University Press, 1987).

Nazih M. Ayubi, *Political Islam: Religion and Politics in the Arab World* (London and New York: Routledge, 1991).

Dale F. Eickelman and James Piscatori (eds), *Muslim Politics* (Princeton, NJ: Princeton University Press, 1996).

R.P. Mitchell, *The Society of the Muslim Brothers* (New York: Oxford University Press, 1993).

Baqer Moin, *Khomeini: Life of the Ayatollah* (London: I.B. Tauris, 1999).

Sayyid Qutb, *Maalim fi al-Tariq*, translated as *Milestones* (Cedar Rapids, IA: Unity, n.d.,1981–5?).

Olivier Roy, *The Failure of Political Islam*, trans. (Cambridge, MA: Harvard University Press, 1994).

Emmanuel Sivan, *Radical Islam: Medieval Theology and Modern Politics* (New Haven, CT: Yale University Press, 1985).

Emmanuel Sivan and Menachem Friedman (eds), *Religious Radicalism and Politics in the Middle East* (Albany, NY: State University of New York Press, 1990).

Chapter 10   The military in and out of politics

Mehmet Ali Birand, *The Generals' Coup in Turkey: An Inside Story of 12 September 1980*, trans. (London: Brassey's, 1987).

—— *Shirts of Steel: An Anatomy of the Turkish Armed Forces*, trans. (London and New York: I.B. Tauris, 1991).

William M. Hale, *Turkish Politics and the Military* (London and New York: Routledge, 1994).

Yoram Peri, *Between Battles and Ballots: Israeli Military in Politics* (Cambridge: Cambridge University Press, 1983).

Elizabeth Picard, 'Arab military in politics: From revolutionary plot to authoritarian regime', in Giacomo Luciani (ed.), *The Arab State* (London: Routledge, 1990).

Robert Springborg, *Mubarak's Egypt: Fragmentation of the Political Order* (Boulder, CO: Westview Press; London: Kegan Paul International, 1989).

P.J. Vatikiotis, *Politics and the Military in Jordan: A Study of the Arab Legion 1921–1957* (London: Frank Cass, 1967).

Sepehr Zabih, *The Iranian Military in Revolution and War* (London and New York: Routledge, 1988).

Chapter 11   Some important non-state actors

Sheila Carapico, *Civil Society in Yemen: The Political Economy of Activism in Modern Arabia* (Cambridge: Cambridge University Press, 1998).

Michael Gilsenan, *Lords of the Lebanese Marches: Violence and Narrative in an Arab Society* (Berkeley, CA.: University of California Press, 1996).

Ellis J. Goldberg (ed.), *The Social History of Labor in the Middle East* (Boulder, CO and Oxford: Westview Press, 1996).

Yezid Sayigh, *Armed Struggle and the Search for State: The Palestinian National Movement 1949–1993* (Oxford: Oxford University Press, 1997).

Mustafa K. Al-Sayyid, 'A civil society in Egypt?', *Middle East Journal*, 47/2 (Spring, 1993), pp. 228–42.

Diane Singerman, *Avenue of Participation: Family, Politics and Networks in Urban Quarters of Cairo* (Princeton, NJ: Princeton University Press, 1995).

Judith E. Tucker (ed.), *Arab Women: Old Boundaries and New Frontiers* (Bloomington and Indianapolis, IN: Indiana University Press, 1993).

Jenny B. White, *Money Makes Us Relatives: Women's Labor in Urban Turkey* (Austin, Texas: University of Texas Press, 1994).

Index